C000070819

Street by Street

EAST SUSSEX

PLUS BURGESS HILL, EAST GRINSTEAD, ROYAL TUNBRIDGE WELLS

Enlarged Areas Brighton, Eastbourne, Hastings, Lewes, Newhaven

Ist edition May 2001

© Automobile Association Developments Limited 2001

Published by AA Publishing (a trading name of Automobile Association Developments Limited, whose registered office is Norfolk House, Priestley Road, Basingstoke, Hampshire, RG24 9NY. Registered number 1878835).

Mapping produced by the Cartographic Department of The Automobile Association.

A CIP Catalogue record for this book is available from the British Library.

Printed by in Italy by Printer Trento srl

Ref: MD022

Key to map pages .... ii-iii

Key to map symbols iv-1

Enlarged scale pages 2-11

Street by Street 12-237

Index – towns & villages 238-240

Index – streets 241-273

Index – featured places 273-280

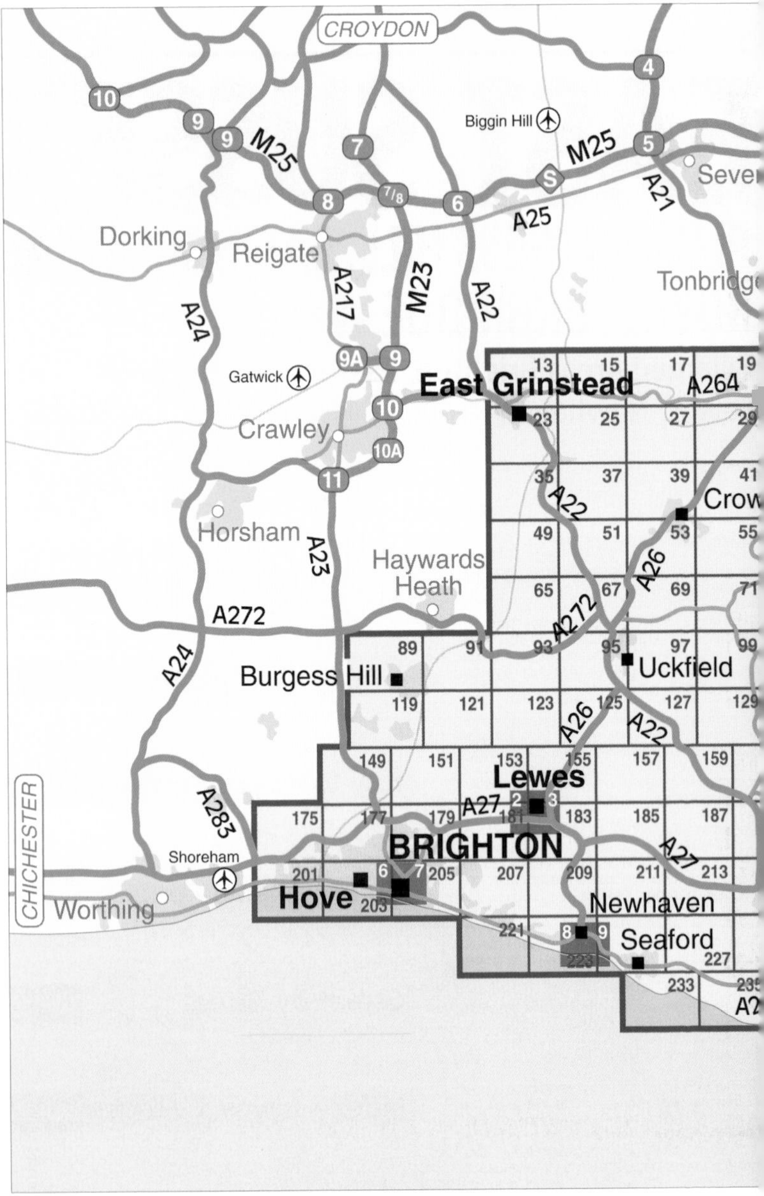

ii

CROYDON

10

9

9
M25

7

Biggin Hill ✈

M25

4

5

Seve

8

7/8

6

A25

S

A21

Dorking

Reigate

A217

M23

A22

Tonbridge

A24

Gatwick ✈

9A

9

East Grinstead

A264

	13	15	17	19
	23	25	27	29
35	37	39	41
49	51	53	55

Crawley

10

10A

11

Crow

A22

A26

Horsham

A23

Haywards
Heath

| 65 | 67 | 69 | 71 |

A272

A24

A272

| 89 | 91 | 93 | 95 | 99 |
| | | | | 97 |

Uckfield

Burgess Hill

| 119 | 121 | 123 | 125 | 129 |
| | | | 127 | |

A26

A22

| 149 | 151 | 153 | 155 | 157 | 159 |

CHICHESTER

A283

| 175 | 177 | 179 | 181 | 183 | 185 | 187 |

Lewes

A27

2

3

BRIGHTON

A27

Shoreham ✈

| 201 | 205 | 207 | 209 | 211 | 213 |
| | 203 | | | | |

6

7

Hove

Worthing

| 221 | | | |
| 223 | 227 | |

Newhaven

8

9

Seaford

| 233 | 235 |

A2

Enlarged scale pages | 1:17,500 | 3.6 inches to 1 mile

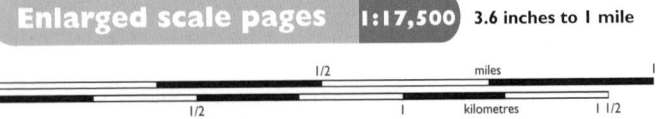

0   1/2   miles   1

0   1/2   1   kilometres   1 1/2

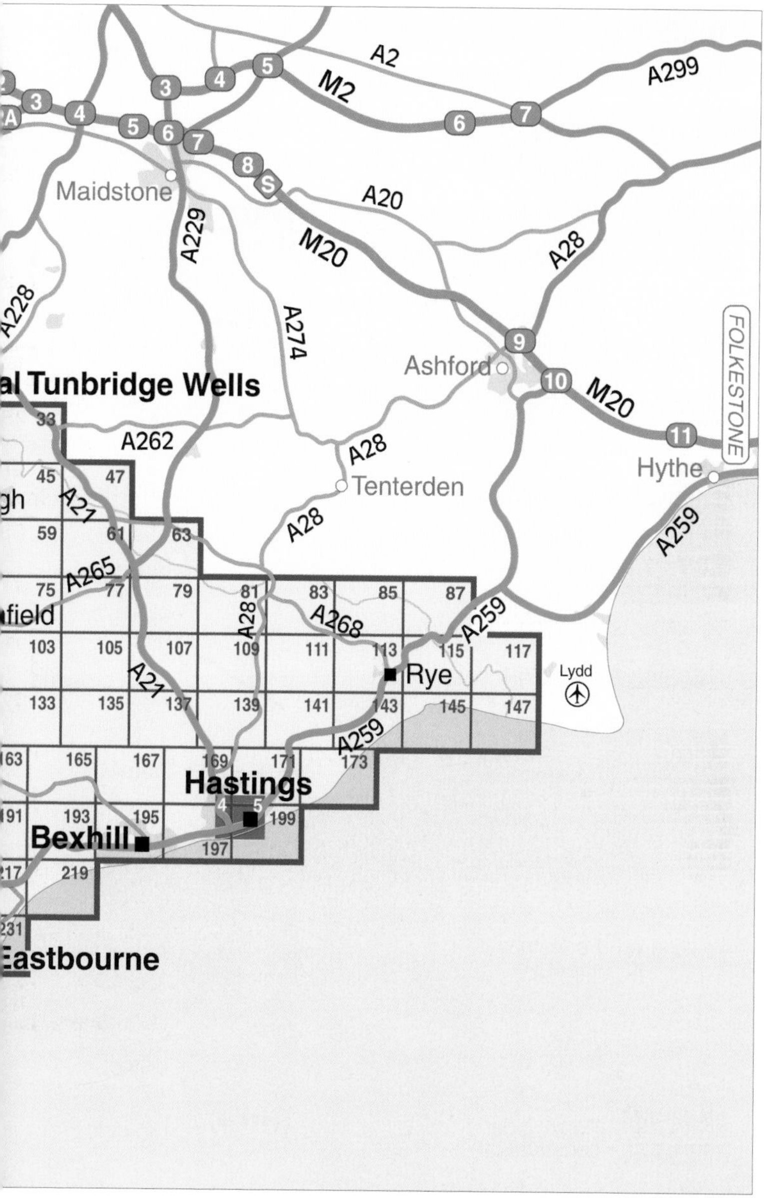

A2

A299

M2

A20

A28

M20

Maidstone

A229

A228

A274

Ashford

FOLKESTONE

M20

Hythe

al Tunbridge Wells

33

A262

A28

Tenterden

A259

45 47

A21

A28

59 61 63

A265

75 77 79 81 83 85 87 A259

field

A28

A268

103 105 107 109 111 113 115 117 Lydd

A21

133 135 137 139 141 143 145 147

Rye

163 165 167 169 171 173

A259

Hastings

191 193 195 199

Bexhill

197

217 219

231

Eastbourne

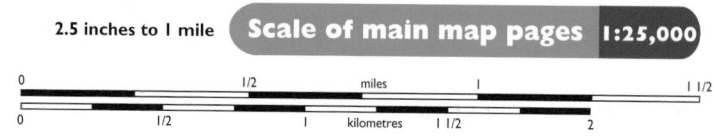

0 1/2 miles 1 1 1/2

0 1/2 1 kilometres 1 1/2 2

Junction 9	Motorway & junction		P+🚌	Park & Ride
Services	Motorway service area		🚌	Bus/coach station
	Primary road single/dual carriageway			Railway & main railway station
Services	Primary road service area			Railway & minor railway station
	A road single/dual carriageway		⊖	Underground station
	B road single/dual carriageway		⊖	Light railway & station
	Other road single/dual carriageway		++++++++++	Preserved private railway
	Restricted road		LC	Level crossing
	Private road		●—●—●	Tramway
← ←	One way street		- - - - - -	Ferry route
	Pedestrian street		....	Airport runway
- - - - -	Track/ footpath		— · — · — ·	Boundaries- borough/ district
	Road under construction		ᐯᐯᐯᐯᐯᐯ	Mounds
⊏ = = = ⊐	Road tunnel		93	Page continuatio 1:25,000
P	Parking		7	Page continuatio to enlarged scale 1:17,500

Symbol	Description
	River/canal lake, pier
	Aqueduct lock, weir
465 ▲ Winter Hill	Peak (with height in metres)
	Beach
	Coniferous woodland
	Broadleaved woodland
	Mixed woodland
	Park
	Cemetery
	Built-up area
	Featured building
⊓⊔⊓⊔⊓	City wall
A&E	Accident & Emergency hospital
	Toilet

Symbol	Description
	Toilet with disabled facilities
	Petrol station
PH	Public house
PO	Post Office
	Public library
i	Tourist Information Centre
	Castle
	Historic house/ building
Wakehurst Place NT	National Trust property
M	Museum/ art gallery
†	Church/chapel
	Country park
	Theatre/ performing arts
	Cinema

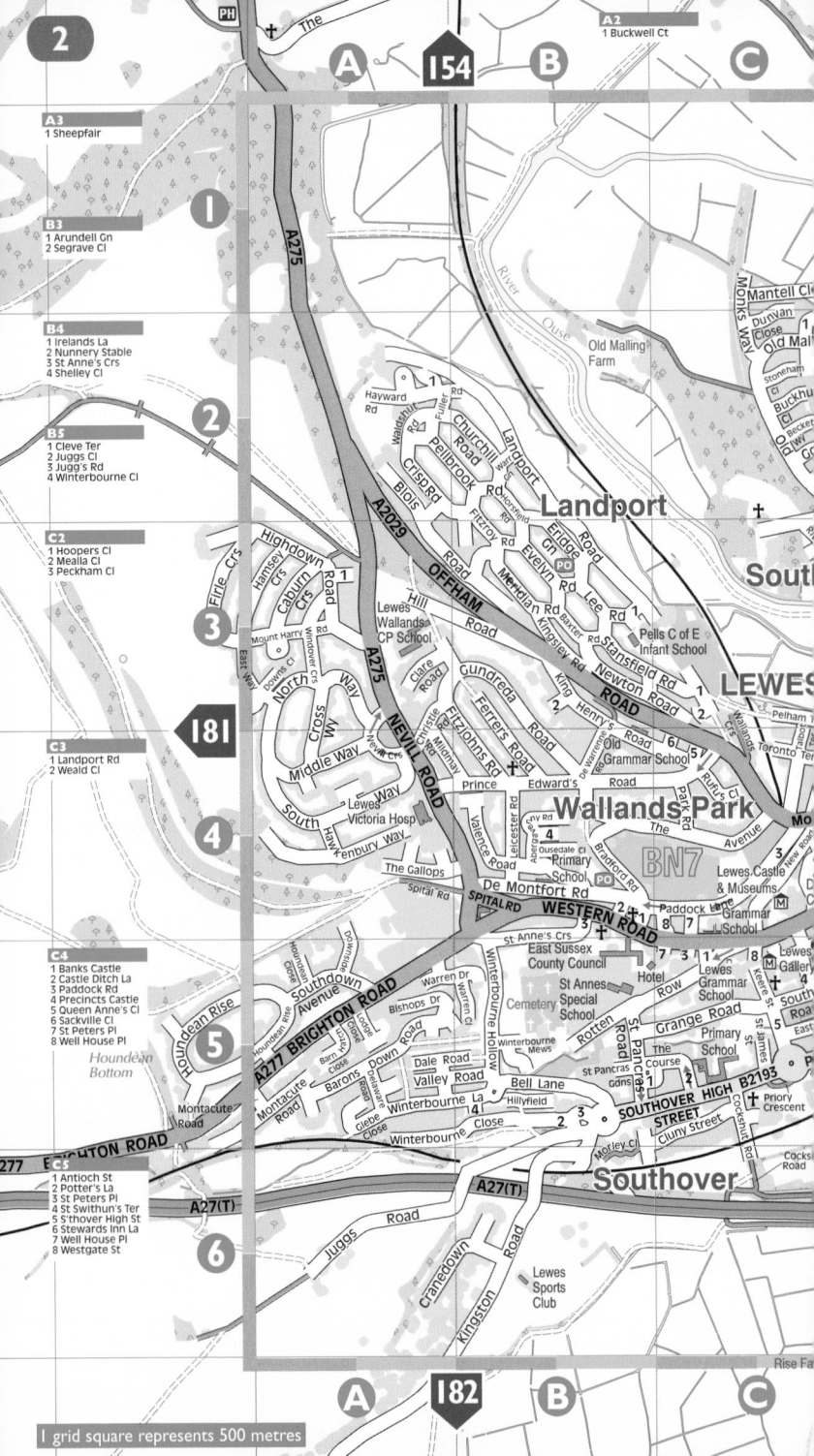

2

A3
1 Sheepfair

B3
1 Arundell Gn
2 Segrave Cl

B4
1 Irelands La
2 Nunnery Stable
3 St Anne's Crs
4 Shelley Cl

B5
1 Cleve Ter
2 Juggs Cl
3 Jugg's Rd
4 Winterbourne Cl

C2
1 Hoopers Cl
2 Mealla Cl
3 Peckham Cl

C3
1 Landport Rd
2 Weald Cl

C4
1 Banks Castle
2 Castle Ditch La
3 Paddock Rd
4 Precincts Castle
5 Queen Anne's Cl
6 Sackville Cl
7 St Peters Pl
8 Well House Pl

C5
1 Antioch St
2 Potter's La
3 St Peters Pl
4 St Swithun's Ter
5 S'thover High St
6 Stewards Inn La
7 Well House Pl
8 Westgate St

A2
1 Buckwell Ct

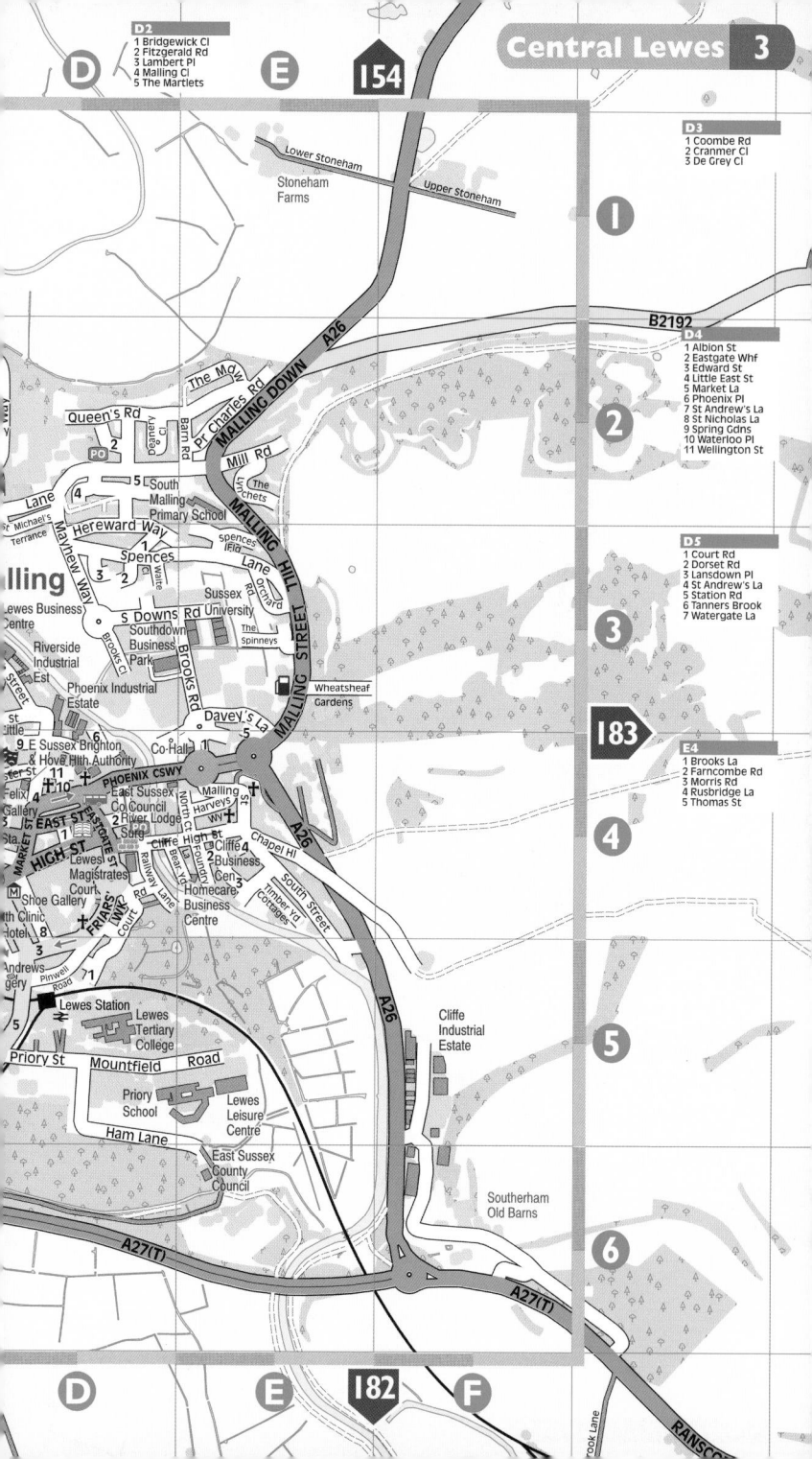

D2
1 Bridgewick Cl
2 Fitzgerald Rd
3 Lambert Pl
4 Malling Cl
5 The Martlets

D3
1 Coombe Rd
2 Cranmer Cl
3 De Grey Cl

D4
1 Albion St
2 Eastgate Whf
3 Edward St
4 Little East St
5 Market La
6 Phoenix Pl
7 St Andrew's La
8 St Nicholas La
9 Spring Gdns
10 Waterloo Pl
11 Wellington St

D5
1 Court Rd
2 Dorset Rd
3 Lansdown Pl
4 St Andrew's La
5 Station Rd
6 Tanners Brook
7 Watergate La

E4
1 Brooks La
2 Farncombe Rd
3 Morris Rd
4 Rusbridge La
5 Thomas St

154

B2192

183

182

Lower Stoneham

Stoneham Farms

Upper Stoneham

The Mow

Pr Charles Rd

A26

Queen's Rd

PO

Avenue

Barn Rd

MALLING DOWN

Mill Rd

The Virchets

South Malling Primary School

Michael's Terrace

Lane

Mayhew Way

Hereward Way

Spences

MALLING HILL

Spences field

Spences Lane

Water

Orchard Lane

lling

Lewes Business Centre

Sussex University

S Downs Rd

Southdown Business Park

Brooks Rd

The spinneys

Riverside Industrial Est

Phoenix Industrial Estate

Davey's La

Wheatsheaf Gardens

MALLING STREET

St

Little

E Sussex Brighton & Hove Hlth Authority

9

6

Co-Hall

Felix Gallery

11

10

PHOENIX CSWY

East Sussex Co Council

River Lodge

Malling

Harveys

Surg

A26

Chapel HI

HIGH ST

EAST STREET

MARKET STREET

Cliffe High St

Cliffe Business Cen

Homecare Business Centre

South Street

Timber Yd Cottages

Lewes Magistrates Court

Railway Lane

Station Yd

Lewes College

Shoe Gallery

lth Clinic

Hotel

FRIARS WLK

Court

Andrews gery

Pinwell Road

Lewes Station

Lewes Tertiary College

Priory St

Mountfield Road

Priory School

Lewes Leisure Centre

Ham Lane

East Sussex County Council

A26

Cliffe Industrial Estate

Southerham Old Barns

A27(T)

A27(T)

RANSCO

rook Lane

D   E   F

I

2

3

4

5

6

D   E   F

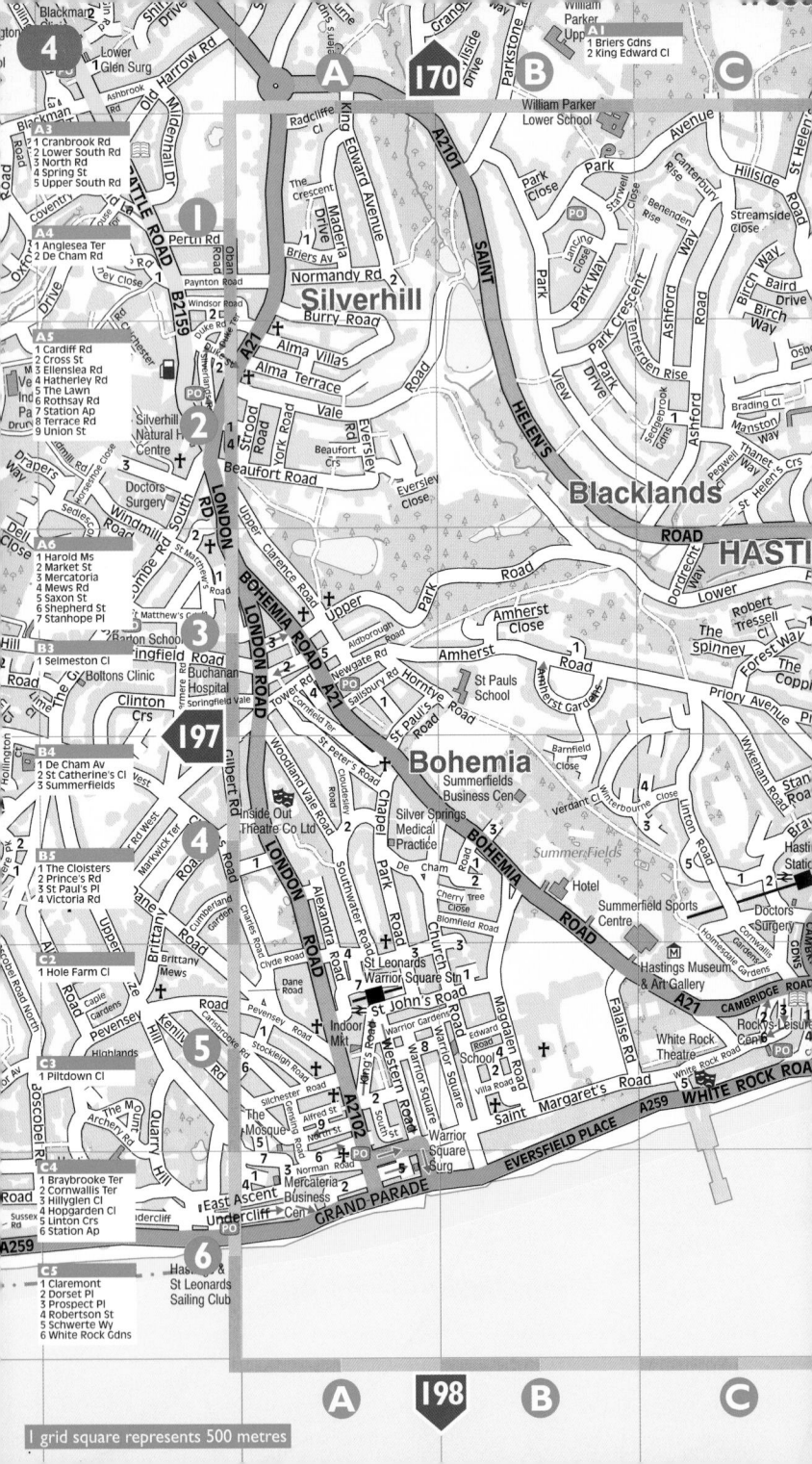

TN34

Broomsgrove

West Hill

Old Town

Hastings Castle

The Fishermans Museum

Sea Life Centre

Rock-A-Nore Parade

CARLISLE PARADE

PELHAM PLACE A259

D4
1 Brook St
2 Castle Hill Pas
3 Cornwallis St
4 Elford St
5 Middle St
6 Portland Pl
7 Station Rd
8 Stonefield Pl
9 Stone St
10 Waldegrave St
11 Wellington Ms
12 Wellington Sq

D5
1 Castle Gdns
2 Castle St
3 Harold Pl
4 Queen's Rd
5 Robertson Pas
6 Robertson Ter
7 Wellington Pl
8 York Gdns

E4
1 Becket Cl
2 Gladstone Rd
3 Saunders Cl

1 Alpine Rd
2 Castledown Av
3 Exmouth Pl
4 Gordon Rd
5 Swan Ter

E5
1 Cutter La
2 East St
3 Pelham Crs
4 Shell La
5 Sun La

F1
1 Clement Hill Rd

F2
1 Broomgrove Rd
2 Robertsons Hl

F3
1 The Glebe

F4
1 Courthouse St
2 Crown La
3 East Beach St
4 East Bourne St
5 Ebenezer Rd
6 Roebuck St
7 Winding St

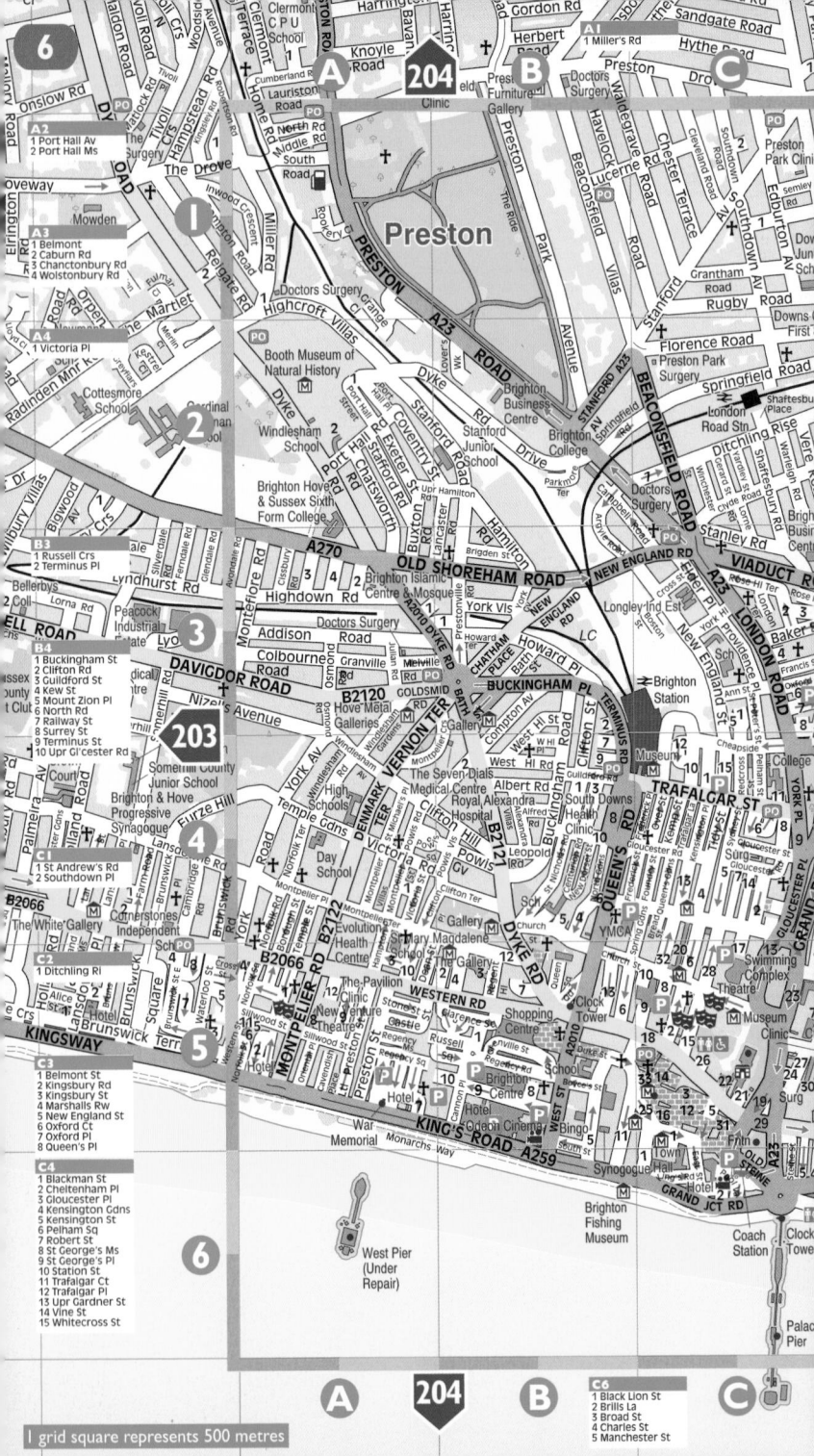

1 grid square represents 500 metres

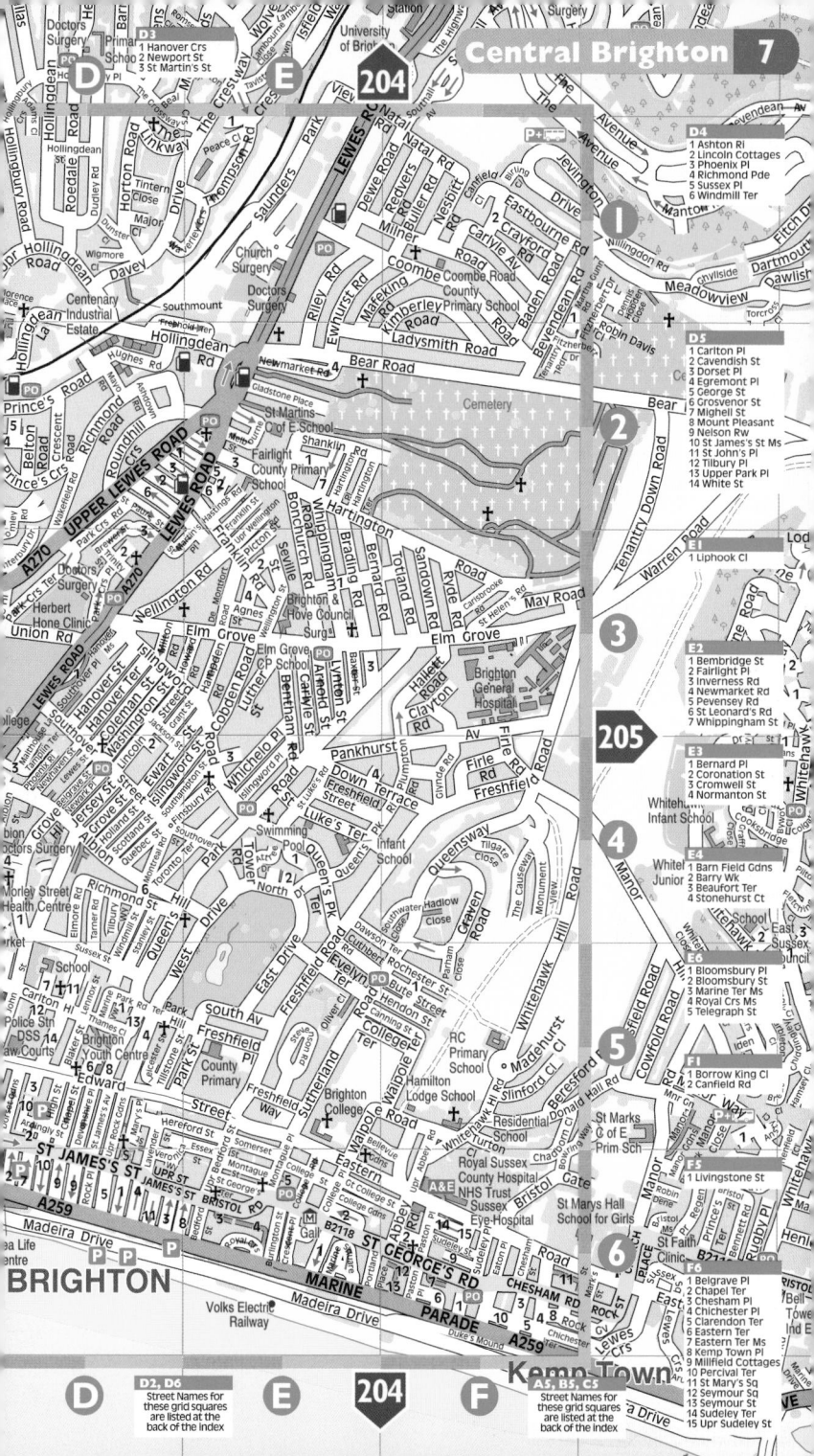

8

B2
1 Piddinghoe Mead

B3
1 Hawthorn Rl
2 Hazel Cl
3 Lapierre Rd
4 Lewry Cl

C2
1 Ship St

C3
1 Cloisters
2 Jackson Ms
3 Lower Pl
4 Murray Av
5 Neill's Cl
6 Newfield La
7 Newfield Rd

C4
1 Northdown Cl

Nore
Down

Cemetery †

Cemetery

Bush Road

Lewes Road

BN9

Robinson Rd

Elphick Road

Lewe
Distri
Cour

Metcalfe Av

Valley Close

Willow Wk

Lee Way

Maple Leaf Cl

Kennedy Way

Valley

Road

Fullwood Av

Evelyn Av

Lawes Av

Anderson Close

PO

LEWES RD

N

Meeching Valley
CP School

Chestnut Way

Elm Ct

Va Dene

Rose Wk Cl

The Rose Wk

East Sussex
County Council

East Sussex
County Council
School

church hill

Meeching Road

Brazen Close

Rothwell Ct

BRIGHTON

ROAD

Nore
Rd

(gr Valley Rd)

Rectory Close

First Avenue

New
Mkt

Links Avenue

Chichester Close

Cliff Pk Close

222

The Fairway

A259

Northdown Road

Second Av

Third

Western
Hill

Road

Cresta Road

Blakeney Avenue

Outlook Avenue

Cheyne Road

Gibbon

Hanson Road

Crest

Road

Ringmer Road

Pagler Av

Southdown Road

Sourhdown
Close

Warrington

East Sussex Co
Council
ington

ROAD

Highway

The

Park Road

The Leas

Road

Pevensey

Charlston Avenue

Cuckmere Rd

Westdean Av

Cornelius Avenue

Harbour View Road

Tideway
School

**Harbour
Heights**

Friars'
Bay

Court

Quar
Farm

The Or

1

2

3

4

5

6

I

I grid square represents 500 metres

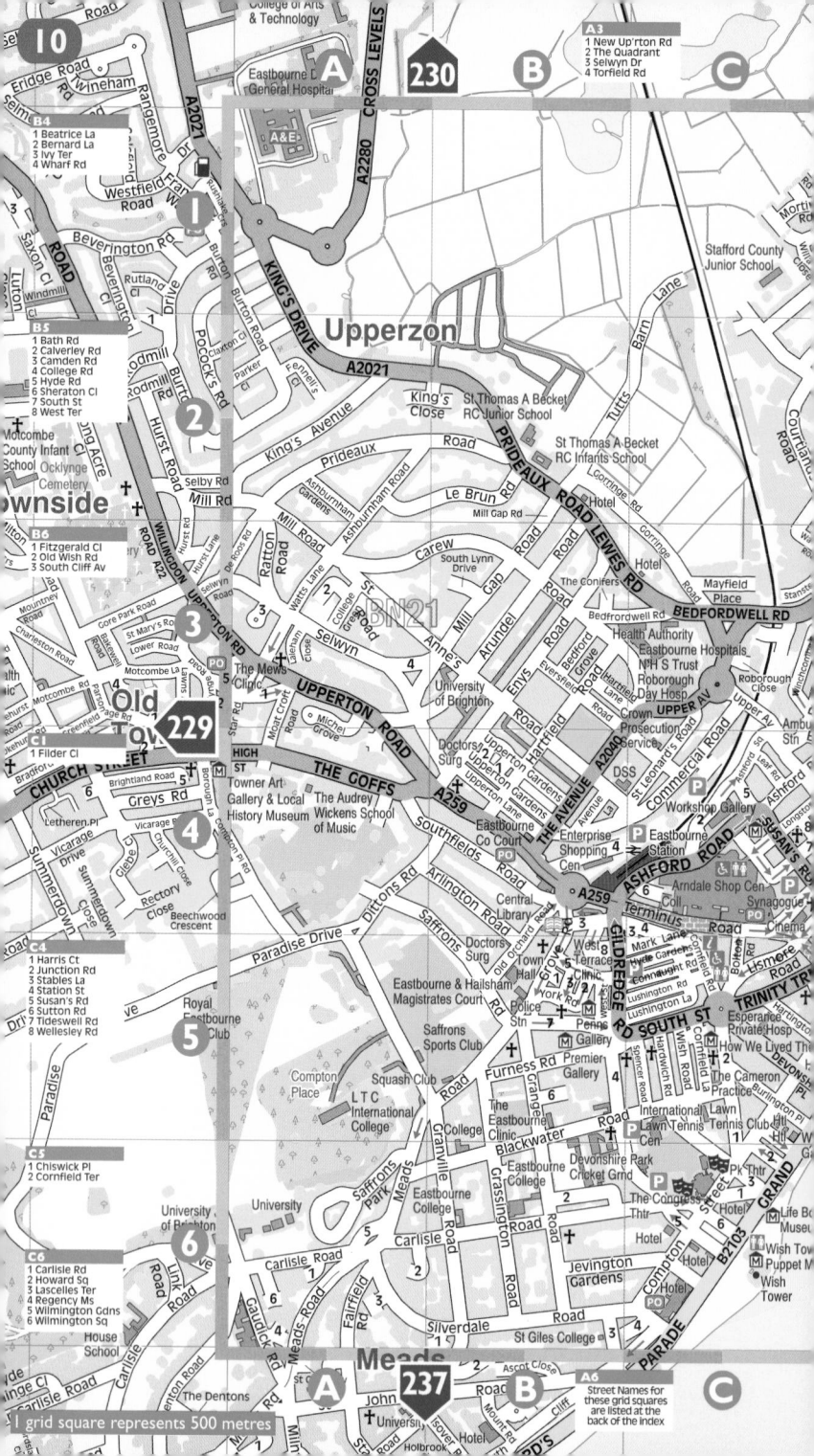

230
231
237

D1
1 Churchdale Pl

D2
1 Avondale Rd
2 Clarence Rd

D3
1 Albion Rd
2 Beltring Ter
3 Chawbrook Rd
4 Havelock Rd
5 Hoad Rd
6 Neville Rd
7 Oxford Rd
8 St George's Rd
9 Sheen Rd
10 Springfield Rd
11 Stanley Rd
12 Willowfield Rd

D4
1 Burfield Rd
2 Cavendish Pl
3 Colonade Rd
4 Leaf Hall Rd
5 Lion La
6 Marine Rd
7 Qu's Col'ade Gdns
8 St Aubyn's Rd
9 Willowfield Sq

D5
1 Burlington Rd
2 Cavendish Pl
3 Elms Rd

E1
1 Burleigh Pl
2 Roseveare Rd

E2
1 Belle Vue Rd
2 Romney St
3 Roselands Cl

E3
1 Bayham Rd
2 Halton Rd
3 St James Rd
4 Taddington Rd

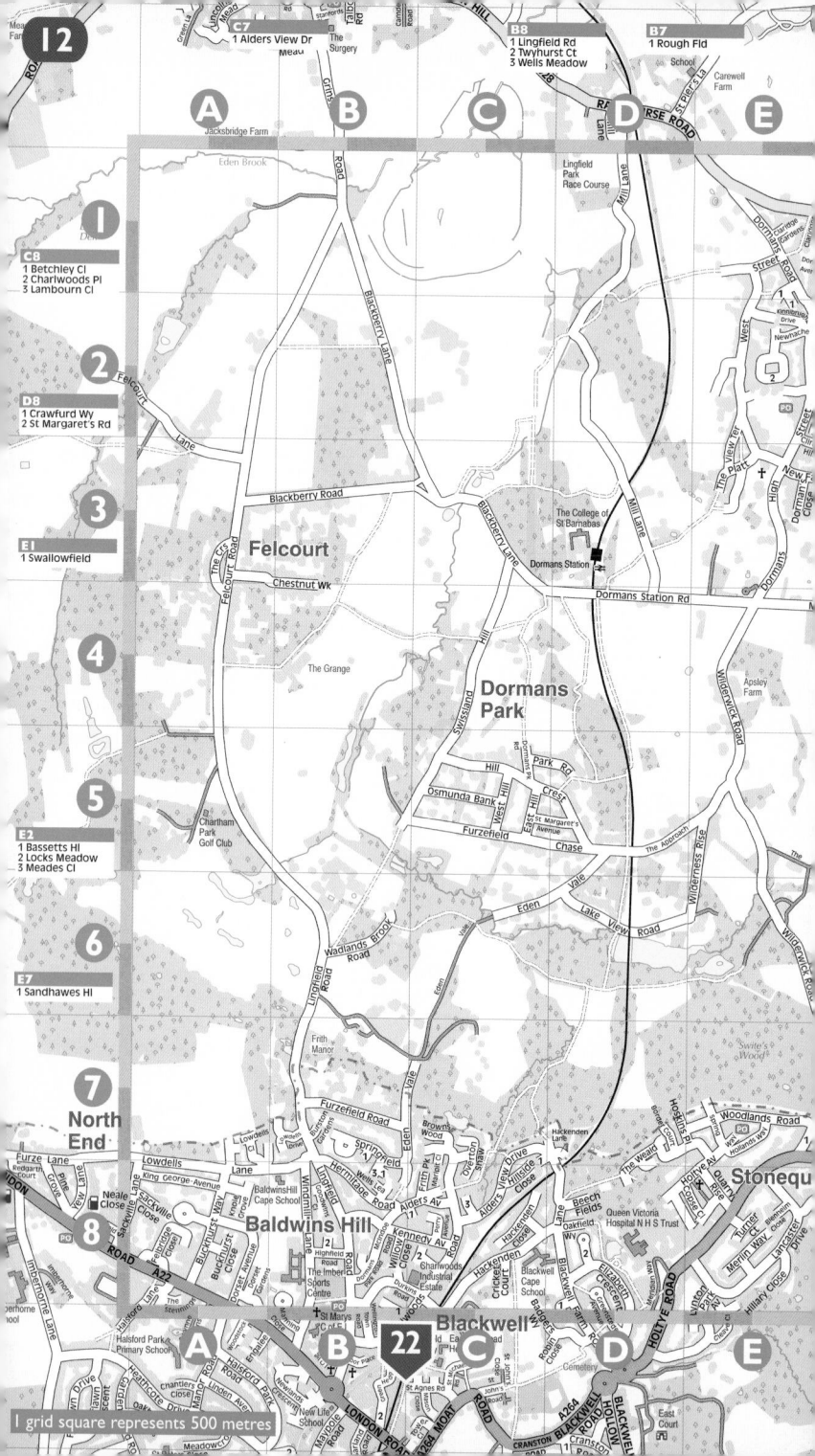

F8
1 Kindersley Cl

F G H J K

1
2
3
4
14
5
6
7
8

I

Hoopers
Farm

Ford Manor Road

Dormansland

Greathed
Manor

Vanguard Way

Moons Lane

Kent County
Surrey County

Old Lodge
Farm

Vanguard Way

Sussex Border Path

Beacon Hill Lane

Hollow Lane

Farindons

Hill

Ladycross
Farm

Upper Stonehurst
Farm

Moons Lane

Hollow Lane

Lower Stonehurst
Farm

Lullenden

Shepherdsgrove Lane

Avenue

Wilderwick
House

Blackwell
Wood

Vanguard Way

Sussex Border Path

Gotwick Manor

Surrey County
West Sussex County

Gotwick Farm

Orchards

Gotwick Farm

ry

Stirling Way

Imar Drive

HOLTYE ROAD

A264

Vanguard Way

East Sussex County
West Sussex County

Chords
Wood

Fairlight

Fairlfrd

Shovelstrode
Manor

Brooklands

Mindenheim Avenue

Shovelstrode Lane

F G H 23 J K

14

New Barns Farm

Greybury Lane

Ockhams

A　**B**　**C**　**D**　**E**

Cobhambury Farm

Hoopers Farm

1

Greybury Farm

Shernden Wood

2

Jackson's Lane

Kent County
Surrey County

Beechenwood Farm

3

Vanguard Way

Ludwells Farm

Sussex Border Path

4

Beeches Farm

13

5

Sussex Border

Lower Stonehurst Farm

enden

6

Shovelstrode Lane

Basing Farm

Scarletts

Vanguard Way

Furnace Farm

Gotwick Manor

7

Kent Water

A264

8

Hammerwood

Holty

AD

ovelstrode
anor

A　**B**　**24**　**C**　**D**　**E**

Brooklands

Hamm Park

Camston

1 grid square represents 500 metres

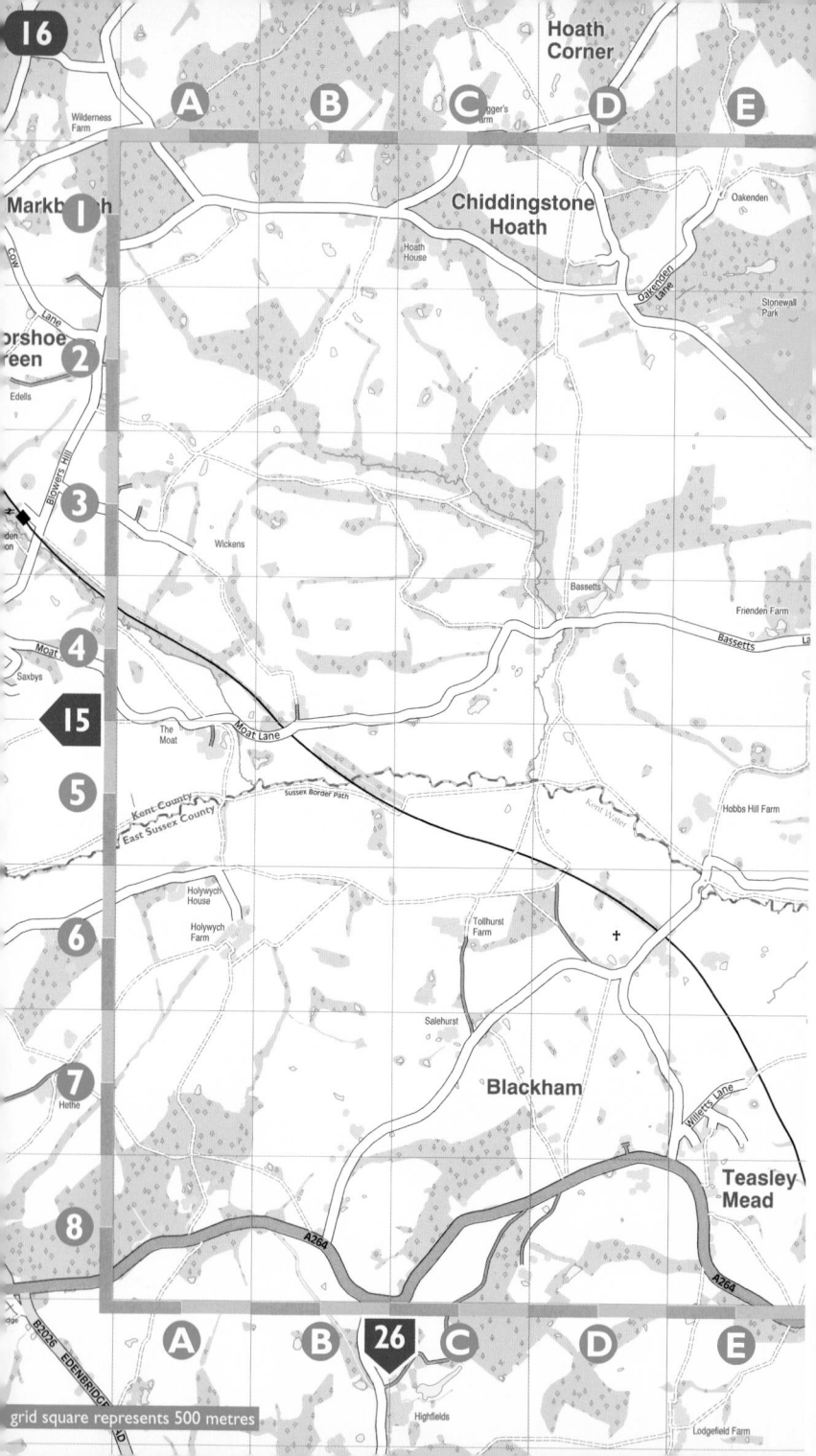

16

A   B   C   D   E

Hoath
Corner

Wilderness
Farm

Markbeech **1**

Chiddingstone
Hoath

Digger's
Farm

Oakenden

Hoath
House

Oakenden
Lane

Stonewall
Park

Horshoe
Green **2**

Edells

Blowers Hill

3

Wickens

Bassetts

Frienden Farm

Bassetts Lane

Moat

4

Saxbys

15

The
Moat

Moat Lane

5

Kent County
East Sussex County

Sussex Border Path

Kent Water

Hobbs Hill Farm

Holywych
House

6

Holywych
Farm

Tollhurst
Farm

✝

Salehurst

7

Hethe

Blackham

Willetts Lane

Teasley
Mead

8

A264

A264

A B036 EDENBRIDGE RD

A   B   **26**   C   D   E

Highfields

Lodgefield Farm

grid square represents 500 metres

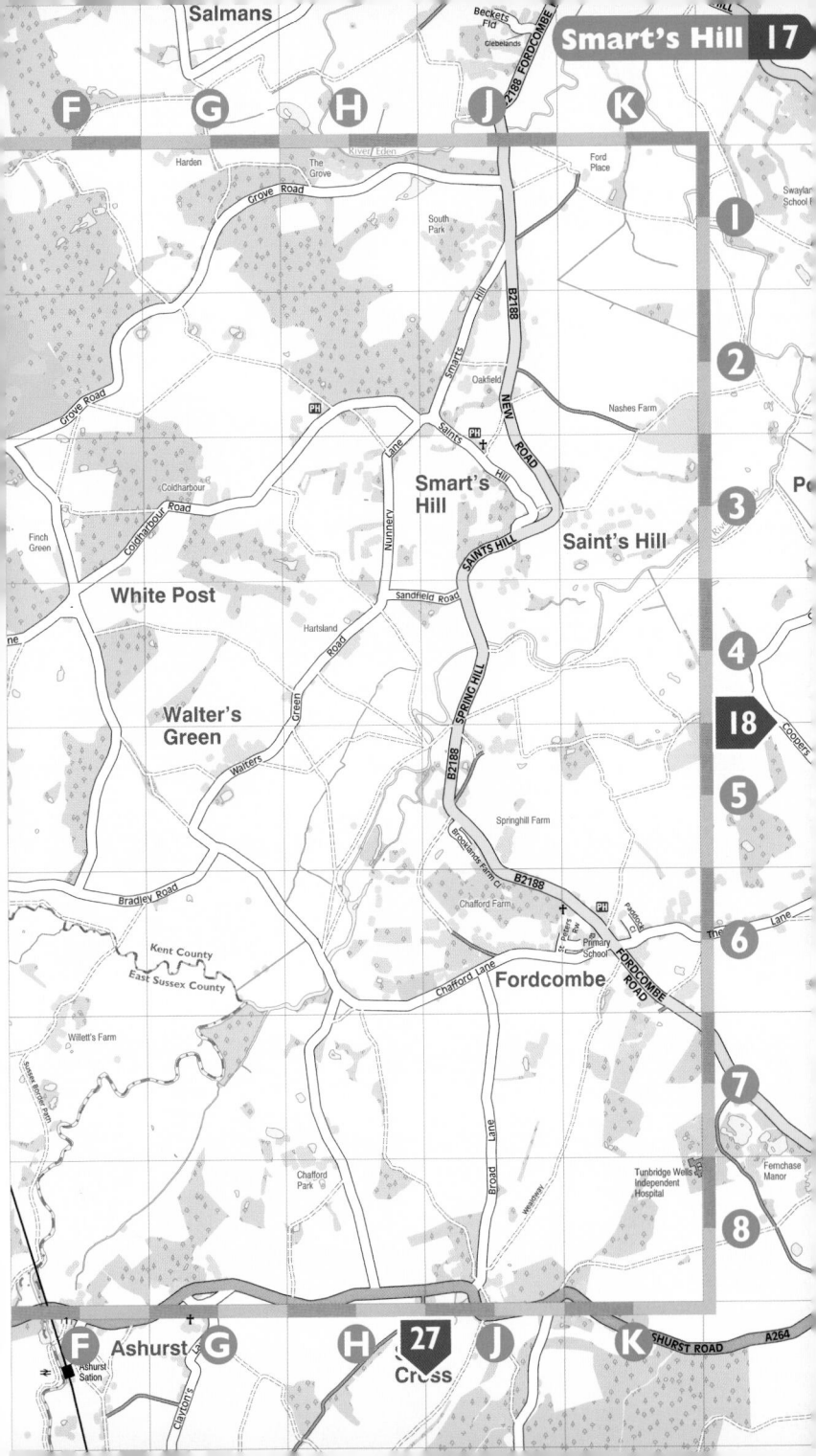

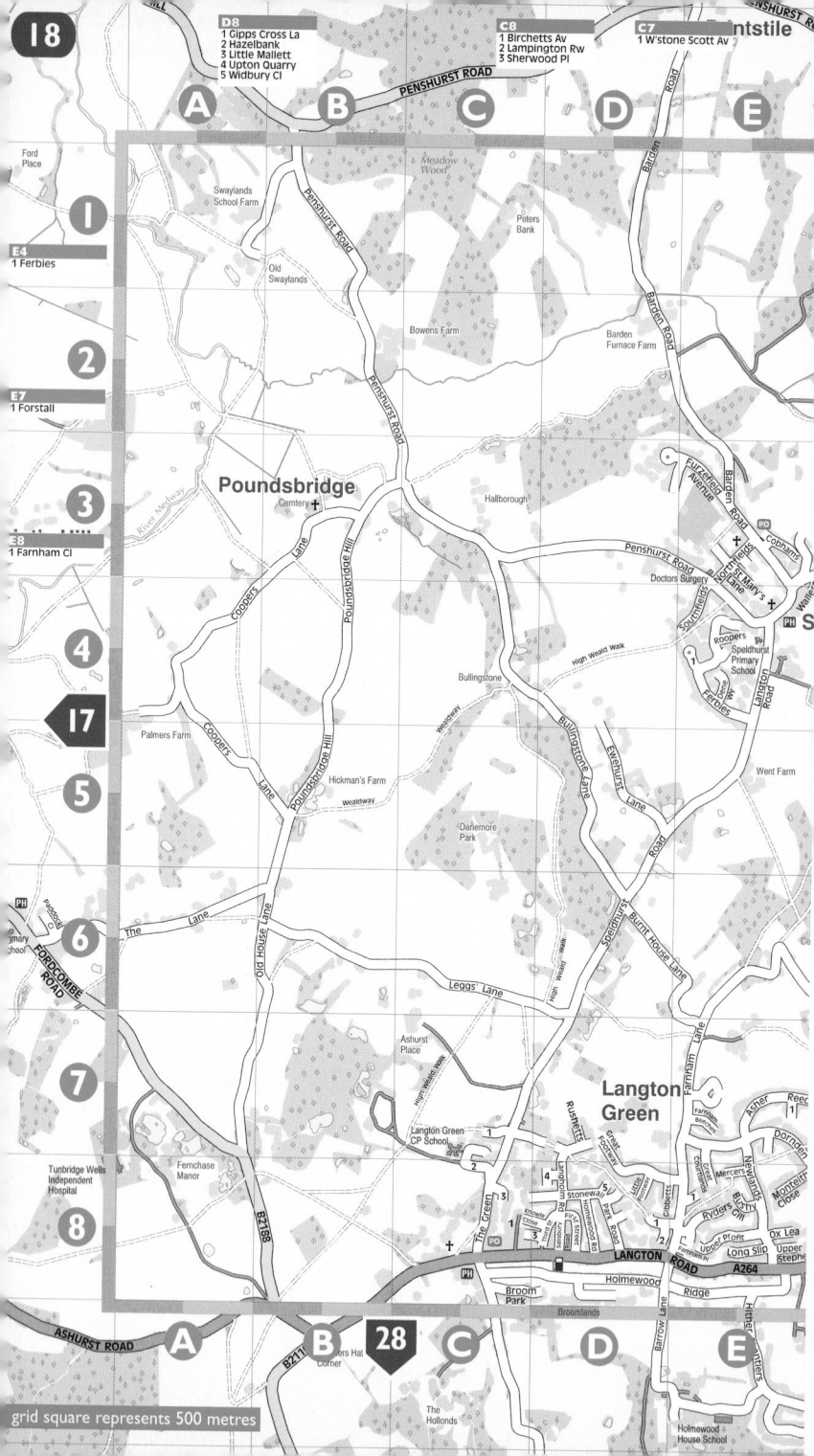

H5
1 Cornford Cl
2 Woodgate Wy

K4
1 Beech Hurst
2 Knight's Rdg
3 Pembury Cl
4 Ridgeway
5 Sweeps Hill Cl

F   G   H   J   K

Kenward

Pembury Walks

Pembury Hall

Pembury Hall Road

High Weald Walk

Kent Co for Girls

Kingstanding Business Park

Colebrooke

Pembury Walks

Old Church Road

Reawings

High Weald Walk

I

K5
1 Stabledene Wy

Yew Tree Farm

Home Farm Lane

Knights Way

Knights Park

2

Maidstone

Stone Court Lane

A228

Tonbridge Road

A21(T)

The Grove

Old Church Road

Rowley Hill

3

Pembury Primary School

Lower Green

Cemetery

Barchester

Birchfields

Doctors Surgery

4

Pembury Hospital

Ridgeway

Berkeley Close

Romford Road

5

MAIDSTONE ROAD

A228

Tonbridge Road

Woodhill Park

Greenleas

The Paddock

High Street

Camden

Cornford

Lower Green

Bellfield Road

Henwoods Crescent

Henwood Road

Woodside Road

Marlon Way

Maltmans Drive

Vauxhall Drive

Blockhouse

Pembury Grange

Havering Close

Thornfield Gardens

Sandown Park

PEMBURY

Hastings

A21(T)

6

ROAD

A264

St Georges School

TN2

Chalket Lane

Chalket Farm

Blackhurst

Larkfield Hall

Fletchers Farm

7

Mouseden

High Weald Walk

Little Bayhall

Great Bayhall

River Teise

8

F   G   H   **31**   J   K

Dodhurst

Dundale Farm

22

London Road · A22
Imberhorne School

A **B** **12** **C** **D** **E** Stoneq

Blackwell

EAST GRINSTEAD

Sunnyside

A **B** **34** **C** **D** **E**

Weir Woo
Resevoir

1 grid square represents 500 metres

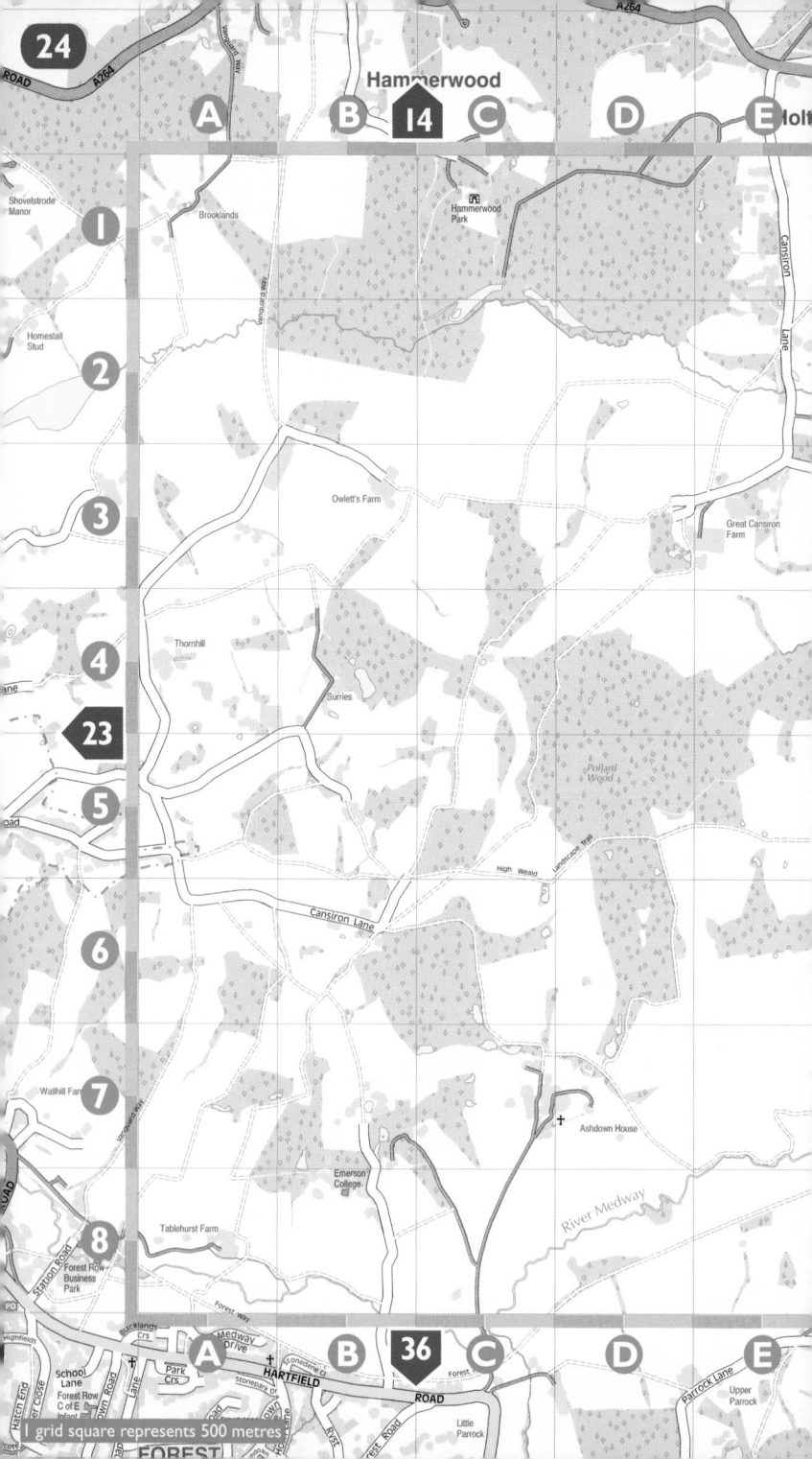

Hammerwood

14

A264

ROAD   A264

A   B   C   D   E   Holt

Shovelstrode Manor

Brooklands

Hammerwood Park

1

Homestall Stud

2

Cansiron Lane

Owlett's Farm

3

Great Cansiron Farm

Thornhill

4

Surries

23

Pollard Wood

5

Landscape Trail

High Weald

Cansiron Lane

6

Wallhill Farm

7

Ashdown House

Emerson College

River Medway

8

Forest Row Business Park

Tablehurst Farm

School Lane   Forest Row C of E Infant

Blacklands Crs   Medway Drive   HARTFIELD   36   Park Crs

Forest Way

A   B   C   D   E

ROAD

Little Parrock

Parrock Lane

Upper Parrock

FOREST

F G H **15** J K

Cullinghurst Farm

Edenbridge Road

B2026

EDENBRIDGE ROAD

I

Tye Farm

Goodyers Lane

Chantlers Farm

2

3

Beeches Farm

Bassett's Manor

Perryhill Farm

Butcherfield Lane

4

ROAD

Butcherfield Lane

26

Hartwell

5

EDENBRIDGE

St Ives Farm

High Weald Landscape Trail

Chartners Farm

6

Forest Way

Forest Way

CASTLEFIELD

Motts Field

HIGH STREET

Hartfield

St Mary the Virgin School

7

TN7 PH

Church Street

Newton's Hill

B2026

8

Gallypot Street

GALLYPOT HILL B2110

High Weald La

F G H **37** J K

JACKS HILL

Parrock Lane

Upper Hartfield

F G H **19** J **K** YAL
TUNBRIDGE
WELLS

Denny
Bottom

Tunbridge
Wells Golf
Club

SHOP'S DOWN A264

Nevill
Ridge

Nevill
Park

The Crossway

The Midway

Hungershall
Park

Hungershall Park

Cabbage Stalk Lane

Park
Close

High Rocks Lane

High Weald Walk

High
Rocks

Kent County
East Sussex County

Summervale Road

Ramslye

Waterdown

Friezland

Ramslye
Primary
School

Fox Garden Lane

The Surgery

I

1
1 Eastlands Rd

The
Mead
School

2

Roedean
Road

**Strawberry
Hill**

Kentish
Gardens

Broadmead

Strawberry Close

St. Mark's

Glenmore

Broadw **Down**
Wallace

3

Waterfield
Road

FRANT ROAD A267

MOAT RD

4

30

5

Hargate
Forest

A26

The
Warren

Spratsbrook
Farm

6

7

Whitehill
Wood

Eridge
Park

8

Warren Farm
Lane

Eridge Green

High Weald Walk

F G H **41** J K

Forge
Wood

30

A264

ROYAL
TUNBRIDGE
WELLS

20

42

29

A **B** **C** **D** **E**

B1
1 Cambridge Gdns
2 Clifton Pl
3 Farmcombe Cl
4 Grecian Rd
5 Madeira Pk
6 Norfolk Rd

A2
1 Broad Gv
2 Clarendon Gdns

A1
Street Names for
these grid squares
are listed at the
back of the index

B2
1 Beau Nash Wy

B3
1 Elphick's Pl

C1
1 Camden Hl
2 Hollyshaw Cl

C3
1 Cypress Gv

D1
1 Camden Pk
2 Hawkenbury Cl
3 Polesden Rd
4 Rookley Cl

D2
1 Hawkenbury Md

Camden Park

Hawkenbury

Broadwater Down

Frant

TN3

F G H 21 J K

I
Dund
Farm

2

3

4

32

5

6

7

8

F G H 43 J K

Mouseden

Little
Bayhall

Great

River Tyse

High Woods Lane

Dodhurst

Palmers
Farm

Road

Kent County
East Sussex County

Dundale Road

Brown's
Wood

Dundale Road

Sunninglye
Farm

Road

Rushlye
Down

Furnace
Wood

Oxpasture
Wood

Tollslye

Rushlye
Farm

Court Lodge
Down

Abbots
Down

Jews
Wood

Rushye
Green

Frant
Station

Middle   Road

Bells Yew Green

B2169

Barr
Oak

Higham
Farm

Barelands Farm

Camden
Wood

Great Shoesmiths
Farm

32

A B C D E

Elmhurst
Farm

1

Great
Sandhurst
Wood

Dundale
Farm

Dundale Road

2

Sandhurst
Farm

3

Rear
Wood

Furnace
Wood

4

Tollslye

31

Bayham
Abbey

5

Bayham Lake

River Teise

Jews
Wood

6

B2169

7

Bartley Mill Road

Little
Bayham

8

Wickhurst
Farm

Buss's
Green

A B 44 C D E

Kent County
East Sussex County

Free Heath Road

Stiver's
Wood

Bartley Mill Rd

1 grid square represents 500 metres

Old Farm

F G H J K

Cuckoo Lane

Tong Lane

1

Little
Dunks Farm

Coldharbour

Lamberhurst Quarter

Lane

2

The Grange

B2162

LAMBERHURST

Lindridge
Lodge Farm

A21(T)

Clay Hill Cotts

Windmill
Farm

3

Fay Hill Road

A21(T)

A262

Toy & Model
Museum

Owl
House

Grantham
Hall

4

B2162

Forstal Farm

Mount
Pleasant

Mount   Pleasant   Lane

Church

5

School Hill

Lamberhurst
Golf Club

Court
Lodge

Hoathly
Farm

Parsonage
Lane

Lamberhurst
C of E
School

Lamberhurst

Furnace
Mill

Brewer Street

Lamberhurst
Surgery

A21(T)

Hazelstub Drive

6

PO

FURNACE

B2100

High Street

Pearse
Place

Spray Hill

7

Hook Green

LANE

Furnace
Farm

Town Hill

Sand Road

The Priory

Nellis Road

B2169

Furnace Avenue

Spray
Hill

8

**The
Down**

The Slade

Widgate

A21(T)

F G H **45** J K

Owls
Castle Farm

Hogpole   Lane

Nellis Road

Lane

East Sus

Kent County

Wiskett's
Wood

Ⓐ   Ⓑ   **22**   Ⓒ   Ⓓ   Ⓔ

West Hoathly Road

Admiral's
Bridge
Lane

Landscape trail

Weir Wood
Resevoir

Charlwood

Ⓘ

❷

Neylands
Farm

❸

Mayes

Blackland
Farm

Cansfield Lane

East Sussex County

West Sussex County

Legsheath
Farm

New Coombe
Farm

❹

Plaw
Wood

Legsheath Lane

❺

Plawhetch
Hall

Coldharbour
Manor

Imberhorne Lane

Tyes
Cross

Top Road

Plaw-Hatch Lane

❻

Courtlands

Horsted Lane

❼

Deanlands
Farm

Chilling Street

Horncastle
Wood

Cripps Manor

❽

Wickenden
Farm

Ⓐ   Ⓑ   **48**   Ⓒ   Ⓓ   Ⓔ

Rest

Twyford
Lodge

Imberhorne Lane

Shunt

1 grid square represents 500 metres

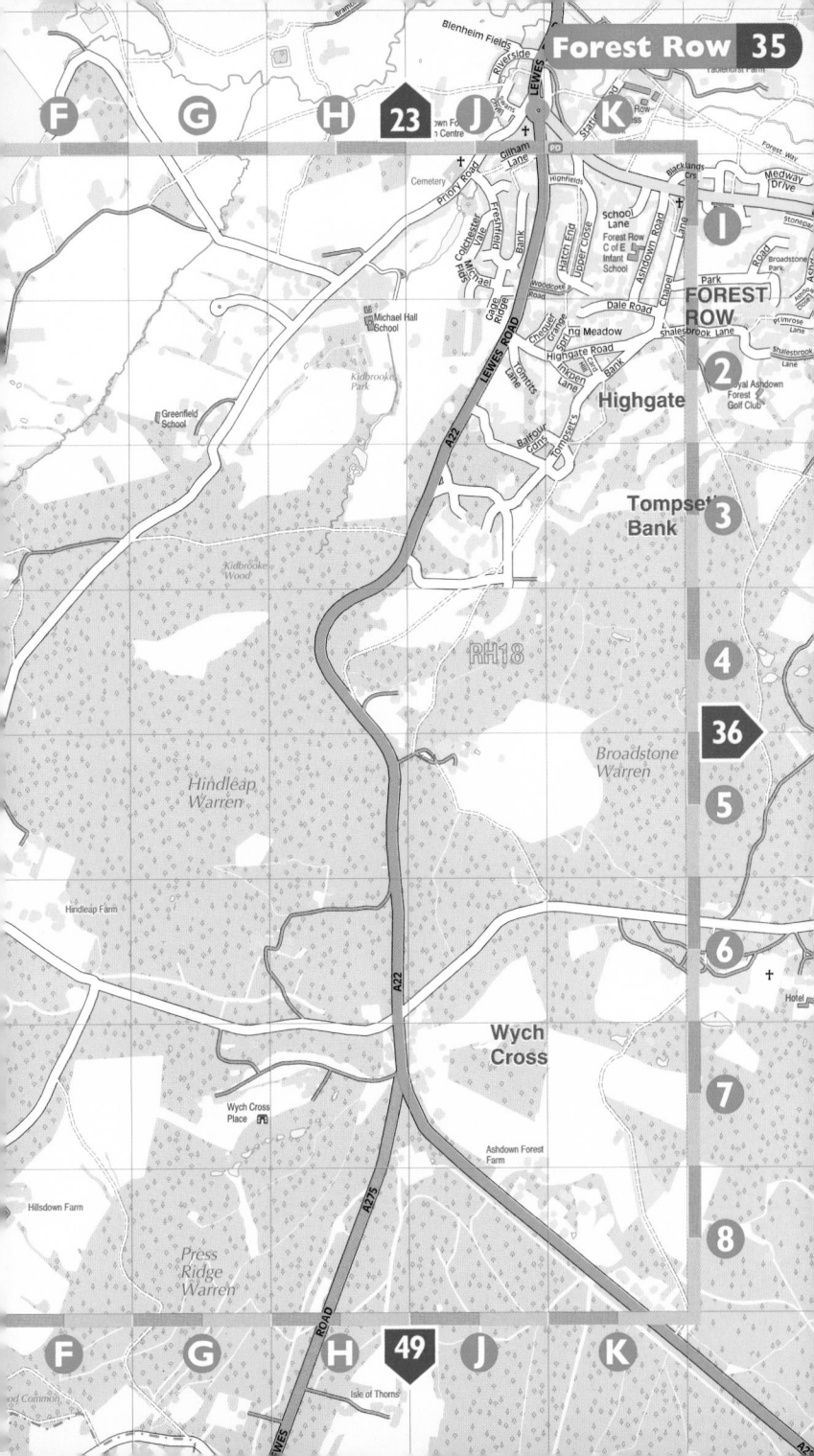

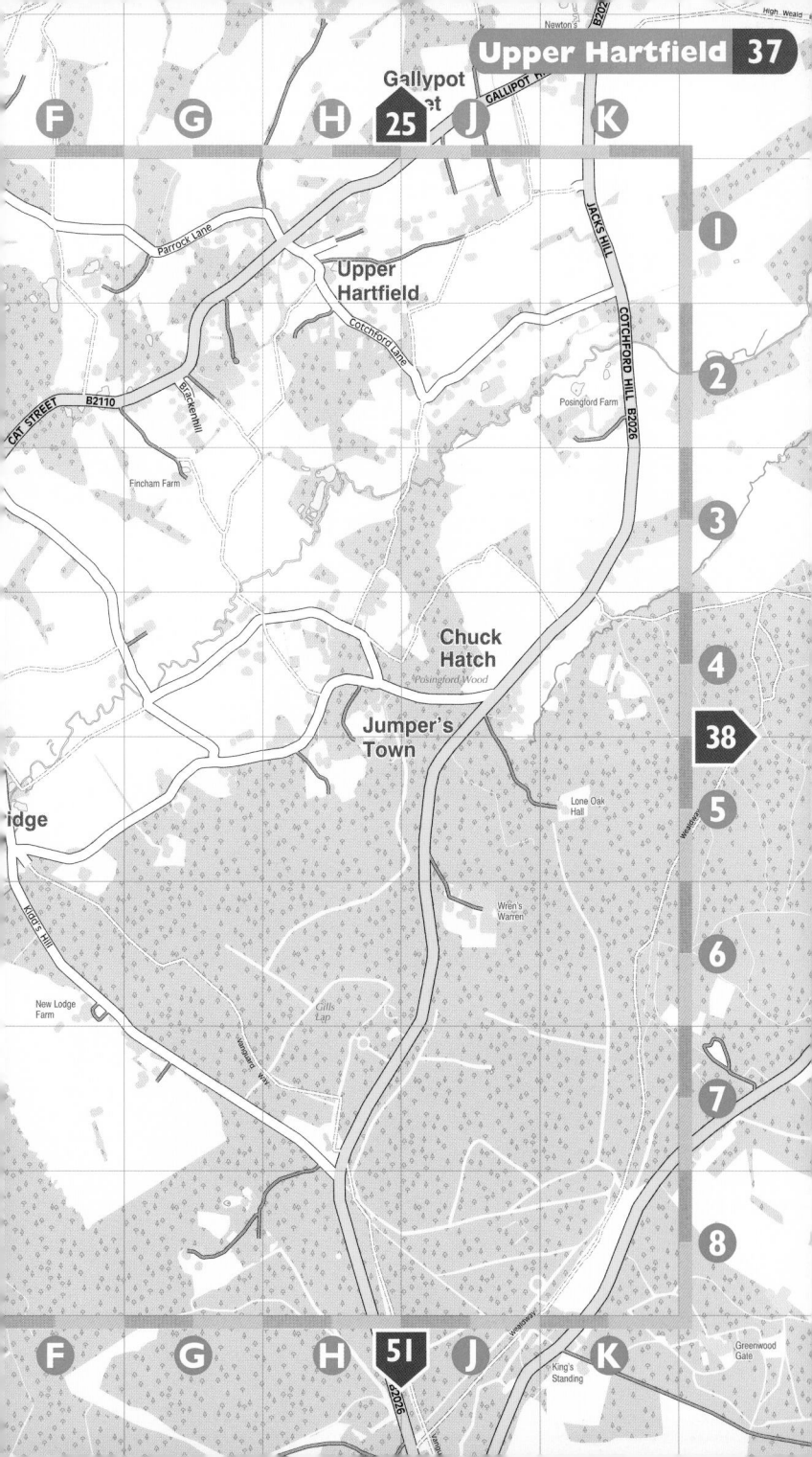

Newton's
High Weald
B2026

Gallypot
et
GALLIPOT
JACKS HILL

Parrock Lane

**Upper
Hartfield**

Cotchford Lane

Posingford Farm

CAT STREET B2110

Brackenhill

COTCHFORD HILL B2026

Fincham Farm

**Chuck
Hatch**

Posingford Wood

**Jumper's
Town**

Lone Oak
Hall

ldge

Webbs

FOG'S HILL

Wren's
Warren

New Lodge
Farm

Gills
Lap

Westerhill

Westerhill

Greenwood
Gate

King's
Standing

B2026

Westerhill

F G H 25 J K
I
2
3
4
38
5
6
7
8
F G H 51 J K

38

Withyham

Forstal Farm

A **B** **26** **C** **D** **E**

Buckhurst Park

I

JACKS HILL

Westway

COTCHFORD LANE B2026

2

Posingford Farm

Buckhurst Farm

Fisher's Gate

3

Westway

4

Friar's Gate

37

5

Lone Oak Hall

Westway

Five Hundred Acre Wood

Marden's Hill

Marden's Hill

6

B2188

7

St John's Church School

SAINT JOHN'S ROAD

Wood Eaves

8

A **B** **52** **C** **D** **E**

King's Standing

Home Farm

Glenn

I grid square represents 500 metres

Crowborough

H7
1 Gillridge Gn

H8
1 Elphick Pl
2 Mill Crs
3 Park Crs

F G H 27 J Mott's Mill K

Corseley Road

Leyswood

I

J8
1 The Farthings
2 Sefton Wy

2

High Weald Landscape Trail

Penns in the Rocks

Lye Green

Park Grove

Landscape Trail

3

Littlebrook

Brean Wood

4

Orznash Farm

40

Gillridge Farm

5

Boarshead

B2188

Beechen Wood

A26

6

Hoadley's Lane

Smugglers Lane

Lane

Innham's Wood

7

Norbury Close

Cooper's Wood

Coopers Lane

Ashleigh Gdns

Elm Cl

Carv

Common Wood Side

Pleasant View

Goldsmith Leisure Centre

Hourne Farm

Ridge Road

John's

Pinmet

London Road

High Cross Fields

Steel Cross

Pinewood Chase

Old Lane

Knowle Lane

Glenmore Road East

Kings Road

Beacon Avenue

Goldsmith Avenue

Ellison Close

Beacon Gardens

Pine Grove

Doctors Surgery

Highlands Close

Shelling Road

Hotel

HIGH

PO

THE BROADWAY

Oldham Road

Wealden Close

Sefton Chase

Fridge Drive

Mill Drive

Oakhurst Rd

Charity Farm Way

Millbrook

Hookswood Close

BRIDGE ROAD

GREEN LANE

Beacon Community College

Methodist Church

8

F G H 53 J K

Bampach Lane

Beacon Rd West

BEACON ROAD

Woodside

Mill Lane

Forest Park

Water Lane

Walters Close

Saxonborough Surgery

Saxonbury Close

Church Road

Tennis

St Marys Primary Catholic School

Cantelupe Rd

Fermor School

Beacon Community College

East Beaches Road

West

Beeches Lane

Hillrise

Poundfield

B2157

PO

F G H **29** J K

I

2

3

4

42

5

6

7

8

High Weald Walk

Forge
Wood

Danegate

Stonewall

Sussex Border Path

Pocacksgate F

Blackdon Hill

Great
Danegate

Saxonbury
Farm

Green Hedges
Farm

Brickyard Lane

Moth Wood

Entry
Hill

Forest Farm

**Mark
Cross**

Greenhouse
Farm

Mark Cross
C of E
School

Hornshuck Road

Edridge Lane

F G H **55** J K B2100

Cent...

Heathfield

Highgate
Farm

MAYFIELD R...

A B **30** C D E

Frant

Manor Farm

I
High Weald Walk

Shernfold Park

Sleeches Cross

2
The Platt

WADHURST ROAD B2099

Woodside

Knowle

Frant Place

3
Sussex Border Path

Comptons

Down Lane

Pococksgate Farm

4

Earlye Farm

Nap Wood

5
Saxonbury Farm

Green Hedges Farm

6
Brickyard Lane

Partridge Lane

7
Frankham Wood

Frankham

Mark Cross

Mark Cross C of E School

WADHURST ROAD

Houndsell Place

8
Sandyden Home

B2100

MAYFIELD ROAD

A B **56** C D E

Renhurst Farm

Earl's Farm

F   G   H   J   K

I
2
3
4
5
6
7
8

BEDGEBURY

Twyssenden
Manor

Three
Chimneys
Farm

Rogers Rough Road
Bedgebury Cross

Bedgebury
Cross

Bedgebury Park

Bedgebury Park
School

Bedgebury Junior
School

National
Pinetum &
Garden

Combwell
Wood

Park
House

LADY OAK LANE

Bedgebury
Forest

Combwell
Priory
Farm

B2079

A21(T)

Flimwell
Grange

Farm
Close

Kent County
East Sussex County

Old Vicarage Dr
Bewl Bridge
Close

Blenheim
Way

LONDON ROAD

B2087

**Union
Street**

Flimwell

HIGH STREET

A268

HAWKHURST

Quedley

61

**Seacox
Heath**

F   G   H   J   K

F G H 35 J K

I

2

3

4

50

5

6

7

8

F G H 65 J K

Hillsdown Farm

Pipps Warren

Common

Isle of Thorns

Birch Grove House

Chelwood Gate

Forest Farm

Sandy Lane

Laundry Lane

Launder Lane

Beaconsfield Road

Stone Quarry Road

Chelwood Beacon

Chelwood Common

Fairplace Farm

Chapelwood Manor

Stone Quarry Road

Lane

Box's

Baxters Lane

Coach and Horses Lane

Coach Lane

Curnnor House School

E School

Danehill Lodge

Chelwood Gate Rd

Annwood Farm

Hole and Alchorne Farm

Tanyard Lane

Collingford La

ehill

Tanyard Farm

Brookhouse

Bottom

Penmans Lane

Pollardsland Wood

LEWES ROAD

LEWES ROAD

A275

A275

A275

A22

(A) (B) 36 (C) (D) (E)

Ash Down

1

Pippingford
Park

Raven
Wood

2

Chelwood
Vachery

A22

3

4

Gl
Bi

49

Londonderry
Farm

Marlpits

ate Road

Fairplace Farm

Cheh

5

Chapelwood
Manor

Mill
Wood

A22

6

Outback
Farm

Ridge Cl

School Lane

Court
House

7

Jessop's
Hill

Nutley
Primary School

HILL

Clock House Lane

Bell Lane

Hole and Alchorne
Farm

Nursery Lane

Nutley

Misbourne
Farms

8

STREET

Ford's
Green

Nether Lane

Prickets Hatch

A22

Wilmshurst

(A) (B) 66 (C) (D) A22 (E)

Dodd
Bank

Courtlands

I grid square represents 500 metres

Funnell's Farm

F G H **39** J K

CROWBOROUGH

Blackness

Whitehill

Alderbrook

Stone
Cross

Burnt
Oak

Poundfield

G1
1 Holly Ct
2 Warren Gdn

The Brook

G2
1 Pratt's Folly La
2 Southview Cl
3 Twyfords

H1
1 Chapel Gn
2 Graycoats Dr
3 Lower Saxonbury
4 Pollington Pl

Tubwell Farm

54

Hayward

H2
1 Little Sunnyside
2 Sandridge

J1
1 Chequers Cl

J2
1 Coldharbour Cl
2 Simons Cl
3 Tanners Wy
4 Troy Cl
5 Wallis Cl

F1
1 The Drive
2 Rannoch Rd West
3 Warren Rdg

F2
1 Winscote Cl

F G **H** **69** J K

K2
1 Kemps Farm Rd
2 Shawfield

K1
1 Springfield Cl

A2
1 Bracken Cl
2 Osborne Rd
3 Rochester Wy
4 Rodwell
5 Shepherds Wk

shurst Wood

A   B   40   C   D   E

Old Lodge
Warren
Farm

Poundfield Road

Poundfield

1

TN6

Lime Kiln
Oast

Beacon
Community
College

GREEN LANE

Beeches
Road

Beeches
Road

/BOROUGH

2

B2100

Palesgate Road

The Brook
Health Centre

Rochester Way

Medway

Hillrise

Brigos

Forest Rd

Forest Lane

Jarvis
Brook

Lexden
Lodge
Industrial Est

CROWBOROUGH HILL

Osborne Road

Windsor Road

St Michaels Cl

3

Tollwood Road

Millbrook
Business
Park

Sybron Way

ROTHERFIELD   ROAD   CHURCH ST

Rotherfield

Wealden Industrial
Estate

Crowborough
Station

Farmingham Road

Knowle
Close

Western Road

Tubwell Road

Treblers Road

Clackhams Lane

Palesgate Road

Old Forest La

4

Mount Pleasant

Road

Jarvis
Brook CP School

Tubwell Farm

53

Finnart
House

5

Steep Road

Haywards

Rotherfield
Hall

Sandhill
Farm

6

Castle
Hill Farm

Owlsbury Farm

Trebler's Farm

Treblers Road

Castle
Hill

Castle Hill

7

(Steep
Park)

Holly Grove
Farm

Dewlands Hill

8

Limney Farm

Great
Dewlands

A   B   70   C   D   E

Pinehurst Farm

Steep Road

Stone
Mill Farm

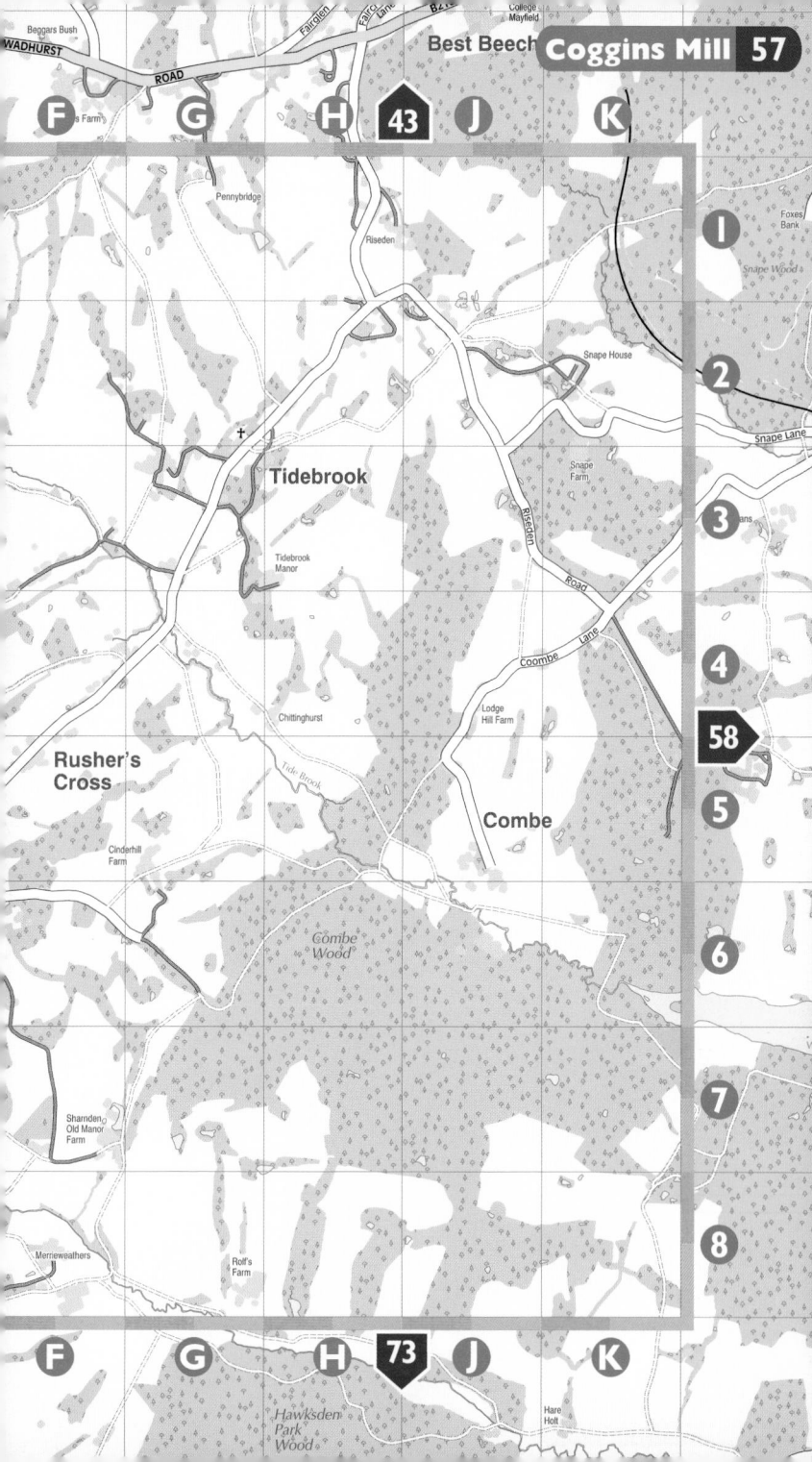

F G H **43** J K

I
Foxes Bank
Snape Wood

2
Snape Lane

Snape House

3
ans

Tidebrook

Snape Farm

Riseden

4

Road

Coombe Lane

58

Tidebrook Manor

Lodge Hill Farm

5

Chittinghurst

Tide Brook

Rusher's Cross

Combe

6

Cinderhill Farm

Combe Wood

7

Sharnden Old Manor Farm

8

Merrieweathers

Rolf's Farm

F G H **73** J K

Hawksden Park Wood

Hare Holt

Pennybridge

Riseden

WADHURST ROAD

Beggars Bush

Farglen

College Mayfield

46

59

76

C2
1 Lavender Gdns
2 Reeves Ter

Three
Leg Cross

Berner
Hill

Dale Hill

Ticehurst

Downash
House

Tinkers Lane

Dale Hill Hotel
& Golf Club

Broomden

Ridgeway Farm

Ticehurst House

Brick Kiln
Farm

B2099

Cross Lane Gardens

The
Surgery

Hillbury
Gardens

Farthing
Hill

The Warren

Springfields
Springfields

HIGH STREET

St Mary's Lane

Doctors Surgery

Ticehurst
C of E Primary School

Oakover

LOWER PLATTS

Steellands Rise

Acres Rise

B2099

Birchenwood
Farm

Gibbs
Reed Farm

Wardsbrook Road

Wedd's

Wardsbrook
Farm

Chestnutfield
Wood

Myskyns

Cottenden

Bearhurst
Farm

Burgham

Sheepstreet Lane

Fox Farm

Shoyswell
Manor

Shortridge Farm

Sheep

Old Shoyswell
Manor

Battenhurst
Farm

Farm

Boarders Lane

Huntley Mill Road

Three Leg Cross Road

Vineyard Lane

Green Lane

Burnt Lodge Lane

Ship Lane

Padgbury Lane

Steellands Rise

Highgrove Avenue

B2087

I grid square represents 500 metres

F1
1 Northgrove Rd
2 Post Office Rd

G1
1 Hammonds
2 Murton-neale Cl

Gun Green

Highgate

Fowler's
Park

Dickens Way

Pipsden

RYE   ROAD   A268   Hotel

Four
Throws

RYE

Risden

Clayhill

Four
Throws

The Moor

Hawkhurst
C of E Primary School

Hall
House

Stream Lane

Thorpes

Collingwood
House

Risden Lane

TN18

East
Heath

Little
Conghurst

Conghurst Lane

Conghurst Lane

Sussex Border Path

Conghurst
Farm

Sussex Border Path

Bourne
Farm

Northlands

Sussex Border Path

San
Cro

Lower
Northlands Farm

Heron's Ghyll

A B 52 C D E

1

Temple Grove with St Nicholas School

Preeymans Lane

2 Claygate Farm

High Hurstwood

Chillies Lane

High Hurstwood C of E School

Burnt Oak Road

Royal Oak Lane

3 Preeymans Lane

Parkhurst

PO

Maypole Cottages

The Homestead

Stonehouse

4

67

Herns Wood

A26

Tudor Rocks

Rocks Lane

Fowly Lane

5 Bevingford

Hurstwood Road

6

Lane

Five Ash Down

New House Farm

7 PO

Millwood Close

Lephams Bridge House

Westdene

Saint Marys Farm

Littlewood Road

Park View

Nursery Field

8 Cooper's Green

Buxted C of E Primary School

Buxted

A272

Buxted Station

Church Road

PO

HIGH STREET

Framfield Road

Coldon Road

Nan

A B 96 C D E

Hotel

Grovehurst Farm

Chillies Lane

Burnt Oak Road

Furnace Wood

Burnt Oak

F G H 53 J K

Inchreed Farm

Fordbrook Hill

Hadlow Down Road

Fordbrook

Mill Lane

Tipps

I

2

Huggett's Furnace

Sleeches

Hastingford Farm

River Uck

3

4

greenhurst

Howbourne Farm

70

Foxhole Farm

Smallberry Hill

Stockland Lane

Stockland Lane

School Lane

Weights

Stockland Farm

5

Howbourne Lane

Lane

Five Chimneys Lane

Hadl Dow

Buxted Wood Lane

A272

St Mary's Prim School

E

6

Redbrook Lane

Howbourne Lane

Five Chimneys

Hall Lane

Pound Green

Saxon Court

Wilderness Lane

7

Vanguard Way

Limes Lane

Waste Wood

8

Wilderness Farm

Popeswood Farm

Potter's Green

Hole Wood

Sleeves Wood

F G H 97 J K

Hole Farm

Warren Farm

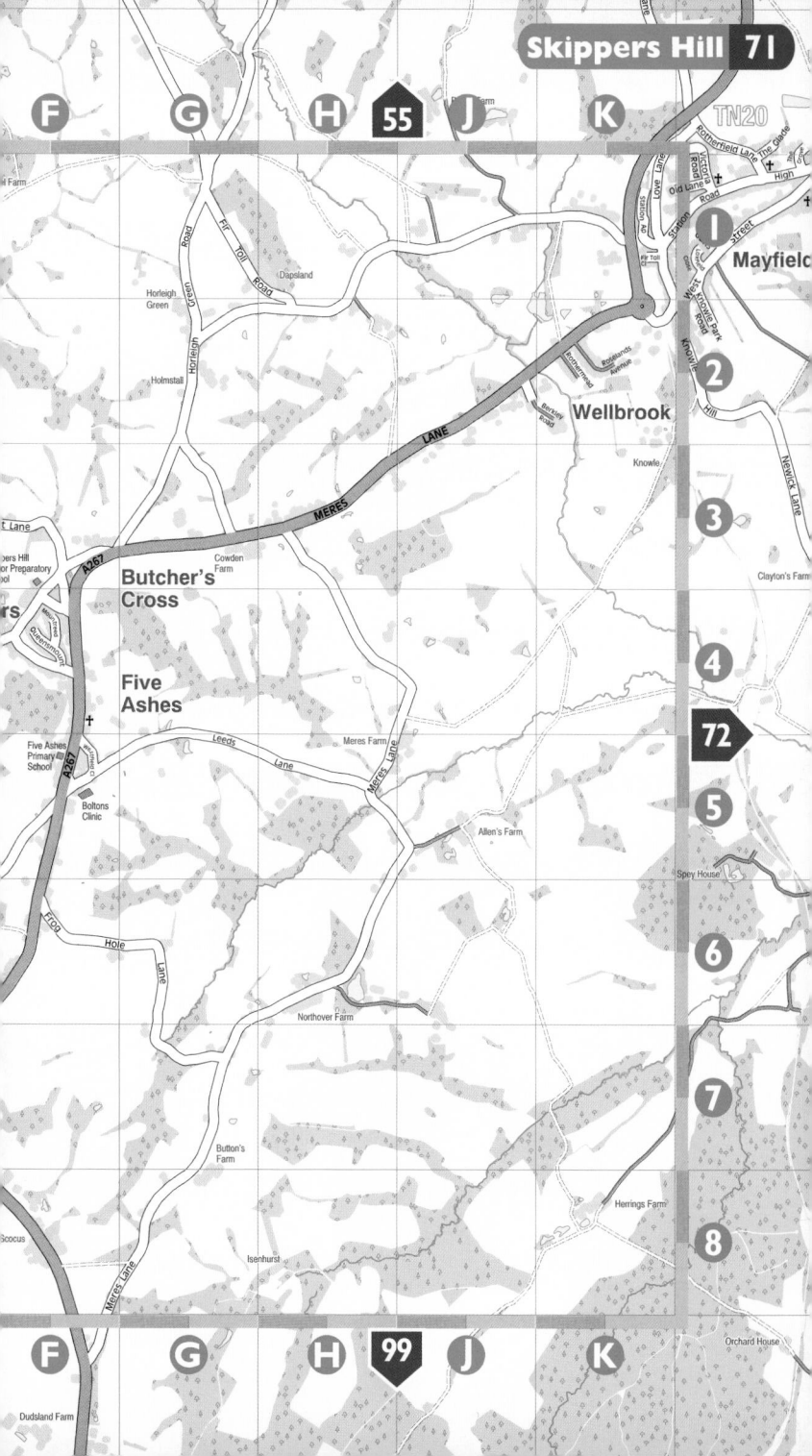

F G H 55 J K

TN20

Rotherfield Lane   The Glebe
Victoria Road   Old Lane   High
West   Station Road   Street

I

Mayfield

Love Lane
Fir Toll

Knowle Park Road

2

Knowle Hill
Newick Lane

Dapsland

Horleigh
Green

Fir Toll Road

Green Road

Rowlands
Avenue

Brookers

Bankery Road

Wellbrook

Holmstall

Horleigh

MERES LANE

Knowle

3

Clayton's Farm

MERES

A267

Cowden
Farm

ers Hill
or Preparatory
ool

Butcher's
Cross

4

72

Five
Ashes

rs

Dudsmarsh

Leeds Lane

Meres Farm

Meres Lane

5

Spey House

Five Ashes
Primary
School

A267

Boltons
Clinic

Allen's Farm

Fir Toll

Hole Lane

6

Northover Farm

7

Meres Lane

Button's
Farm

Herrings Farm

8

Isenhurst

Scocus

Orchard House

F G H 99 J K

Dudsland Farm

A B **58** C D E

bridge
Wood

River Rother

I

Hare
Holt

Bivelham Forge
Farm

Witherenden Hill

2

Bivelham Farm

Great
Bines

Woodkne
Farm

Turk's Bridge

3

Spring La

Sou

Holmshurst

4

Great
Broadhurst Farm

73

Swife

Ponts Farm

5

6

7

Oakdown

Foxhole Farm

Lower
Bough Farm

**Burwash
Common**

**Burwash
Weald**

A265

20

Vicarage Road

8

Holban's
Farm

Vicarage
Lane

Westdown Lane

Foot's Lane

A265

†

Willi

A B **102** C D E

Kingsdown
Farm

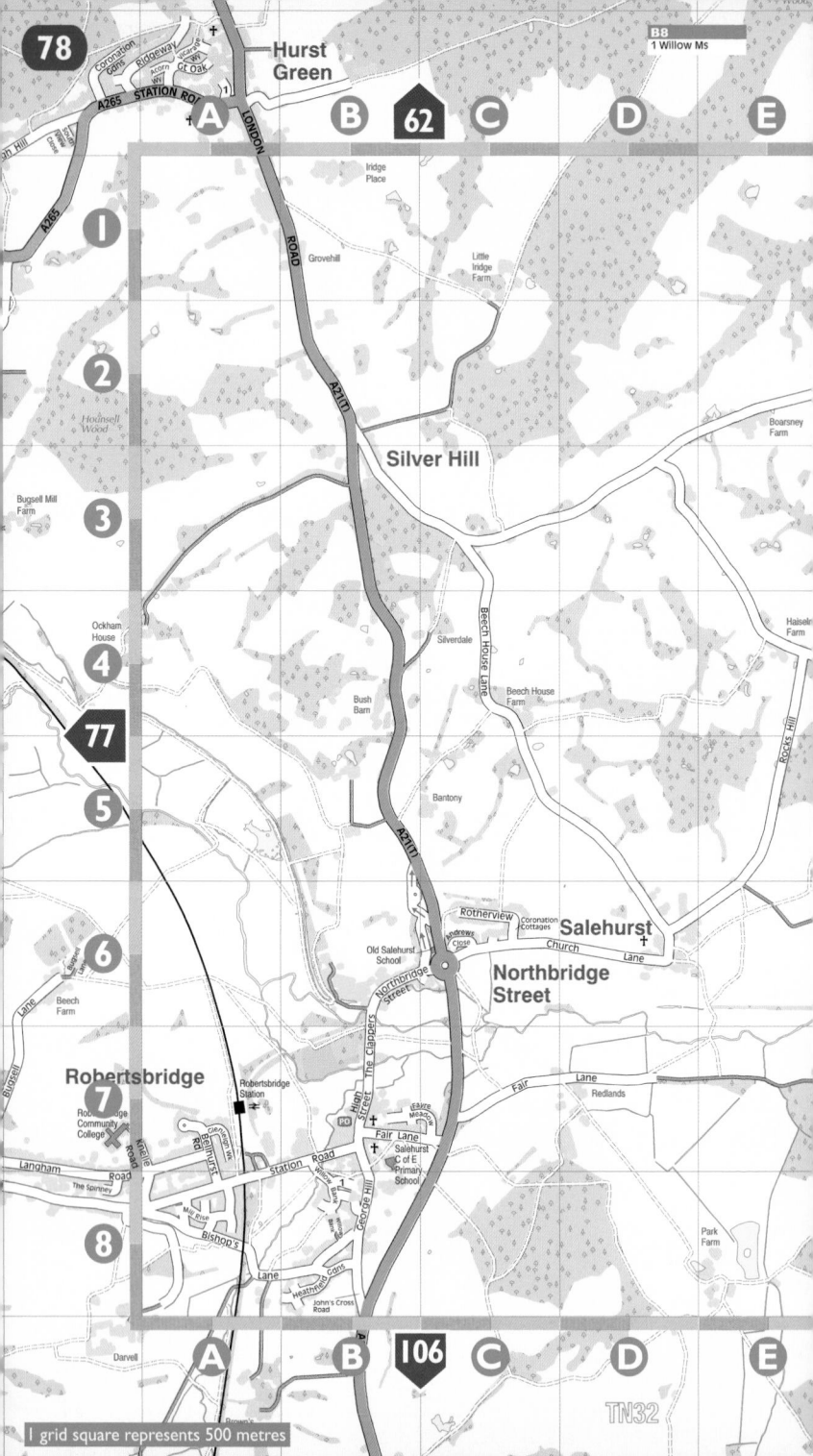

Moon's
Green

Swan Street

Swan
Street

Swan
Cottages

Forge
Meads

POPLAR ROAD

Wittersham

B2082

Cemetery

The

Wittersham
Primary School

A **B** **C** **D** **E**

Wittersham
Manor

Blackbrook
Farm

Budd's
Farm

1

Ham
Green

2

River Rother

3

Kent County
East Sussex County

Sussex Border Path

Sussex Border Path

Sussex Border Path

4

Sussex Border Path

Kitchenham

5

Mackerel Hill

6

New House
Farm

Moat
Farm

Forstal
Farm

7

Iden
Wood

Old House
Farm

8

Hotel

Flackley
Ash

A268

Mill Lane

Tanhouse
Lane

A **B** **C** **D** **E**

Farleys
Way

112

STREET

MAIN

The
Old Hop
Garden

Farm
Cottages

A268

Peasmarsh

Lane

1 grid square represents 500 metres

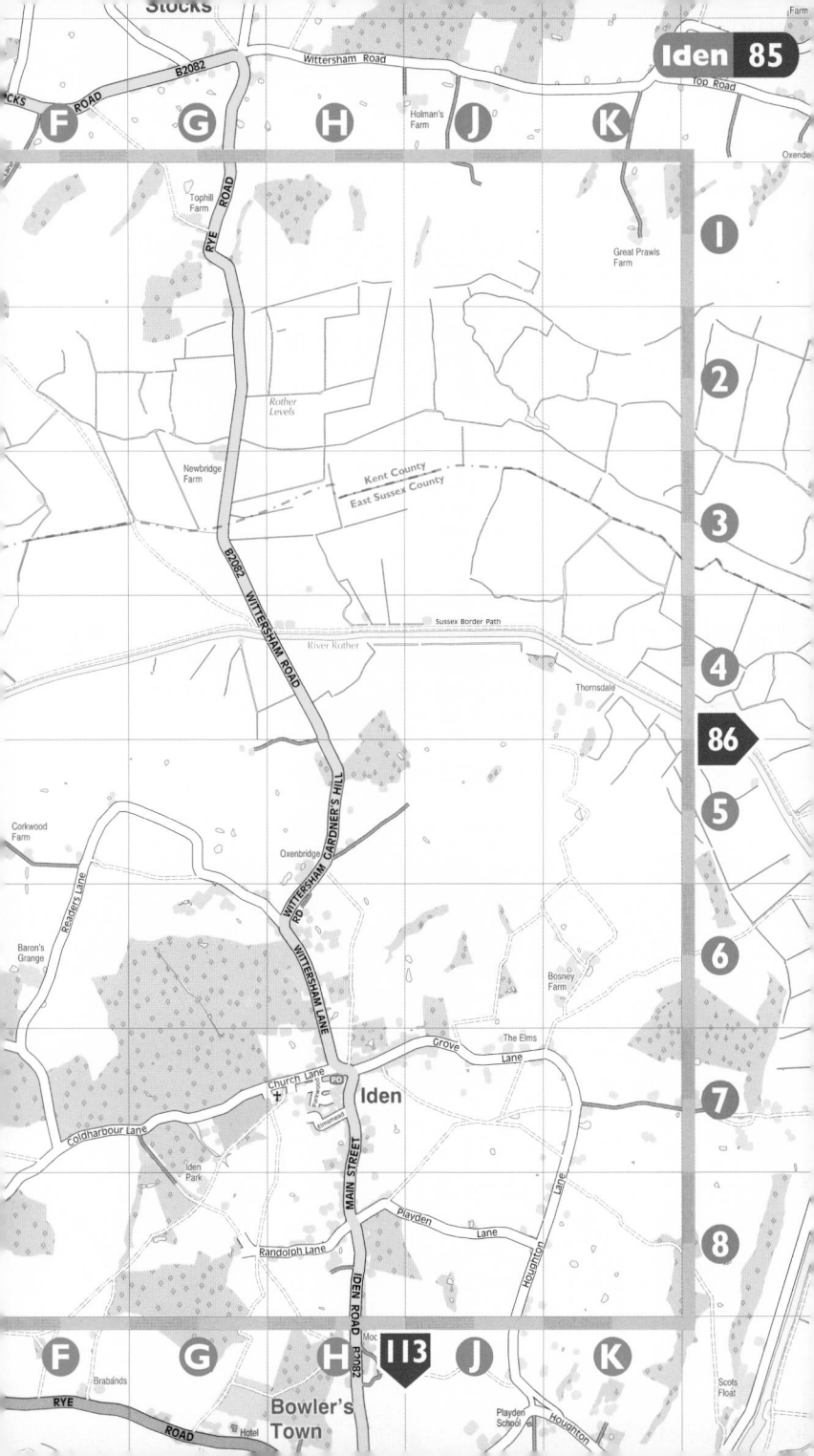

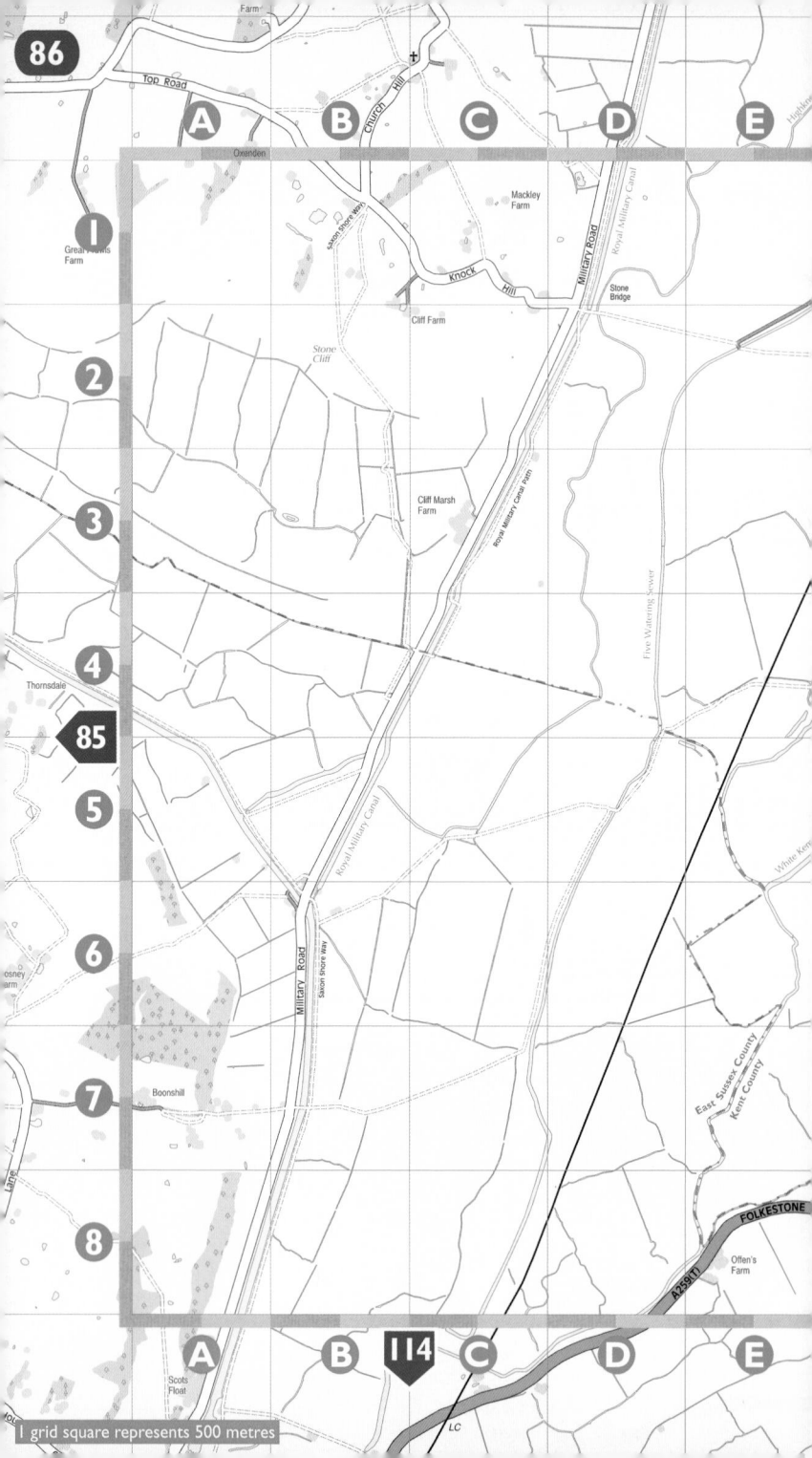

86

A B C D E

Top Road

Church Hill

Oxenden

Savers Shore Way

Mackley Farm

1

Great Farms Farm

Knock Hill

Military Road

Royal Military Canal

Stone Bridge

Cliff Farm

2

Stone Cliff

3

Royal Military Canal Path

4

Thornsdale

85

Five Watering Sewer

5

Royal Military Canal

Whan Kent

6

osney arm

Military Road

Saxon Shore Way

East Sussex County

Kent County

7

Boonshill

Lane

FOLKESTONE

8

Offen's Farm

A259(T)

A B C D E

114

Scots Float

LC

1 grid square represents 500 metres

F G H J K

I

2

3 Salter's Lane

4

5

6

7

8

Fairfield Court

Brattle House

Old Farm

Poplar Hall

Puddock

Dean Court

New Buildings Farm

Whitehouse Farm

LC

Becket Barn Farm

Fairfield

Salter's Lane

Wall

Hook Lane

A259(T)

GUILDEFORD LANE

Lamb Farm

Guldeford Lane Corner

F G H **115** J K

E7
1 Baylis Crs
2 Pannett
3 Wallis Wy
4 Withy Bush

E6
1 Withy Bush

D7
1 Chaffinch Cl

Ansty

A   B   C   D   E

A272

CUCKFIELD ROAD

Pickwell Farm

1

E8
1 Colmer Pl
2 Victoria Av
3 Victoria Cl
4 Weald Rd

West Riddens

HARVEST HILL

Harvesthill

2

ovell's Farm

Hilders Farm

Legh Manor

Bishopstone Lane

B2036

3

Greenacres

Cuckfield Road

Lye's Farm

PAIN'S FLAT

4

Paynes Place Farm

B2036 CUCKFIELD

Abbotsford

5

Job's Lane

A2300

6

Dumbrell's F.

A2300

A275 SUSSEX W

Bretton

THE BROOKS

Perrryvale

Goddards' Green

Bishopstone Road

Cuckfield Road

Gatehouse Lane

The MORNS

Primrose Cl

Saxby

The Meadows

Bramble Cv

Gatehouse Surgery

Cupeter

Howard

West Pk Crs

West

7

Dumworth

Oaklands Park

JANE MURRAY WAY

The Gatehouse

Barley Dr

Malthouse Lane

Denham Road

Southway County Junior School

Gatons CP School

Wester

Co Co

Royal G Clinic

Southway

8

Naldretts Farm

Lane

Mill

Lane

Northend   Lane

Cuckfield Road

Pomper   Lane

Doveys Close

Woodpecker Crs

JANE MURRAY

Victoria Road

Consort Way

Regent Business Centre

Braybon Business Park Drive

Newhouse Farm

Kent's Farm

Edward Way

Jubilee Road

Albert

A   B   **118**   C   D   E

F6
1 Chiltington Cl
2 Spicers Cl
3 Tate Crs
4 Woodcroft

F7
1 Packham Wy
2 Shepherds Mead
3 South Lodge Cl
4 Tudor Gdns
5 Turners Wy

F8
1 Commercial Rd
2 London Rd
3 Orchard Wy

G6
1 Gander Cl
2 The Hawthorns

G7
1 Marle Av
2 Sheddingdean Cl

H6
1 Bedelands Cl

H7
1 Midfields Cl
2 Midfields Wk
3 The Ridgeway
4 The Twitten

H8
1 Crescent Cl
2 Turkey La

J5
1 Valebridge Cl

J6
1 Ladymead
2 Valebridge Dr

J7
1 Woodland Cl

K8
1 St Andrews Rd
2 Tilers Cl
3 Tindal Cl

K6
1 Hawthorn Cl
2 Laurel Cl

K1
1 Pinewood Wy

90

119

A   B   64   C   D   E

1

Hammond's
Farm

Sennotts
Farm

Wapsbourne
Farm

Lindfield
Farm

Warr's
Farm

2

Vale
Farm

Great
Noven
Farm

New
Heritage

Banks   Road

Warren
Ridge

Warrenwood

Lane End
Common

The
Warre

3

West Sussex County
East Sussex County

Warren
Lane

Cox's Fa

4

Leylands
Farm

North
Common

PD

Hangleton
Lane

Cockhaise
La

91   North Common Road

Chailey Heritage
Clinical Services
La Chailey
Heritage
School

B2183

Old
Heritage

A272   STATION ROAD

Downs Vw
Close

A275

Lower St

5

BEGGAR'S   WOOD   ROAD

North
Chailey

6

Townings
Farm

7

Roeheath

St Peters
Primary
School

8

Chailey

Ades

Cinder   Hill

A   B   122   C   D   E

A275

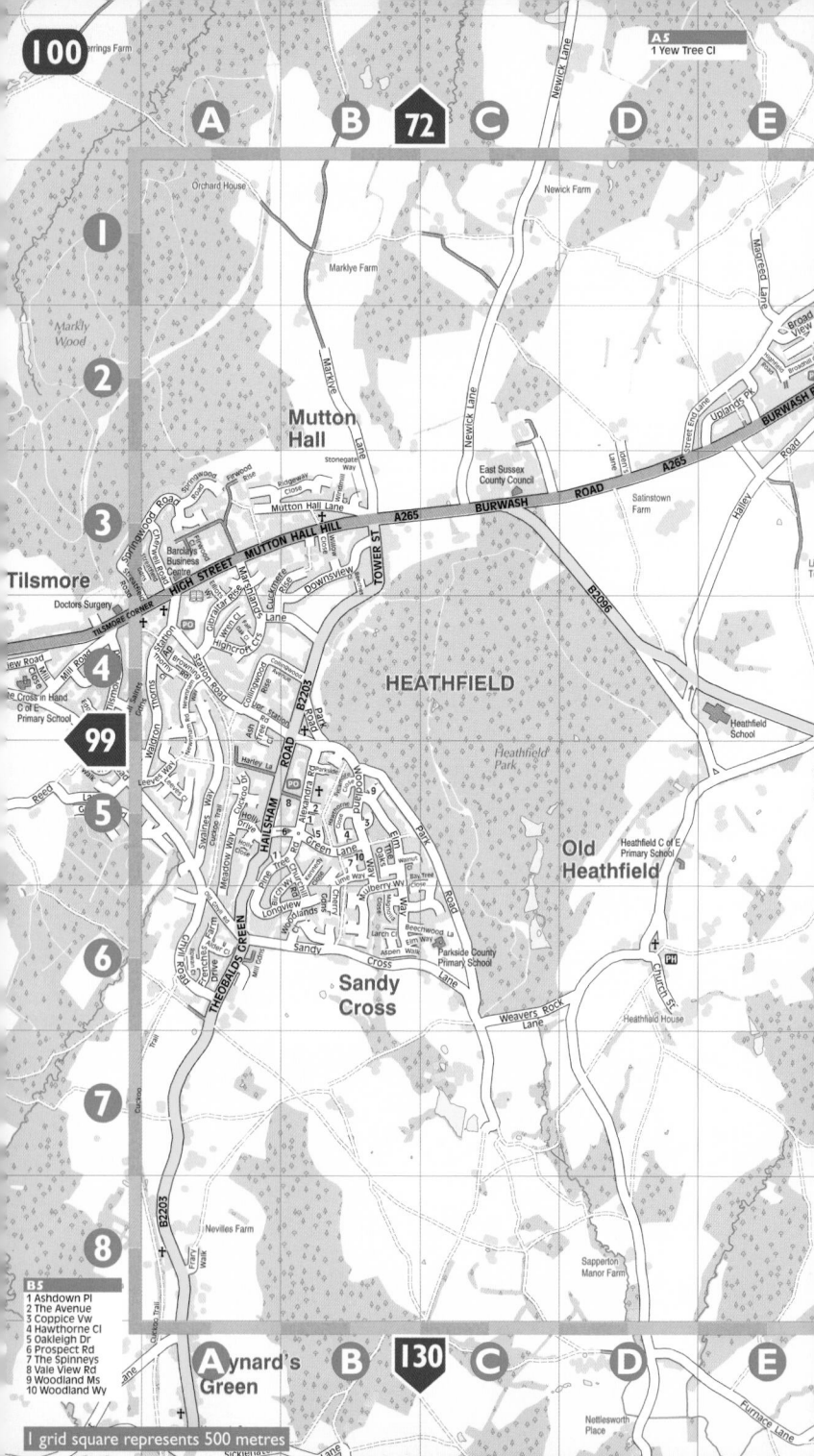

A5
1 Yew Tree Cl

A   B   72   C   D   E

1

Orchard House   Newick Farm

Marklye Farm

Markly
Wood

2

Mutton
Hall

Stonegate
Way
Mutton Hall Lane   East Sussex
                          County Council   Satinstown
                                            Farm

3 Tilsmore   HIGH STREET MUTTON HALL HILL   A265   BURWASH   ROAD   A265

Barclays
Business

Doctors Surgery   TOWER ST

TILSMORE   B2096

4 Cross in Hand
   C of E
   Primary School

99

Reed   HEATHFIELD

5   HAILSHAM

                     Heathfield
                     Park   Heathfield
                                   School

6   Old   Heathfield C of E
   THEOBALDS GREEN   Heathfield   Primary School

   Sandy
   Cross   Park Road   PH

7   Cross Lane
                   Weavers Rock Lane   Heathfield House

8   Nevilles Farm
                   Priory
                   Walk
B5
1 Ashdown Pl   Sapperton
2 The Avenue   Manor Farm
3 Coppice Vw
4 Hawthorne Cl
5 Oakleigh Dr
6 Prospect Rd
7 The Spinneys   A   Aynard's   B   130   C   D   E
8 Vale View Rd   Green
9 Woodland Ms   Nettlesworth
10 Woodland Wy   Place

1 grid square represents 500 metres

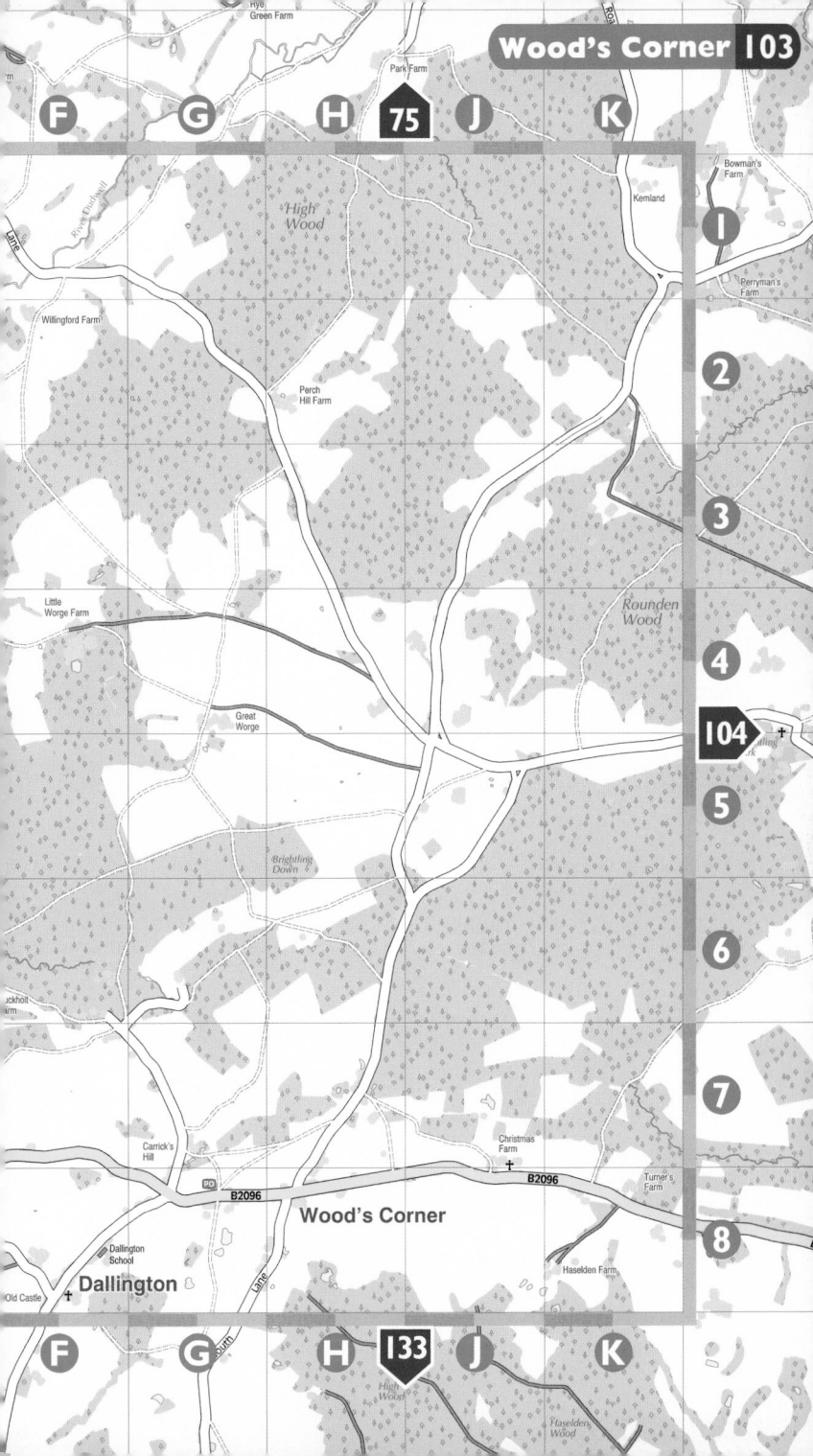

F G H **75** J K

Rye
Green Farm

Park Farm

Bowman's
Farm

Kemland

I

Perryman's
Farm

'High'
Wood

River Dudwell

2

Willingford Farm

Perch
Hill Farm

3

Rounden
Wood

Little
Worge Farm

4

Great
Worge

104

5

Brightling
Down

6

7

uckholt
arm

Carrick's
Hill

Christmas
Farm

B2096

Turner's
Farm

8

PO

B2096

Wood's Corner

Dallington
School

Haselden Farm

Old Castle

Dallington

Sorn Lane

F G H **133** J K

High
Wood

Haselden
Wood

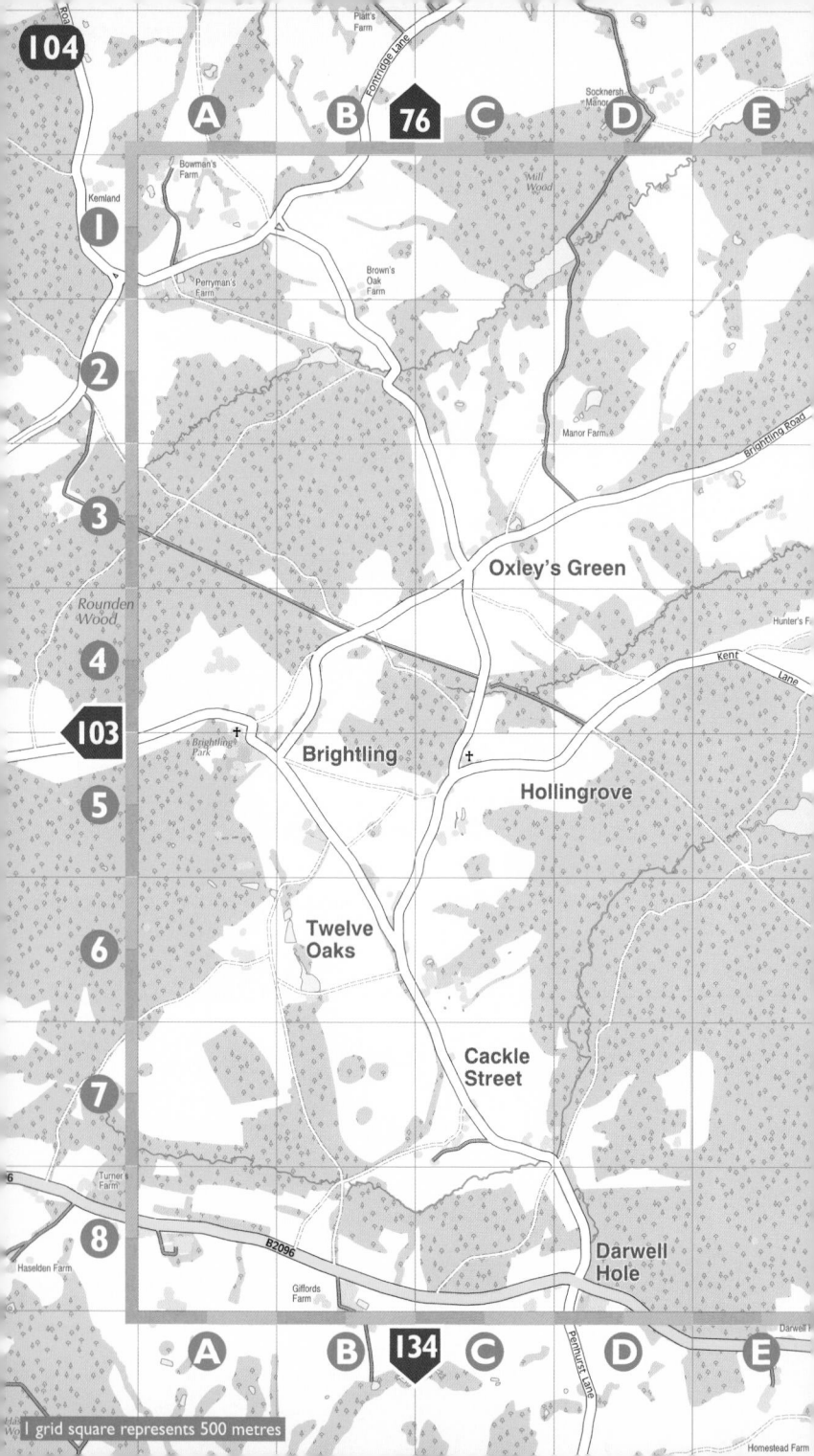

104

A   B   **76**   C   D   E

1 Kemland
Bowman's Farm
Platt's Farm
Fairlight Lane
Will Wood
Socknersh Manor

Perryman's Farm

2

Brown's Oak Farm

3

Manor Farm

Brightling Road

Oxley's Green

Rounden Wood

4

Kent Lane

Hunter's F

103
Brightling Park

5 Brightling
Hollingrove

6

Twelve Oaks

7
Turner's Farm

6

8 Haselden Farm
B2096
Cackle Street

Giffords Farm

Darwell Hole

Penhurst Lane

Darwell

A   B   **134**   C   D   E

Homestead Farm

1 grid square represents 500 metres

F G H **77** J K

Brightling Road

Peans

Newhouse
Farm

Brightling
Hall

Scalands
Farm

Darvell

Bishop's
Lane

Brown's
Farm

1

Scalands
Wood

Glottenham Stream

Glottenham
Manor

2

Mountfield Park
Farm

Park
Pale

3

Mountfield Lane

Darwell Reservoir

Tunstall
Farm

4

Taylor's
Cottage

106

Baldwin's
Farm

5

Mountfie

The
Banks

Castle Farm

6

Darwell
Wood

7

Crowhurst Wood

8

Crowhurst
Farm

Durley Down

Neth of E.
Primary School

PO

Netherfield
Court

Netherfield
Way

Netherfield

Eatenden Lane

Eatenden Wood

Netherfield Road

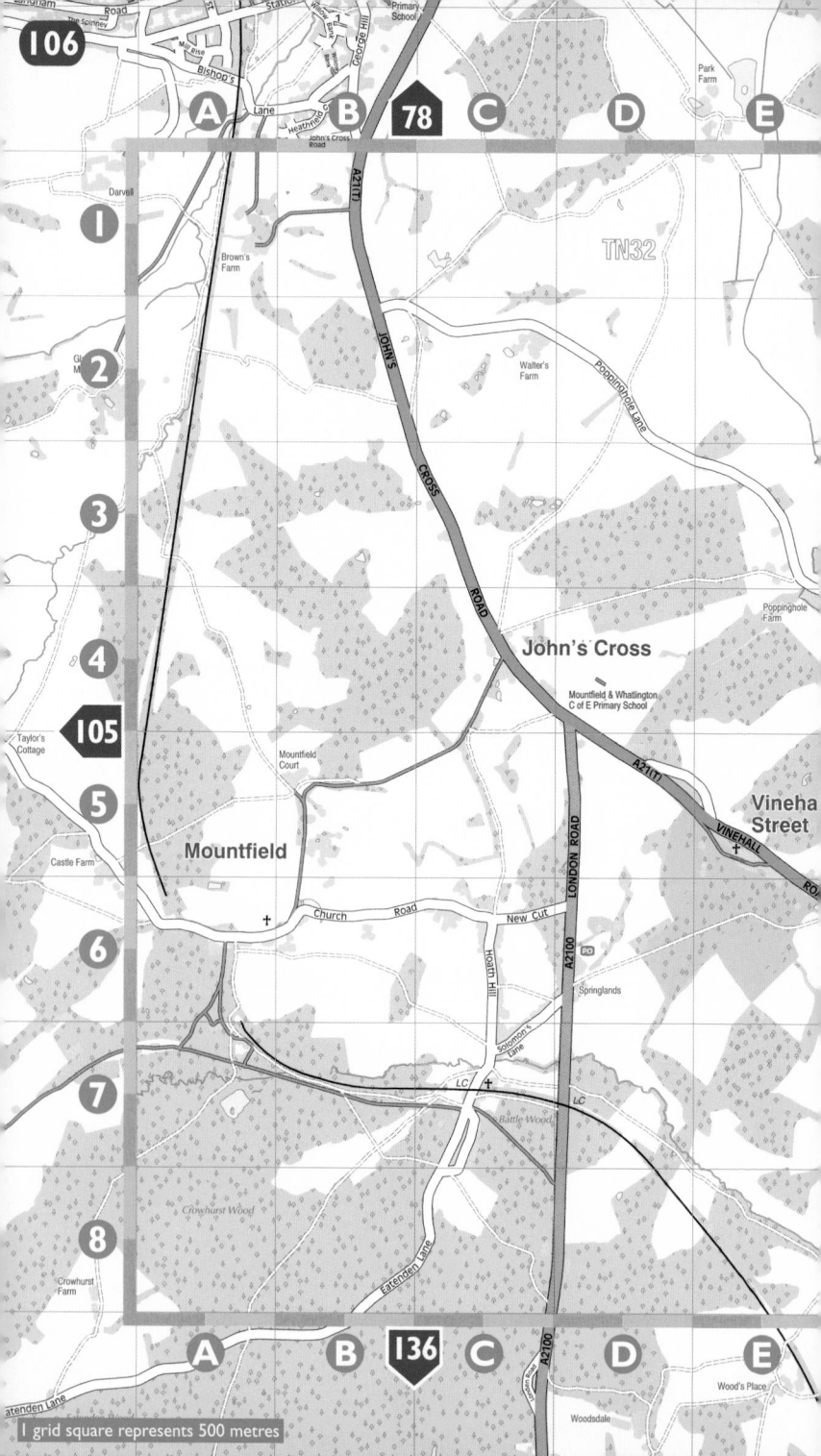

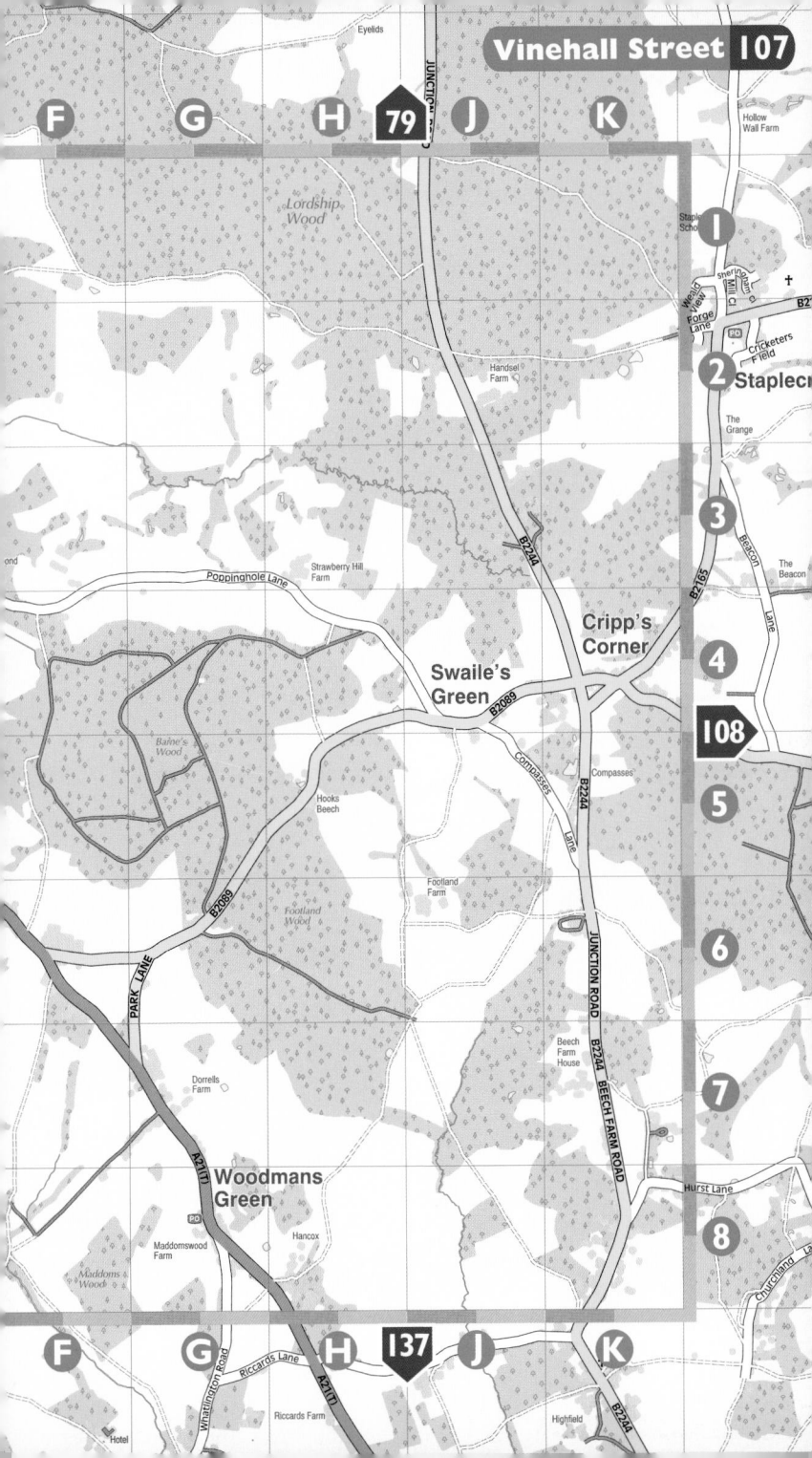

A Farm
B
80
C
D
E Martinshaw Farm

Sandhurst Lane

I
Staplecross School
Lordine Court

Sherington
Mill CI
Weald View
Forge Lane
† B2165
Collier's Green
B2165

2
Cricketers Field
Staplecross
Gate Farm
Sparks

The Grange
Stockwood Farm

3
Beacon Lane
The Beacon
Ellenwhorne
Ellenwhorne Lane
B2165

Cripp's Corner

4
Miles Farm
Stocklands Farm
Ellenwhorne Lane

107
Calts Green Farm
Compasses
B2244 Lane

5
Streetfield Wood
B2069
Brede High Wood
B2089

6
JUNCTION ROAD

Beech Farm House
B2244 BEECH FARM ROAD

7
Powdermill Reservoir

8
Hurst Lane
Hurst Wood
Churchland Lane

Hurst House
Jacob's Farm

A
B
I38
C
D
E

Hurst Lane
Brede Lane

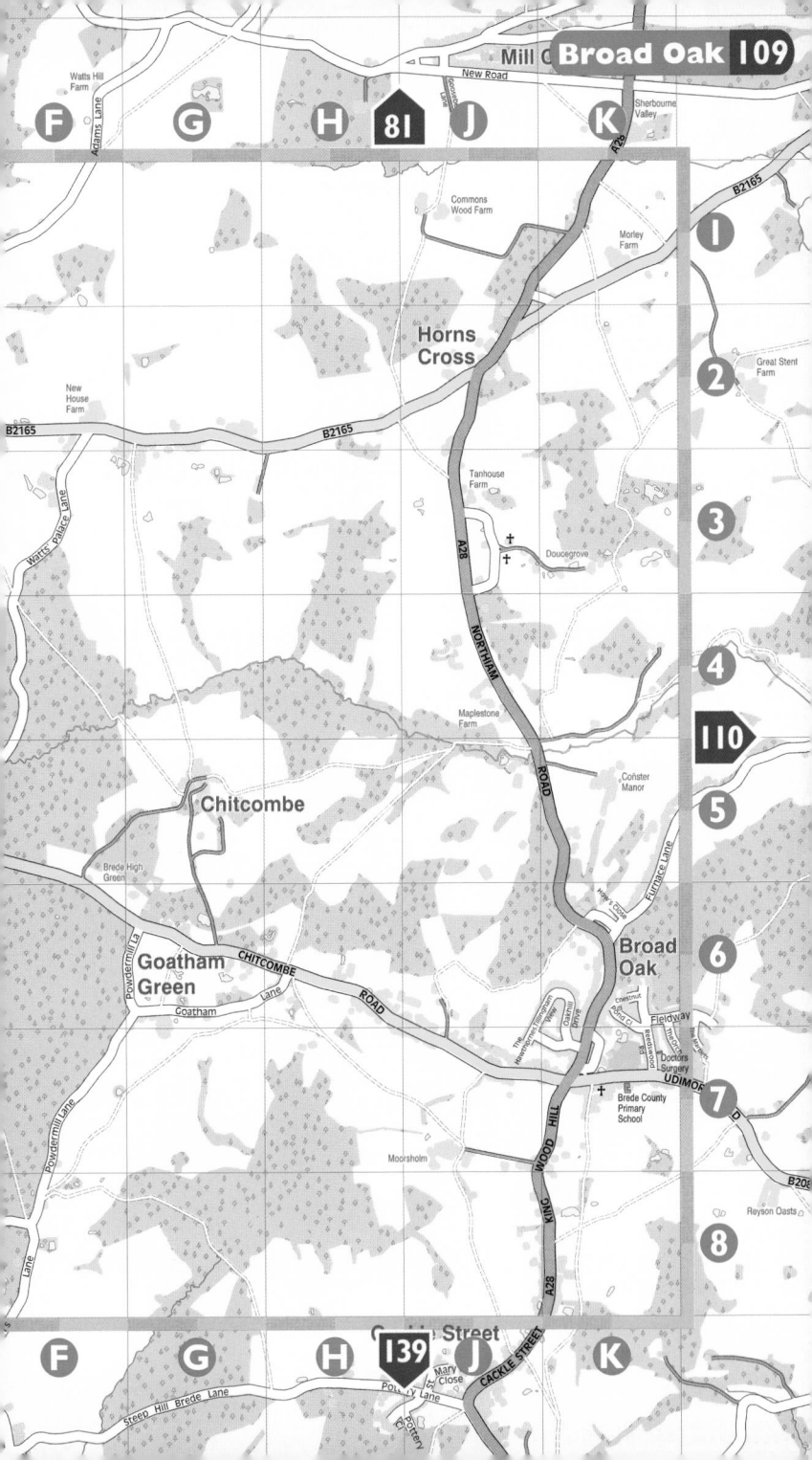

F G H 81 J K

Watts Hill Farm
New Road
Sherbourne Valley
Adams Lane

Commons Wood Farm

Morley Farm

I

B2165

New House Farm
B2165

Great Stent Farm
2

Horns Cross

Watts Palace Lane

Tanhouse Farm

3
Doucegrove

A28 NORTHIAM ROAD

4

Maplestone Farm

110

Chitcombe

Brede High Green

Conster Manor

Furnace Lane

5

Hog's Hole

Broad Oak

6

Goatham Green

CHITCOMBE

Powdermill La

ROAD

Goatham Lane

The Hawthorns
Oaklea Gardens
Oakhill Drive
Chestnut
Fieldway
Doctors Surgery
UDIMOR

7

Powdermill Lane

Brede County Primary School

B20

Moorsholm

Reyson Oasts

8

WOOD HILL

KING

A28

Lane

Street

F G H 139 J K

Steep Hill Brede Lane
Poundry Lane
Mary Close
CACKLE STREET
Pottery

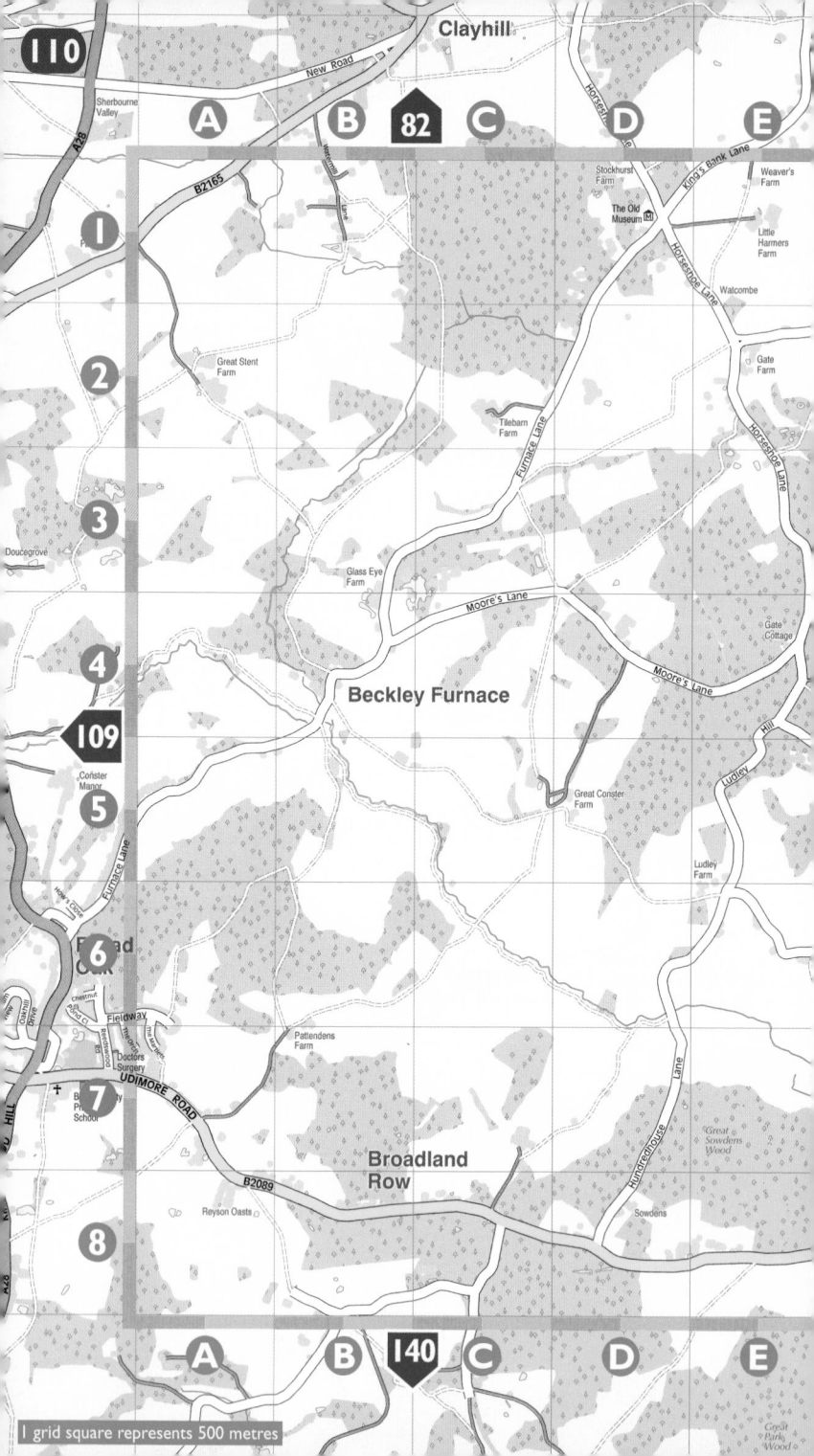

Clayhill

New Road

110

Sherbourne
Valley

B2165

A

B

82

C

D

Stockhurst
Farm

King's Bank Lane

Weaver's
Farm

E

The Old
Museum

Horseshoe Lane

Little
Harmers
Farm

Walcombe

1

Horseshoe Lane

Great Stent
Farm

2

Gate
Farm

Tilebarn
Farm

Furnace Lane

3

Doucegrove

Glass Eye
Farm

Moore's Lane

Gate
Cottage

Moore's Lane

4

109

Beckley Furnace

Hill

Conster
Manor

5

Great Conster
Farm

Ludley

Ludley
Farm

Furnace Lane

6

Broad
Oak

Chestnut

Fieldway

Doctors
Surgery

7

UDIMORE ROAD

B Pri
School

Pattendens
Farm

Broadland
Row

Hundredhouse Lane

Great
Sowdens
Wood

8

B2089

Reyson Oasts

Sowdens

A

B

140

C

D

E

Great
Park
Wood

1 grid square represents 500 metres

F G H **83** J
Flackley Ash K

Mill Lane

A268

Tannouse Lane

1

Peas

Woodlands Farm

2

Peasmar Place

The Hermitage

Starvecrow Lane

Drew Lane

3

Lower Gate Farm

Beckley Woods

Tillingham Lane

4

Groves

Starvecrow Lane

New Lane

112

Partridge Farm

Pelsham

5

Hayes Farm

Hayes Lane

Hayes Lane

Dinglesden

6

River Tillingham

7

Billingham Farm

Newman's Farm

Billingham Lane

8

F G Udim **H** **141** J K

Court Lodge

Little Park Wood

Knellstone

Cock Marling

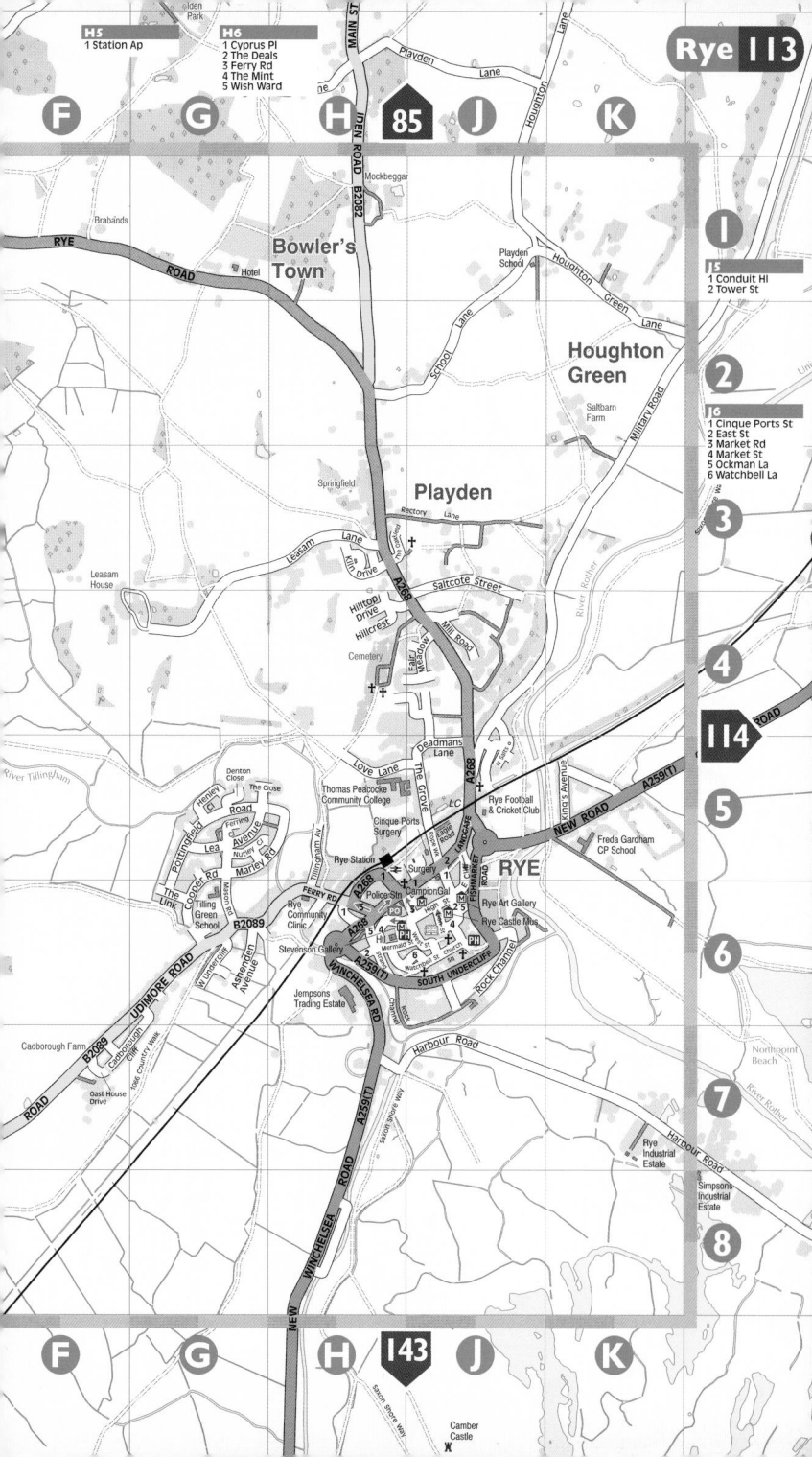

A B C D E

Little Cheyne
Court

Lower
Agney

Re
Hou

Broomhill Level

A B 146 C D E

F G H J K

I
2
3
4
5
6
7
8

Corner

Newland Farm

Newland

H
Bones
Farm

Little Scotney

Kent County
East Sussex County

Pigwell

Gap Road

Jury's

Gap Road

Jury's

Scotney
Court

LC

West Rise

LC LC LC

LC

The Forelands

Marsh Bridge Road

LC

F G H **147** J K

Heath Road Ferguson Road Ferguson Road LC Rivers Road

Keymer 119

F1
1 Albion Ct

F2
1 Colchins
2 Fox Cl
3 Grovelands Cl
4 Hammonds Gdns
5 Mayhouse Rd
6 Pepper Dr

F6
1 Brambles

F7
1 Woodlands Cl

F8
1 Keymer Rd

G1
1 Ashway
2 Wolstonbury Wy

G7
1 Clerks Acre

G8
1 The Poplars
2 Willowbrook Wy

H1
1 Keymer Ct
2 Keymer Pde

H2
1 Franklands Cl
2 Woodwards Cl

H6
1 Sweetlands

K1
1 Badgers Wk

K8
1 Boddingtons La
2 The Dymock's

J2
1 Bough Beeches
2 Hambrook
3 Kirdford Cl
4 Lurgashall
5 Pendean

J1
1 Wykeham Wy

KEYMER

Ditchling

G5
1 The Paddocks

G6
1 Station Cl

F G H 91 J K

I

H6
1 South Downs

2

Southam

3

4

122

Yokehurst

5

Heath Farm

St Helena Farm

Great Home Wood

Shaw Park

Inholms Farm

Homewoodgate Farm

Honeypot

Lane

Shepherds Way

Pouchnards Drive

Chapel Rd

Woodgate Mews

Wells Cl

West Gate

Station Road

Rigdens Lane

Rigdens Cl

PO

East Fields

LC

Plumpton Green

North Barnes Farm

North Hall

North Barnes Lane

Plumpton New Primary School

Barnfield

LC

Plumpton Station

6

Highbridge Lane

Plumpton Race Course

Rylands

Mount Pleasant

Novington Lane

Brookhouse

7

Chiltington

Ashurst

Plumpton Lane

East Chiltington

Crabtree Lane

PH

LC

Woofton Farm

8

The Old Mill Ho

Chilt

A B **92** C Chailey D E

C4
1 Appledene Cnr
2 Grantham Cl
3 Green La
4 Hornbuckles Cl

B4
1 Whitegates Cl

Ades

1

Wilding Wood

The Hooke

Markstakes Lane   Markstakes

Markstakes Farm

2

Southam

South Street

PO

3

Caveridge Lane

Markstakes Commons

South Common

St John Bank Lane

Ba W

4

Honey   Lane

Mill Lane

Mill Brooks

Green Lane

Marewood Lane

South Chailey

Balneath Manor

Chailey Comprehensive School

Shepherds Way

Pouchlands Drive

Swan Close

◄ 121

5

Yokehurst

Old Barns Farm

North Hall

A275

6

Woodbrooks Farm

Hurst Barns

Mount Pleasant Lane

Highbridge Lane

7

Novington Lane

Hewenstreet Farm

Shelley's

ouse

LC

Chiltington Lane

RESTING OAK HL

8

Wootton Farm

Wickham Lane

Lane

Chiltington

A B **153** C Wins... D E

Lane

RESTING

MacKerel's
Rocks

Vuggles
Farm

Gipp's
Barn

A   **B**   **94**   **C**   **D**   **E**

Constantia
Manor

New
House Farm

1

Gipp's
Wood

Sutton
Hall

Longford Str

2

Beaks
Farm

Longford
Farm

River Ouse

station
road

Tile Barn
Cl

3

Isfield

Spithurst

PO

Lavendr

4

Burtenshaw
Farm

123

Birches Farr

**Mount
Pleasa**

5

Dallas Lane

Spithurst

Anchor Lane

Scufflings

Boathouse
Farm

Lewes Road

Lane

Delves Farm

6

Banks
Farm

Isfield Road

Oaklands
Park

Kiln

7

PH

Iron River

8

Clink Hill

Upper Clay
Hill Farm

Barcombe Mills
Road

Barcombe
House

A   **B**   **155**   **C**   **D**   **E**

F G H 95 J K

Ridgewood
House
New
Lewes
Mo
Eph

A22

I

Ridgewood
Stream

Horstedpont
Farm

2

Hotel
Horsted
Place

Little
Horsted
School

**Little
Horsted**

East Sussex
National
Golf Club

3

Worth
Farm

Bradford's
Farm

4

Wicklands

1

Lane

Old
Farm

126

5

Brockwells
Farm

Crump's
Wood

**Rose
Hill**

Plashett
Park

6

lor's

Moatpark
Farm

Cooper's
Hatch

7

Plashett
Wood

Harvey's Lane

Mount Farm

8

Red
Barn Farm

Upper
Lodge Farm

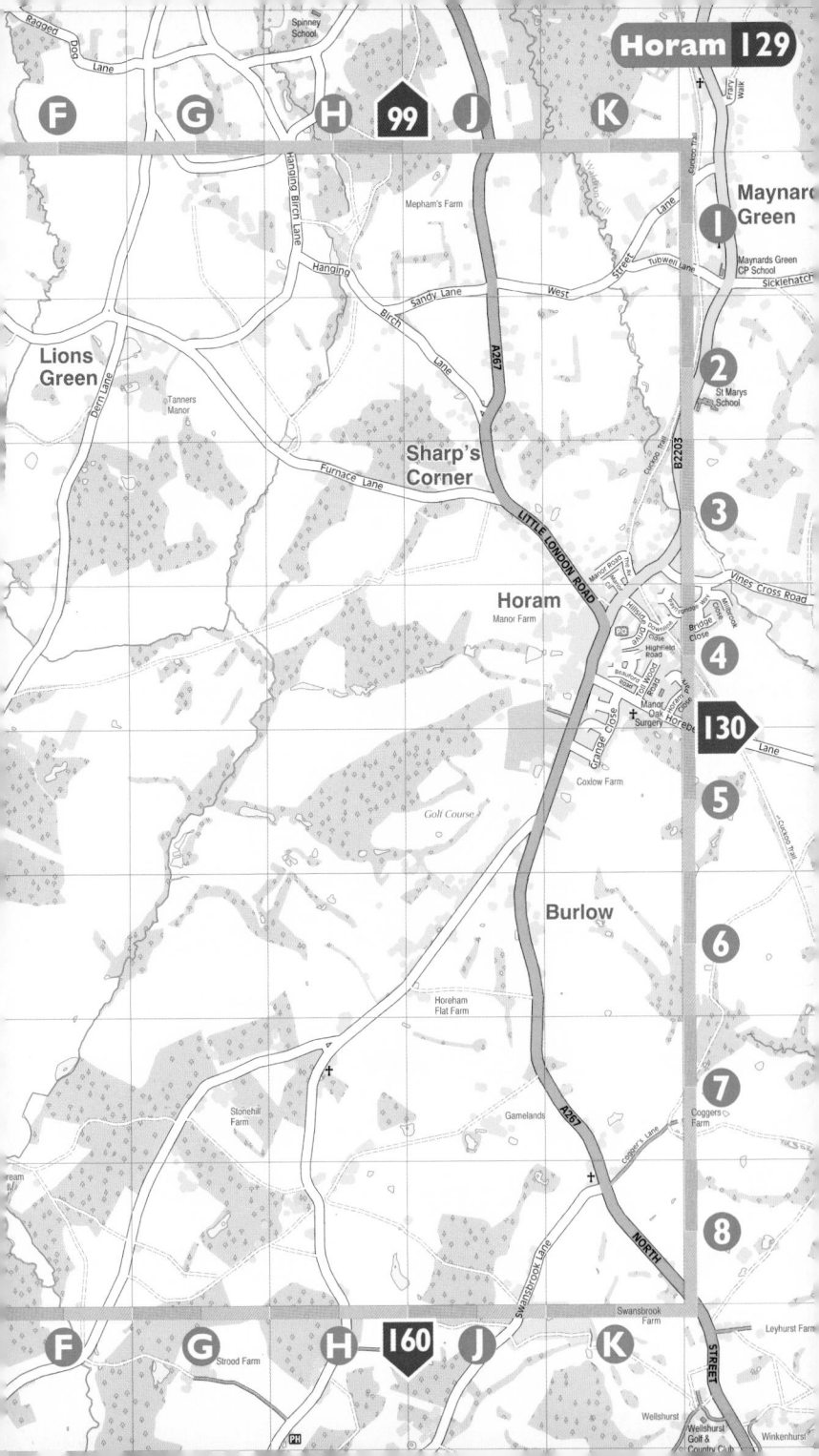

F G H **99** J K

Maynard
Green

Spinney
School

Ragged Dog Lane

Priory Walk

I

Mepham's Farm

Hanging Birch Lane

Maynards Green
CP School

Sicklehatch

Hanging

Sandy Lane

West

Street

Tubwell Lane

Birch

Lions
Green

2

St Marys
School

Tanners
Manor

Fern Lane

Lane

B2203

Coggers Trail

Sharp's
Corner

Furnace Lane

3

Vines Cross Road

Horam

Manor Road

Manor Farm

130

4

Highfield
Road

Bridge
Close

Ellacroft

PO

Grange Close

Manor Oak
Surgery

Horebe

Lane

Coxlow Farm

5

Coggers Trail

Golf Course

Burlow

6

Horeham
Flat Farm

Stonehill
Farm

7

Coggers
Farm

Gamelands

Coggers Lane

A267

Swansbrook Lane

NORTH

8

F G H **160** J K

Strood Farm

Swansbrook
Farm

Leyhurst Farm

STREET

PH

Wellshurst

Wellshurst
Golf &
Country Club

Winkenhurst

130

A B **100** C D E

I

Maynard's Green

Nevilles Farm

Friary Walk

B2203

Cuckoo Trail

Street Lane

Tubwell Lane

West

Maynards Green CP School

Sicklehatch Lane

Sapperton Manor F

Nettlesworth Place

Furnace Lane

2

St Marys School

B2203

Cuckoo Trail

Hale Hill Farm

3

LONDON ROAD

Manor Road

Hillside

Birchbank

Bridge Close

Runnybrook

Vines Cross

PO

Ballsocks Lane

4

Broadview

Vines Cross Road

Gardner Close

129

Forebeech Lane

Coxlow Farm

Foord's Farm

Brookside

5

Clappers Wood

Norman Norris

Beestons

Burlow

6

Marle Green

Cowden Hall Lane

Cowden Hall

A267

7

Coggers Farm

Coggers Lane

Cuckoo Trail

Lewhurst Farm

8

HIGH

Swansbrook Farm

Leyhurst Farm

Grovebridge Farm

Knightsbridge Farm

A STREET B **161** C D Grove Park E

Grove Hill

Golf & Country Club

Winkenhurst

Wood's Corner

F **Dallington** **G** **H** 103 **J** **K**

Haselden

B2096

B2096

Old Castle

Dallington School

Hill

PO

Turner's

I

2

3

4

134

5

6

7

8

High Wood

Haselden Wood

's Gill

Pinnelridge Wood

Lakehurst Lane

South Lane

Herrings Road

Lakehurst Lane

Herrings Farm

Padgham Down Farm

Tigham Lane

Silverick's Lane

Silvericks Farm

Buckwell Farm

Thornden Farm

Lattenden Farm

Woodlands Farm

Redpale Farm

Bucksteep Manor

Farthing Lane

Glyde's Farm

Brigden Hill Farm

Pear Tree Farm

Court Lodge

Ponts Green

PO

1066 Country Walk

Merrie Field

New Buildings Farm

Brownbread Street

F **G** **H** 164 **J** PH **K**

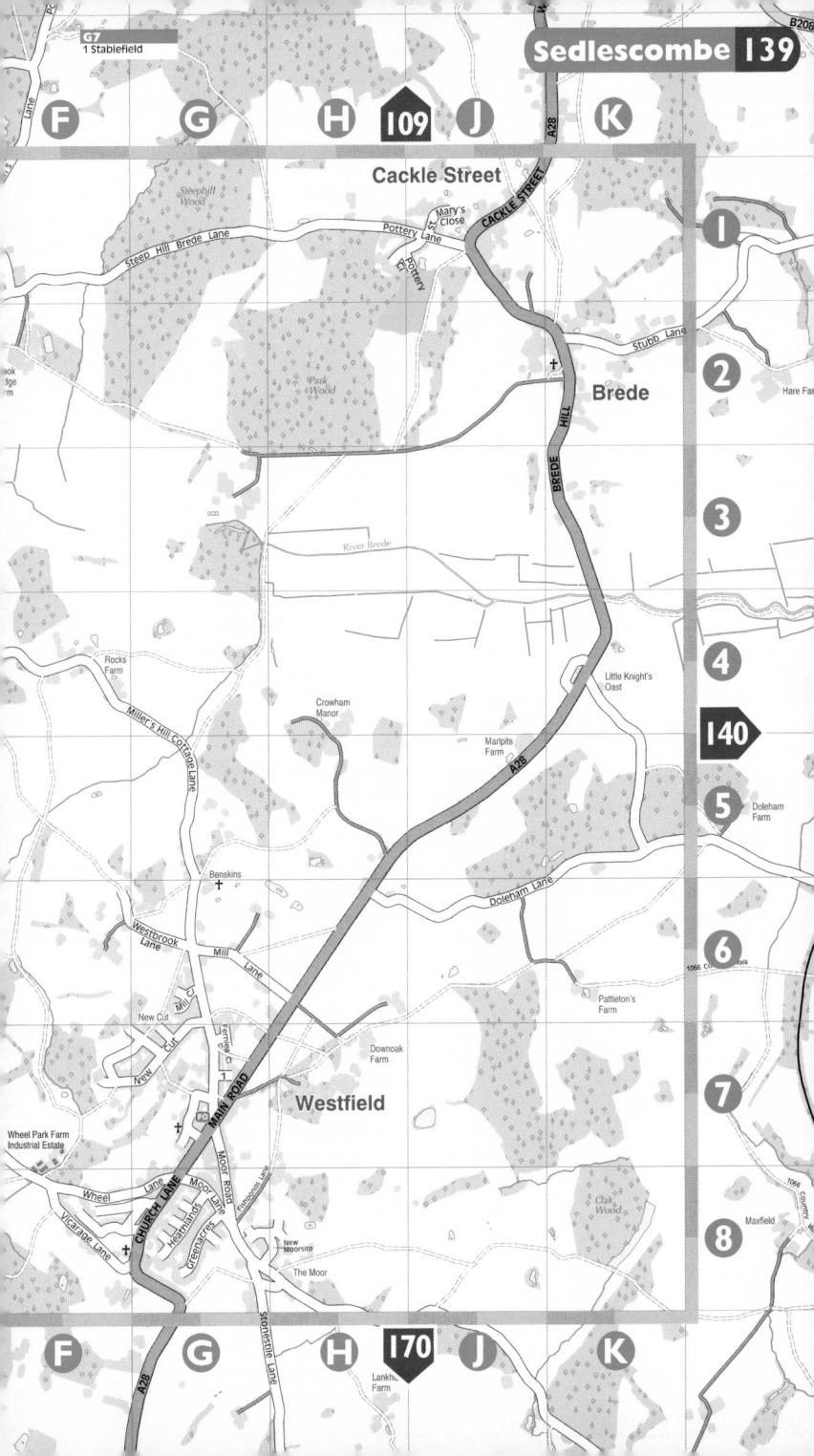

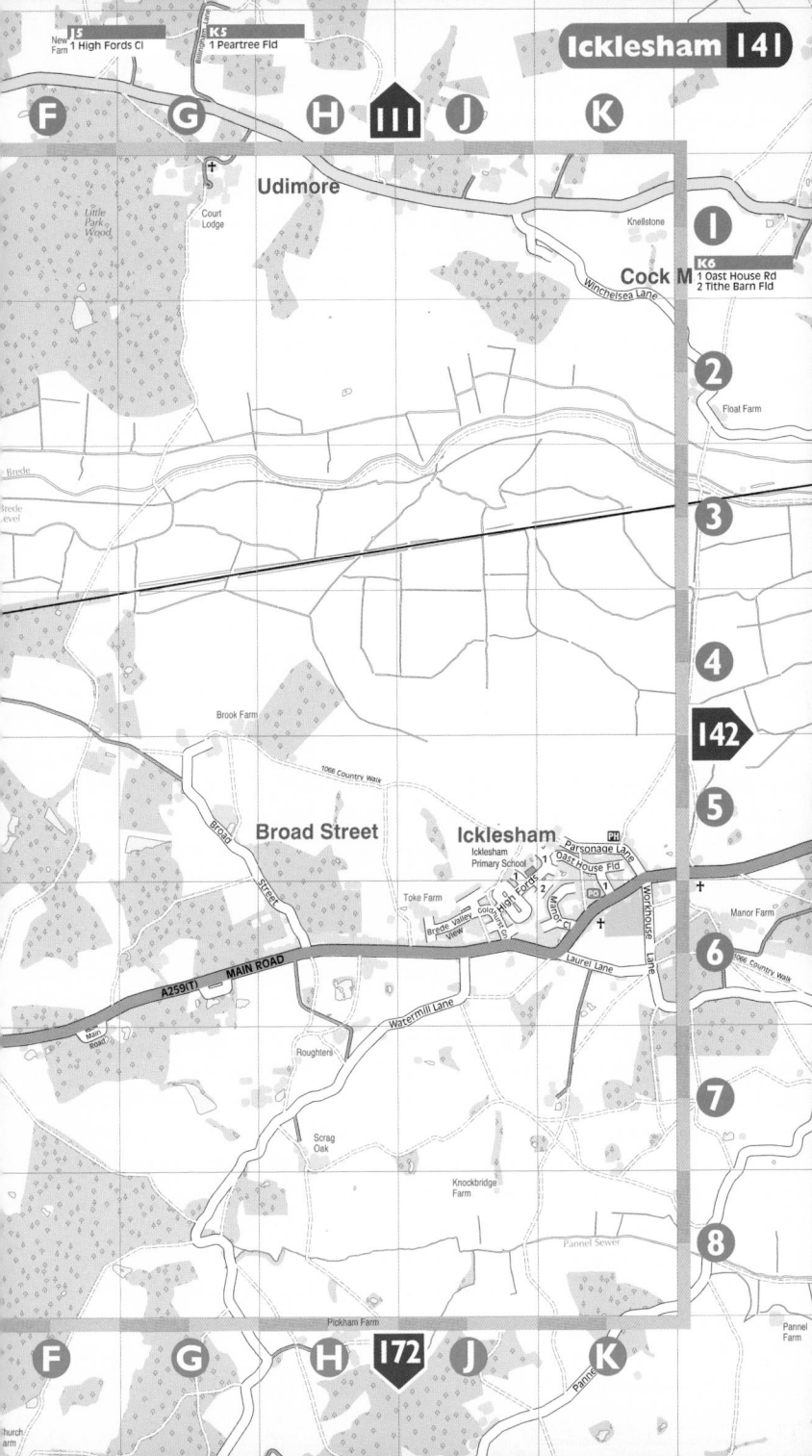

F G H J K

J5
New Farm 1 High Fords Cl

K5
1 Peartree Fld

Udimore

Little Park Wood

Court Lodge

Knellstone

I

K6
1 Oast House Rd
2 Tithe Barn Fld

Cock M

Winchelsea Lane

2

Float Farm

Brede

Brede Level

3

4

142

5

Brook Farm

1066 Country Walk

Broad Street

Icklesham

Icklesham Primary School

Parsonage Lane
Oast House Fld

PH

Broad Street

Toke Farm

Brede Valley View

High Forge

Manor Cl

Workhouse Lane

6

Manor Farm

1066 Country Walk

Laurel Lane

A259(T) MAIN ROAD

Main Road

Watermill Lane

Roughters

7

Scrag Oak

Knockbridge Farm

Pannel Sewer

8

Pickham Farm

Pannel

Pannel Farm

F G H J K

172

Church arm

H4 1 Windmill Wy
H5 1 Greyfriars Pl

F G H 113 J K

I
2
3
4
144
5
6
7
8

F G H J K

Rye Marsh Farm

Camber Castle

Saxon Shore Way

Nook Beach

Watch House

ROYAL MILITARY ROAD
A259(T)
NEW WINCHELSEA ROAD
A259(T)

LANE
A259(T)

Barrack

PO

St Thomas of E Primary School

Friars

Sea Road

Castle Farm

Saxon Shore Way

Sutton Ind Park

Sea Road
Old River Way
Morlais Ridge

Morlais Place

Sea Road

Harley Farm

Willow Lane

Dimsdale Sewer

Saxon Shore Way

Winchelsea Beach

The Ridge

The Ridge

Streamside Lane

The Ridge

Donald Wy
Windsor Way
Windsor Way

Pett Level Road

Rye Bay Club House

Pett Level Road

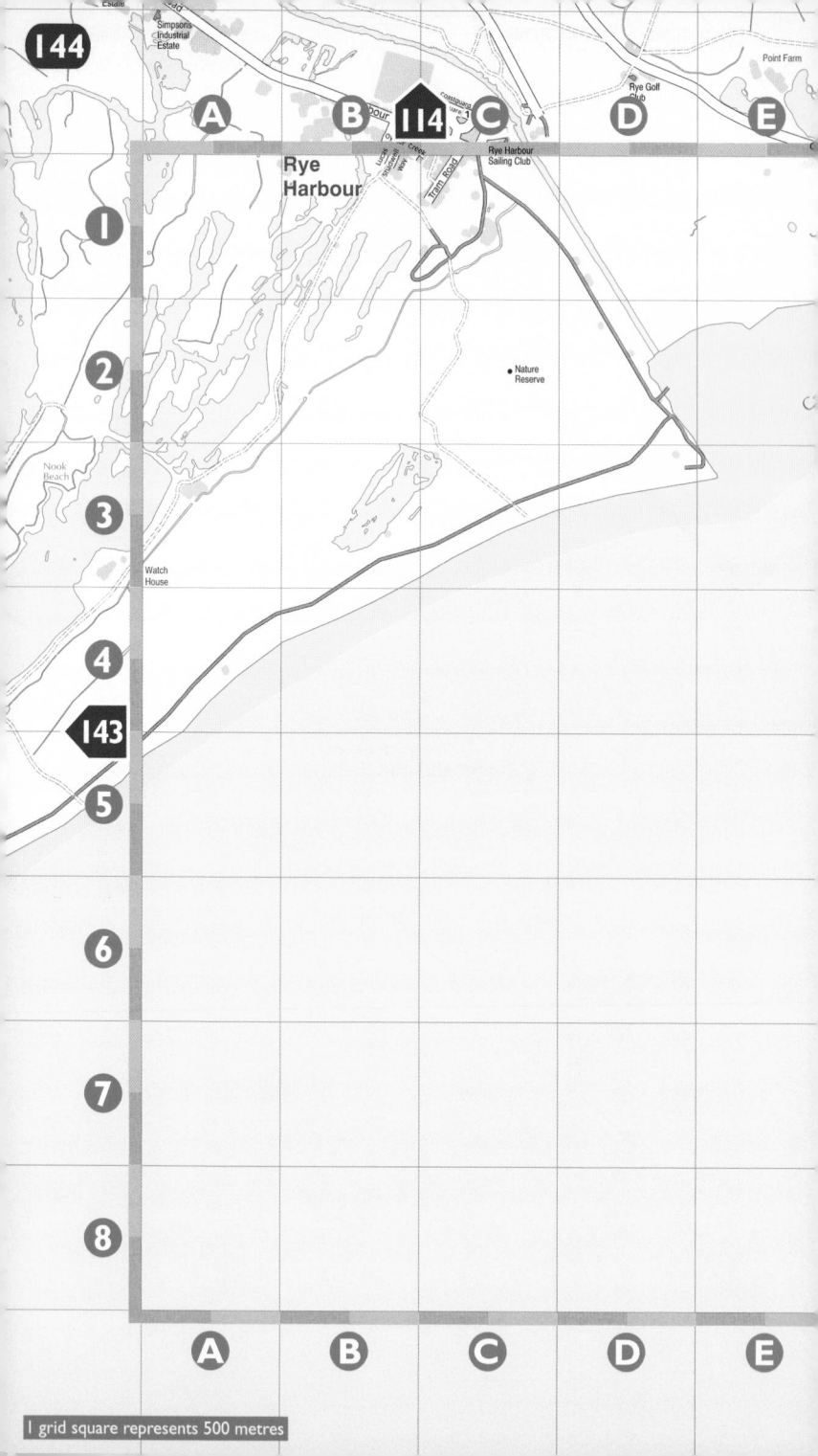

A   B   114   C   D   E

Rye Harbour

Rye Harbour Sailing Club

Simpsons Industrial Estate

Rye Golf Club

Point Farm

1

2

Nature Reserve

Nook Beach

3

Watch House

4

143

5

6

7

8

A   B   C   D   E

I grid square represents 500 metres

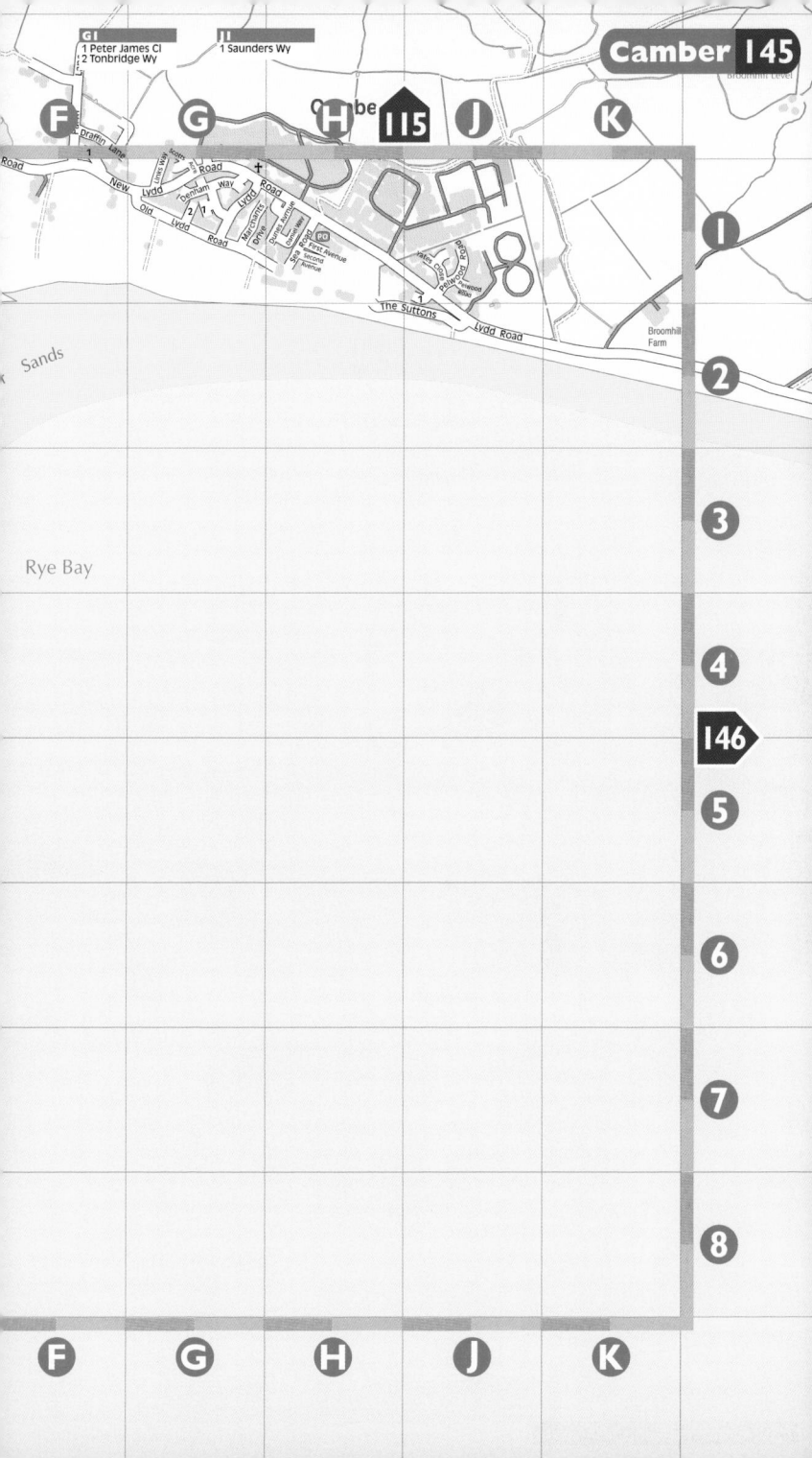

F **G** O Cambe **H** 115 **J** **K**

Road

Draffin Lane

New Lydda Links Vw Denham Way Road
Old Lydd Road Marshlands Dray Road Dunes Av Dunes Wy PO First Avenue Yates Clo Peter Clo Birch Wood Golf Clo Second Avenue The Suttons Lydd Road

I

2

Broomhill Farm

Sands

Rye Bay

3

4

146 ›

5

6

7

8

F **G** **H** **J** **K**

A   B   116   C   D   E

I

Broomhill Level

Broomhill Farm

2

Lydd Road

Jury's Gap

Broomhill Sands

3

4

145

5

6

7

8

A   B   C   D   E

Neam Road

Neam Road

Midrips

I grid square represents 500 metres

F G H 117 J K

Neath Road
Ferguson Road

Holmstone
Ferguson Road

LC

Lydd
Ranges

LC

LC

South
Brooks

LC

LC

The
Wicks

East Sussex County
Kent County

South Brooks Road

Invicta

I

2

3

4

5

6

7

8

F G H J K

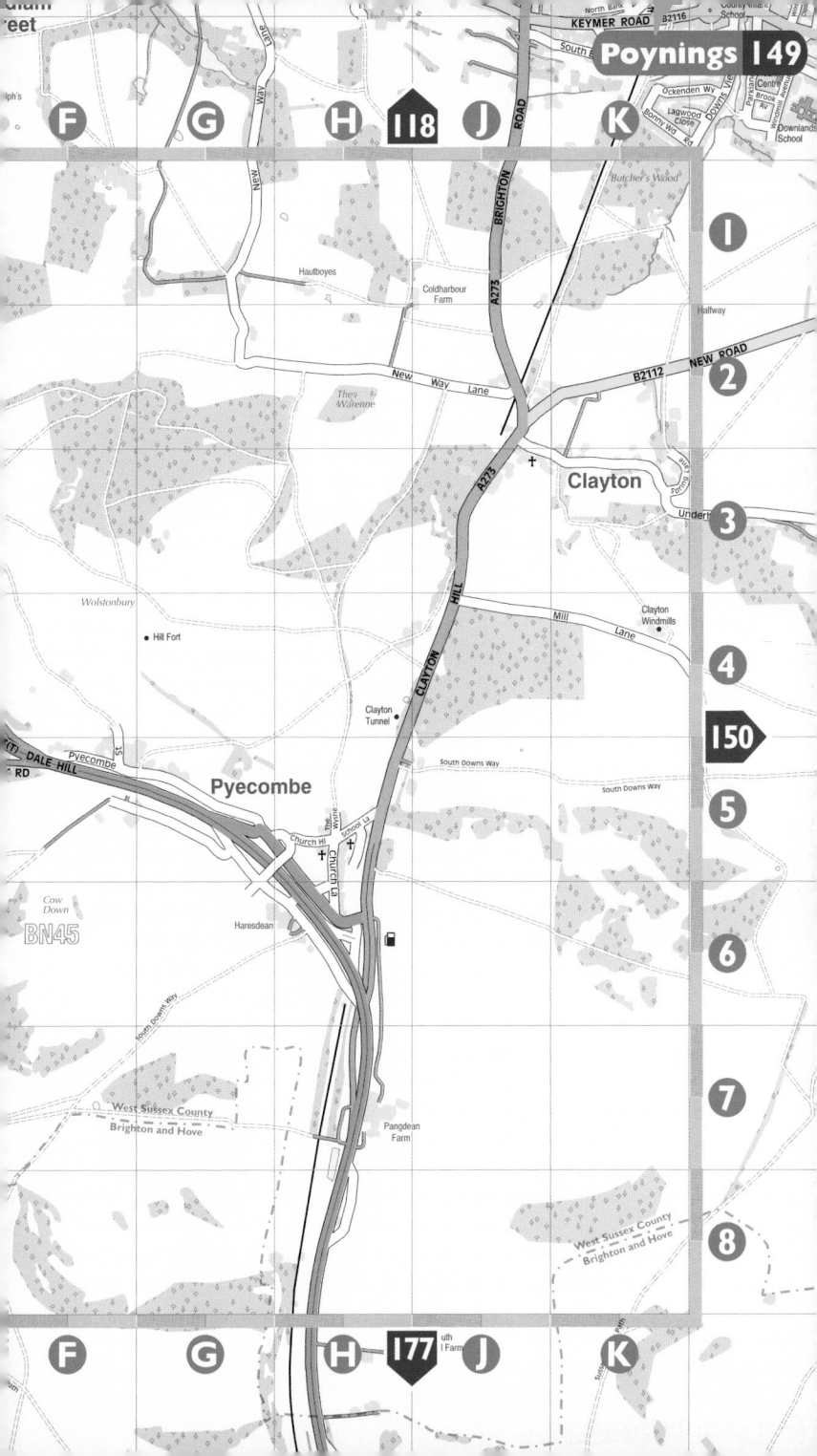

Downlands School

KEYMER ROAD
B2116

South

Ockenden Wy
Lagwood Close
Bonny Wd

F G H **118** J K

BRIGHTON

ROAD

A273

Haulboyes

Coldharbour Farm

I

Halfway

B2112 NEW ROAD

2

New Way Lane

The Wellenne

Clayton

3

Under

Wolstonbury

Mill Lane

Clayton Windmills

Hill Fort

CLAYTON HILL

4

Clayton Tunnel

150

(T) DALE HILL
RD

Pyecombe

South Downs Way

South Downs Way

5

Church Hl

The

School La

Church La

6

Cow Down

BN45

Haresdean

South Downs Way

7

West Sussex County
Brighton and Hove

Pangdean Farm

West Sussex County
Brighton and Hove

8

F G H **177** J K

Streat

F   G   H   120   J   K

I

2

3

4

152

5

6

7

8

F   G   H   179   J   K

LEWES

ROAD

B2116

Sedlow
Wood

Brock's
Wood

Middleton
Manor

Westmeston

The
Gote

Street Lane

Street Bostall

B2116

Wales Farm

Plumpton

South Downs Way

Streathill
Farm

Lane

Boxtall

Ditching

Road

High Park
Farm

Stanmer
Down

St Mary's
Farm

152

A   **B**   **121**   **C**   **D**   **E**

East
Chiltington

Ashurst

Old
Hill Ho

PH
Chapel Lane

Wootton Far

1

Stantons
Farm

Street Lane

2

Novington
Manor

Plumpton Lane

Novington Lane

3

Wales Farm

Warningore
House

Warningore
Farm

4   B2116   **Plumpton**

151

Novington
Farm

Plumpton Bostall

5

South Downs Way

Plumpton Plain

Blackcap

6

7

South Downs Way

Ashcombe
Bottom

8

Buckland
Bank

South Downs Way

A   **B**   **180**   **C**   **D**   **E**

Balmer
Down

I grid square represents 500 metres

A   B   125   C   D   E

A4
1 Manor Cl

1

Red
Barn Farm

Plashett
Park Farm

2

Little Norlington

Green Lane

Broyle Lane

3

Broyle
Cl
Broyle Rd
Broyle Kiln

Broyle Side

Broyle Mill Farm

THE BROYLE

Yew
Tree

Foxglove
Close
1

Broyle
Paddock

4

Eding
Road

Yeomans

155

Half Mile Drove

Lower
Lodge Farm

Broyle
Place

Chamberlaines Lane

B2192

5

Trinity Flds
Green Cl
ROAD
3

LAI

Greater
Paddock

Ringmer
Business
Centre

Shepherds Wy
Harrisons
Lane
Pursey Close
2
1

Arches
Farm

Neaves Lane

6

Ringmer
School

shy Green

BN8

Md

Potato Lane

7

**Ashton
Green**

Moorland
Farm

Neaves Lane

Moor Lane

8

Oldhouse
Farm

Road

Wakelands

Glynde ourne

A   B   184   C   D   E

I grid square represents 500 metres

F G H **126** ho **J** te K

I

Laughton
Park Farm

Upper
Lodge Farm

Walls Farm

2

Raystede Centre
for Animal Welfare

Laughton
Common

3

Birkhurst Lane

Brickhurst Farm

Laughton

4

Sportgate Lane

Pound Lane

Laughton
Manor

Elm Close

LAUGHTON ROAD

158

ROAD

B2124

Colbrans
Farm

County
Primary
School

Church Lane

B

5

6

Old
Barn

Church Lane

7

Cleaver's Farm

8

F G H **185** J K

Mark
Cross

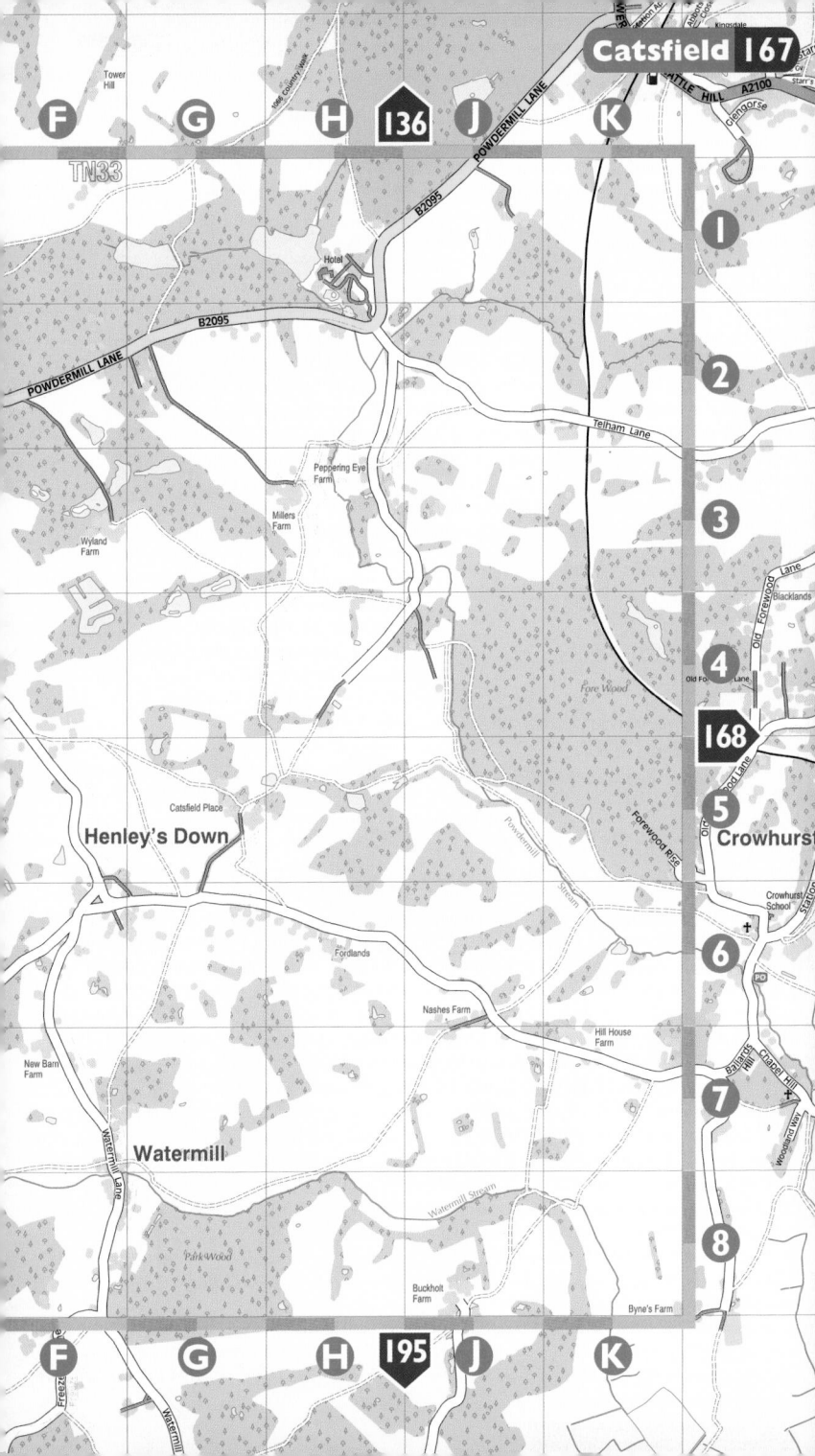

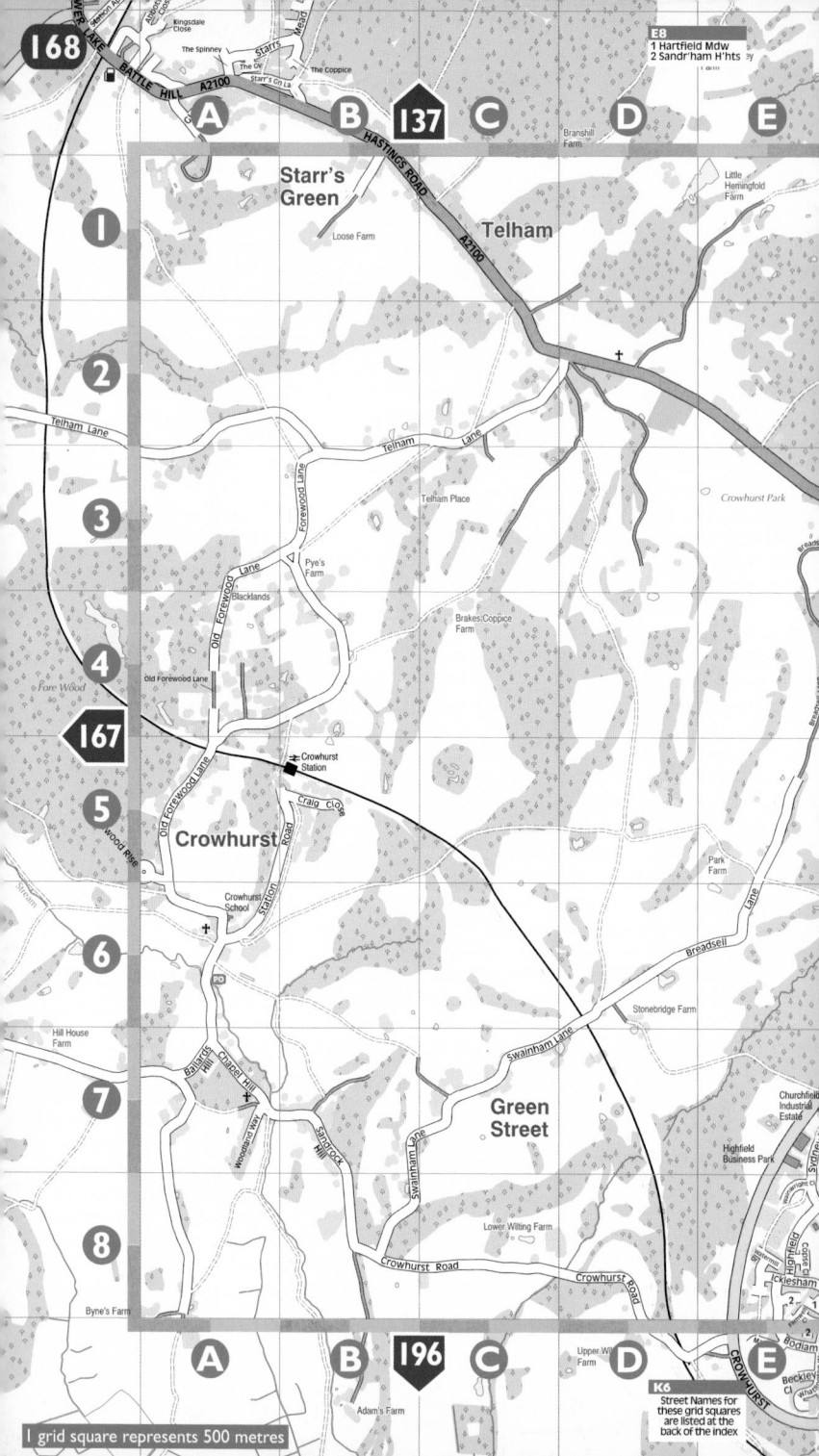

Hollington 169

F7
1 Coneybur'w Gdns

F8
1 Curlew Ct
2 Silvan Rd
3 Wren Ct

138

F G H J K

G6
1 The Kestrels

G7
1 Beecham Pl

I

H5
1 Hadrian Gdns

2
Cockmartin's

H6
1 Carinus Gdns
2 Cooper Ri
3 The Finches
4 Willingdon Wy

3 WESTFIELD

H7
1 Beauchamp Rd
2 Edward Ter
3 Meadow Cl
4 Northampton Wy

4

170

5 Silverhill Park

H8
1 Beauchamp Rd
2 Larkfield Cl

J4
1 Maplehurst Ri

6

J6
1 Ledsham Cl
2 Thom Brassey Cl

7

J7
1 Battle Crs
2 Bellingham Cl
3 Clarendon Cl
4 Hollinghurst Rd

8

J8
1 Menzies Rd
2 Stevenson Rd

4

Silverhill
Burry Road

Baldslow

Hollington

F **197** G H J K

K6
1 Briers Gdns
2 King Edward Cl

K7
1 Blackthorn Cl
2 Copper Beeches

K5
1 Beaulieu Gdns
2 Chalvington Dr
3 Westdene Rd

A2100 BATTLE ROAD
THE RDG WEST
A2100
A21(T)
A28
A21(T)
QUEENSWAY B2092
BATTLE ROAD
B2159
SEDLESCOMBE ROAD NORTH
SILVERHILL AVENUE
KING EDWARD AVENUE
A21
THE RIDGE
EBDEN'S HILL
STONEHOUSE DRIVE

Broomham School

A
B
141
C
D
E

E7
1 Fairlight Gdns

Knockbridge Farm
D6
1 Knowle Av

Pannel Sewer

I

Pickham Farm

Pannel Lane

Church Farm

Pound F

Guestling Wood

2

Church Lane

Watermill Lane

French Court Farm

Elms

The Oak Field

Guestling School

Guestling Green

The Thorns

3

PO

Elva Chapel Lane

Pett Road

Pett

Allards

PO

Guestling Surgery

Friar's Bank

Friar's Hill

4

Pett Road

Peter James Lane

Marsham Sewer

New Barn Farm

Humphrey's Farm

171

Rosemary Lane

Wakehams Farm

5

Cherry Garden Farm

Pett Level

The Hall

6

Mallydams Wood

Stonelynk Farm

Battery Hill

PO

Fairlight Cove

Farley Way

Waites

Broad Oak

Pinmore Cl

Knowle Rd

Church Way

Waites

7

Fairlight Road

Battery Hill Road

Fairlight

The Close

Coastguard Lane

Warren Road

Hill Road

Knowle Road

Woodland Way

Meadow Way

Lower

Blackwood

Stock Dale

Rockmead Road

Commanders Walk

Corsehorn Way

Bramble Wy

Shepherds Way

Fyrsway

Channel Way

8

Hastings County Park

Fire Hills

Saxon Shore Way

Fairlight Glen

A
B
C
D
E

Covehurst

F
G
H
142
J
K

Pannel Farm

Carter's Farm

Lane

Lunsford

Pett Road

Pett Level

Chick Hill

Pett Road

Saxon Shore Way

Pett Level Road

Saxon Shore Way

Cliff End Lane

Cliff End

Saxon Way

Stream Lane

Sea Road

I
2
3
4
5
6
7
8

F
G
H
J
K

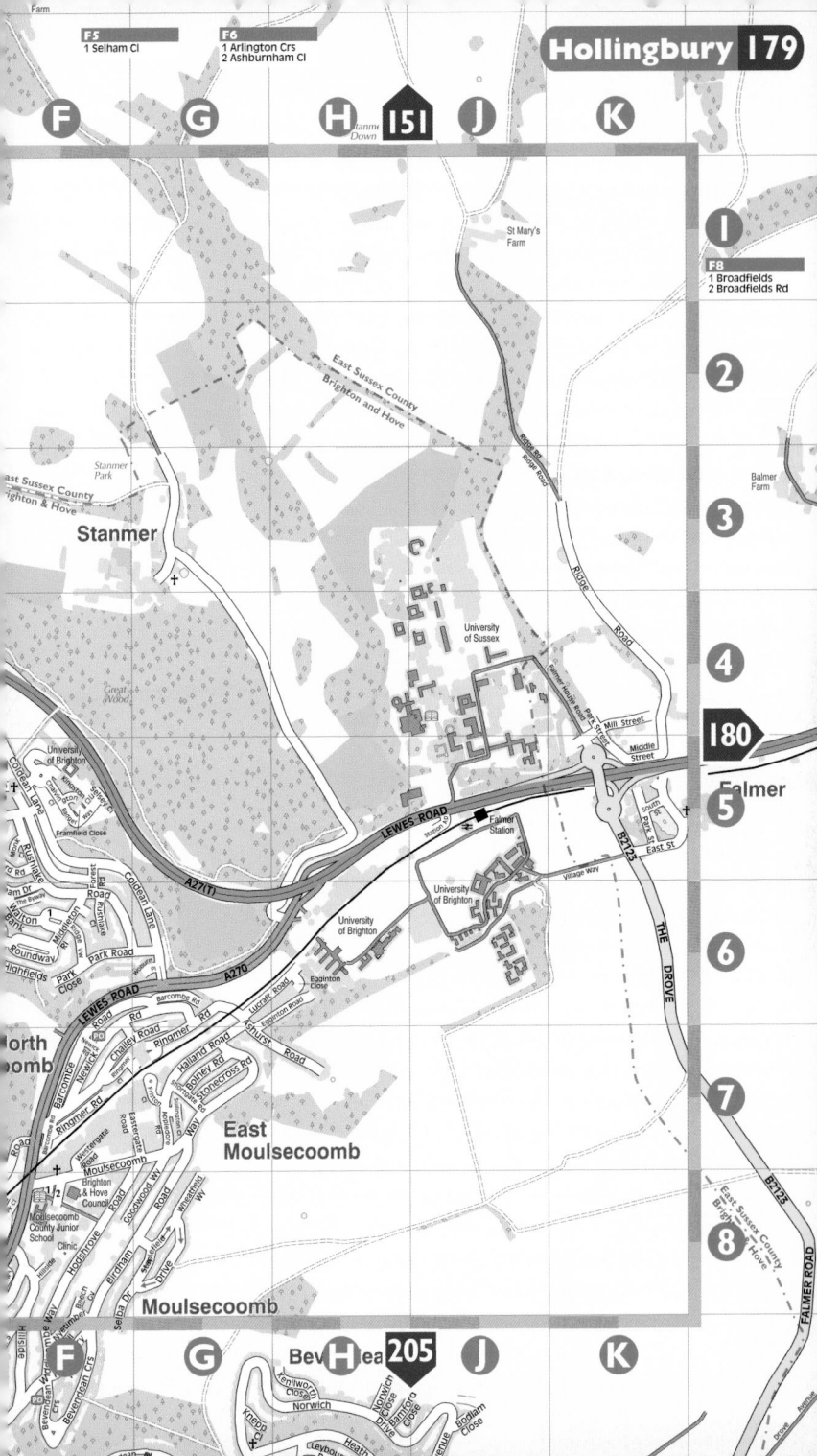

A   B   **152**   C   D   E

1

2

Buckland Bank

Balmer Down

Bankershill Plantation

South Downs Way

South Downs Way

3

Balmer Farm

RIDGE ROAD

Lower House Road

Park Street

179

4

Housedean Farm

A27(T)

Falmer

5

East St

B2123

Village Way

New Barn

6

THE DROVE

Loose Bottom

South Downs Way

7

8

B2123

East Susex County Brighton & Hove

FALMER ROAD

Wildl Reser

A   B   **206**   C   D   E

Newmarket Hill

184

A   B   156   C   D   E

Oldhouse
Farm

Wakelands

Glyndebourne

1

Glyndebourne

2

3

Lacys Hill

Glynde
Palace

4 Glynde

183

P.O.

5 Glynde Station

Glynde Reach

6

Lower
Wood

Newho
Farm

Bur

Wick Street

Gibraltar

7

Preston Home

Firle
Park

Little
Dene

Preston Court

Firle C of E
School

Bostal Rd

8

The
Furlongs

Newelm

PH

P.O.

The Street

The Dock

West Firle

Firle
Place

A   B   210   C   D   E

1 grid square represents 500 metres

F   G   H   **157**   J   K

1

Mark
Cross

2

3

Lulhams Farm

4

Hall
Court Farm

186

Middle
Barn

Sheeplands
Farm

5

Bushy
Lodge Farm

LC

6

Lane

Middle
Farm

7

Pookhill
Barn

Sherrington
Manor

8

F   G   H   **211**   J   K

Charleston
Farmhouse

Tilton Farm

A2101

186

A B 158 C Lane D E

1 Mark Cross

2 PO Ripe
Eckington Corner
Channers Lane
Church Lane

3

Chalvington

4

185 Langtye Farm

Sheeplands Farm

Langtye Lane

5 Lower Claverham House

6 Lower Mays Farm

Cobb Court

7 Mays Farm

Ludlay

8 Sherrington Manor

Selmeston

A A271 B 212 C Vanguard Way D E Berwick Station LC

Green Fa...

Vanguard Way

Vanguard Way

I grid square represents 500 metres

F   G   H   159   J   K

Limekiln Farm

Vanguard

Field House

1

Camberlot Road

2

Clover Farm

Colgat

Mount Pleasant Farm

Vanguard Way

The Dicker St Bedes School

Upper Dicker

Cackleway

3

PH

Weavering

High Barn

Park Mead School

4

188

Lower Claverham Farm

Michl Prio

5

Parkwood Farm

Wenderes

Wickstreet

6

Weavering

Sessingham Farm

Cuckmere River

7 PH

Raylands Farm

Tye

Hill Road

Arlington

Wealdway

8

Wilbees Farm

Bakers Lane

F   G   H   213   J   K

Arlington Reservoir

HAILSHAM

Summer Hill

161
190
215

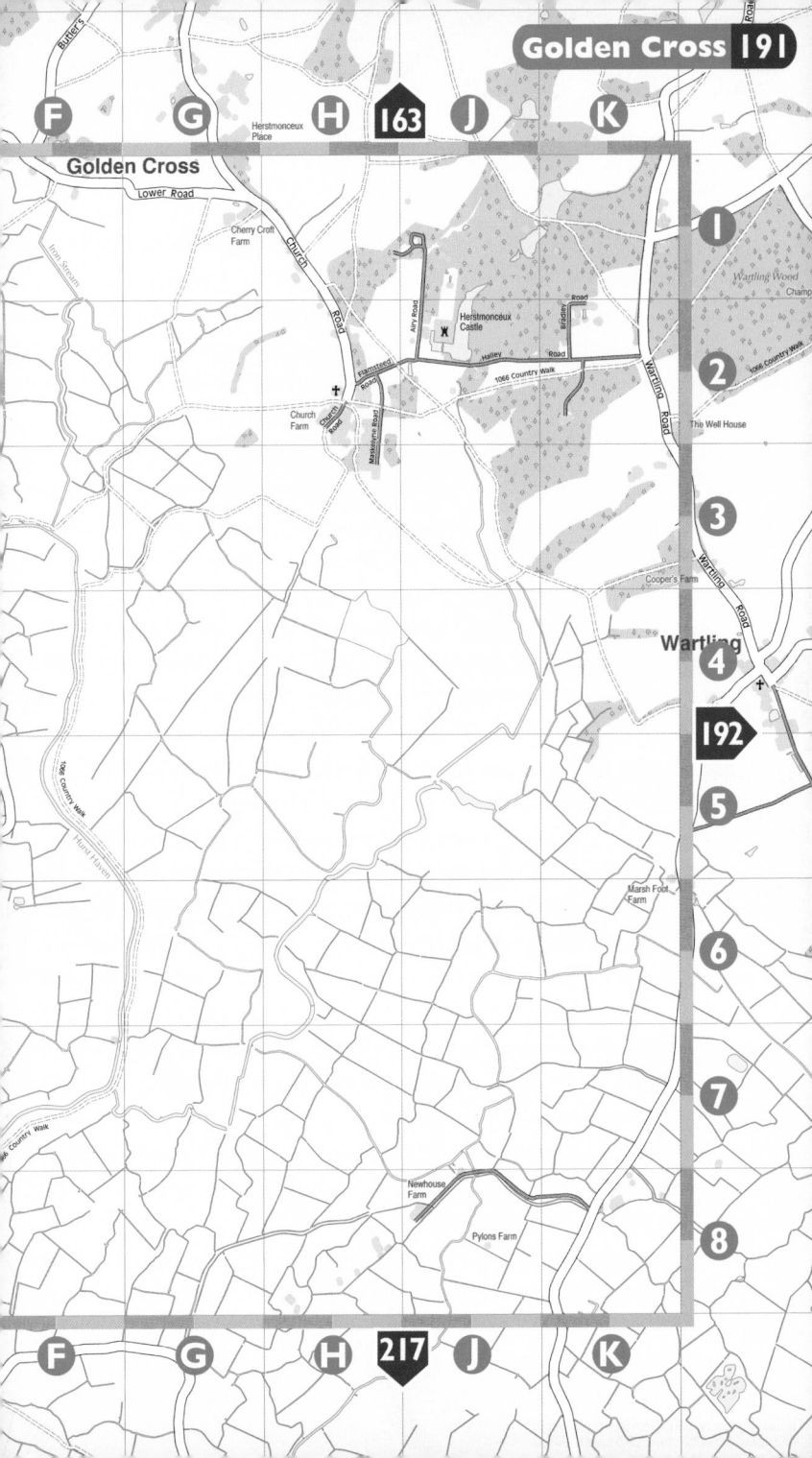

F G H **163** J K

Golden Cross

Lower Road

Herstmonceux Place

Cherry Croft Farm

Iron Stream

Church Road

Alyn Road

Herstmonceux Castle

Church Farm

Flimstead Road

Mackleyne Road

Halley

1066 Country Walk

Widden Road

1066 Country Walk

Wartling Road

Wartling Road

The Well House

Cooper's Farm

Wartling

192

1066 Country Walk

Hunt Haven

Marsh Foot Farm

Newhouse Farm

Pylons Farm

I 2 3 4 5 6 7 8

Wartling Wood
Champ

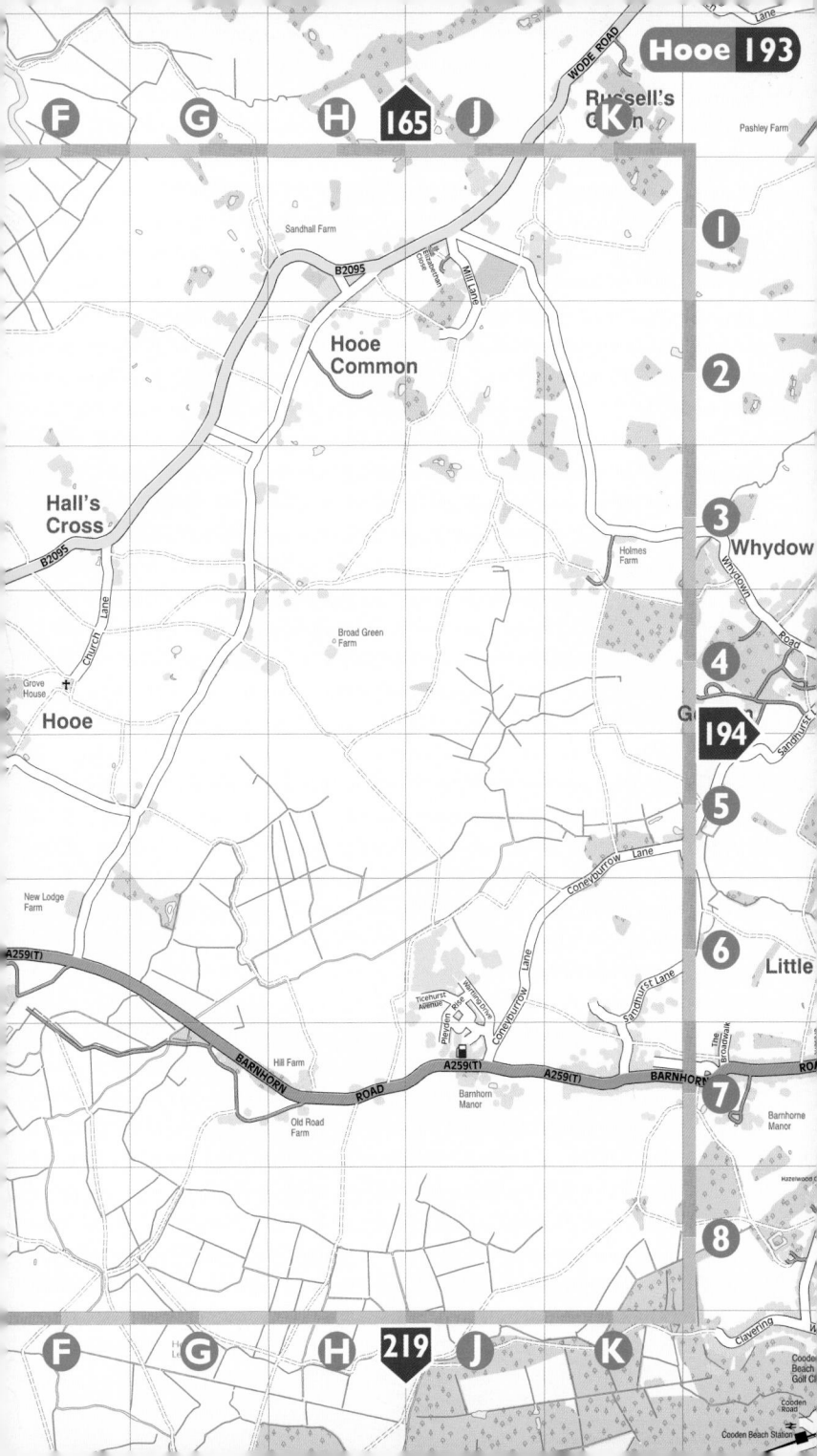

E8
1 St Augustine's Cl

E5
1 Roselands

D8
1 Tanglew'd Cop'ce
2 Tangmere Cl
3 Westham Cl

A   **B**   **166**   **C**   **D**   **E**

I

Thorne Farm

Hollis Street Farm

Messens Farm

Lunsford's Cross

2

NINFIELD ROAD

The Thorne

Freezeland

A269

Freezeland Farm

3

Holmes Farm

Whydown

High Woods

Bexhill Cemetery

The Highla

The Ridings

4

Turkey Road

Gotham

193

Whydown Road

Sandhurst Lane

Peartree Lane

TN39

Highwoods Golf Club

Greenways

5

Holly Close

Wealden Way

Cowdray Park Road

Woodstock Way

Oakfield Way

Levant Close

Berwick Close

Cowdray Close

Easter Gate

Ellerslie Lane

Fryatts Way

Broadoak

The Fairway

The Fairway View

Summer Hill

Concorde

6

Coneyburrow Lane

Sandhurst Lane

Little Common

Chestnut Walk

Fontwell Avenue

Green Lane

The Byeway

Foxhill

Courthope Drive

Piders Lane

Byelands Croft

Bushy Croft

Duke Street

Knelworth

7

259(T)

BARNHORN ROAD

The Broadwalk

Barnhorne Manor

Sycamore Close

Norman's Close

Coghurst Road

Prowting Mead

St Marks Close

Hillborough

LITTLE COMMON ROAD

A259(T)

Whitel Id Av

High Branches

Fairlie Chase

East

Collington Park Cr

Pinewoods

Grenada Close

Little Common Primary School

Collington Grove

Eden Drive

Copse Road

Alexander Drive

Collington

Winston Drive

Cranston Rise

Crans

Brampton Avenue

Thornbank Crescent

8

Hazelwood Cl

Kennel Lane

Tyndale Avenue

Birk Dale

Drayton Rise

The Mead

Lakelands Drive

Collington Lane

Cooden Sea Road

SEA ROAD

Cooden

Kewhurst Avenue

Ashcombe Drive

Falconbury Drive

Maple Avenue

Maple Walk

Maple Close

Osborn Close

Ravens Close

Cooden

Collington

Wrestwood Avenue

The Barnhams

The Finden

Horn Oak Close

A   **B**   **C**   **D**   **E**

Cooden Beach Golf Club

Cooden Close

B2182

COODEN DRIVE

The Close

Elsted Road

Chelgates

Wynham

Jevington Dr

Brackerne Close

Mossbank

Beaulieu Road

Gatehouse Close

Shipley Lane

Wartmann Gardens

B2182

COODEN DRIVE

Hartfield Road

South

Southway

Cooden

F3
1 Pankhurst Cl

F6
1 Leasingham Gdns

F   **G**   **H**   **167** olt   **J**   **K**

F7
1 Downlands Cl

I

G3
1 Faygate Cl
2 Morgan Cl
3 Redwell Av

2

G4
1 Oakwood Av

3

G5
1 Dane Court Cl

4

196

5

H4
1 Bank Rd

Pe

6

H5
1 Maberley Rd

7

H6
1 Bowrey Pl
2 Edinburgh Rd
3 Hanover Cl
4 Jacobs Acre
5 Pipers Cl

8

H7
1 Cookham Dene

K7
1 Brookfield Rd

K6
1 Compton Cl
2 Gleneagles Cl
3 Martlets

K5
1 Gainsborough Rd

196

168
195

E1
1 Catsfield Cl
2 Salehurst Gdns

C6
1 Hythe Av

A4
1 Angela Cl

Lower Wilting Farm

Crowhu

A B C D E

Byne's Farm

CROWHURST

Mayfield

Beckley

I

Acton's Farm

Adam's Farm

Upper Wilting Farm

2

3

Worsham Lane

4

Pebsham Farm

TN40

Ur

Amanda Close
Ian Close
Gyneth Grove
Top Cross Road
Pebsham Drive
Pebsham Lane
Diana Close
Pebsham Lane

5

St Marys School
Clades
St Mary Magdalene School

Seabourne
Pebsham
Doctors Surgery

Road
Grand Avenue

Lane

A259
Bexhill

A259

Bulverhythe
Cliffonville

BEXHILL ROAD

A2036
Battle Abbey Preparatory School
Charters Ancaster School
Second Avenue
Martyns
Glyne Barn Close
Way

6

Dorset
HASTINGS ROAD
First Avenue
Wentworth Close
Claxton Row
Gloucester Av
Bexhill Road

A259

Glassenbury Dr
Primary School
School Place
Kent Cl

Bulverhythe

DE LA WARR ROAD
A259(T)

Glyne
Gap

7

Links
College
St Richards School
Ridgewood Gardens
The Finches
Boxgrove Close
Megabowl

Ashdown Road
Sutton Pl
Hill View

Bexhill Squash Rackets Club
Parade
Bethune Road

8

A B C D E

1 grid square represents 500 metres

F

G

Hollington

H

169

J

K

Silverhill

I **St Helen's**

2

Bohemia

Summerfields
Business Cen

Silver Springs
Medical
Practice

Summer Fields

3

Harley
Shute

St Leonards

4

198

FIELD PLACE

5

West Marina

Hastings &
St Leonards
Sailing Club

4

6

7

8

F

G

H

J

K

198

170

197

Burry Road
Blacklands
HASTINGS
Broomsgrove
Bohemia
West Hill
Old

1 grid square represents 500 metres

F1
1 High Bank Cl
2 Richmond St

F2
1 Lodge Rd

F **G** **H** 171 **J** **K**

Clive Vale

Fairlight Glen

I

Covehurst

G1
1 Hawthorn Rd

All Saints
Junior School

Doctors Surgery

Glenview
Close

Belmont

2

Ecclesbourne Glen   Saxon Shore Way

East Hill

Town

3

Rock-A-Nore
Parade

4

5

6

7

8

F **G** **H** **J** **K**

200

174

C2
1 Amberley Cl
2 Annington Gdns
3 Buckingham Ms
4 Mill Av
5 Newtimber Gdns
6 Ravensbourne Cl

B4
1 Buckingham St
2 Little High St

A6
1 Fishermans Wk
2 Mariners Cl
3 Seahaven Gdns

A   B   C   D   E

C3
1 The Cygnets
2 Northbourne Cl

C4
1 St Mary's Cl

C5
1 Collingwood Ct
2 Hardy Cl

D3
1 Buckingham Cl

E2
1 Berberis Ct
2 Marjoram Pl
3 New Barn Cl
4 Tottington Wy

E3
1 Glebelands Cl

Old Shoreham

SHOREHAM-BY-SEA

Shoreham Beach

A   B   C   D   E

I grid square represents 500 metres

F2
1 Bay Tree Cl
2 Thyme Cl

G2
1 Paythorne Cl

F G H 175 J K

Mile Oak

Portslade Village

I

G3
1 Crossroad Cl
2 Westmount Cl

2

G4
1 Montague Cl
2 Querneby Cl

H2
1 Southview Cl

3

H3
1 Green Field Cl

4

202

Southwick

Southern Cross

Fishersgate

5

POR BY-S

H4
1 The Cotswolds
2 Green Cl
3 School Cl
4 Twitten Cl
5 Waterdyke Av
6 Watling Cl

6

J1
1 Lodge Cl

J2
1 Ridgeway

7

K1
1 The Crossway

8

F G H J K

K4
1 Chapel Rd
2 Fishergate Cl

K3
1 St Louie Cl

K2
1 High Cl

176

201

A4
1 Church St
2 St Aubyn's Crs

A3
1 Bampfield St
2 Barnes Rd
3 Buckler St

A1
1 Blackthorn Cl
2 Brackenbury Cl
3 Cornford Cl
4 Foredown Cl
5 Highways
6 Meadow Cl

Hangleton

A **B** **C** **D** **E**

Portslade
Village

B1
1 Cottage Bush Cl

B3
1 Southdown Av

2

B4
1 George St
2 Symbister Rd

West

Souther Cross

3

B5
1 Camden St
2 Clarendon Pl

VICTORIA ROAD

4

Aldrington

NEW CHURCH ROAD

WELLINGTON ROAD

5

C1
1 Dale View Gdns
2 Northease Cl

PORTSLADE-
BY-SEA

KINGSWAY

6

C4
1 Mornington Crs

7

D1
1 Ashlings Wy
2 Storrington Cl
3 Sunninghill Cl
4 Thornhill Cl

8

D4
1 Ingram Crs

A **B** **C** **D** **E**

E1
1 Fallowfield Cl

E2
1 Acacia Av
2 Torrance Cl
3 Wayfield Cl

E4
1 Mainstone Rd
2 Scott Rd

I grid square represents 500 metres

204

Home Farm Business Centre

Hollingdean

178

1

2

Preston

3

4

203

5

6

7

8

6

BRIGHTON

7

MARINE PARADE

A   **B**   **C**   **D**   **E**

1 grid square represents 500 metres

Moulsecoomb

Bevendean

Woodingdean

Whitehawk

BN2

Wick Bottom

Sheepcote Valley

Golf Course

Black Rock

Roedean

Brighton Marina

Iford

A B **182** C D E

I

2

White Way

Northease Manor School

Northease Farm

South Downs Way

3

Rodmell Primary School

Rodmell

The Dicklands

Badger's Dene

The Paddocks

Mill Lane

4

Breaky Bott

207

Southease

5

6

7

Telscombe

Dean's Farm

Money Burgh

8

Bullock Down

The Lookout

Roderick Avenue North

Halcombe Farm

A B **222** C D E

Waterford Close

Jonns

Brett's Field

Bretts Road West

Telscombe Road

Rustic

Oval

Road

Valley

High

Road

Wendale Drive

Highstead Park

Greenacre

Telscombe Road

185

F G H J K

1

2

3 Alcist

4

212

5

6

7

8

F G H 225 J K

Charleston Farmhouse

Tilton Farm

south Downs Way

219
▲
Firle
Beacon

Bopeep Lane

Bopeep Lane

Bopeep Farm

Bopeep Road

Jerry's
Pond

south Downs Way

Five Lord's
Burgh

A2711

Arlington
Reservoir

Arlington

F G H **187** J K

Wealdway

Wilbees
Farm

Barley's

1

Hayreed

Endiewick
Farm

2

Robin

Po

Thornwell Road

Monkyn
Pyn

3

LC

4

**Wilmington
Green**

A27(T)

214

Sherman
Bridge

Wealdway

Thornwell Road

Wealdway

A27(T) ES ROAD

5

Ades
Fld

Wilmington Street

Wilmington

BN26

6

Wilmington
Prior

**Milton
Street**

Wealdway

Wealdway

Hunter's
Burgh

7

The Long Man
of Wilmington

8

South Downs Way

Tenantry

F G H **227** J K

South Downs Way

Polgate 215

F3
1 Mapleleaf Gdns

F4
1 High St
2 Mimosa Cl
3 Minster Cl
4 Old School La
5 Westfield Ct

F5
1 Burnside
2 Fairlight Cl

F8
1 Brocks Gyhll
2 Downsview Rd
3 Scanion Cl
4 The Triangle
5 Willingdon Ct

G5
1 Oaklands Cl

G7
1 Thurrock Cl

G8
1 Short Brow Cl
2 Windover Wy

H5
1 Drockmill Cl
2 Levett Cl
3 Levett Wy

H8
1 Berwick Cl
2 Burlow Cl

J5
1 Blenheim Wy

J8
1 Croxden Wy
2 Limetree Av
3 Rosedale Pl
4 St Martins Rd
5 St Pauls Cl
6 Sycamore Cl
7 Walsingham Cl
8 Welbeck Cl

POLEGATE

Dittons

Foulride Green

Lower Willingdon

C7
1 Eskdale Cl
2 Hickling Cl
3 Horning Cl
4 Ranworth Cl
5 Reedham Rd
6 Whitbread Cl

B7
1 Boship Cl
2 Broad Oak Cl
3 Caburn Cl
4 Chyngton Cl
5 Laughton Cl
6 Michelham Cl
7 Ringmer Wy

A8
1 Shepherds Cl

A B **190** C D E

Rickney

Glynleigh Level

Glynley Manor

1

C8
1 Lavender Cl

Glynleigh Road

The Horns

B2104

Glynleigh Road

Lusteds

1066 Country Walk

2

D6
1 Blatch'ton Mill Dr

Presthawes

3

D7
1 Borrowdale Cl
2 Buttermere Wy
3 Coniston Rd
4 Elmwood Cl
5 Elmwood Gdns
6 Middleham Wy
7 Wildwood

HAILSHAM

Montague

Hankham CP School

Hankham

ROAD

Street Hankham

4

215

Milton Street

Hankham Road

Foords Lane

Hankham Hall Road

Peelings

Mill Hill

DITTONS ROAD

5

A27(T)

Peelings Lane

D8
D
1 Cleveland Cl
2 Harebell Cl
3 Magdalen Cl
4 Milfoil Dr
5 Sorrel Cl

B2247 DITTONS ROAD

Barn Close

Peelings Lane

Rattle Road

Mill View

Rattle Road

Windmill Gn

Stone Cross

6

E8
1 Marlborough Cl
2 Pentland Cl

Milfram Rd Stone Cross CP School

LION HILL

Mounting Level

Regnum Cl

7

Catsfield Cl
Ditchling Cl

ROTHERFIELD AVENUE

Burwash

Sorrel

Doctors Surg

Health Centre

Pennine

FRIDAY STREET

Pantiln Wy

B2104

HIDE HOLLOW

8

MAYWOOD AVENUE

HEYWOOD

Causeway Secondary School

SORREL DRIVE

FOXGLOVE ROAD

DROVE

Langney Shopping Cen

Acacia Road

Hampden Park Infants School

A B **230** C D E

Crawley Rd

Midhurst Rd

Minor Rd

Fletching

LINGDON

Infant School

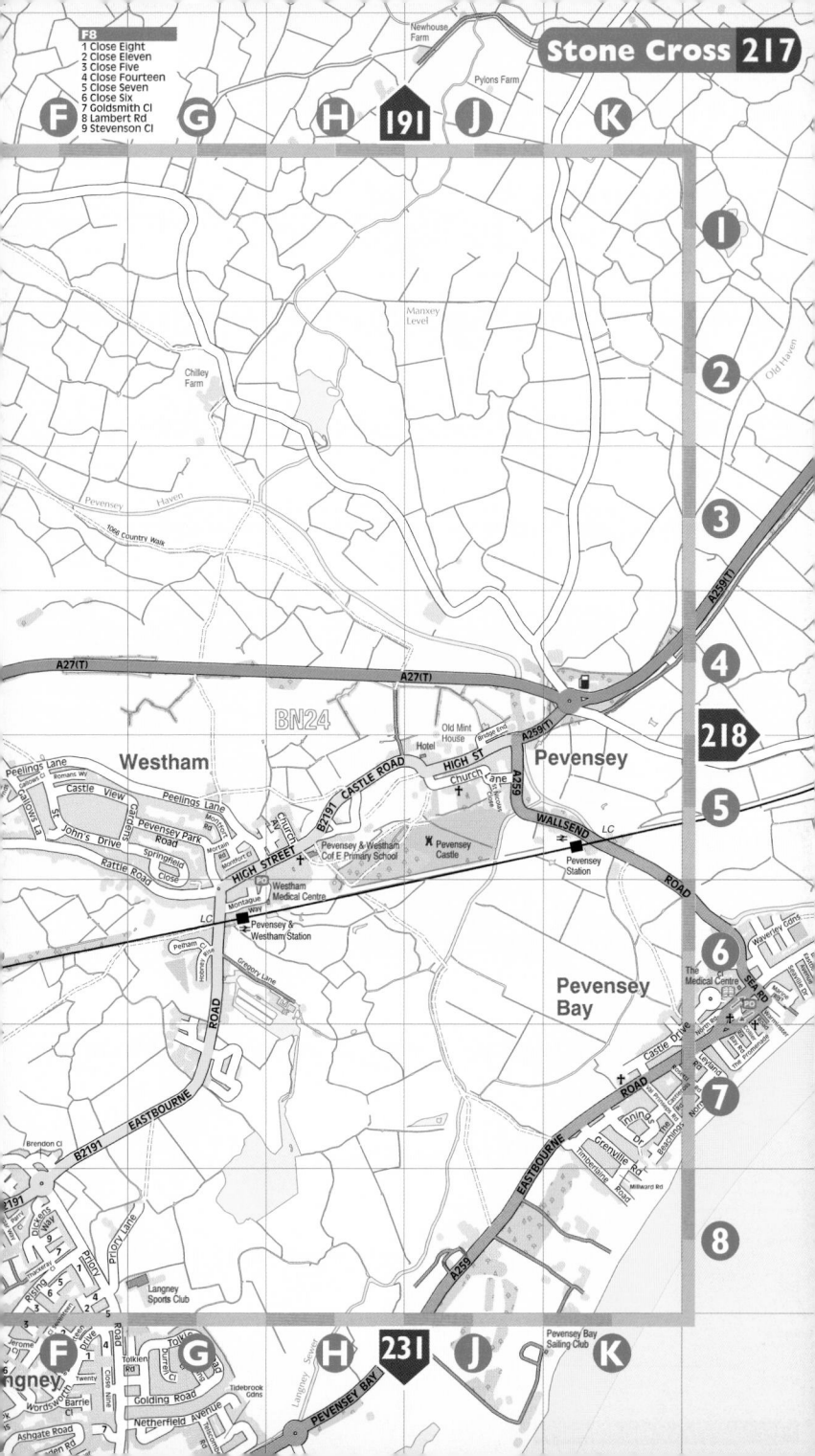

Stone Cross **217**

A　　B　192　C　　D　　E

1

2

3

4

Pevensey

Middle
Bridge

Waller's Haven

A259(T)

A259(T)

Old Haven

Rockhouse
Bank

5

ALLSEND　LC

Pevensey
Station

ROAD

Mountney Dr

Sunset
Close

Arundel
Close

The Boulevard

Hazel
Cl

Maresfield Drive

Tower Close

Dr
South

Drive

Cam

Memorial
Close

Close

Coast Road

Westham Drive

The Square

Westham
Dr

Coast Road

Beachlands

6

Pevensey
Bay

Waverley Gdns

Priory

The
Medical Centre

Coast Road

SEA RD

The Parade

Close
Rd

7

Castle Drive

Norman Rd

Innings
Dr

8

Grenville
Rd

Timberlaine

Millward Rd

Pevensey
Bay
Pevensey Bay
Sailing Club

Pevensey
Bay

A　　B　　C　　D　　E

I grid square represents 500 metres

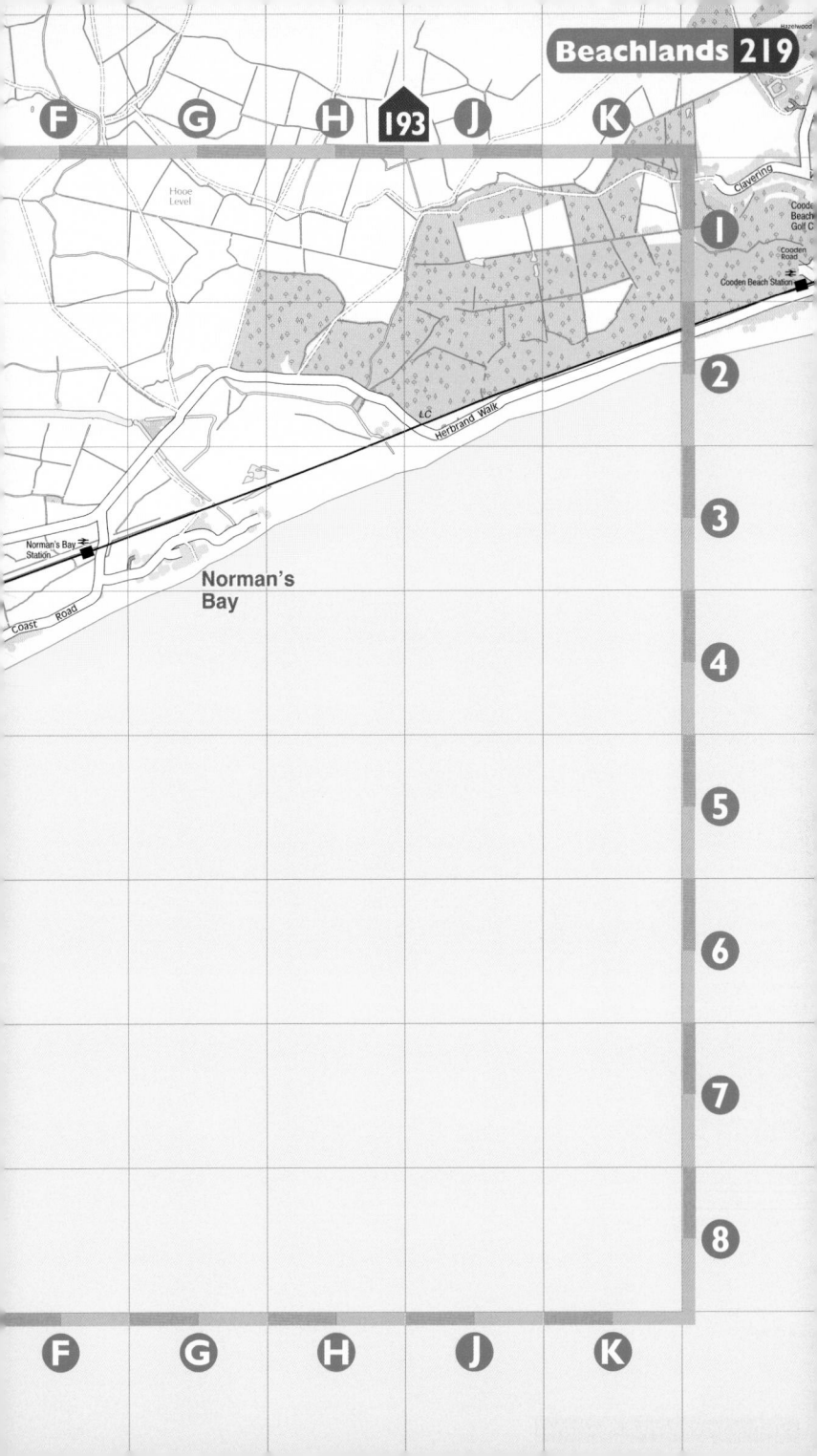

F G H **193** J K

Hazelwood

Clavering

Coode
Beach
Golf C

Cooden
Road

Cooden Beach Station

Hooe
Level

Herbrand Walk

LC

Norman's Bay
Station.

Norman's
Bay

Coast Road

I
2
3
4
5
6
7
8

F G H J K

Roedean School

Roedean

Ainsworth Avenue

Dover Road

Beacon Hill

Ovi Bea **206**

Rottingdean Football Club

A B C D E

DRIVE

A259

The Rotyngs
Challoner's Ms

ROTTINGDEAN

Rottingdean
Primary School

Our Lady of
Lourdes School

Whiteway
Lane

Neville
Road

The Gallery

St Aubyns
School

MARINE

Marine
Clinic

DRIVE

Westmeston Avenue

Steyning Road

Founthill
Road

Lenham Rd W

Eileen
Av

Marine Cl

I grid square represents 500 metres

1 grid square represents 500 metres

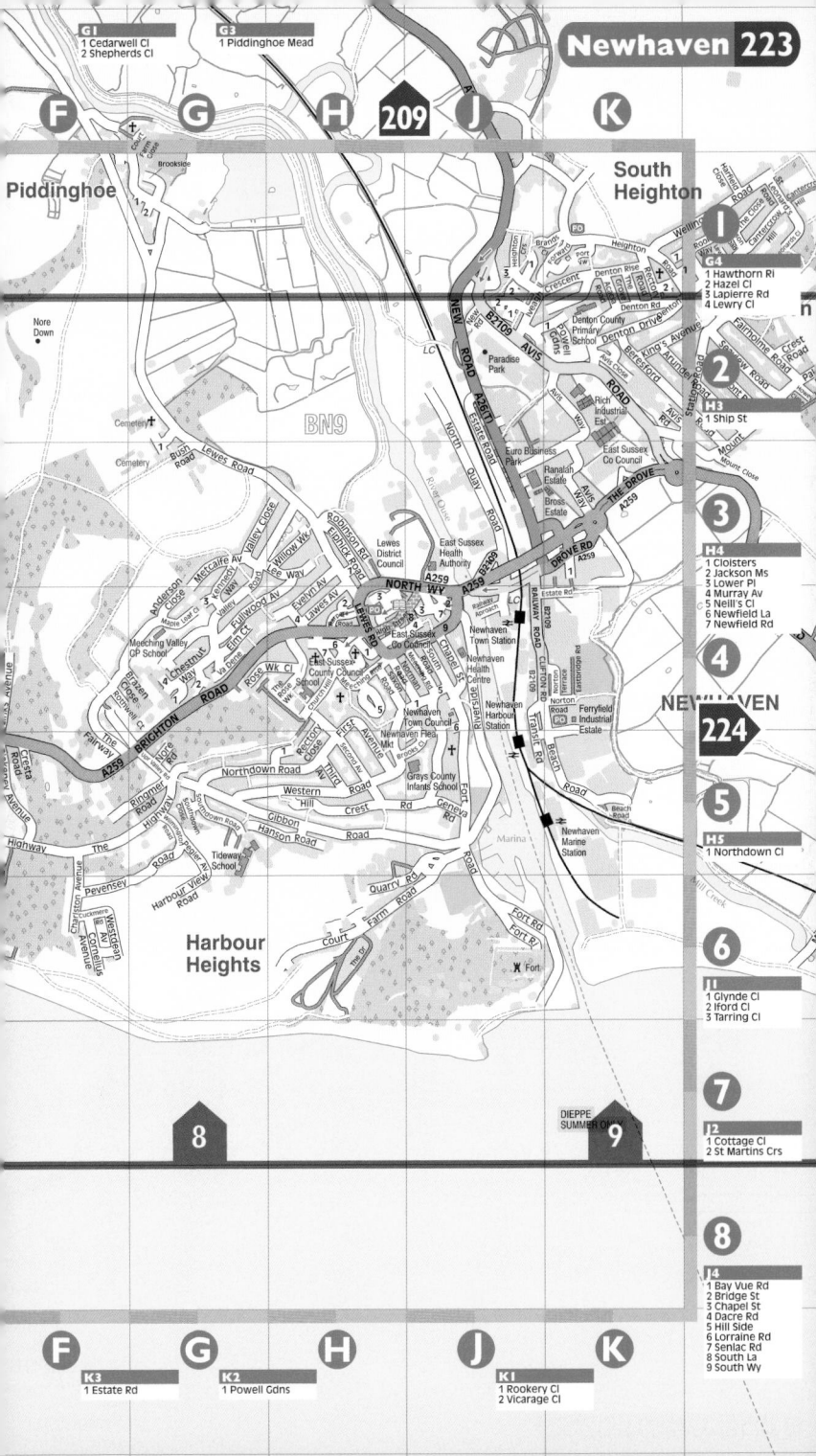

C5
1 Harbour View Cl
2 Norman Cl
3 Roman Cl

B5
1 Edward Cl
2 Seagrave Cl
3 Troon Cl

A1
1 Orchard Ms

A **B** 210 **C** **D** **E**

South
Heighton

1

D6
1 Earls Cl
2 Hawth Gv
3 Hawth Park Rd
4 Hawth Rl

Denton County
Primary
School

Denton

Mount
Pleasant

2

E6
1 Caroline Cl
2 Charles Cl
3 Eleanor Cl
4 Kingsmead
5 Princess Dr

Norton

3

E7
1 Berwick Cl
2 Birling Cl

4

NEWHAVEN

Stud Farm

Bishopstone

Ferryfield
Industrial
Estate

223

Gleneagles
Close

Elizabeth
Close

Freeland
Close

Hurdis
Close

Windsor
Close

Hanover
Close

Antony
Close

Rochford
Way

Rookery
Hill

5

Newhaven
Marine
Station

Rookery Way

6

Mill Creek

LC

Tide
Mills

Grand Avenue

Clementine

Katherine

Churchill Drive

Hill Rise

BUCKLE BY-PASS

Princes

Duke

7

DIEPPE
SUMMER ONLY

9

Bishopstone Station

Station Road

Hawth Crescent

Hawth Park Road

Hawth

Surrey

Bishops
Close

Kingsway

Tudor Road

Beacon Road

Westdown

Marine Parade

claremont Road

CLAREMONT

St Crispian

8

Seaford

SEAFORD

A **B** **C** **D** **E**

Seaford
Bay

F5
1 Chartwell Cl

F6
1 Adelaide Cl
2 Alexandra Cl

F7
1 Buckingham Cl
2 Kingsmead Cl

F8
1 Croft Ct
2 Richmond Ter
3 Sutton Croft La
4 Warwick Rd

G6
1 Buckland Rd
2 Offham Cl

G7
1 Blatchington Cl
2 Esher Cl
3 Homefield Cl
4 Northcliffe Cl
5 Pinewood Cl

G8
1 Cornfield Cl

H5
1 Normansal Cl
2 Sandringham Cl

H6
1 Jubilee Gdns
2 Monarch Gdns
3 The Peverells
4 Sovereign Cl

H7
1 Benenden Cl
2 Hindover Crs
3 Lexden Ct
4 Roadean Cl
5 Sandore Cl

H8
1 Aquila Pk
2 Went Hill Pk

I6
1 Hillside Av
2 Landsdown Rd
3 Seafield Cl
4 Upr Chy'on Gdns

J7
1 Dulwich Cl

K7
1 Bodiam Cl
2 Dymock Cl
3 Hythe Crs
4 Hythe Vw
5 Stonewood Cl

K8
Street Names for these grid squares are listed at the back of the index

K6
1 Folkestone Cl
2 Winchelsea Cl

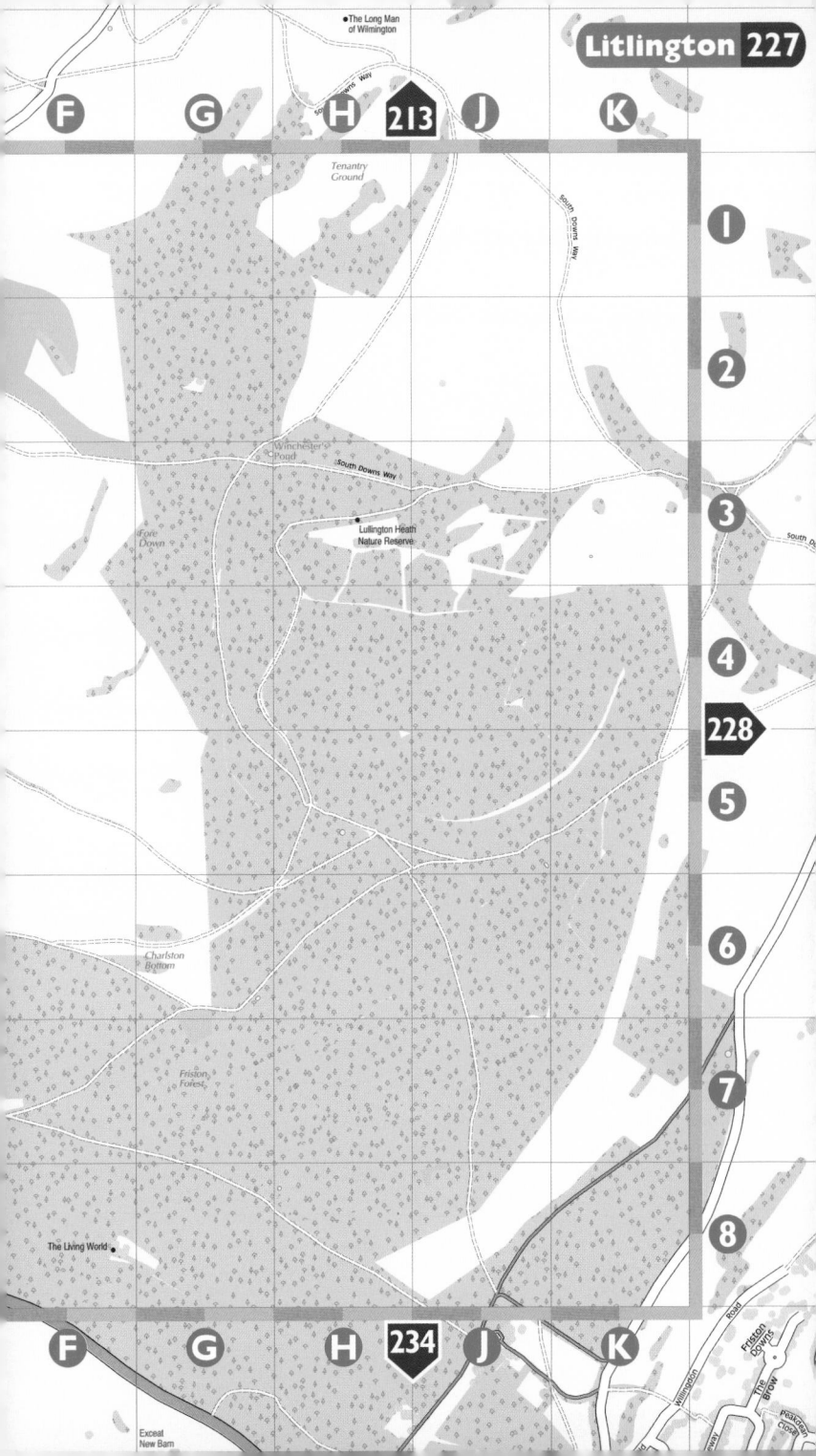

The Long Man
of Wilmington

Tenantry
Ground

F G H 213 J K

I

2

3

South Downs Way

South Downs Way

Winchester's
Pond

Fore
Down

Lullington Heath
Nature Reserve

South D

4

228

5

Charlston
Bottom

6

Friston
Forest

7

8

The Living World

F G H 234 J K

Exceat
New Barn

Friston
Downs

Willington
Road

The
Brow

Peace
Close

Wannoc

A B **214** C D E

Mill
Fitching
Close

Wannock
The
Lane

1

Ash Farm

Fitching
Manor

Westdean Drove

Wesdway

2

Green Lane

Jevington Road

Weald way

3

South Down Way

Wealdway

Wealdway

Jevington

Church La

Willingdon Lane

4

Eastboune
Lane

South Downs Way

227

Oxendean

5

6

7

8

Hillingdon Road

The Brow

Peacehaven

The Link

A B **235** C Pea D Ring E

G1
1 Cleevelands
2 Willingdon Wy

G2
1 Hoo Gdns
2 Willingdon Cl

G6
1 Lennox Cl
2 Maxfied Cl
3 Victoria Rd

G7
1 The Sanctuary

H1
1 Canterbury Cl

H2
1 Shortlands Cl

H3
1 Warburton Cl

H4
1 Chalvington Rd
2 Jack O'dandy Cl

H5
1 Gresham Cl
2 Newick Rd
3 Willingdon Rd

H7
1 Victoria Gdns

H8
1 Ridge Lands Cl

I7
1 Halland Cl

J6
1 Yielding's Cl

I7
1 Bay Pond Rd
2 Brodie Pl
3 Gore Park Av
4 Old Motc'be Ms
5 Prospect Gdns
6 Shortdean Pl

K7
1 New Upp'ton Rd
2 The Quadrant
3 Selwyn Dr
4 Torfield Rd

K1
1 Blackthorn Cl
2 Petworth Pl
3 Thornwood Cl

J8
1 Baker's Rd
2 Church La
3 New Pl
4 Park Cl
5 St Mary's Cots
6 Vicarage La

F1
1 Close Eighteen
2 Close Fifteen
3 Close Four
4 Close Ten
5 Close Twelve
6 Close Twentyfour
7 Spring Lodge Cl

F2
1 Chailey Cl
2 Redford Cl
3 Slindon Crs

F3
1 Ethelred Cl
2 Fair Isle Cl

F4
1 Cochrane Cl
2 Foley Cl
3 Gardner Cl
4 Middleton Dr
5 Somerville Cl
6 Vernon Cl
7 Woodward Cl

F5
1 Cook Av
2 Nelson Dr
3 Palliser Cl

G4
1 Ayscue Cl
2 Boscawen Cl
3 Cornwallis Cl
4 Rodney Cl
5 Vincent Cl

G5
1 Pound Cl
2 Royal Sover'n Vw

1 The Close
E2

The Living World

A   B   227   C   D   E

1

Exceat
New Barn

2   Friston

Windmill Lan

Gayles

3   Crowlink

South Downs W

4

Seven
Sisters

233   south Downs Way

5

6   Bi
G

7

8

A   B   C   D   E

I grid square represents 500 metres

F2
1 Downlands Wy
2 Lindon Cl

F3
1 Wayside

F G H 228 J K

Ringwood

Pea Down

I

Eastbour
Golf Club
Ho

G2
1 Elven La
2 Michel Dene Cl
3 Went La

A259

2

B2103 WARREN

Friston Downs

The Brow

Road

Pankdean Lane

Peascean Close

The Link

Summerdown Lane

Dene Road

Michel Close

Birch Close

HillSide

Dene

Side

Lane Close

Dene

Elven La

Downsview Lane

Warren Lane

EAST DEAN ROAD

3

Doctors
Surgery

Michel

A259

Bramley
Coppice
Gorsses Close

Summerdown
Lane

Mill Close

Eastdean
Down

BN20

4

Upper Street

Lower Street

Drive

East
Dean

236

Crapham
Down

5

Gilberts Road

Birling
Farm

Long
Down

Bullock
Down

6

g

Birling Gap Road

Cornish
Farm

Beachy Head Road

7

Hodcombe
Farm

8

South Downs Way

F G H J K

F1
1 Bath Rd
2 Calverley Rd
3 Camden Rd
4 College Rd
5 Hyde Rd
6 Sheraton Cl
7 South St
8 West Ter

F2
1 Fitzgerald Cl
2 Old Wish Rd
3 South Cliff Av

230

F3
1 Chatsworth Gdns
2 Jephson Cl
3 Ravens Cft

G1
1 Chiswick Pl
2 Cornfield Ter

G2
1 Carlisle Rd
2 Howard Sq
3 Lascelles Ter
4 Regency Ms
5 Wilmington Gdns
6 Wilmington Sq

H1
1 Burlington Rd
2 Cavendish Pl
3 Elms Rd

Abbotsford 88 E5
Alciston 212 A3
Alderbrook 53 H4
Aldrington 202 D4
Alfriston 226 C1
Argos Hill 55 J6
Arlington 187 J7
Ashburnham Forge 134 B6
Ashburnham Place 165 H1
Ashton Green 156 A7
Ashurst 27 F1
Ashurst Wood 23 J5
Bachelor's Bump 171 H5
Baldslow 169 J4
Baldwins Hill 12 A8
Balls Green 26 C6
Barcombe 154 D2
Barcombe Cross 123 J7
Bardown 59 F4
Battle 136 C5
Beachlands 218 C5
Beacon Down 98 E4
Beckley 82 E7
Beckley Furnace 110 B4
Beddingham 183 J7
Bells Yew Green 31 H6
Belmont 199 F2
Berner's Hill 60 E1
Berwick 212 C4
Best Beech Hill 43 J8
Bevendean 205 H1
Bexhill 195 F7
Birchden 28 B5
Birchett's Green 45 C8
Birchgrove 48 E2
Birling Gap 234 E6
Bishopstone 224 D4
Blackboys 97 K5
Blackham 16 C7
Blacklands 4 B2
Blackness 53 J2
Black Rock 205 H8
Blackwell 22 C1
Boarshead 39 K5
Bodiam 80 A3
Bodle Street Green 163 K1
Bohemia 4 A4
Boreham Street 164 B7
Bowler's Town 113 H1
Bray's Hill 164 D2
Brede 139 K2
Brightling 104 B5
Brighton 7 D6
Broadland Row 110 B7
Broad Oak 101 F2
Broad Oak 109 K6
Broad Street 141 C5
Broadwater Down 29 K3
Broomham 158 C5
Broomhill Bank 19 G4
Broomsgrove 5 E2
Brownbread Street 133 J8
Broyle Side 156 B3
Buckham Hill 94 E5
Budlett's Common 67 J8
Bulverhythe 196 E6
Burgess Hill 89 G8
Burgh Hill 61 J8
Burgh Hill 159 H5
Burlow 129 K6
Burnt Oak 53 H8
Burrswood 27 J3
Burwash 75 J5
Burwash Common 74 C8
Burwash Weald 74 E8
Butcher's Cross 71 G3
Buxted 68 C8
Cackle Street 66 E1
Cackle Street 104 C7
Cackle Street 139 H1
Cade Street 100 E5
Camber 115 H8
Camden Park 30 C1
Canadia 136 C3
Castle Hill 54 E7
Catsfield 166 E3
Catsfield Stream 166 D4
Chailey 92 C8
Chalvington 186 D4
Chapel Cross 101 G6
Chapel Row 163 G6
Chapman's Town 131 H1
Charlwood 34 C2
Chelwood Common 49 H5

Chelwood Gate 49 G2
Chiddingly 159 H2
Chiddingstone Hoath 16 C1
Chilsham 163 G3
Chiltington 153 F1
Chitcombe 109 G5
Chuck Hatch 37 J4
Churches Green 132 D3
Clayhill 82 C8
Clayton 149 K3
Cliff End 173 G4
Clive Vale 199 G1
Cock Marling 141 K1
Coggins Mill 56 C7
Coldean 178 E6
Coleman's Hatch 36 E2
Collier's Green 108 C2
Combe 57 J5
Cooden 194 C8
Cooksbridge 153 K3
Cooper's Green 67 K8
Cousley Wood 44 E4
Cowbeech 162 D2
Cowbeech Hill 162 C4
Cowden 15 G5
Cripp's Corner 107 K4
Cross in Hand 99 F4
Crowborough 53 H2
Crowborough Warren 52 E1
Crowhurst 168 A5
Dale Hill 60 D1
Dallington 103 F8
Danegate 41 G5
Danehill 48 E7
Darwell Hole 104 D8
Davis's Town 127 K4
Denny Bottom 19 H8
Denton 9 F1
Ditchling 119 K8
Dittons 215 K5
Dormansland 13 F2
Dormans Park 12 C4
Downside 229 H6
Down Street 66 D6
The Down 33 H8
Duddleswell 51 G7
Durgates 44 A6
Earl's Down 102 D7
Eason's Green 127 F2
East Blatchington 225 F7
Eastbourne 229 H6
East Chiltington 121 J7
East Dean 235 F3
East Grinstead 22 C2
East Guldeford 114 B4
East Hoathly 127 K6
East Moulsecoomb 179 G7
Eckington Corner 186 B3
Eridge Green 29 G7
Etchingham 77 F2
Etchingwood 97 F2
Ewhurst Green 80 D6
Exceat 226 C7
Fairfield 87 G2
Fairlight 172 B7
Fairlight Cove 172 E6
Fairwarp 67 H2
Falmer 180 A5
Felcourt 12 A3
Ferndale 20 C6
Fishersgate 201 J4
Five Ash Down 68 A6
Five Ashes 71 G4
Flackley Ash 83 K8
Fletching 66 A7
Fletching Common 93 F3
Flimwell 47 G8
Flowers Green 163 G7
Folkington 214 B7
Foothcombe 17 J6
Ford's Green 50 C8
Forest Row 35 K2
Foul Mile 131 J7
Foulride Green 215 G7
Four Oaks 83 G6
Four Throws 63 J3
Foxhunt Green 128 D2
Framfield 96 C5
Frant 30 C5
Friar's Gate 38 D4
Friar's Hill 172 A4
Friston 234 D2
Furner's Green 65 G2
Gallypot Street 25 H8

Ginger's Green 162 D5
Glenleigh Park 195 F4
Glynde 183 K4
Glyndebourne 183 K1
Glyne Gap 196 D6
Goatham Green 109 G6
Goddards' Green 88 A6
Godleys Green 91 H7
Golden Cross 159 G5
Golden Cross 191 H7
Gotham 193 K4
Green Street 168 C7
Groombridge 27 J4
Grove Hill 161 K2
Guestling Green 171 K3
Guestling Thorn 140 E7
Gun Green 63 J1
Gun Hill 160 B2
Hadlow Down 70 A6
Hailsham 189 H3
Hale Green 159 K2
Halland 126 E5
Hall's Close 193 F3
Ham Green 84 C2
Hammerwood 14 B8
Hampden Park 229 K2
Hamsey 154 B5
Hangleton 202 D1
Hankham 216 B2
Harbour Heights 8 B5
Harley Shute 197 G3
Hartfield 25 J7
Hassocks 118 E7
Hastings 4 C3
Hawkenbury 30 D1
Hawkhurst 62 E2
Hawkhurst Common 127 J2
Hazard's Green 165 G6
Heathfield 55 G1
Heathfield 100 B4
Hellingly 160 E6
Henley's Down 167 F5
Heron's Ghyll 51 K8
Herstmonceaux 163 G5
High Brooms 20 C3
High Cross 55 G4
Highgate 35 K2
Highgate 63 G1
High Hurstwood 68 B2
The Highlands 194 E3
High Street 62 D1
Hollingbury 178 C6
Hollingdean 178 C8
Hollingrove 104 C5
Hollington 169 G8
Holmes's Hill 159 F5
Holtye 14 E8
Hooe 193 F4
Hooe Common 193 H2
Hook Green 33 F7
Horam 129 J4
Horney Common 66 E3
Horns Cross 109 J2
Horshoe Green 15 K2
Horsted Green 95 H8
Horsted Keynes 48 A6
Houghton Green 113 K2
Hove 203 G6
Hungershall Park 29 J1
Hurst Green 62 A8
Hurst Wickham 118 C5
Icklesham 141 J5
Iden 85 H7
Iford 182 A8
Isfield 124 E3
Jarvis Brook 54 B3
Jevington 228 B3
John's Cross 106 C4
Jumper's Town 37 H4
Jury's Gap 146 C2
Kemp Town 204 E8
Keymer 119 H7
Kilndown 46 E1
Kingston by Sea 200 E4
Kingston near Lewes 181 H6
Lamberhurst 33 K6
Lamberhurst Quarter 33 F1
Landport 2 B2
Langney 230 E1
Langton Green 18 D7
Laughton 157 K4
Lewes 2 C3
Lidham Hill 140 C5
Lions Green 129 F2

Litlington	226 D3
Little Bayham	32 B7
Little Common	194 A6
Little Horsted	125 J2
Little London	99 H7
Little Norlington	155 K2
Lower Cousley Wood	45 G3
Lower Dicker	160 A7
Lower Green	19 G6
Lower Green	21 K3
Lower Horsebridge	160 D7
Lower Street	166 A6
Lower Willingham	215 G8
Lunsford's Cross	194 E1
Lye Green	39 G2
Lyewood Common	26 D4
Magham Down	162 A7
Manor Park	96 A2
Marden's Hill	38 D6
Maresfield Park	67 G6
Markbeech	15 K1
Mark Cross	42 A7
Mark Cross	185 K1
Marle Green	130 B6
Marlpits	50 D5
Marlpits	166 A4
Mayfield	72 A1
Maynard's Green	130 A1
Meads	236 E3
Mile Oak	175 J8
Mill Corner	81 J8
Mill Hill	216 E5
Milton Street	213 G6
Modest Corner	19 J1
The Moor	63 F3
Mott's Mill	27 J8
Moulsecoomb	179 G8
Mount Ephraim	96 A8
Mountfield	106 A5
Mount Pleasant	123 K5
Mount Pleasant	224 B2
Muddles Green	159 H4
Mutton Hall	100 B2
Nash Street	159 J5
Netherfield	135 G1
Newbridge	36 E5
Newhaven	9 E3
Newick	93 J3
New Town	96 A5
Ninfield	166 A5
Norlington	155 J4
Norman's Bay	219 G3
Northbridge Street	78 C6
North Chailey	92 B5
North Common	92 C4
Northiam	81 K5
North Moulsecoomb	178 E7
Norton	224 D3
Nutley	50 C8
Offham	153 K6
Old Heathfield	100 D5
Old Shoreham	200 B2
Old Town	5 F4
Old Town	195 H5
Old Town	229 J7
Ore	171 F8
Ovingdean	206 B8
Oxley's Green	104 C3
Palehouse Common	126 D1
Park Corner	28 C6
Park Corner	158 C1
Patcham	178 A5
Peacehaven	222 B4
Peacehaven Heights	222 A6
Peasmarsh	112 A1
Pebsham	196 A5
Pell Green	44 D4
Pembury	21 J5
Penhurst	134 D5
Pett	172 D3
Pett Level	173 G3
Pevensey	217 J5
Pevensey Bay	217 K6
Piddinghoe	223 F1
Piltdown	94 C2
Pipsden	63 K2
Playden	113 J3
Plumpton	152 C4
Plumpton Green	121 G5
Polegate	215 F6
Ponts Green	133 K7
Portslade-by-Sea	202 A5
Portslade Village	201 K1
Potter's Green	69 F8
Poundfield	53 K1
Poundford	70 E6
Poundgate	52 C4
Pound Green	69 F7
Poundsbridge	18 A3
Pounsley	97 J3
Poynings	148 A6
Preston	6 A1
Punnett's Town	101 J5
Pyecombe	149 G5
Quabrook	36 C2
Ramslye	29 H2
Rickney	216 E1
Ridgewood	95 J7
Ringles Cross	95 J1
Ringmer	155 H5
Ripe	186 B2
Robertsbridge	77 K7
Rockrobin	43 K4
Rocks Park	95 G4
Rodmell	208 C3
Roedean	205 K8
Rose Hill	125 F5
Roselands	230 D4
Roser's Cross	98 D5
Rotherfield	54 E3
Rottingdean	220 D1
Royal Tunbridge Wells	19 K8
Rusher's Cross	57 F5
Rushlake Green	131 J2
Rushy Green	155 K6
Russell's Green	165 K8
Rusthall	19 G7
Rye	113 J5
Rye Foreign	112 E2
Rye Harbour	144 B1
Saddlescombe	148 D8
St Helen's	170 D6
St Helen's Wood	170 B7
St John's	19 K5
St John's	38 E7
St Leonards	197 H4
Saint's Hill	17 K3
Salehurst	78 C6
Saltdean	221 G1
Sandown Park	21 F5
Sandy Cross	100 B6
Seacox Heath	61 J1
Sedlescombe	137 K2
Selmeston	186 B8
Sharpsbridge	94 C5
Sharp's Corner	129 J3
Sheffield Green	65 F4
Sherwood Park	20 E5
Shoreham Beach	200 E6
Shoreham-by-Sea	200 C6
Shortbridge	94 E3
Shortgate	126 D8
Shover's Green	58 E1
Sidley	195 G5
Silver Hill	78 B3
Silverhill	4 A1
Silverhill Park	169 K5
Skippers Hill	70 E4
Sleeches Cross	42 B1
Smart's Hill	17 H3
Snagshall	80 B6
Southborough	20 A2
South Chailey	122 C4
Southease	208 D4
Southern Cross	201 K3
South Heighton	223 K1
South Malling	2 C3
Southover	2 B6
Southover	74 E3
South Street	122 C2
Southwick	201 H3
Sparrow's Green	44 B6
Speldhurst	18 E4
Spithurst	123 K4
Splayne's Green	66 A6
Stanmer	179 F3
Staplecross	108 A2
Starr's Green	168 B1
Steel Cross	39 K8
Steven's Crouch	135 F8
Stockland Green	19 G3
Stone Cross	27 H1
Stone Cross	
Stone Cross	
Stone Cross	38
Stonecrouch	46 C4
Stonegate	59 J5
Stonequarry	12 E8
Strawberry Hill	29 H3
Streat	120 D8
Stunts Green	162 E4
Summer Hill	189 F7
Sunnyside	22 C5
Sutton	225 H7
Swaile's Green	107 J4
Sweethaws	52 E5
Tarring Neville	209 J7
Teasley Mead	16 E8
Telham	168 C1
Telscombe	208 A8
Telscombe Cliffs	221 K3
Three Cups Corner	101 J6
Three Leg Cross	46 B8
Three Oaks	171 G1
Thunder's Hill	159 J4
Ticehurst	60 C1
Tidebrook	57 H3
Tilsmore	99 K3
Tolhurst	59 H1
Tompset's Bank	35 K3
Town Littleworth	123 G2
Town Row	55 G2
Trollilloes	162 E1
Turner's Green	44 A5
Turner's Green	102 B7
Twelve Oaks	104 B6
Uckfield	95 K4
Udimore	141 H1
Union Street	47 F8
Upper Dicker	187 K3
Upper Hartfield	37 H1
Upper Horsebridge	160 D8
Upperton	10 A2
Upper Wellingham	155 F3
Vinehall Street	106 C5
Vines Cross	130 C3
Wadhurst	44 C7
Waldron	98 D8
Waldron Down	98 B3
Wallands Park	2 B4
Wallcrouch	59 H2
Walter's Green	17 G4
Wannock	214 E7
Warbleton	131 G2
Wartling	191 K4
Watermill	167 G7
Wellbrook	71 K2
West Blatchington	202 E2
Westdean	226 E7
Westdene	177 G6
Westfield	139 H7
West Firle	184 D8
Westham	217 F5
West Hill	5 E3
West Marina	197 G5
Westmeston	151 F3
Whatlington	137 G2
Whitehawk	205 G5
Whitehill	53 G3
White Post	17 F4
Whitesmith	158 E3
Whydown	194 A3
Wickstreet	187 H5
Willard's Hill	77 G6
Willingdon	229 F2
Wilmington	213 H5
Wilmington Green	213 H4
Winchelsea	142 D4
Winchelsea Beach	143 H5
Windmill Hill	163 J6
Winton	212 D7
Withdean	177 K7
Witherenden Hill	74 C2
Withyham	26 C8
Wivelsfield	90 C6
Woodingdean	205 K4
Woodmans Green	107 G8
Wood's Corner	103 H8
Wood's Green	44 B3
World's End	89 K7
Wych Cross	35 J7

USING THE STREET INDEX

Street names are listed alphabetically. Each street name is followed by its postal town or area locality, the Postcode District, the page number, and the reference to the square in which the name is found.

Example: **Abbey Wy** *BAT* TN3................................ **136** D6 🔟

Some entries are followed by a number in a blue box. This number indicates the location of the street within the referenced grid square. The full street name is listed at the side of the map page.

GENERAL ABBREVIATIONS

ACC............ACCESS	GA............GATE	PL............PLACE
ALY............ALLEY	GAL............GALLERY	PLN............PLAIN
AP............APPROACH	GDN............GARDEN	PLNS............PLAINS
AR............ARCADE	GDNS............GARDENS	PLZ............PLAZA
ASS............ASSOCIATION	GLD............GLADE	POL............POLICE STATION
AV............AVENUE	GLN............GLEN	PR............PRINCE
BCH............BEACH	GN............GREEN	PREC............PRECINCT
BLDS............BUILDINGS	GND............GROUND	PREP............PREPARATORY
BND............BEND	GRA............GRANGE	PRIM............PRIMARY
BNK............BANK	GRG............GARAGE	PROM............PROMENADE
BR............BRIDGE	GT............GREAT	PRS............PRINCESS
BRK............BROOK	GTWY............GATEWAY	PRT............PORT
BTM............BOTTOM	GV............GROVE	PT............POINT
BUS............BUSINESS	HGR............HIGHER	PTH............PATH
BVD............BOULEVARD	HL............HILL	PZ............PIAZZA
BY............BYPASS	HLS............HILLS	QD............QUADRANT
CATH............CATHEDRAL	HO............HOUSE	QU............QUEEN
CEM............CEMETERY	HOL............HOLLOW	QY............QUAY
CEN............CENTRE	HOSP............HOSPITAL	R............RIVER
CFT............CROFT	HRB............HARBOUR	RBT............ROUNDABOUT
CH............CHURCH	HTH............HEATH	RD............ROAD
CHA............CHASE	HTS............HEIGHTS	RDG............RIDGE
CHYD............CHURCHYARD	HVN............HAVEN	REP............REPUBLIC
CIR............CIRCLE	HWY............HIGHWAY	RES............RESERVOIR
CIRC............CIRCUS	IMP............IMPERIAL	RFC............RUGBY FOOTBALL CLUB
CL............CLOSE	IN............INLET	RI............RISE
CLFS............CLIFFS	IND EST............INDUSTRIAL ESTATE	RP............RAMP
CMP............CAMP	INF............INFIRMARY	RW............ROW
CNR............CORNER	INFO............INFORMATION	S............SOUTH
CO............COUNTY	INT............INTERCHANGE	SCH............SCHOOL
COLL............COLLEGE	IS............ISLAND	SE............SOUTH EAST
COM............COMMON	JCT............JUNCTION	SER............SERVICE AREA
COMM............COMMISSION	JTY............JETTY	SH............SHORE
CON............CONVENT	KG............KING	SHOP............SHOPPING
COT............COTTAGE	KNL............KNOLL	SKWY............SKYWAY
COTS............COTTAGES	L............LAKE	SMT............SUMMIT
CP............CAPE	LA............LANE	SOC............SOCIETY
CPS............COPSE	LDG............LODGE	SP............SPUR
CR............CREEK	LGT............LIGHT	SPR............SPRING
CREM............CREMATORIUM	LK............LOCK	SQ............SQUARE
CRS............CRESCENT	LKS............LAKES	ST............STREET
CSWY............CAUSEWAY	LNDG............LANDING	STN............STATION
CT............COURT	LTL............LITTLE	STR............STREAM
CTRL............CENTRAL	LWR............LOWER	STRD............STRAND
CTS............COURTS	MAG............MAGISTRATE	SW............SOUTH WEST
CTYD............COURTYARD	MAN............MANSIONS	TDG............TRADING
CUTT............CUTTINGS	MD............MEAD	TER............TERRACE
CV............COVE	MDW............MEADOWS	THWY............THROUGHWAY
CYN............CANYON	MEM............MEMORIAL	TNL............TUNNEL
DEPT............DEPARTMENT	MKT............MARKET	TOLL............TOLLWAY
DL............DALE	MKTS............MARKETS	TPK............TURNPIKE
DM............DAM	ML............MALL	TR............TRACK
DR............DRIVE	ML............MILL	TRL............TRAIL
DRO............DROVE	MNR............MANOR	TWR............TOWER
DRY............DRIVEWAY	MS............MEWS	U/P............UNDERPASS
DWGS............DWELLINGS	MSN............MISSION	UNI............UNIVERSITY
E............EAST	MT............MOUNT	UPR............UPPER
EMB............EMBANKMENT	MTN............MOUNTAIN	V............VALE
EMBY............EMBASSY	MTS............MOUNTAINS	VA............VALLEY
ESP............ESPLANADE	MUS............MUSEUM	VIAD............VIADUCT
EST............ESTATE	MWY............MOTORWAY	VIL............VILLA
EX............EXCHANGE	N............NORTH	VIS............VISTA
EXPY............EXPRESSWAY	NE............NORTH EAST	VLG............VILLAGE
EXT............EXTENSION	NW............NORTH WEST	VLS............VILLAS
F/O............FLYOVER	O/P............OVERPASS	VW............VIEW
FC............FOOTBALL CLUB	OFF............OFFICE	W............WEST
FK............FORK	ORCH............ORCHARD	WD............WOOD
FLD............FIELD	OV............OVAL	WHF............WHARF
FLDS............FIELDS	PAL............PALACE	WK............WALK
FLS............FALLS	PAS............PASSAGE	WKS............WALKS
FLS............FLATS	PAV............PAVILION	WLS............WELLS
FM............FARM	PDE............PARADE	WY............WAY
FT............FORT	PH............PUBLIC HOUSE	YD............YARD
FWY............FREEWAY	PK............PARK	YHA............YOUTH HOSTEL
FY............FERRY	PKWY............PARKWAY	

POSTCODE TOWNS AND AREA ABBREVIATIONS

BAT ....Battle
BEX ....Bexhill
BEXW ....Bexhill west
BRI ....Brighton
BUR/ETCH ....Burwash/Etchingham
BURH ....Burgess Hill
CRBK ....Cranbrook
CROW ....Crowborough
EAST ....Eastbourne
EDEN ....Edenbridge
EDN/EASTW ....East Dean/Eastbourne west
EGRIN ....East Grinstead
FROW ....Forest Row
HAIL ....Hailsham
HAS ....Hastings
HAWK ....Hawkhurst
HFD ....Henfield
HOVE ....Hove
HPPT/KEY ....Hurstpierpoint/Keymer
HRTF ....Hartfield

HTHF ....Heathfield
HWH ....Haywards Heath
LEW ....Lewes
LGNY ....Langney
LING ....Lingfield
LW/ROSE ....Lower Willingdon/Roselands
LYDD ....Lydd
MAYF ....Mayfield
NEWHV ....Newhaven
NROM ....New Romney
PEAHV ....Peacehaven
PEV ....Pevensey
POLE ....Polegate
POY/PYE ....Poynings/Pyecombe
PTSD ....Portslade
RBTBR ....Robertsbridge
RHAS ....Rural Hastings
RHWH ....Rural Haywards Heath
RING/NEW ....Ringmer/Newick
ROTT ....Rottingdean

RRTW ....Rural Royal Tunbridge Wells
RTON ....Rural Tonbridge
RTW ....Royal Tunbridge Wells
RTWE/PEM ....Royal Tunbridge
                    Wells east/Pembury
RYE ....Rye
SBGH/RUST ....Southborough/Rusthall
SEAF ....Seaford
SHOR ....Shoreham
SLVH ....Silverhill
STEY/UB ....Steyning/Upper Beeding
STHW ....Southwick
STLEO ....St Leonards
STPH/PW ....Staplehurst/Paddock Wood
TENT ....Tenterden
UCK ....Uckfield
WADH ....Wadhurst
WSEA ....Winchelsea

106 - Arr

Index - streets

1066 Country Wk *BAT* TN33 .... **137** J7
  HAIL BN27 .... **191** F5
  RHAS TN35 .... **140** A8
  RHAS TN35 .... **199** F3
  WSEA TN36 .... **141** H5

A

Abberton Fld *HPPT/KEY* BN6 .... **118** B6
Abbey Cl *PEAHV* BN10 .... **222** B2
Abbey Dr *STLEO* TN38 .... **196** C6
Abbey Rd *EDN/EASTW* BN20 ...... **229** C6
  ROTT BN2 .... **7** F6
Abbey Vw *BEX* TN40 .... **195** H8
Abbey Wy *BAT* TN33 .... **136** D6 🔢
Abbotsbury Cl *ROTT* BN2 .... **220** E2 🔢
Abbots Cl *BAT* TN33 .... **137** F8
  HPPT/KEY BN6 .... **118** E7
Abbotsfield Cl *HAS* TN34 .... **5** D1
Aberdale Rd *POLE* BN26 .... **215** H5
Aberdeen Rd *ROTT* BN2 .... **7** D2 🔢
Abergavenny Rd *LEW* BN7 .... **2** B4
Abinger Pl *LEW* BN7 .... **2** C4
Abinger Rd *PTSD* BN41 .... **202** A3
  ROTT BN2 .... **206** B5
Acacia Av *HOVE* BN3 .... **202** E2 🔢
Acacia Rd *LW/ROSE* BN22 ...... **229** J1
  NEWHV BN9 .... **223** K1
Acer Av *RTWE/PEM* TN2 .... **30** C3
Acorn Cl *EGRIN* RH19 .... **22** C3
  SLVH TN37 .... **169** K7
The Acorns *HPPT/KEY* BN6 .... **88** D7
  WADH TN5 .... **59** H5
Acorn Wy *BUR/ETCH* TN19 .... **62** A3
Acre Cl *HWH* RH16 .... **89** K1
Acres Ri *WADH* TN5 .... **60** C2
Adam Cl *CROW* TN6 .... **53** J5
  STLEO TN38 .... **169** C7
Adams Cl *BRI* BN1 .... **204** C1
Adams La *RYE* TN31 .... **81** F8
Adastra Av *HPPT/KEY* BN6 .... **119** C7
Addingham Sq *LW/ROSE* BN22 ... **11** E5
Addington Cl *STLEO* TN38 ...... **197** G4
Addison Rd *HOVE* BN3 .... **6** A3
Adelaide Cl *SEAF* BN25 .... **225** F4 🔢
Adelaide Crs *HOVE* BN3 .... **203** H6
Adelaide Rd *STLEO* TN38 .... **169** J8
Adelaide Sq *SHOR* BN43 .... **200** E4
Ades Fld *POLE* BN26 .... **213** J5
Admiral's Bridge La *EGRIN* RH19 ... **34** A3
Adur Av *SHOR* BN43 .... **200** B2
Adur Dr *PEV* BN24 .... **216** B6
  SHOR BN43 .... **200** D4
Adur Rd *BURH* RH15 .... **89** J7
  SHOR BN43 .... **200** B3
Agincourt Cl *STLEO* TN38 .... **169** G4
Agnes St *ROTT* BN2 .... **7** E3
Ainsworth Av *ROTT* BN2 .... **206** A8
Ainsworth Cl *ROTT* BN2 .... **206** A7
Airy Rd *HAIL* BN27 .... **191** J2
Akehurst Fld *BAT* TN33 .... **133** K8
Alan Wy *ROTT* BN2 .... **205** G5
Albany Cl *RTWE/PEM* TN2 .... **20** C6
Albany Ms *HOVE* BN3 .... **203** G5
Albany Rd *BEX* TN40 .... **195** H8
  SEAF BN25 .... **224** D8
  STLEO TN38 .... **197** J3
Albany Vls *HOVE* BN3 .... **203** G6
Albert Dr *BURH* RH15 .... **118** E1
Albert Ms *HOVE* BN3 .... **203** G5

Albert Rd *BEX* TN40 .... **195** H8
  BRI BN1 .... **6** B4
  POLE BN26 .... **214** E4
  STHW BN42 .... **201** G4
  UCK TN22 .... **95** K5 🔢
Albert Ter *EAST* BN21 .... **229** H4
Albion Ct *BURH* RH15 .... **119** F1 🔢
Albion Hl *ROTT* BN2 .... **7** D4
Albion Rd *LW/ROSE* BN22 .... **11** D3 🔢
  RTW TN1 .... **20** B6
Albion St *LEW* BN7 .... **3** D4 🔢
  PTSD BN41 .... **201** G5
  ROTT BN2 .... **7** D4
  STHW BN42 .... **201** K4
Albourne Cl *ROTT* BN2 .... **205** F4
  STLEO TN38 .... **197** G3
Aldborough Rd *SLVH* TN37 .... **4** A3
Alderbrook Cl *CROW* TN6 .... **53** J5
Alderbrook Wy *CROW* TN6 .... **53** J5
Alder Cl *HTHF* TN21 .... **100** A6
  RTWE/PEM TN2 .... **20** C2
  SLVH TN37 .... **169** K6
Alders Av *EGRIN* RH19 .... **12** B8
Alders View Dr *EGRIN* RH19 ...... **12** C7 🔢
Aldervale Cottages *CROW* TN6 ... **53** J4
Aldrich Cl *ROTT* BN2 .... **205** G5
Aldington Av *HOVE* BN3 .... **202** C4
Aldrington Cl *HOVE* BN3 .... **202** C4
Alexander Dr *BEXW* TN39 .... **194** D7
Alexandra Cl *SEAF* BN25 .... **225** F6 🔢
Alexandra Rd *BURH* RH15 .... **119** J1
  HTHF TN21 .... **100** B5
  LW/ROSE BN22 .... **11** F1
  MAYF TN00 .... **56** C8
  SLVH TN37 .... **4** A4
  UCK TN22 .... **95** K5
Alexandra Vls *BRI* BN1 .... **6** B4
Alford Wy *BEX* TN40 .... **195** K5
Alfray Rd *BEX* TN40 .... **196** B6
Alfred Rd *BRI* BN1 .... **6** B4
  LGNY BN23 .... **231** G3
  RHAS TN35 .... **171** F8
Alfred St *STLEO* TN38 .... **4** A5
Alfriston Cl *BEXW* TN39 .... **194** B5
  EDN/EASTW BN20 .... **236** C1
  ROTT BN2 .... **205** G5
Alfriston Pk *SEAF* BN25 .... **225** K6
Alfriston Rd *SEAF* BN25 .... **225** J6
  SLVH TN37 .... **203** J6
Alice Bright La *CROW* TN6 .... **53** H4
Alice St *HOVE* BN3 .... **203** J6
Allan Cl *SBGH/RUST* TN4 .... **19** C7
Allandale Rd *RTWE/PEM* TN2 .... **20** D5
Allards Rd *HAS* TN34 .... **172** B3
Allen's Cl *EGRIN* RH19 .... **23** H5
Allen Wy *BEX* TN40 .... **196** A5
Allfrey Rd *LW/ROSE* BN22 .... **11** F1
Allfreys La *CROW* TN6 .... **53** F5
Allington Crs *RING/NEW* BN8 .... **93** G4
Allington La *LEW* BN7 .... **153** F4
Allington Rd *RING/NEW* BN8 ..... **93** G5
All Saints Gdns *HTHF* TN21 .... **99** K4
All Saints La *BEXW* TN39 .... **195** G4
All Saints Rd *HAWK* TN18 .... **63** G2
  SBGH/RUST TN4 .... **20** A5
All Saints' St *HAS* TN34 .... **5** F4
Allwood Crs *RHWH* RH17 .... **90** E7
Alma Ter *SLVH* TN37 .... **4** A2
Alma Vls *SLVH* TN37 .... **4** A2
Alpine Rd *HAS* TN34 .... **5** E4 🔢
  HOVE BN3 .... **202** E3
Alverstone Cl *LGNY* BN23 .... **216** C7
Amanda Cl *BEX* TN40 .... **196** A4
Amberleaze Dr *RTWE/PEM* TN2 ... **21** K5

Amberley Cl *BURH* RH15 .... **89** G7
  SHOR BN43 .... **200** C2 🔢
Amberley Dr *HOVE* BN3 .... **176** D8
Amberley Rd *LW/ROSE* BN22 .... **229** H2
Amberstone Cl *HAS* TN34 ...... **170** D7 🔢
Amberstone Vw *HAIL* BN27 ..... **189** H1
Ambleside Av *PEAHV* BN10 ...... **221** K4
Amesbury Crs *HOVE* BN3 .... **202** D4
Amherst Cl *SLVH* TN37 .... **4** B3
Amherst Crs *HOVE* BN3 .... **202** E3
Amherst Gdns *HAS* TN34 .... **4** B3
Amherst Rd *BEX* TN40 .... **195** H7
  SBGH/RUST TN4 .... **20** A6
  SLVH TN37 .... **4** B3
Amhurst Rd *PEAHV* BN10 .... **221** J4
Anchor Cl *SHOR* BN43 .... **200** D5
Anchor Fld *RING/NEW* BN8 ..... **155** J6
Anchor La *RING/NEW* BN8 ...... **124** A5
Anderida Rd *LW/ROSE* BN22 .... **215** G3
Anderson Cl *NEWHV* BN9 .... **8** B3
Andrew Rd *SBGH/RUST* TN4 ..... **20** C3
Andrews Cl *RBTBR* TN32 .... **78** C6
  RTWE/PEM TN2 .... **20** D6 🔢
Angela Cl *BEX* TN40 .... **196** A4 🔢
Anglesea Ter *STLEO* TN38 .... **4** A4 🔢
Anglesey Av *HAIL* BN27 .... **189** F1
Angus Cl *EDN/EASTW* BN20 ..... **229** G3
Ann Cl *HPPT/KEY* BN6 .... **119** G6
Annington Gdns *SBGH/RUST* BN43 ... **200** C2 🔢
Annington Rd *LW/ROSE* BN22 ... **11** D2
Ann St *BRI* BN1 .... **6** C2
  HAS TN34 .... **5** F2
Anson Cl *LGNY* BN23 .... **231** F4 🔢
Ansty Cl *ROTT* BN2 .... **205** F6
Antioch St *LEW* BN7 .... **2** C5 🔢
Antony Cl *SEAF* BN25 .... **224** C5
Antrona Cl *BEXW* TN39 .... **194** B8
Anvil Cl *PTSD* BN41 .... **202** A1
  UCK TN22 .... **95** H5
Anvil Ct *SLVH* TN37 .... **169** K6 🔢
Anzac Cl *PEAHV* BN10 .... **222** B2
Appledene Cnr *RING/NEW* BN8 ... **122** C4 🔢
Appledore Cl *LGNY* BN23 .... **230** E1 🔢
Appledore Rd *ROTT* BN2 .... **179** G2
Applesham Av *HOVE* BN3 .... **202** D1
Applesham Wy *PTSD* BN41 ..... **201** K2
Apple Tree La *RTWE/PEM* TN2 .... **20** D3
Applewood Cl *SLVH* TN37 .... **169** J7
The Approach *BRI* BN1 .... **177** K8
  EGRIN RH19 .... **12** D5
Apsley St *SBGH/RUST* TN4 .... **19** H7
Aquarius Cl *PEAHV* BN10 .... **222** B5 🔢
Aquila Pk *SEAF* BN25 .... **225** H8 🔢
Arbourvale *STLEO* TN38 .... **197** H2
Archery Rd *STLEO* TN38 .... **197** J4
Archery Wk *HAIL* BN27 .... **189** H5
Ardingly Rd *ROTT* BN2 .... **221** C3
Ardingly St *ROTT* BN2 .... **7** D5
Argent Cl *SEAF* BN25 .... **225** H6
Argos Hill Rd *MAYF* TN20 .... **57** H7
Argyle Rd *BRI* BN1 .... **6** B2
  SBGH/RUST TN4 .... **20** A1
Arlington Crs *BRI* BN1 .... **179** F6 🔢
Arlington Gdns *ROTT* BN2 ...... **221** C1
Arlington Rd *EAST* BN21 .... **10** A4
Arlington Rd East *HAIL* BN27 .... **188** E5
Arlington Rd West *HAIL* BN27 ... **188** E5
Armstrong Cl *STLEO* TN38 ...... **169** F7
Arnbury Ms *STLEO* TN38 .... **197** F5
Arnold St *ROTT* BN2 .... **7** E3
Arnside Rd *STLEO* TN38 .... **197** F5
Arran Cl *HAIL* BN27 .... **189** F1

Arthur Rd *BEXW* TN39 .... 195 G7
Arthur St *HOVE* BN3 .... 203 F3
Arundel Cl *HAIL* BN27 .... 189 H1
   PEV BN24 .... 218 C5
   SHOR BN43 .... 201 F3
Arundel Dr East *ROTT* BN2 .... 221 F2
Arundel Dr West *ROTT* BN2 .... 220 E2
Arundel Gn *LEW* BN7 .... 2 B3 🔲
Arundel Pl *ROTT* BN2 .... 205 F7
Arundel Rd *EAST* BN21 .... 10 B3
   NEWHV BN9 .... 9 E1
   PEAHV BN10 .... 222 B4
   ROTT BN2 .... 205 F8
   RTW TN1 .... 30 B1
   SEAF BN25 .... 225 H8
Arundel Road Central *PEAHV* BN10... 222 A4
Arundel Rd West *PEAHV* BN10 .... 221 K3
Arundel St *ROTT* BN2 .... 205 F8
Arundel Ter *ROTT* BN2 .... 205 F8
Arun Wy *PEV* BN24 .... 216 A6
Ascham Pl *EDN/EASTW* BN20 .... 10 A6 🔲
Ascot Cl *EDN/EASTW* BN20 .... 237 F3
Ascot Ms *STLEO* TN38 .... 197 H3 🔲
Ashbrook Rd *SLVH* TN37 .... 169 J7
Ashburnham Cl *BRI* BN1 .... 179 F6 🔲
Ashburnham Dr *BRI* BN1 .... 178 E5
Ashburnham Gdns *EAST* BN21 .... 10 A2
Ashburnham Pl *HAIL* BN27 .... 189 F1 🔲
   RHAS TN35 .... 199 F2
Ashby Cl *BEXW* TN39 .... 195 F4
Ash Cl *HOVE* BN3 .... 177 H6
   LW/ROSE BN22 .... 215 K8
   RTWE/PEM TN2 .... 30 D3
Ashcombe Dr *BEXW* TN39 .... 194 C8
Ashcombe Hollow *LEW* BN7 .... 181 G4
Ashcombe La *LEW* BN7 .... 181 H5
Ash Ct *HAIL* BN27........................... 189 F4
Ashcroft Cl *RING/NEW* BN8 .... 155 J6
   SHOR BN43 .... 201 G4
Ashdown Av *ROTT* BN2 .... 220 E2
Ashdown Cha *UCK* TN22 .... 50 C6
Ashdown Cl *FROW* RH18 .... 36 A1
   SBGH/RUST TN4 .... 19 K7
   STLEO TN38 .... 197 F1
Ashdown Pl *HTHF* TN21 .... 100 B5 🔲
Ashdown Rd *BEX* TN40 .... 195 K7
   FROW RH18 .... 35 K1
   ROTT BN2 .... 7 D2
Ashdown Vw *EGRIN* RH19 .... 22 C4
   UCK TN22 .... 50 D5
Ash Dr *LEW* BN7 .... 225 K8
Ashenden Av *RYE* TN31 .... 113 C6
Ashenden Wk *RTWE/PEM* TN2 .... 20 E3
Ashford Cl *HAIL* BN27 .... 189 H4 🔲
Ashford Rd *BRI* BN1 .... 204 B1
   EAST BN21 .... 10 C4
   HAS TN34 .... 4 C2
Ashford Sq *EAST* BN21 .... 10 C4
Ashford Wy *HAS* TN34 .... 4 C2
Ashgate Rd *LGNY* BN23 .... 231 F1
Ash Gv *HWH* RH16 .... 89 K1
   PEV BN24 .... 216 E5
Ashington Gdns *PEAHV* BN10 .... 222 D5
Ashington Rd *LW/ROSE* BN22 .... 230 B2
Ashleigh Gdns *CROW* TN6 .... 39 G7
Ashley Cl *BRI* BN1 .... 177 K4
Ashley Gdns *HAIL* BN27 .... 161 H8
   MAYF TN20 .... 72 A1
   SBGH/RUST TN4 .... 19 G6
Ashley Park Cl *SBGH/RUST* TN4 ..... 19 G6
Ashley Rd *CROW* TN6 .... 55 H2
Ashlings Wy *HOVE* BN3 .... 202 D1 🔲
   SHOR BN43 .... 200 E2
Ashmore Cl *PEAHV* BN10 .... 222 C1
Ashton Ri *ROTT* BN2 .... 7 D4 🔲
Ashtonville Cl *RING/NEW* BN8 .... 155 K6 🔲
Ash Tree Cl *HTHF* TN21 .... 100 A4
Ashurst Av *ROTT* BN2 .... 221 H3
Ashurst Rd *ROTT* BN2 .... 179 G6
   RRTW TN3 .... 27 K1
   SEAF BN25 .... 232 B1
Ashway *BURH* RH15 .... 119 G1 🔲
Aspen Cl *LW/ROSE* BN22 .... 229 K1
Aspen Wk *HTHF* TN21 .... 100 B6
Aspen Wy *BEXW* TN39 .... 194 B7
   RTWE/PEM TN2 .... 20 C2
Astaire Av *LW/ROSE* BN22 .... 11 D1
Asten Cl *STLEO* TN38 .... 197 F4
Asten Flds *BAT* TN33 .... 136 B7
Athelstan Cl *LGNY* BN23 .... 231 G3 🔲
Athelstan Rd *RHAS* TN35 .... 199 C1
Atlantic Dr *LGNY* BN23 .... 231 G4
Atlingworth St *ROTT* BN2 .... 7 D6 🔲
Attree Dr *ROTT* BN2 .... 7 E4
Auckland Dr *ROTT* BN2 .... 205 G2
Auckland Rd *RTW* TN1 .... 20 C5
Audrey Cl *BRI* BN1 .... 177 K6
   SEAF BN25 .... 224 E6
Augustus Wy *STLEO* TN38 .... 169 G7
Austen Wy *RHAS* TN35 .... 171 G6
Avard Crs *EDN/EASTW* BN20 .... 229 G5
Avards Cl *HAWK* TN18 .... 62 E3
Avenue La *EAST* BN21 .... 10 B4

The Avenue *EAST* BN21 .... 10 B4
   EGRIN RH19 .... 12 E5
   HAIL BN27 .... 189 C5
   HTHF TN21 .... 100 B5 🔲
   HTHF TN21 .... 129 K3
   LEW BN7 .... 2 B3
   LEW BN7 .... 181 C6
   MAYF TN20 .... 72 B1
   RHAS TN35 .... 172 E7
   ROTT BN2 .... 204 E1
   SHOR BN43 .... 200 B2
Avery Cl *PTSD* BN41 .... 175 J7
Aviemore Rd *CROW* TN6 .... 53 F1
Avis Cl *NEWHV* BN9 .... 9 E1
Avis Rd *NEWHV* BN9 .... 9 D1
Avis Wy *NEWHV* BN9.......................... 9 E2
Avondale Rd *HOVE* BN3 .... 203 J4
   LW/ROSE BN22 .... 11 D2 🔲
   SEAF BN25 .... 225 C8
   STLEO TN38 .... 197 H2
Avonhurst *BURH* RH15 .... 89 H8
Avon St *RTW* TN1 .... 20 C6
Aylesbury Av *LGNY* BN23 .... 231 F3
Aymer Rd *HOVE* BN3 .... 203 F5
Ayscue Cl *LGNY* BN23 .... 231 G4 🔲

Babylon Wy *EDN/EASTW* BN20........ 229 C3
Back La *HTHF* TN21 .... 99 C4
   HTHF TN21 .... 131 K3
   UCK TN22 .... 67 H1
   WSEA TN36 .... 142 E4
Baden Rd *ROTT* BN2 .... 7 F2
Badens Cl *RING/NEW* BN8 .... 93 G5 🔲
Badger Cl *PTSD* BN41 .... 202 A1
Badgers Brow *EDN/EASTW* BN20 ..... 229 C3
Badgers Cl *CROW* TN6 .... 39 G8
Badgers Copse *SEAF* BN25 .... 225 K8
Badgers Dene *LEW* BN7 .... 208 C3
Badgers Fld *PEAHV* BN10 .... 222 B2
Badgers Holt *RTWE/PEM* TN2.......... 20 E6
Badgers Mt *BEXW* TN39 .... 194 D6
Badgers Wk *BURH* RH15 .... 119 K1 🔲
Badgers Wy *EGRIN* RH19 .... 12 C3
   HAS TN34 .... 170 A6
Badger Wy *BRI* BN1 .... 179 F5
Badlesmere Rd *LW/ROSE* BN22 .... 10 C1
Bagham La *HAIL* BN27 .... 163 C5
Bahram Rd *POLE* BN26 .... 214 D5
Bailey Crs *LW/ROSE* BN22 .... 215 C8
Baillie Av *LW/ROSE* BN22 .... 11 E2
Bainbridge Cl *SEAF* BN25 .... 232 B1
Baird Dr *HAS* TN34 .... 4 C1
Baker's Rd *EAST* BN21 .... 229 J8 🔲
Baker St *BRI* BN1.............................. 6 C2
   UCK TN22 .... 95 K5
Bakewell Rd *EAST* BN21 .... 229 J7
Balaclava La *WADH* TN5 .... 44 B4
Balcombe La *RHWH* RH17 .... 48 C1
Balcombe Rd *PEAHV* BN10 .... 222 A3 🔲
Baldock Rd *WADH* TN5 .... 43 K7
Baldslow Down *SLVH* TN37 .... 169 K2
Baldslow Rd *HAS* TN34 .... 5 D2
Baldwin Av *EAST* BN21 .... 229 H5
Bale Cl *BEXW* TN39 .... 194 D6
Balfour Gdns *FROW* RH18 .... 35 J3
Balfour Rd *BRI* BN1 .... 204 A1
Ballard Dr *RING/NEW* BN8 .... 156 A3
Ballards Hl *BAT* TN33 .... 168 A7
Ballsocks La *HTHF* TN21 .... 130 C3
Balmoral Cl *SEAF* BN25 .... 225 H5
Balsdean Rd *ROTT* BN2 .... 206 A2
Bamford Cl *ROTT* BN2 .... 205 H1
Bampfield St *PTSD* BN41 .... 202 A3 🔲
Bancroft Rd *BEXW* TN39 .... 195 C6
Bank Rd *BEXW* TN39 .... 195 H4 🔲
Bankside *BRI* BN1 .... 177 H6
   HPPT/KEY BN6 .... 119 F6
   WADH TN5 .... 44 A6
Banks Rd *RING/NEW* BN8 .... 92 C2
Banner Farm Rd *RTWE/PEM* TN2 ..... 30 B1
Bannings V *ROTT* BN2 .... 221 C3
Bannisters Fld *RING/NEW* BN8 .... 93 J4
Baranscraig Av *BRI* BN1 .... 178 B4
Barcombe Av *SEAF* BN25 .... 225 K8
Barcombe Cl *SEAF* BN25 .... 225 K8 🔲
Barcombe Mills Rd
   RING/NEW BN8................. 154 E1
Barcombe Rd *BRI* BN1 .... 179 F7
Barden Rd *LW/ROSE* BN22.............. 11 E3
   RRTW TN3 .... 18 D1
Bardown Rd *WADH* TN5 .... 59 C5
Bargate Cl *BEXW* TN39 .... 195 H4
Barham Cl *HAS* TN34 .... 170 A7
Barkdale *BURH* RH15 .... 89 K6
Barley La *PEAHV* BN10 .... 222 A1
Barley Dr *BURH* RH15 .... 88 C7
Barley La *RHAS* TN35 .... 199 F2
Barley Mow La *HTHF* TN21 .... 101 H6

Barming Cl *LGNY* BN23 .... 230 E1 🔲
Barn Cl *HAIL* BN27 .... 189 H2
   HEAT BN1 .... 181 H6
   PEV BN24 .... 216 B5
   SEAF BN25 .... 225 H5
   SLVH TN37 .... 169 K6
Barnes Rd *PTSD* BN41 .... 202 A3 🔲
Barnett Rd *BRI* BN1 .... 204 C1
Barnetts Cl *RTWE/PEM* TN2 .... 20 C2
Barnetts Wy *SBGH/RUST* TN4 .... 20 C2
Barnett Wy *UCK* TN22 .... 95 K4
Barnet Wy *HOVE* BN3 .... 176 D8
Barnfield *CROW* TN6 .... 53 J1
   LEW BN7 .... 121 C6
   RTWE/PEM TN2 .... 29 K4
Barnfield Cl *SLVH* TN37..................... 4 B4
Barnfield Gdns *HPPT/KEY* BN6 .... 120 A8 🔲
Barn Field Gdns *ROTT* BN2 .... 7 E4 🔲
The Barnhams *BEXW* TN39 .... 194 D8
Barn Hatch Cl *LEW* BN7 .... 2 A5
Barnhorn Cl *BEXW* TN39 .... 194 B7
Barnhorn Rd *BAT* TN33 .... 193 G7
   BEXW TN39 .... 193 K7
Barn La *UCK* TN22 .... 97 F3
Barn Ri *BRI* BN1 .... 177 J6
   SEAF BN25 .... 225 H6
Barn Rd *LEW* BN7 .... 3 E2
Barnside Av *BURH* RH15 .... 119 J2
Barons Cl *SEAF* BN25 .... 224 D6
Barons Ct *BURH* RH15 .... 119 H1
Barons Down Rd *LEW* BN7 .... 2 A5
Barons Wy *POLE* BN26 .... 214 E6
Barrack Rd *BEX* TN40 .... 195 H6
Barrack Sq *WSEA* TN36 .... 143 F4
Barretts Rd *HAWK* TN18 .... 63 G1
Barrhill Av *BRI* BN1 .... 178 A4
Barrie Cl *LGNY* BN23 .... 231 F1
Barrow Cl *BRI* BN1 .... 204 D1 🔲
Barrowfield Cl *HOVE* BN3 .... 177 H8 🔲
Barrowfield Dr *HOVE* BN3 .... 203 H1
Barrow Hl *BRI* BN1 .... 204 D1
Barrow La *RRTW* TN3 .... 28 D2
Barrow Ri *SLVH* TN37 .... 169 K6
Barry Wk *ROTT* BN2 .... 7 E4 🔲
Bartholomews *BRI* BN1 .... 6 C5 🔲
Bartley Mill Cl *PEV* BN24 .... 216 C6
Bartley Mill Rd *RRTW* TN3 .... 32 A7
Barton Crs *EGRIN* RH19 .... 22 E3
Basin Rd South *PTSD* BN41 .... 201 J5
Baslow Rd *EDN/EASTW* BN20 .... 236 D4
Bassetts Hl *LING* RH7 .... 12 E2 🔲
Bassetts La *CROW* TN6 .... 42 E8
   EDEN TN8 .... 16 E4
   MAYF TN20 .... 95 G4
Batchelor Wy *UCK* TN22 .... 95 G4
Bateman's La *BUR/ETCH* TN19 .... 75 J7
Batemans Rd *ROTT* BN2 .... 206 A1
Bates Rd *BRI* BN1 .... 204 A1
Bathford Cl *LGNY* BN23 .... 230 E1 🔲
Bath Rd *EAST* BN21 .... 10 B5 🔲
Bath St *BRI* BN1............................... 6 B3
Battery Hl *RHAS* TN35 .... 172 A7
Battle Cl *SEAF* BN25 .... 225 K6
Battle Crs *HAIL* BN27 .... 189 H3
   SLVH TN37 .... 169 F3
Battle Gates *BAT* TN33 .... 136 B7
Battle Hl *BAT* TN33 .... 136 E8
Battle Rd *BAT* TN33 .... 169 F3
   HAIL BN27 .... 189 G3
   SLVH TN37 .... 169 G5
Batts Bridge Rd *UCK* TN22 .... 49 K4
Bavant Rd *BRI* BN1 .... 203 K1
Baxter Rd *LEW* BN7 .... 2 B5
Baxters La *RHWH* RH17 .... 49 C5
Baxter St *ROTT* BN2 .... 7 E3
Bay Av *PEV* BN24.............................. 218 B6
Bayencourt North *BEXW* TN39......... 195 G6
Bayhall Rd *RTWE/PEM* TN2 .... 20 D8
Bayham Rd *HAIL* BN27 .... 189 J4
   LW/ROSE BN22 .... 11 E3 🔲
   RTWE/PEM TN2 .... 30 A3
Bayley's La *POLE* BN26 .... 187 K8
Baylis Crs *BURH* RH15 .... 88 E7 🔲
Bay Pond Rd *EAST* BN21 .... 229 J7 🔲
Bay Rd *PEV* BN24 .... 218 A7
Bay Tree Cl *HTHF* TN21 .... 100 B5
   SHOR BN43 .... 201 F2
Bay Tree La *POLE* BN26 .... 214 E3
Bayview Rd *PEAHV* BN10 .... 222 D6
Bay Vue Rd *NEWHV* BN9 .... 9 D3 🔲
Baywood Gdns *ROTT* BN2 .... 205 K2
Bazehill Rd *ROTT* BN2 .... 206 D8
Beach Cl *SEAF* BN25 .... 224 E8
Beach Gn *SHOR* BN43 .... 200 A5
The Beachings *PEV* BN24 .... 217 K7
Beach Rd *LW/ROSE* BN22.............. 11 E2
   NEWHV BN9 .... 9 E4
   SHOR BN43 .... 200 B6
Beachy Head Rd
   EDN/EASTW BN20 .... 235 F6
   EDN/EASTW BN20 .... 236 B3
Beacon Cl *BRI* BN1 .... 204 B1
   CROW TN6 .... 53 G1
   SEAF BN25 .... 224 E6
Beacon Dr *SEAF* BN25 .... 224 E6

Beacon Gdns *CROW* TN6 .... 39 G8
Beacon Hl *BEXW* TN39 .... 194 E3
　　LING RH7 .... 13 F3
　　ROTT BN2 .... 206 B8
Beacon Hurst *HPPT/KEY* BN6 .... 119 H8
Beacon La *RBTBR* TN32 .... 108 A3
Beacon Rd *CROW* TN6 .... 52 E3
　　HPPT/KEY BN6 .... 150 E2
　　RHAS TN35 .... 171 H7
　　SEAF BN25 .... 224 E7
Beacon Rd West *CROW* TN6 ...... 53 F1
Beaconsfield Rd *BEX* TN40 ...... 195 H5
　　BRI BN1 .... 6 C2
　　HAS TN34 .... 5 D2
　　PTSD BN41 .... 202 A5
　　RHWH RH17 .... 49 H3
Beaconsfield Vls *BRI* BN1 .... 6 B1
Beal Crs *BRI* BN1 .... 204 C1
Beales La *RYE* TN31 .... 81 K5
Beale St *BURH* RH15 .... 118 E2
Beamsley Rd *LW/ROSE* BN22 .... 11 E3
Beaney's La *HAS* TN34 .... 170 B5
　　RHAS TN35 .... 170 C3
Bear Rd *ROTT* BN2 .... 7 E2
Bear Yd *LEW* BN7 .... 3 D4
Beatrice La *EAST* BN21 .... 10 B4
Beatrice Wk *BEXW* TN39 .... 195 F5
Beatty Av *BRI* BN1 .... 178 E4
Beatty Rd *LGNY* BN23 .... 231 F5
Beauchamp Rd *STLEO* TN38 ...... 169 H8
　　STLEO TN38 .... 169 H7
Beauford Rd *HTHF* TN21 .... 129 K4
Beaufort Crs *SLVH* TN37 .... 4 A2
Beaufort Ter *ROTT* BN2 .... 7 E4
Beauharrow Rd *SLVH* TN37 ...... 169 H5
Beaulieu Dr *PEV* BN24 .... 216 B6
Beaulieu Gdns *SLVH* TN37 ...... 169 K5
Beau Nash Wy *RTWE/PEM* TN2 .. 30 B2
Beauport Gdns *SLVH* TN37 ...... 169 H4
Beauport Home Farm Cl
　　SLVH TN37 .... 169 H5
Beaver Cl *CROW* TN6 .... 53 C4
Beckenham Rd *HAIL* BN27 ...... 161 G8
Becket Cl *HAS* TN34 .... 5 E5
Beckets Wy *UCK* TN22 .... 96 D6
Beckett Wy *EGRIN* RH19 .... 22 D5
　　LEW BN7 .... 2 C2
Beckley Cl *ROTT* BN2 .... 206 E1
　　STLEO TN38 .... 196 F1
Bedelands Cl *BURH* RH15 .... 89 H6
Bedford Av *BEX* TN40 .... 195 J3
Bedford Ct *UCK* TN22 .... 95 J3
Bedford Gv *EAST* BN21 .... 10 B3
Bedford Pl *BRI* BN1 .... 6 A5
Bedford Rd *RHAS* TN35 .... 199 F1
　　SBGH/RUST TN4 .... 20 A2
Bedford Sq *BRI* BN1 .... 6 A5
Bedford St *ROTT* BN2 .... 7 E6
Bedfordwell Rd *EAST* BN21 ...... 10 C3
Bedgebury Cl *STLEO* TN38 ...... 197 F1
Bedgebury Cross *CRBK* TN17 .... 47 C1
Beecham Rd *STLEO* TN38 ...... 169 G7
Beech Cl *BAT* TN33 .... 136 B4
　　BEXW TN39 .... 194 B5
　　PTSD BN41 .... 175 J8
Beechers Cl *PTSD* BN41 .... 175 J8
Beeches Cl *HTHF* TN21 .... 100 B3
　　UCK TN22 .... 95 K3
The Beeches *BRI* BN1 .... 177 J8
Beech Farm Rd *CROW* TN6 ...... 53 J2
Beechfield Cl *PEV* BN24 .... 216 D5
Beech Flds *RTWE/PEM* TN2 ...... 12 D8
Beech Green La *HRTF* TN7 ...... 36 E3
Beech Gv *ROTT* BN2 .... 79 F9
Beech House La *RBTBR* TN32 .. 78 C4
Beech Hurst *RTWE/PEM* TN2 .. 21 K4
Beeching Cl *EGRIN* RH19 .... 22 C2
Beeching Rd *BEXW* TN39 .... 195 G7
Beeching Wy *EGRIN* RH19 .... 22 C2
Beech St *RTW* TN1 .... 20 B6
Beechwood Av *BRI* BN1 .... 178 A4
Beechwood Cl *BRI* BN1 .... 178 A4
　　BUR/ETCH TN19 .... 75 G4
　　HAIL BN27 .... 189 H6
Beechwood Crs
　　EDN/EASTW BN20 .... 229 J8
Beechwood Gdns *HAS* TN34 .... 170 A6
Beechwood La *HTHF* TN21 ...... 100 B6
　　LEW BN7 .... 153 H2
Beechwood Ms *RTWE/PEM* TN2 .. 20 E7
Beechwoods *BURH* RH15 .... 119 G2
Beechy Av *EDN/EASTW* BN20 .... 229 G7
Beechy Gdns *EDN/EASTW* BN20 .. 229 G7
Beechy Rd *UCK* TN22 .... 127 H2
Beeding Av *HOVE* BN3 .... 176 E8
Bee Rd *PEAHV* BN10 .... 222 B3
Beggar's La *POY/PYE* BN45 ...... 148 C6
Beggar's Wood Rd *RING/NEW* BN8 .. 92 A5
Belfast St *HOVE* BN3 .... 203 G5
Belfield Rd *RTWE/PEM* TN2 ...... 21 K5
Belfry Orch *UCK* TN22 .... 95 K5
The Belfry *HAIL* BN27 .... 189 F3

Belgrave Crs *SEAF* BN25 .... 225 G6
Belgrave Pl *ROTT* BN2 .... 7 F6
Belgrave Rd *RTW* TN1 .... 20 A7
　　SEAF BN25 .... 224 E7
Belgrave St *ROTT* BN2 .... 7 D4
Bell Alley Rd *BUR/ETCH* TN35 .. 75 K5
Bell Banks Rd *HAIL* BN27 ...... 189 H4
Belle Hl *BEX* TN40 .... 195 H6
Bellevue Gdns *ROTT* BN2 .... 7 E5
Belle Vue Rd *LW/ROSE* BN22 .. 11 E2
Bell Hammer *EGRIN* RH19 ...... 22 C5
Bellhurst Rd *RBTBR* TN32 ...... 78 A7
Bellingham Cl *SLVH* TN37 ...... 169 J7
Bellingham Crs *HOVE* BN3 ...... 202 C3
Bell La *LEW* BN7 .... 2 E5
　　UCK TN22 .... 50 A7
　　UCK TN22 .... 95 J5
　　UCK TN22 .... 95 H5
Bell Wk *UCK* TN22 .... 95 J4
Belmont *BRI* BN1 .... 6 A3
Belmont Cl *HPPT/KEY* BN6 ...... 118 E6
Belmont La *HPPT/KEY* BN6 ...... 118 C7
Belmont Rd *RHAS* TN35 .... 199 F2
　　UCK TN22 .... 95 J4
Belmont St *BRI* BN1 .... 6 C3
Belmore Rd *LW/ROSE* BN22 .... 11 D3
Belton Rd *ROTT* BN2 .... 7 D2
Beltring Rd *LW/ROSE* BN22 .... 11 D3
　　SBGH/RUST TN4 .... 20 A5
Beltring Ter *LW/ROSE* BN22 .... 11 D3
Belvedere Gdns *CROW* TN6 .... 53 J2
　　SEAF BN25 .... 225 H6
Belvedere Pk *CROW* TN6 .... 197 H5
Bembridge Rd *LGNY* BN23 ...... 216 C8
Bembridge St *ROTT* BN2 .... 7 E2
Bembrook Rd *HAS* TN34 .... 5 F3
Benchfield Cl *EGRIN* RH19 ...... 22 E3
Benenden Cl *SEAF* BN25 .... 225 H7
Benenden Ri *HAS* TN34 .... 4 C1
Benett Av *HOVE* BN3 .... 203 G1
Benett Dr *HOVE* BN3 .... 203 G1
Benfield Cl *PTSD* BN41 .... 202 B3
Benfield Crs *PTSD* BN41 .... 202 B3
Benfield Wy *PTSD* BN41 .... 202 B3
Bengairn Av *BRI* BN1 .... 178 B4
Benhall Mill Rd *RTWE/PEM* TN2 .. 30 C3
Benjamin Cl *LW/ROSE* BN22 .. 230 A1
Bennett Av *HOVE* BN3 .... 203 G1
Bennett Rd *ROTT* BN2 .... 205 F7
Bentham Hl *RRTW* TN3 .... 19 H2
Bentham Rd *ROTT* BN2 .... 7 E5
Berberis Ct *SHOR* BN43 .... 200 C2
Beresford Rd *NEWHV* BN9 .... 9 E1
　　ROTT BN2 .... 7 F5
Bergamot Crs *SHOR* BN43 ...... 201 F2
Beristede Cl *EDN/EASTW* BN20 .. 10 A6
Berkeley Rd *RTW* TN1 .... 30 A1
Berkley Rd *MAYF* TN20 .... 71 K2
Berlin Rd *RHAS* TN35 .... 199 F1
Bermuda Pl *LGNY* BN23 .... 231 H4
Bernard La *EAST* BN21 .... 10 B4
Bernard Pl *ROTT* BN2 .... 7 E3
Bernard Rd *ROTT* BN2 .... 7 E3
Bernhard Gdns *POLE* BN26 .... 214 E6
Berriedale Av *HOVE* BN3 .... 202 D5
Berry Cl *BURH* RH15 .... 89 G6
　　PEAHV BN10 .... 221 K2
Berwick Cl *BEXW* TN39 .... 194 B5
　　LW/ROSE BN22 .... 215 H8
　　SEAF BN25 .... 224 E7
Berwick Rd *ROTT* BN2 .... 207 G8
Betchley Cl *EGRIN* RH19 .... 12 C8
Bethune Rd *BEX* TN40 .... 195 K3
Bethune Wy *HAS* TN34 .... 5 D5
Beulah Rd *RTW* TN1 .... 20 C7
Beuzeville Av *HAIL* BN27 ...... 189 G3
Bevendean Av *ROTT* BN2 ...... 221 G2
Bevendean Crs *ROTT* BN2 ...... 205 F1
Bevendean Rd *ROTT* BN2 ...... 7 F2
Beverington Cl *EAST* BN21 ...... 229 J5
Beverington Rd *EAST* BN21 .... 229 J5
Bewl Bridge Cl *WADH* TN5 ...... 47 F8
Bewlbridge La *RRTW* TN3 ...... 46 A2
Bexhill Rd *BAT* TN33 .... 166 A6
　　LW/ROSE BN22 .... 11 E2
　　ROTT BN2 .... 206 A2
　　STLEO TN38 .... 196 C6
Bexleigh Av *STLEO* TN38 .... 196 C6
Bexley Cl *HAIL* BN27 .... 189 G1
Bicton Gdns *BEXW* TN39 .... 194 D7
Biddenden Cl *LGNY* BN23 ...... 230 E1
Bidwell Av *BEXW* TN39 .... 195 F5
Bigwood Av *HOVE* BN3 .... 203 J4
Billingham La *RYE* TN31 .... 111 G8
Binsted Cl *LW/ROSE* BN22 ...... 229 K1
Birch Cl *RTWE/PEM* TN2 .... 20 D4
　　UCK TN22 .... 96 A3
Birches Cl *CROW* TN6 .... 39 H7
Birchetts Av *RRTW* TN3 .... 18 C8
Birchetts Green La *WADH* TN5 .. 45 C8
Birch Grove Crs *BRI* BN1 .... 178 B6
Birchgrove La *RHWH* RH17 ...... 48 D2
Birchgrove Rd *RHWH* RH17 .... 48 B6

Birchington Cl *BEXW* TN39 ...... 194 C7
Birch Rd *LGNY* BN23 .... 230 D4
Birch Vw *BEXW* TN39 .... 195 H5
Birch Wy *HAIL* BN27 .... 189 G5
　　HAS TN34 .... 4 C1
　　HTHF TN21 .... 100 A6
　　HWH RH16 .... 90 C1
　　RTWE/PEM TN2 .... 20 D4
Birchwood Grove Rd *BURH* RH15 .. 119 G2
Birdham Rd *ROTT* BN2 .... 179 F8
Bird in Eye Hl *UCK* TN22 .... 96 A5
Bird in Hand St *RRTW* TN5 ...... 28 A3
Bird La *WADH* TN5 .... 43 H7
Birk Dl *BEXW* TN39 .... 194 C7
Birken Rd *RTWE/PEM* TN2 ...... 20 D5
Birling Cl *ROTT* BN2 .... 7 F1
　　SEAF BN25 .... 224 E7
Birling Dr *RTWE/PEM* TN2 ...... 30 A3
Birling Gap Rd *EDN/EASTW* BN20 .. 235 F6
Birling Park Av *RTWE/PEM* TN2 .. 30 B3
Birling Rd *RTWE/PEM* TN2 ...... 30 B3
Birling St *EDN/EASTW* BN20 .... 229 H7
Bishop's Cl *RING/NEW* BN8 ...... 155 K5
　　SEAF BN25 .... 224 D7
Bishop's Down *SBGH/RUST* TN4 .. 19 J8
Bishop's Down Park Rd
　　SBGH/RUST TN4 .... 19 J7
Bishop's Down Rd *SBGH/RUST* TN4 .. 19 J8
Bishops Dr *LEW* BN7 .... 2 A5
Bishop's La *RBTBR* TN32 .... 78 A8
　　RING/NEW BN8 .... 155 J5
Bishops Rd *HOVE* BN3 .... 203 H2
Bishopstone Dr *ROTT* BN2 ...... 220 E1
Bishopstone La *HPPT/KEY* BN6 .. 88 A6
　　RHWH RH17 .... 88 A4
Bishopstone Rd *SEAF* BN25 .... 224 D5
Bishop's Wk *BEX* TN40 .... 196 A5
Bixley La *RYE* TN31 .... 110 E2
Blackberry La *LING* RH7 .... 12 B1
Blackberry Rd *EGRIN* RH19 ...... 12 A3
Blackdon Hl *CROW* TN6 .... 41 G5
Blackdown Rd *HTHF* TN21 ...... 101 K5
Blackfields Av *BEXW* TN39 ...... 194 E6
Blackhouse La *BURH* RH15 ...... 89 H7
Blackhurst La *RTWE/PEM* TN2 .. 21 G4
Blacklands Crs *FROW* RH18 .... 35 K1
Blacklands Dr *HAS* TN34 .... 5 D2
Black Lion St *BRI* BN1 .... 6 C6
Blackman Av *STLEO* TN38 ...... 169 H8
Blackman St *BRI* BN1 .... 6 C4
Blackmill Cl *BEXW* TN39 .... 195 F5
Blackness Rd *CROW* TN6 .... 53 H2
Black Pth *POLE* BN26 .... 215 F5
Blacksmiths Copse *HAIL* BN27 .. 189 F5
Blacksmiths La *BAT* TN33 ...... 166 D3
　　WADH TN5 .... 44 C6
Blackstone Wy *BURH* RH15 ...... 89 G6
Blackthorn Av *RTWE/PEM* TN2 .. 20 C2
Blackthorn Cl *BRI* BN1 .... 177 J8
　　LW/ROSE BN22 .... 229 K1
　　PTSD BN41 .... 202 A1
　　SLVH TN37 .... 169 K7
The Blackthorns *BURH* RH15 .. 89 H6
Blackthorn Wy *RHAS* TN35 ...... 172 E7
Blackwater Rd *EDN/EASTW* BN20 .. 10 B6
Blackwell Farm Rd *EGRIN* RH19 .. 12 D8
Blackwell Hollow *EGRIN* RH19 .. 22 D1
Blackwell Rd *EGRIN* RH19 ...... 22 D1
Blakeney Av *NEWHV* BN9 .... 8 A4
Blaker St *ROTT* BN2 .... 7 D5
Blakes Wy *LGNY* BN23 .... 231 G5
Blake Wy *RTWE/PEM* TN2 ...... 20 D4
Blatchington Cl *SEAF* BN25 .... 225 G7
Blatchington Hl *SEAF* BN25 .... 225 F7
Blatchington Mill Dr *PEV* BN24 .. 216 D6
Blatchington Rd *HOVE* BN3 .... 203 G4
　　RTW TN1 .... 30 A2
　　SEAF BN25 .... 225 F8
Blenheim Cl *EGRIN* RH19 ...... 12 E8
Blenheim Flds *FROW* RH18 ...... 23 J8
Blenheim Wy *POLE* BN26 ...... 215 J5
　　WADH TN5 .... 47 G8
Bletchinglye La *CROW* TN6 .... 55 J2
Blind La *RING/NEW* BN8 .... 93 J5
Blois Rd *LEW* BN7 .... 2 A2
Blomfield Rd *SLVH* TN37 .... 4 A4
Bloomsbury Pl *ROTT* BN2 .... 7 E6
Bloomsbury St *ROTT* BN2 .... 7 E6
Blount Av *EGRIN* RH19 .... 22 A2
Blowers Hl *EDEN* TN8 .... 15 K3
Blue Haze Av *SEAF* BN25 ...... 225 J7
Bluemans La *BAT* TN33 .... 138 C8
Bluestone Cl *STLEO* TN38 ...... 197 C1
Boarders La *WADH* TN5 .... 46 A8
Boast La *RING/NEW* BN8 .... 123 J6
Bocking Cl *WADH* TN5 .... 44 A7
Boddingtons La *HPPT/KEY* BN6 .. 119 K8
Bodiam Av *BEX* TN40 .... 195 J3
　　ROTT BN2 .... 205 J2
Bodiam Cl *ROTT* BN2 .... 205 J1
　　SEAF BN25 .... 225 K7
Bodiam Crs *LW/ROSE* BN22 .... 230 B1
Bodiam Dr *STLEO* TN38 .... 196 E1
Bodiam Rd *HAWK* TN18 .... 80 B1
Bodle Crs *BEXW* TN39 .... 195 G4

Bohemia Rd *SLVH* TN37 .... 4 B4
  STLEO TN38 .... 197 J2
Bolding Wy *HWH* RH16 .... 89 K1
Bolebrooke Rd *BEX* TN40 .... 195 J8
Bolney Av *PEAHV* BN10 .... 222 B5
Bolney Rd *ROTT* BN2 .... 179 G7
Bolsover Rd *EDN/EASTW* BN20 .. 236 E3
  HOVE BN3 .... 202 D4
Bolton Cl *UCK* TN22 .... 95 G5
Bolton Rd *EAST* BN21 .... 10 C5
Bonchurch Rd *ROTT* BN2........... 7 E2
Bondfield Cl *SBGH/RUST* TN4 ..... 20 A2
Bond St *BRI* BN1 .... 6 C5 🔲
Bonfire La *RHWH* RH17 .... 48 A7
Boniface Cl *PEV* BN24 .... 216 D5
Bonny Wood Rd *HPPT/KEY* BN6 .. 118 E8
Booker Cl *CROW* TN6 .... 53 J2
Bopeep Bostal *POLE* BN26 ...... 211 J4
Bopeep La *POLE* BN26 .... 211 J3
Border Ct *EGRIN* RH19 .... 12 D7
Borders La *BUR/ETCH* TN19 ...... 76 E3
Boreham Hl *HAIL* TN21 .... 164 D8
Boreham La *HAIL* BN27 .... 192 B2
Borough La *EDN/EASTW* BN20 .. 229 J8
Borough St *BRI* BN1 .... 6 A5
Borrowdale Cl *LGNY* BN23 .... 216 D7 🔲
Borrow King Cl *ROTT* BN2 .... 7 F1 🔲
Boscawen Cl *LGNY* BN23 .... 231 G4 🔲
Boscobel Rd *STLEO* TN38 .... 197 H4
Boscobel Rd North *STLEO* TN38 .. 197 H3
Boship Cl *LGNY* BN23 .... 216 B7 🔲
Bostal Rd *RING/NEW* BN8 .... 184 C7
Boston Cl *LGNY* BN23 .... 231 G4
Boston St *BRI* BN1 .... 6 C3
Bough Beeches *BURH* RH15 ...... 119 J2 🔲
Boughey Pl *LEW* BN7 .... 2 C2
The Boulevard *BN24* 218 B5
Boundary & Station Roads
  PTSD BN41 .... 202 B5
Boundary Rd *ROTT* BN2 .... 205 F8
  RTWE/PEM TN2 .... 30 D2
The Boundary *RRTW* TN3 .... 19 F8
  SEAF BN25 .... 232 A1
Bourg-de-peage Av *EGRIN* RH19 .. 22 E2
Bourne La *RBTBR* TN32 .... 79 F3
Bourne St *LW/ROSE* BN22 .... 10 C4
The Bourne *HAS* TN34 .... 5 F4
  HPPT/KEY BN6 .... 118 C5
Bowden Ri *SEAF* BN25 .... 225 F5
Bowen Rd *SBGH/RUST* TN4 .... 19 F6
Bower Cl *SLVH* TN37 .... 169 J7
Bowley Rd *HAIL* BN27 .... 189 H4
Bowmans Dr *BAT* TN33 .... 136 D5
Bowood Av *LW/ROSE* BN22 ...... 11 D1
Bowrey Pl *BEX* TN40 .... 195 H6 🔲
Bowring Wy *ROTT* BN2 .... 7 F6
Bowsprit Ms *STLEO* TN38 .... 169 F4
Boxes La *RHWH* RH17 .... 48 A7
Boxgrove Cl *BEX* TN40 .... 196 A7
Box La *EGRIN* RH19 .... 23 J5
Box's La *RHWH* RH17 .... 49 C5
Boyce's St *BRI* BN1 .... 6 B5
Boyne Pk *SBGH/RUST* TN4 .... 19 E7
Boyne Rd *RHAS* TN35 .... 199 F2
Brackenbury Cl *PTSD* BN41 ...... 202 A1 🔲
Bracken Cl *CROW* TN6 .... 54 A2 🔲
  RTWE/PEM TN2 .... 20 E6 🔲
Brackendale *RHAS* TN35 .... 199 G1
Brackenhill *HRTF* TN7 .... 37 G2
Bracken Rd *EDN/EASTW* BN20 .. 229 F6
  RTWE/PEM TN2 .... 20 E6
  SEAF BN25 .... 232 C1
Bracken Wy *HTHF* TN21 .... 100 E2
Bradford Rd *LEW* BN7 .... 2 B4
Bradford St *EAST* BN21 .... 229 H8
Brading Cl *HAS* TN34 .... 4 C2 🔲
  LGNY BN23 .... 216 C7
Brading Rd *ROTT* BN2 .... 7 E3
Bradley Rd *HAIL* BN27 .... 191 K2
  RRTW TN3 .... 17 F6
Braemore Rd *HOVE* BN3 .... 202 D5
Braeside Av *HOVE* BN3 .... 178 A4
Bramber Av *HOVE* BN3 .... 176 E8
  PEAHV BN10 .... 222 B4
Bramber Av North *PEAHV* BN10 .. 222 B3
Bramber Cl *PEAHV* BN10 .... 222 B3 🔲
  SEAF BN25 .... 232 B1 🔲
Bramber La *SEAF* BN25 .... 232 B1
Bramber Rd *SEAF* BN25 .... 232 B1
Bramber Wy *BURH* RH15 .... 89 G7
Bramble Cl *LGNY* BN23 .... 216 C8
Bramble Cft *CROW* TN6 .... 53 J1
Brambledean Rd *PTSD* BN41 .... 202 A4
Bramble Dr *HAIL* BN27 .... 189 F4
Bramble Gdns *BURH* RH15 .... 88 D7
Bramble Ri *BRI* BN1 .... 177 H6
Brambles *HPPT/KEY* BN6 .... 119 F6 🔲
Brambleside *UCK* TN22 .... 95 G5
Brambletye La *FROW* RH18 .... 23 H8
Brambletye Av *ROTT* BN2 .... 221 G2
Bramble Wy *RHAS* TN35 .... 172 E7
Bramley Rd *POLE* BN26 .... 215 H5
Bramleys *LEW* BN7 .... 181 H6
Brampton Av *BEXW* TN39 .... 194 E7
Brampton Rd *LW/ROSE* BN22 .... 230 A2

Brand Rd *LW/ROSE* BN22........... 229 K2
Brands Cl *NEWHV* BN9 .... 223 J1
Brangwyn Av *BRI* BN1 .... 177 K5
Brangwyn Crs *BRI* BN1 .... 177 K5
Brangwyn Dr *BRI* BN1 .... 177 J5
Brangwyn Wy *BRI* BN1 .... 177 K6
Branksome Rd *STLEO* TN38 ...... 197 H3
Branston Rd *LW/ROSE* BN22 ..... 229 J2
Brassey Av *LW/ROSE* BN22 ...... 229 K2
Brassey Rd *BEX* TN40 .... 195 J8
Brasslands Dr *PTSD* BN41 .... 201 J2
Braybon Av *BRI* BN1 .... 178 A7
Braybrooke Rd *HAS* TN34 .... 4 C4
Braybrooke Ter *HAS* TN34 .... 4 C4 🔲
Braypool La *BRI* BN1 .... 177 J3
Brazen Cl *NEWHV* BN9 .... 8 A5
Breadsell La *BAT* TN33 .... 168 D6
Bread St *BRI* BN1 .... 6 C4
Brede Cl *LW/ROSE* BN22 .... 11 F1
  ROTT BN2 .... 205 F6
  STLEO TN38 .... 169 G4
Brede Hl *RYE* TN31 .... 139 K3
Brede La *BAT* TN33 .... 138 B2
Brede Valley Vw *WSEA* TN36..... 141 J6
Breedon Av *SBGH/RUST* TN4 ..... 19 K2 🔲
Brendon Cl *LGNY* BN23............. 217 F7
  RTWE/PEM TN2 .... 20 D6 🔲
Brendon Ri *HAS* TN34 .... 5 F1
Brentwood Cl *BRI* BN1 .... 178 C8 🔲
Brentwood Crs *BRI* BN1 .... 178 C8
Brentwood Rd *BRI* BN1 .... 178 C8
Bretland Rd *SBGH/RUST* TN4 ..... 19 H7
Brett Dr *BEX* TN40 .... 196 A6
Bretton *BURH* RH15 .... 88 E6
Bretts Fld *PEAHV* BN10 .... 222 B1
Brewers Gy *MAYF* TN20 .... 72 B1 🔲
Brewer St *ROTT* BN2 .... 7 D3
  RRTW TN3 .... 33 J6
Brian Crs *SBGH/RUST* TN4 .... 20 B3
Briar Cl *RHAS* TN35 .... 173 F6
  ROTT BN2 .... 206 A3
Briarcroft Rd *ROTT* BN2 .... 206 A4
Briar Pl *LGNY* BN23 .... 216 C8
Brickhurst La *RING/NEW* BN8 .... 157 K3
Brick Kiln La *UCK* TN22 .... 70 B5
Brickyard La *CROW* TN6 .... 41 K7
The Bricky *PEAHV* BN10 .... 222 C3
Bridge Cl *BURH* RH15 .... 89 F7
  HTHF TN21 .... 130 A4
Bridge End *PEV* BN24 .... 217 J5
Bridge Farm Rd *UCK* TN22 .... 95 J5
Bridgelands *RING/NEW* BN8 ..... 123 H7
Bridgemere Rd *LW/ROSE* BN22 .. 11 D1
Bridger Wy *CROW* TN6 .... 53 H2
Bridge St *NEWHV* BN9 .... 9 D3 🔲
Bridge Wy *STLEO* TN38............. 196 D5
Bridgewick Cl *LEW* BN7 .... 3 D2 🔲
Bridle Wy *PEAHV* BN10 .... 221 K2
Briers Av *SLVH* TN37 .... 4 A1
Briers Gdns *SLVH* TN37 .... 4 A1 🔲
Brigden St *BRI* BN1 .... 6 B3
Brightland Rd *EDN/EASTW* BN20 .. 229 J8
Brightling Av *RHAS* TN35 .... 171 G7
Brightling Rd *POLE* BN26 .... 215 F6
  RBTBR TN32 .... 104 E3
Brighton Pl *BRI* BN1 .... 6 C5 🔲
Brighton Rd *HPPT/KEY* BN6 ...... 148 C1
  HPPT/KEY BN6 .... 149 J1
  LEW BN7 .... 181 H4
  NEWHV BN9 .... 8 B4
  SHOR BN43 .... 200 A5
Bright Rdg *SBGH/RUST* TN4 ..... 19 J3
Brills La *BRI* BN1 .... 6 C5 🔲
Brincliffe *CROW* TN6 .... 39 G8
Brinkers La *WADH* TN5 .... 58 C1
Bristol Gdns *ROTT* BN2 .... 205 F7
Bristol Ga *ROTT* BN2 .... 7 F6
Bristol Ms *ROTT* BN2 .... 205 F7
Bristol Pl *ROTT* BN2 .... 205 F7
Bristol Rd *ROTT* BN2 .... 205 F7
  STLEO TN38 .... 169 H8
Bristol St *ROTT* BN2 .... 205 F7
Brittany Ms *STLEO* TN38 .... 197 J4
Brittany Rd *HOVE* BN3 .... 202 C5
  STLEO TN38 .... 197 J4
Britten Cl *LGNY* BN23 .... 216 E8
Brittenden La *HTHF* TN21 .... 98 C6
Britts Farm Rd *UCK* TN22 .... 68 E8
Broadcroft *RTWE/PEM* TN2 ...... 29 K3
Broadfields *ROTT* BN2 .... 179 F8 🔲
Broadfields Rd *ROTT* BN2 .... 179 F8 🔲
Broad Gn *ROTT* BN2 .... 206 B5
Broad Green Av *BURH* RH15 ..... 119 J1
Broad Gv *RTWE/PEM* TN2 .... 30 A2 🔲
Broadhill Cl *HTHF* TN21 .... 100 E2
Broadlands *BURH* RH15 .... 119 H3
  RHAS TN35 .... 199 F1
Broad La *RRTW* TN3 .... 17 J8
Broadmead *RTWE/PEM* TN2 ..... 29 K3
Broadmead Av *RTWE/PEM* TN2 .. 29 K5 🔲
Broad Oak *RRTW* TN3 .... 27 K5
Broad Oak Cl *LW/ROSE* BN22 ... 216 B7 🔲
  RTWE/PEM TN2 .... 29 K2
Broadoak La *BEXW* TN39 .... 194 D6
Broad Rig Av *HOVE* BN3............ 176 C7

Broad Rd *EDN/EASTW* BN20 ...... 214 E7
Broadstone Pk *FROW* RH18 .... 36 A1
Broad St *ROTT* BN2 .... 6 C6 🔲
  SEAF BN25 .... 225 F8
  WSEA TN36 .... 141 G5
Broad Vw *BEXW* TN39 .... 194 E5
  HTHF TN21 .... 100 E2
Broadview Cl *EDN/EASTW* BN20 .. 214 E7 🔲
The Broadwalk *BEXW* TN39 ...... 194 C4
Broadwater Down
  RTWE/PEM TN2 .... 29 K3
Broadwater La *RTWE/PEM* TN2 .. 29 K2
Broadwater Ri *RTWE/PEM* TN2 .. 29 K2
Broadwater Wy *LW/ROSE* BN22 .. 230 A3
Broad Wy *RHAS* TN35 .... 172 E6
The Broadway *CROW* TN6 .... 53 H1
  LW/ROSE BN22 .... 229 J2
  POLE BN26 .... 212 C8
  RHAS TN35 .... 171 G7 🔲
  RRTW TN3 .... 33 K6
Brockley Rd *BEXW* TN39 .... 195 F8
Brocks Gyhll *EDN/EASTW* BN20 .. 215 F8 🔲
Brodie Pl *EAST* BN21 .... 229 J7 🔲
Brodrick Cl *LW/ROSE* BN22 ...... 230 A2
Brodrick Rd *LW/ROSE* BN22 ..... 229 J1
Brokes Wy *SBGH/RUST* TN4 ..... 20 C2
Bromley Cl *HPPT/KEY* BN6 .... 119 C7
  LGNY BN23 .... 230 D1
Bromley Rd *ROTT* BN2 .... 7 D3
  SEAF BN25 .... 225 J7
Brompton Cl *BRI* BN1 .... 177 K5
The Brontes *EGRIN* RH19 .... 22 B2 🔲
Brook Av *HPPT/KEY* BN6 .... 119 F8
Brook Cl *CROW* TN6 .... 54 B2
  RTWE/PEM TN2 .... 23 F2
Brooke Gdns *RING/NEW* BN8 .... 93 H5
Brooker Pl *HOVE* BN3 .... 203 F4
Brooker St *HOVE* BN3 .... 203 F4
Brookfield Rd *BEX* TN40 .... 195 K7 🔲
Brookhouse Bottom *RHWH* RH17 .. 49 G8
Brookhouse La *UCK* TN22 .... 96 C8
Brookland Cl *HAS* TN34 .... 5 D2
  PEV BN24 .... 218 B5
Brooklands *RTWE/PEM* TN2 ..... 20 D4 🔲
Brooklands Av *CROW* TN6 .... 53 H4
Brooklands Farm Cl *RRTW* TN3 .. 17 J5
Brooklands Wy *EGRIN* RH19 ..... 22 B3
Brook La *RING/NEW* BN8 .... 183 F5
Brooklyn Rd *SEAF* BN25............ 225 F8
Brookmead Cl *LW/ROSE* BN22 .. 11 D2
Brook Rd *RTWE/PEM* TN2 .... 20 C4
Brooks Cl *LEW* BN7 .... 3 D3
  NEWHV BN9 .... 8 C4
Brookside *NEWHV* BN9 .... 8 C4
  UCK TN22 .... 95 C5
Brookside Av *POLE* BN26 .... 214 E4
Brooks La *LEW* BN7 .... 3 E4 🔲
Brooks St *LEW* BN7 .... 3 D3
The Brooks *BURH* RH15 .... 88 E6
Brook St *HAS* TN34 .... 5 D4 🔲
  LEW BN7 .... 2 C3
  POLE BN26 .... 214 C5
Brookway *BURH* RH15 .... 89 J8
Broom Cl *LW/ROSE* BN22 .... 229 J1
Broomfield Av *PEAHV* BN10 ...... 221 J4
Broomfield Dr *PTSD* BN41 .... 175 K7
Broomfield St *EDN/EASTW* BN20 .. 229 H7
Broomgrove Rd *HAS* TN34 .... 5 F2 🔲
Broomham La *RING/NEW* BN8 ... 147 F8
Broomhill Park Rd *SBGH/RUST* TN4 .. 19 J3
Broomhill Rd *RRTW* TN3 .... 18 D2
Broom La *RRTW* TN3 .... 28 D2
Broom Pk *RRTW* TN3 .... 18 C8
Browning Rd *HTHF* TN21 .... 100 A4
The Brownings *EGRIN* RH19 ..... 22 A2 🔲
Brown Jack Av *POLE* BN26 .... 214 E5 🔲
Brownleaf Rd *ROTT* BN2 .... 206 B5
Browns Cl *UCK* TN22 .... 95 K3
Browns La *HTHF* TN21 .... 99 F5
  UCK TN22 .... 95 K2
Browns Wd *EGRIN* RH19 .... 12 C7
The Brow *BURH* RH15 .... 119 C1
  EDN/EASTW BN20 .... 235 F1
  ROTT BN2 .... 206 A3
Broyle Cl *RING/NEW* BN8 .... 156 A3
Broyle La *RING/NEW* BN8 .... 156 A4
Broyle Paddock *RING/NEW* BN8 .. 156 A4
The Broyle *RING/NEW* BN8 .... 156 E3
Brunel Rd *STLEO* TN38 .... 169 F8
Brunswick Ms *HOVE* BN3 .... 203 J6 🔲
Brunswick Pl *HOVE* BN3 .... 203 J5
Brunswick Rd *HOVE* BN3 .... 203 J6
  SHOR BN43 .... 200 C4
Brunswick Sq *HOVE* BN3 .... 203 J6
Brunswick St East *HOVE* BN3 ... 203 J6
Brunswick St West *HOVE* BN3 ... 203 J6 🔲
Brunswick Ter *HOVE* BN3 .... 203 J6
Bryants Fld *CROW* TN6 .... 39 G8
Brydges Cl *LW/ROSE* BN22 ...... 11 E1
Buci Crs *SHOR* BN43 .... 201 F3
Buckholt Av *BEX* TN40 .... 196 B5
Buckholt La *BEXW* TN39 .... 195 H2
Buckhurst Cl *EDN/EASTW* BN20 .. 229 G3
  EGRIN RH19 .... 12 A8
  LEW BN7 .... 2 C2

Buckhurst La *CROW* TN6 .... 43 F7
Buckhurst Rd *BEX* TN40 .... 195 H7
  PEAHV BN10 .... 221 J4
Buckhurst Wy *EGRIN* RH19 .... 12 A8
Buckingham Av *SHOR* BN43 .... 200 B2
Buckingham Cl *SEAF* BN25 .... 225 F7 🔲
  SHOR BN43 .... 200 D3 🔲
Buckingham Dr *EGRIN* RH19 .... 22 E4
Buckingham Ms *SHOR* BN43 .... 200 C2 🔲
Buckingham Pl *BRI* BN1 .... 6 B3
Buckingham Rd *BRI* BN1 .... 6 B4
  RTW TN1 .... 30 B1
  SHOR BN43 .... 200 C4
  STLEO TN38 .... 169 H7
Buckingham St *BRI* BN1 .... 6 B4 🔲
  SHOR BN43 .... 200 B4 🔲
Buckland Dr *SEAF* BN25 .... 225 G6 🔲
Buckle By-pass *SEAF* BN25 .... 224 D6
Buckle Cl *SEAF* BN25 .... 224 D7
Buckle Dr *SEAF* BN25 .... 224 D7
Buckle Ri *SEAF* BN25 .... 224 D7
Bucklers Cl *RTWE/PEM* TN2 .... 20 C8 🔲
Buckler St *PTSD* BN41 .... 202 A3 🔲
Buckley Cl *HOVE* BN3 .... 176 D7
Buckthorn Cl *SEAF* BN25 .... 225 K8 🔲
The Bungalows *UCK* TN22 .... 96 D6
Burchetts Cl *HWH* RH16 .... 89 K1
Burden Pl *STLEO* TN38 .... 169 H8
Burdett Rd *CROW* TN6 .... 54 A2
  SBGH/RUST TN4 .... 19 F7 🔲
Burdocks Dr *BURH* RH15 .... 119 J2
Burfield Rd *LW/ROSE* BN22 .... 11 D4 🔲
Burgh La *BUR/ETCH* TN19 .... 77 J1
Burgh La *RING/NEW* BN8 .... 184 E6
Burhill Wy *STLEO* TN38 .... 197 G4
Burleigh Pl *LW/ROSE* BN22 .... 11 E1 🔲
Burlington Gdns *PTSD* BN41 .... 202 B2 🔲
Burlington Pl *EAST* BN21 .... 10 C5
Burlington Rd *EAST* BN21 .... 11 D5 🔲
Burlington St *ROTT* BN2 .... 7 E6
Burlow Cl *LW/ROSE* BN22 .... 215 H8 🔲
  ROTT BN2 .... 205 F2
Burners Cl *BURH* RH15 .... 119 K2
Burnham Cl *ROTT* BN2 .... 206 C4
Burnside *POLE* BN26 .... 215 F5 🔲
Burns Wy *EGRIN* RH19 .... 22 A2
Burnthouse Bostall
  HPPT/KEY BN6 .... 150 D4
Burnt House La *RRTW* TN5 .... 18 D6
Burnt Lodge La *WADH* TN5 .... 59 K2
Burnt Oak Rd *UCK* TN22 .... 68 D2
Burrells La *UCK* TN22 .... 67 G4
The Burrells *SHOR* BN43 .... 200 E5
Burrow Down *EDN/EASTW* BN20 .... 229 H6
Burry Rd *SLVH* TN37 .... 4 A1
Burslem Rd *RTWE/PEM* TN2 .... 20 E5
Burstead Cl *BRI* BN1 .... 178 C8
Burston Gdns *EGRIN* RH19 .... 12 B7
Burton Rd *EAST* BN21 .... 229 J5
Burton Vls *HOVE* BN3 .... 203 J3 🔲
  LGNY BN23 .... 216 C7
Burwash Cl *HAS* TN34 .... 170 D6 🔲
  LGNY BN23 .... 216 C7
Burwash Rd *HOVE* BN3 .... 176 D8
  HTHF TN21 .... 100 C3
Bushbury La *UCK* TN22 .... 97 J8
Bush Cl *PEAHV* BN10 .... 221 K2
  ROTT BN2 .... 206 A2
Busheyfields *HAIL* BN27 .... 189 F3 🔲
Bush Farm Pr *PTSD* BN41 .... 202 A1
Bush Rd *NEWHV* BN9 .... 8 B2
Bushy Cft *BEXW* TN39 .... 194 E6
Bushy Gill *RRTW* TN3 .... 18 E8
Butcherfield La *HRTF* TN7 .... 25 G4
Butcher's La *RHAS* TN35 .... 171 J1
Bute St *ROTT* BN2 .... 7 F5
Butler's La *HAIL* BN27 .... 163 F8
Butlers Wy *RING/NEW* BN8 .... 155 J6 🔲
Butterbox La *RHWH* RH17 .... 64 B7
Buttercup Wk *BRI* BN1 .... 178 C5
Buttermere Wy *LGNY* BN23 .... 216 D7 🔲
Butts Fld *HAIL* BN27 .... 189 H5
Buttsfield La *RING/NEW* BN8 .... 127 J6
Butts La *EDN/EASTW* BN20 .... 229 F2 🔲
  WADH TN5 .... 44 E4
Butts Rd *STHW* BN42 .... 201 H4
Buxted Ri *BRI* BN1 .... 178 C6
Buxted Wood La *UCK* TN22 .... 69 F6
Buxton Dr *BEXW* TN39 .... 195 G5
Buxton Rd *BRI* BN1 .... 6 A3
  EDN/EASTW BN20 .... 236 C3
Bydown *SEAF* BN25 .... 225 H7
The Byeways *SEAF* BN25 .... 225 G7

The Byeway *BEXW* TN39 .... 194 C6
  HAS TN34 .... 170 C7
Byfields Cft *BEXW* TN39 .... 194 E6
Byland Cl *LW/ROSE* BN22 .... 215 K8
Byng Rd *SBGH/RUST* TN4 .... 19 J6
Byron Gv *EGRIN* RH19 .... 22 A3
Byron St *HOVE* BN3 .... 203 F4
Byways *HAS* TN34 .... 170 A5
The Byway *BRI* BN1 .... 179 F6
Byworth Cl *BEXW* TN39 .... 194 B5
  ROTT BN2 .... 205 G5

C

Cabbage Stalk La *SBGH/RUST* TN4 .... 29 J1
Cabot Cl *LGNY* BN23 .... 231 H5
Caburn Cl *LW/ROSE* BN22 .... 216 B7 🔲
Caburn Crs *LEW* BN7 .... 2 A3
Caburn Rd *HOVE* BN3 .... 6 A3 🔲
Caburn Wy *HAIL* BN27 .... 189 F5
Cacklebury La *HAIL* BN27 .... 189 F5
Cackle St *RYE* TN31 .... 139 J1
  UCK TN22 .... 66 E2
Cadborough Cliff *RYE* TN31 .... 113 F7
Cade St *LW/ROSE* BN22 .... 230 A1
Cairngorm Cl *LGNY* BN23 .... 216 E8
Cairo Av *PEAHV* BN10 .... 221 K4
Cairo Av South *PEAHV* BN10 .... 221 K4
Caister's Cl *HOVE* BN3 .... 203 H3
Caldbec Hl *BAT* TN33 .... 136 D6
Caldicotts La *HAIL* BN27 .... 160 B8
Caledonian Rd *ROTT* BN2 .... 7 D2 🔲
Caley Rd *RTWE/PEM* TN2 .... 20 D3
Calgary Rd *BEXW* TN39 .... 195 G4
Callums Wk *BEX* TN40 .... 195 K6
Calverley Ct *RTWE/PEM* TN2 .... 20 C8 🔲
Calverley Pk *RTWE/PEM* TN2 .... 20 B8
Calverley Park Crs
  RTWE/PEM TN2 .... 20 B8 🔲
Calverley Park Gdns *RTW* TN1 .... 20 B8
Calverley Rd *EAST* BN21 .... 10 B5 🔲
  RTW TN1 .... 20 B7 🔲
  RTWE/PEM TN2 .... 20 B8
Calverley St *RTW* TN1 .... 20 B7
Calvert Cl *UCK* TN22 .... 95 G4
Calvert Rd *HAS* TN34 .... 5 D4 🔲
  UCK TN22 .... 95 G4
Camber Cl *BEX* TN40 .... 195 K5
Camber Dr *PEV* BN24 .... 218 C5
Camberlot Rd *HAIL* BN27 .... 187 K2
Camber Rd *RYE* TN31 .... 114 B7
Camber Wy *PEV* BN24 .... 218 C5
Cambrian Rd *SBGH/RUST* TN4 .... 20 C4
Cambridge Gdns *HAS* TN34 .... 4 C4
  RTWE/PEM TN2 .... 30 D1
Cambridge Gv *HOVE* BN3 .... 203 H4
Cambridge Rd *BEXW* TN39 .... 195 H5
  HAS TN34 .... 4 C4
  HOVE BN3 .... 203 J5
  LW/ROSE BN22 .... 11 D3
Cambridge St *RTWE/PEM* TN2 .... 20 C8 🔲
Cambridge Wy *UCK* TN22 .... 95 J2
Camden Av *RTWE/PEM* TN2 .... 21 J5
Camden Hl *RTWE/PEM* TN2 .... 20 B8 🔲
  RTWE/PEM TN2 .... 30 C1 🔲
Camden Pk *RTWE/PEM* TN2 .... 20 B8 🔲
  RTWE/PEM TN2 .... 30 D1 🔲
Camden Rd *EAST* BN21 .... 10 B5 🔲
  RTW TN1 .... 20 C7
Camden St *PTSD* BN41 .... 202 B5 🔲
Camelford St *ROTT* BN2 .... 7 D6 🔲
Cameron Cl *HAIL* BN27 .... 189 F3
Campbell Cl *UCK* TN22 .... 95 J2
Campbell Rd *BRI* BN1 .... 6 B2
  SBGH/RUST TN4 .... 20 A5 🔲
Camperdown St *BEXW* TN39 .... 195 F4
Canada Cl *PEAHV* BN10 .... 222 A2 🔲
Canada Wy *BEXW* TN39 .... 195 G4
Canadia Rd *BAT* TN33 .... 136 D3
Canfield Cl *ROTT* BN2 .... 7 F1
Canfield Rd *ROTT* BN2 .... 7 F1 🔲
Canning St *ROTT* BN2 .... 7 E5
Cannon Pl *BRI* BN1 .... 6 B5 🔲
  SBGH/RUST TN4 .... 20 A5 🔲
Cansiron La *EDEN* TN8 .... 24 E1
  FROW RH18 .... 24 B6
Canterbury Cl *LW/ROSE* BN22 .... 229 H1 🔲
Canterbury Dr *ROTT* BN2 .... 7 D3
Canterbury Ri *HAS* TN34 .... 4 C1
Cantercrow Hl *NEWHV* BN9 .... 224 A1
Cants Cl *BURH* RH15 .... 89 J8
Cants Ri *BURH* RH15 .... 89 J7
Canute Cl *LGNY* BN23 .... 231 G3 🔲
Canute Rd *RHAS* TN35 .... 171 G8
Capel Av *PEAHV* BN10 .... 222 B5
Capenors *BURH* RH15 .... 119 F2
Caple Gdns *STLEO* TN38 .... 197 J4
Carden Av *BRI* BN1 .... 178 A6
Carden Cl *BRI* BN1 .... 178 B5
Carden Crs *BRI* BN1 .... 178 B5
Carden Hl *BRI* BN1 .... 178 C6

Card Hl *FROW* RH18 .... 35 K2
Cardiff Rd *STLEO* TN38 .... 4 A5 🔲
Cardinals Cl *BEX* TN40 .... 196 A5
Carew Rd *EAST* BN21 .... 10 A3
Carey Down *PEAHV* BN10 .... 222 A2 🔲
Carfax Cl *BEXW* TN39 .... 195 G3
Carinus Gdns *STLEO* TN38 .... 169 H6 🔲
Carisbrooke Cl *LGNY* BN23 .... 216 C7
Carisbrooke Rd *ROTT* BN2 .... 7 F3
  STLEO TN38 .... 4 A5
  STLEO TN38 .... 197 J4
Carlisle Pde *HAS* TN34 .... 4 C5
Carlisle Rd *EAST* BN21 .... 10 C6 🔲
  EDN/EASTW BN20 .... 10 A6
  HOVE BN3 .... 202 E5
Carlton Cl *SEAF* BN25 .... 224 E7
Carlton Crs *RTWE/PEM* TN2 .... 20 C7 🔲
Carlton Hl *ROTT* BN2 .... 7 D5
Carlton Pl *ROTT* BN2 .... 7 D5 🔲
Carlton Rd *LW/ROSE* BN22 .... 11 E2
  RTWE/PEM TN2 .... 20 C7
  SEAF BN25 .... 224 E7
Carlton Ter *HOVE* BN3 .... 202 B3
Carlyle Av *ROTT* BN2 .... 7 F1
Carlyle St *ROTT* BN2 .... 7 E3
Carmel Cl *BEXW* TN39 .... 194 C8
Carol Cl *BRI* BN1 .... 178 A5
Caroline Cl *SEAF* BN25 .... 224 E6 🔲
Carpenter Dr *STLEO* TN38 .... 169 G7
Carpenters Cft *RING/NEW* BN8 .... 127 J6 🔲
Carpenters Wy *HAIL* BN27 .... 189 F5
Carville Av *SBGH/RUST* TN4 .... 19 K2
Castle Ditch La *LEW* BN7 .... 2 C4 🔲
Castledown Av *HAS* TN34 .... 5 E4 🔲
Castle Dr *PEV* BN24 .... 217 K7
Castlefields *HRTF* TN7 .... 25 K7
Castle Gdns *HAS* TN34 .... 5 D5 🔲
Castle Hl *MAYF* TN20 .... 54 E6
Castle Hill Pas *HAS* TN34 .... 5 D4 🔲
Castle Hill Rd *HAS* TN34 .... 5 E4
Castle Hurst *RBTBR* TN32 .... 79 H3
Castle Ri *UCK* TN22 .... 95 K7
Castleross Rd *PEV* BN24 .... 217 K7
  SBGH/RUST TN4 .... 19 K8
Castle St *BRI* BN1 .... 6 A5
  HAS TN34 .... 5 D5 🔲
  RTW TN1 .... 30 A1 🔲
  SBGH/RUST TN4 .... 19 K1
  WSEA TN36 .... 143 F4
Castle View Gdns *PEV* BN24 .... 217 F5
Castle Wk *WADH* TN5 .... 44 A7
Castle Wy *UCK* TN22 .... 95 K7 🔲
Catherine Pl *RTW* TN1 .... 20 B8 🔲
Catherine V *ROTT* BN2 .... 206 B3
Catsfield Cl *POLE* BN26 .... 216 A7
  STLEO TN38 .... 196 E1 🔲
Catsfield Rd *BAT* TN33 .... 135 H8
Cat St *HRTF* TN7 .... 37 F2
Catt's Hl *CROW* TN6 .... 55 H2
The Causeway *ROTT* BN2 .... 7 F4
  SEAF BN25 .... 232 A1
Cavalier Wy *EGRIN* RH19 .... 22 D4
Cavalry Crs *EDN/EASTW* BN20 .... 229 G6
Cavell Av *PEAHV* BN10 .... 222 A4
Cavell Av North *PEAHV* BN10 .... 222 B3
Cavendish Av *LW/ROSE* BN22 .... 11 D3
  STLEO TN38 .... 197 H4
Cavendish Cl *PEAHV* BN10 .... 222 A3
Cavendish Dr *RTWE/PEM* TN2 .... 30 B1
Cavendish Pl *BRI* BN1 .... 6 A5 🔲
  EAST BN21 .... 11 D4 🔲
  EAST BN21 .... 11 D5 🔲
Cavendish St *ROTT* BN2 .... 7 D5 🔲
Caveridge La *RING/NEW* BN8 .... 122 C3
Caves Rd *STLEO* TN38 .... 197 H5
Cedar Cl *BURH* RH15 .... 89 H5
  HAS TN34 .... 170 A6
  LW/ROSE BN22 .... 229 H1
Cedar Rdg *RTWE/PEM* TN2 .... 20 D5
Cedars Cl *UCK* TN22 .... 95 J3 🔲
Cedars Gdns *BRI* BN1 .... 177 J8
The Cedars *HAIL* BN27 .... 189 G2
  PEAHV BN10 .... 222 B2 🔲
  UCK TN22 .... 95 K3
Cedarwell Cl *NEWHV* BN9 .... 223 G1 🔲
Celandine Dr *STLEO* TN38 .... 197 H4
Central Av *EDN/EASTW* BN20 .... 229 G6
  PEAHV BN10 .... 221 K4
  POLE BN26 .... 215 G4
Centurion Ri *HAS* TN34 .... 170 D7
Centurion Rd *BRI* BN1 .... 6 B4
Ceylon Pl *EAST* BN21 .... 11 D4
Ceylon Wk *BEXW* TN39 .... 194 D8
Chadborn Cl *ROTT* BN2 .... 7 F6
Chaffinch Cl *BURH* RH15 .... 88 D7 🔲
Chaffinch Rd *LGNY* BN23 .... 230 D1 🔲
Chaffinch Wk *UCK* TN22 .... 95 K6
Chafford La *RRTW* TN3 .... 17 J6
Chailey Av *ROTT* BN2 .... 220 D2
Chailey Cl *HAS* TN34 .... 170 B6
  LGNY BN23 .... 231 F2 🔲
Chailey Crs *ROTT* BN2 .... 221 H2
Chailey La *RING/NEW* BN8 .... 93 F6
Chailey Rd *BRI* BN1 .... 179 F7

Chain La BAT TN33 .... **136** C6
Chalfont Dr HOVE BN3 .... **177** H8
Chalkers La HPPT/KEY BN6 .... **118** B3
Chalket La RTWE/PEM TN2 .... 21 J6
Chalk Farm Cl EDN/EASTW BN20 ... **229** C5
Chalkland Ri ROTT BN2 .... **206** B3
Chalky Rd PTSD BN41 .... **175** J8
Challoners RHWH RH17 .... 48 A7
Challoners Cl ROTT BN2 .... **220** C1
Challoners Ms ROTT BN2 .... **220** C1
Challow Cl HPPT/KEY BN6 .... **118** E7 ☑
Chalvington Cl BRI BN1 .... **179** F5
  SEAF BN25 .... **225** C5
Chalvington Dr SLVH TN37 .... **169** K5 ☑
Chalvington Rd EAST BN21 .... **229** H4 ☑
Chamberlaines La RING/NEW BN8.. **156** A5
Chamberlain Rd EAST BN21 .... **229** H7
Chambers Crs STLEO TN38 .... **169** G8
Chambers Rd STLEO TN38 .... **197** C1
Chancellors Pk HPPT/KEY BN6 .... **119** F7
Chanctonbury Dr HAS TN34 .... **170** B5
  SHOR BN43 .... **200** B2
Chanctonbury Rd BURH RH15 ..... **119** F2
  HOVE BN3 .... 6 A3 ☑
Chandler Rd BEXW TN39 .... **195** F6
Chandler's Md RING/NEW BN8 .... **153** K4
Chandos Rd RTW TN1 .... 20 C6 ☑
Channel Vw East BEX TN40 .... **195** H4
Channel View Rd LW/ROSE BN22 .. 11 E2
  PEV BN24 .... **218** A5
  ROTT BN2 .... **205** J3
Channel Vw West BEX TN40 .... **195** H8
Channel Wy RHAS TN35 .... **172** D8
Channers La RING/NEW BN8 .... **186** A3
Chant La CROW TN6 .... 55 F2
Chantiers La EGRIN RH19 .... 22 A1
Chantlers Md EDEN TN8 .... 15 G6
Chantry Av BEX TN40 .... **195** H6
Chantry La BEX TN40 .... **195** H6
Chapel Barn Cl HAIL BN27 .... **189** H4 ☑
Chapel Cl BURH RH15 .... 89 F6
  SEAF BN25 .... **225** F7
Chapel Fld RYE TN31 .... 81 J4
Chapel Gn CROW TN6 .... 53 H1 ☑
Chapel Hl BAT TN33 .... **138** A3
  BAT TN33 .... **168** A7
  LEW BN7 .... 3 E4
Chapel La EGRIN RH19 .... 23 H5
  FROW RH18 .... 35 K2
  LEW BN7 .... **121** J8
  RHAS TN35 .... **171** K3
  RHWH RH17 .... 48 A4
  UCK TN22 .... 97 K4
Chapel Ms HOVE BN3 .... **203** J6 ☑
Chapel Park Rd SLVH TN37 .... 4 A4
Chapel Pl PTSD BN41 .... **202** A4
Chapel Rd LEW BN7 .... **121** C4
  PTSD BN41 .... **201** K4 ☑
Chapel St NEWHV BN9 .... 9 D3 ☑
  ROTT BN2 .... 7 D5
Chapel Ter ROTT BN2 .... 7 F6 ☑
Chapman's La EGRIN RH19 .... 22 B2 ☑
Chapmans Town Rd HTHF TN21 ... **131** H2
Chapman Wy RTWE/PEM TN2 .... 20 C3
Charity Farm Wy CROW TN6 ...... 39 J8
Charles Av BURH RH15 .... **118** C1
Charles Cl HOVE BN3 .... **177** F8
  SEAF BN25 .... **224** E6 ☑
Charles Rd STLEO TN38 .... 4 A4
Charles Rd West STLEO TN38 ..... **197** J3 ☑
Charles St ROTT BN2 .... 6 C6 ☑
  SBCH/RUST TN4 .... 20 A3
Charleston Rd EAST BN21 .... **229** H7
Charlotte St ROTT BN2 .... 7 D6 ☑
Charlston Av NEWHV BN9 .... 8 A5
The Charltons BRI BN1 .... **178** E5 ☑
Charlton's Wy SBCH/RUST TN4 ... 29 J2 ☑
Charlwood Gdns BURH RH15 ...... 89 J6
Charlwood Rd BURH RH15 .... 89 J6
Charlwoods Business Centre
  EGRIN RH19 .... 22 B1 ☑
Charlwoods Pl EGRIN RH19 .... 12 C8 ☑
Charlwoods Rd EGRIN RH19 ...... 22 B1
Chartfield HOVE BN3 .... **203** F1
Chartres BEX TN40 .... **195** J5
Chartres Cl BEX TN40 .... **195** J5
Chartwell Cl SEAF BN25 .... **225** F5 ☑
Chatfield Crs LW/ROSE BN22 ...... **229** H2
Chatham Pl BRI BN1 .... 6 B3
  SEAF BN25 .... **232** A1 ☑
Chatham Rd SLVH TN37 .... **197** J1 ☑
Chatsfield Cl STLEO TN38 .... **169** F7
Chatsworth Av PEAHV BN10 ...... **221** K2 ☑
Chatsworth Cl PEAHV BN10 .... **221** K3
Chatsworth Gdns
  EDN/EASTW BN20 .... **237** F3 ☑
Chatsworth Pk PEAHV BN10 ...... **222** A2 ☑
Chatsworth Rd BRI BN1 .... 6 A2
Chaucer Av EGRIN RH19 .... 22 A3
Chawbrook Rd LW/ROSE BN22 ... 11 D3 ☑
Cheal Cl SHOR BN43 .... **200** D5
Cheapside BRI BN1 .... 6 C4
Cheeleys RHWH RH17 .... 48 A6
Chelsea Cl BEX TN40 .... **195** J7
Chelston Av HOVE BN3 .... **202** C4

Cheltenham Pl BRI BN1 .... 6 C4 ☑
Chelwood Cl BRI BN1 .... **178** D5
Chelwood Gate Rd UCK TN22 .... 49 K5
Chelworth Rd LW/ROSE BN22 .... **229** J1
Chene Rd PEAHV BN10 .... **222** E5
Chenies Cl RTWE/PEM TN2 .... 30 A3
Chepbourne Rd BEX TN40 .... **195** C2
Chequer Gra FROW RH18 .... 35 J2
Chequer Rd EGRIN RH19 .... 22 D2 ☑
Chequers Cl CROW TN6 .... 53 J1 ☑
Chequers Wy CROW TN6 .... 53 J1
Cherington Cl HPPT/KEY BN6 .... **118** B6 ☑
Cherry Cl BURH RH15 .... 88 E8
Cherry Garden Rd
  EDN/EASTW BN20 .... **229** C8
Cherry Gdns BRI HTHF TN21 ...... **100** B6
Cherry Side HAIL BN27 .... **189** F4
Cherry Tree Cl SLVH TN37 .... 4 A4
Cherry Tree Gdns BEX TN40 ...... **196** A5
Cherry Tree Rd RTWE/PEM TN2 .. 29 J2
Cherwell Cl POLE BN26 .... **216** A6
Cherwell Rd HTHF TN21 .... **100** A3
Chesham Pl ROTT BN2 .... 7 F6 ☑
Chesham Rd ROTT BN2 .... 7 F6
Chesham St ROTT BN2 .... 7 F6
Chesnut Cl HAIL BN27 .... **189** F2 ☑
Chester Av SBGH/RUST TN4 ...... 20 B3
Chesterfield Gdns
  EDN/EASTW BN20 .... **236** E3
Chesterfield Rd EDN/EASTW BN20.. **236** E3
Chester Ter BRI BN1 .... 6 C1
Chesterton Av SEAF BN25 .... **225** J8
Chesterton Cl EGRIN RH19 .... 22 D4
Chesterton Dr SEAF BN25 .... **225** J8
Chestnut Av SBGH/RUST TN4 .... 20 B3
Chestnut Cl BURH RH15 .... 89 H6
  EGRIN RH19 .... 22 E2
  HAIL BN27 .... **163** F5
  RYE TN31 .... **109** K6
  SBGH/RUST TN4 .... 20 B3
Chestnut Dr POLE BN26 .... **215** F5
The Chestnuts HAWK TN18 .... 62 E3
Chestnut Wk BEXW TN39 .... **194** B6
  EGRIN RH19 .... 12 A4
Chestnut Wy NEWHV BN9 .... 8 B3
Cheviot Cl LGNY BN23 .... **216** D8
The Cheviots HAS TN34 .... **170** E7
Chichester Cl BEXW TN39 .... **195** C5
  HOVE BN3 .... **176** D7
  LW/ROSE BN22 .... **229** C1
  PEAHV BN10 .... **222** E4
Chichester Dr East ROTT BN2 ..... **221** F3
Chichester Dr West ROTT BN2 .... **220** E2
Chichester Pl ROTT BN2 .... 7 F6 ☑
Chichester Rd SEAF BN25 .... **225** F8
Chichester Ter ROTT BN2 .... 7 F6
Chichester Wy BURH RH15 .... 89 J6
Chick Hl RHAS TN35 .... **173** C3
Chicks La CRBK TN17 .... 46 E1
Chiddingley Cl ROTT BN2 .... **205** C6
Chieveley Dr RTWE/PEM TN2 .... 30 C2
Chilcomb BURH RH15 .... **119** J2
Chilham Cl LGNY BN23 .... **230** E1 ☑
Chillies La UCK TN22 .... 68 C2
Chilsham La HAIL BN27 .... **162** E4
Chilston Cl SBGH/RUST TN4 ...... 20 A6
Chilston Rd SBGH/RUST TN4 ..... 20 A6
Chiltern Cl LGNY BN23 .... **216** E8
  SHOR BN43 .... **201** F3
Chiltern Dr HAS TN34 .... 5 F1
Chiltington Cl BURH RH15 .... 89 F6 ☑
  ROTT BN2 .... **221** F1
Chiltington La LEW BN7 .... **122** A8
Chiltington Wy ROTT BN2 .... **221** F1
Chiswick Pl EAST BN21 .... 10 C5 ☑
Chitcombe Rd RYE TN31 .... **109** C6
Chorley Av ROTT BN2 .... **220** E1
Chown's Hl HAS TN34 .... **170** D5
Chrisdory Rd PTSD BN41 .... **175** H8
Christie Av RING/NEW BN8 .... **155** J5
Christie Rd LEW BN7 .... 2 A4
Christies EGRIN RH19 .... 22 B8 ☑
Christopher Rd EGRIN RH19 ...... 22 C2
Church Av PEV BN24 .... **217** H5
Church Cl BRI BN1 .... **178** A6
  BURH RH15 .... 89 C8
  EDN/EASTW BN20 .... **215** F7
Churchdale Pl LW/ROSE BN22 ... 11 D1 ☑
Churchdale Rd LW/ROSE BN22 ... 11 D1
Church Farm Cl BUR/ETCH TN19 .. 77 C2
Churchfields UCK TN22 .... 50 C6
Church Gn SHOR BN43 .... **201** F4
Church Hl BRI BN1 .... **177** K5
  BUR/ETCH TN19 .... 77 F1
  NEWHV BN9 .... 8 C3
  POY/PYE BN45 .... **149** H5
  RING/NEW BN8 .... **155** J5
Church Hill Av BEXW TN39 .... **194** B7
Church House La STHW BN42 ..... **201** H2
Churchill Av RHAS TN35 .... **171** C6
Churchill Cl EDN/EASTW BN20 ... **229** J8
Churchill Rd HTHF TN21 .... **100** D5
  LEW BN7 .... 2 B2
  SEAF BN25 .... **224** E6
Churchill Wy BURH RH15 .... **119** J1

Church in the Wood La
  STLEO TN38 .... **169** C8
Churchland La BAT TN33 .... **108** A8
Church La BAT TN33 .... **166** A6
  BAT TN33 .... **166** D3
  BAT TN33 .... **193** F4
  BUR/ETCH TN19 .... 77 C2
  EAST BN21 .... **229** J8 ☑
  EGRIN RH19 .... 22 D2
  HAIL BN27 .... **161** F6
  HPPT/KEY BN6 .... **119** J8
  HWH RH16 .... 90 B5
  LEW BN7 .... 2 C3
  LEW BN7 .... **181** C6
  PEV BN24 .... **217** J5
  POLE BN26 .... **228** B4
  POY/PYE BN45 .... **148** C4
  POY/PYE BN45 .... **149** H5
  RBTBR TN32 .... 78 C6
  RHAS TN35 .... **139** C8
  RHAS TN35 .... **172** A2
  RHWH RH17 .... 48 A5
  RHWH RH17 .... 48 E8
  RING/NEW BN8 .... **157** K5
  RING/NEW BN8 .... **186** B3
  RRTW TN3 .... 30 B7
  RYE TN31 .... 82 A5
  RYE TN31 .... 82 C7
  RYE TN31 .... 85 H7
  RYE TN31 .... **112** B3
  SEAF BN25 .... **232** A1 ☑
  STHW BN42 .... **201** C4
  UCK TN22 .... 68 E6
Church Marks La RING/NEW BN8.. **127** H6
Church Md HPPT/KEY BN6 .... **119** C8
Church Pl ROTT BN2 .... **205** F7
Church Rd BAT TN33 .... **166** E3
  BURH RH15 .... 89 C8
  BURH RH15 .... **119** C1
  CRBK TN17 .... 46 D1
  CROW TN6 .... 53 C1
  HAIL BN27 .... **191** H2
  HOVE BN3 .... **203** C5
  POLE BN26 .... **215** F5
  PTSD BN41 .... **202** A4
  RBTBR TN32 .... **106** B6
  RING/NEW BN8 .... 93 J7
  RING/NEW BN8 .... **154** D1
  RRTW TN3 .... 33 K5
  SBGH/RUST TN4 .... 19 K8
  SBGH/RUST TN4 .... 19 K1
  SLVH TN37 .... 4 A4
  UCK TN22 .... 68 D8
Churchsettle La WADH TN5 .... 58 E4
Church Sq RYE TN31 .... **113** J6
Church St BEX TN40 .... **195** J6
  BRI BN1 .... 6 B5
  CROW TN6 .... 54 E3
  EDEN TN8 .... 15 H6
  EDN/EASTW BN20 .... **229** C2
  EDN/EASTW BN20 .... **229** J8
  HRTF TN7 .... 25 K7
  HTHF TN21 .... **100** D6
  LW/ROSE BN22 .... **229** H1
  PTSD BN41 .... **202** A4 ☑
  RHAS TN35 .... **171** F8
  SEAF BN25 .... **225** F8
  SHOR BN43 .... **200** C4
  UCK TN22 .... 95 J3
Church Vale Rd BEX TN40 .... **195** H6
Church Wood Dr STLEO TN38 ..... **169** F7
Church Wood Wy STLEO TN38 .... **197** C1
Chyngton Av SEAF BN25 .... **225** J7
Chyngton Cl LGNY BN23 .... **216** B7 ☑
Chyngton Gdns SEAF BN25 .... **225** J7
Chyngton La SEAF BN25 .... **225** K8
Chyngton La North SEAF BN25 ... **225** K8
Chyngton Pl SEAF BN25 .... **232** D1
Chyngton Rd SEAF BN25 .... **232** C1
Chyngton Wy SEAF BN25 .... **232** E1
Cinderford La HAIL BN27 .... **161** K3
Cinder Hl RING/NEW BN8 .... 92 D8
  RING/NEW BN8 .... 93 F6
Cinquefoil PEAHV BN10 .... **222** B3
Cinque Ports St RYE TN31 .... **113** J6 ☑
Cinque Ports Wy SEAF BN25 ..... **225** K7
  STLEO TN38 .... **197** F5
Circus St ROTT BN2 .... 6 C5
The Circus LGNY BN23 .... **230** E3
Cissbury Av PEAHV BN10 .... **222** D5
Cissbury Crs ROTT BN2 .... **221** H2
Cissbury Rd BURH RH15 .... 88 E7
  HOVE BN3 .... 6 A3
Civic Ap UCK TN22 .... 95 J4
Civic Wy BURH RH15 .... 89 C8
Clackhams La CROW TN6 .... 54 B4
Clanricarde Gdns RTW TN1 .... 20 A8 ☑
Clanricarde Rd SBGH/RUST TN4 .. 19 K8 ☑
Clapham La POLE BN26 .... **226** D3
Claphatch La WADH TN5 .... 45 J6
The Clappers RBTBR TN32 .... 78 B7
Claremont HAS TN34 .... 4 C5 ☑
Claremont Gdns RTW TN1 .... 30 B1
Claremont Ri UCK TN22 .... 95 J2
Claremont Rd BEXW TN39 .... **195** C4

NEWHV BN9 .... 9 F1
RTW TN1 .... 30 B1
SEAF BN25 .... 224 E8
Clarence Dr EGRIN RH19 .... 22 D4
Clarence Rd LW/ROSE BN22 ..... 11 D2 🔟
RTW TN1 .... 20 A8 🔟
Clarence Sq BN1 .... 6 B5
Clarendon Cl SLVH TN37 .... 169 J7 🔟
Clarendon Gdns RTWE/PEM TN2 .. 30 A2 🔟
Clarendon Pl PTSD BN41 .... 202 B5 🔟
Clarendon Rd HOVE BN3 .... 203 G4
SHOR BN43 .... 201 F3
Clarendon Ter ROTT BN2 .... 7 F6 🔟
Clarendon Vls HOVE BN3 .... 203 F4
Clarendon Wy RTWE/PEM TN2.... 29 K2
Clare Rd LEW BN7 .... 2 A3
Claridge Gdns LING RH7 .... 12 E1
Claridges Md LING RH7 .... 12 E1
Clarke Av HOVE BN3 .... 176 E8
Claverham Cl BAT TN33 .... 136 B7
Claverham Wy BAT TN33 .... 136 B7
Claxton Cl EAST BN21 .... 229 J6
Claxton Rd BEX TN40 .... 196 B6
Clayfields PEAHV BN10 .... 222 A4 🔟
Clayford LING RH7 .... 12 E1
Clay Hill Rd RRTW TN3 .... 33 F6
Clays Cl EGRIN RH19 .... 22 C3 🔟
Clayton Av HPPT/KEY BN6 .... 118 E8
Clayton Dr BURH RH15 .... 119 F2
Clayton Hl POY/PYE BN45 .... 149 J4
Clayton Mill Rd PEV BN24 .... 216 C6
Clayton Rd HPPT/KEY BN6 .... 150 D1
ROTT BN2 .... 7 F3
Clayton's La RRTW TN3 .... 27 C1
Clayton Wy HOVE BN3 .... 176 E8
Clearwaters La BURH RH15 .... 89 K3
Cleeve Av RTWE/PEM TN2........ 30 D1
Cleevelands LW/ROSE BN22 ..... 229 G1 🔟
Clegg St HAS TN34 .... 5 D4
Clement Hill Rd HAS TN34 .... 5 F1 🔟
Clementine Av SEAF BN25 .... 224 E6
Clement La POLE BN26 .... 215 F6
Clerks Acre HPPT/KEY BN6 ...... 119 G7 🔟
Clermont Rd BRI BN1 .... 203 J1
Clermont Ter BRI BN1 .... 203 K1
Cleve Cl UCK TN22 .... 96 D6
Clevedon Rd BEXW TN39 .... 194 E5
Cleveland RTWE/PEM TN2 .... 20 D6
Cleveland Cl LGNY BN23 .... 216 D3 🔟
Cleveland Gdns BURH RH15 ...... 119 H1
Cleveland Rd HOVE BN3 .... 6 C1
Cleve Ter LEW BN7 .... 2 B5 🔟
Cliff Ap ROTT BN2 .... 205 C2
Cliff Av PEAHV BN10 .... 222 D6
Cliff Cl SEAF BN25 .... 232 B2
Cliffe High St LEW BN7 .... 3 D4
Cliff End La RHAS TN35 .... 173 G4
Cliff Gdns PEAHV BN10 .... 221 J3
SEAF BN25 .... 232 B2
Clifford Av EAST BN21 .... 229 H5
Clifford Rd BEX TN40 .... 195 H7
Cliff Park Cl PEAHV BN10 .... 222 E4
Cliff Rd EDN/EASTW BN20 .... 236 E4
ROTT BN2 .... 205 C8
SEAF BN25 .... 232 B2
The Cliff ROTT BN2 .... 205 C2
Cliff Wy RHAS TN35 .... 172 E6
Clifton Cl LW/ROSE BN22 .... 229 J3
Clifton Hl BRI BN1 .... 6 A4
Clifton Pl BRI BN1 .... 6 A4
RTW TN1 .... 30 B3 🔟
Clifton Ri BEX TN40 .... 196 A6
Clifton Rd BRI BN1 .... 6 B4 🔟
BURH RH15 .... 88 D6
NEWHV BN9 .... 9 D3
RHAS TN35 .... 171 F8
RTWE/PEM TN2 .... 20 C4
Clifton St BRI BN1 .... 6 B4
Clifton Ter BRI BN1 .... 6 B4
Cliftonville Rd STLEO TN38 ...... 196 E5
Clifton Wy PEAHV BN10 .... 221 K3
Clinch Green Av BEXW TN39 .... 194 E4
Clinton Cls STLEO TN38 .... 197 J2
Clinton Hl LING RH7 .... 12 E2
Clinton La SEAF BN25 .... 225 F8
Clinton Pl SEAF BN25 .... 225 F8
Clinton Wy RHAS TN35 .... 172 E6
Clive Av RHAS TN35 .... 199 F1
Clockhouse RTWE/PEM TN2 ...... 21 F5
Clock House La UCK TN22 .... 50 C7
Cloisters NEWHV BN9 .... 8 C3 🔟
The Cloisters BAT TN33 .... 136 D5 🔟
LW/ROSE BN22 .... 229 H1
SLVH TN37 .... 4 B5 🔟
Close Eight LGNY BN23 .... 217 E8 🔟
Close Eighteen LGNY BN23 ...... 231 F1 🔟
Close Eleven LGNY BN23 .... 217 F8 🔟
Close Fifteen LGNY BN23 .... 231 F1 🔟
Close Five LGNY BN23 .... 217 F8 🔟
Close Four LGNY BN23 .... 231 F1 🔟
Close Fourteen LGNY BN23 ...... 217 F8 🔟
Close Nine LGNY BN23 .... 231 F1
Close One LGNY BN23 .... 230 E1 🔟
Close Seven LGNY BN23 .... 217 E8 🔟

Close Seventeen LGNY BN23 .... 231 F1
Close Six LGNY BN23 .... 217 F8 🔟
Close Sixteen LGNY BN23 .... 231 F1
Close Ten LGNY BN23 .... 231 F1 🔟
The Close BRI BN1................ 177 J6
BURH RH15 .... 89 J7
CROW TN6 .... 39 G8
EDN/EASTW BN20 .... 229 G3
EDN/EASTW BN20 .... 234 E2 🔟
EGRIN RH19 .... 22 B3
HPPT/KEY BN6 .... 119 F7
NEWHV BN9 .... 224 A1
RHAS TN35 .... 172 B7
RRTW TN3 .... 28 A5 🔟
RYE TN31 .... 113 G5
SEAF BN25 .... 232 B1
SHOR BN43 .... 200 C3
UCK TN22 .... 97 K5
Close Three LGNY BN23 .... 230 E1 🔟
Close Twelve LGNY BN23 .... 231 F1 🔟
Close Twenty LGNY BN23 .... 231 F1
Close Twentyfive LGNY BN23 ... 230 E1 🔟
Close Twentyfour LGNY BN23 ... 231 F1 🔟
Close Two LGNY BN23 .... 230 E1 🔟
Cloudesley Rd SLVH TN37 .... 4 A4
Cloverlea HAS TN34 .... 170 B6 🔟
Clovers End BRI BN1 .... 178 C4
Clover Wy PTSD BN41 .... 202 A1
Cluny St LEW BN7 .... 2 C5
Clyde Rd BRI BN1 .... 6 C2
STLEO TN38 .... 4 A5
Coach & Horses La RHWH RH17 .. 49 G5
Coach La RHWH RH17 .... 49 G5
Coastguard La RHAS TN35......... 172 A7
Coastguard Sq RYE TN31 .... 114 C8
Coast Rd PEV BN24................... 218 B6
Cobald Rd PEV BN24 .... 218 B6
Cobbett's Ride RTWE/PEM TN2 .. 29 K2 🔟
Cobbold Av EAST BN21 .... 229 H5
Cobden Rd ROTT BN2................... 7 E3
Cobdown La UCK TN22 .... 67 J7
Cobhams RRTW TN3 .... 18 E3
Cobton Dr HOVE BN3 .... 177 F8
Cochrane Cl EAST BN21 .... 231 F4 🔟
Cockcrow Wd HAS TN34 .... 170 A6
Cockmount La WADH TN5 .... 44 A5
Cockshut Rd LEW BN7................. 2 C6
Cogger's La HTHF TN21 .... 129 K8
Coggins Mill Rd MAYF TN20 ...... 56 D5
Coghurst Rd RHAS TN35 .... 171 F7
Colbourne Av HOVE BN3 .... 188 A1
Colbourne Rd HOVE BN3 .... 6 A3
Colchester V FROW RH18........... 35 J1
Colchins BURH RH15 .... 119 F2 🔟
Coldean La BRI BN1 .... 178 D3
Coldharbour Cl CROW TN6 .... 53 J2 🔟
Coldharbour La RING/NEW BN8 .. 92 E4
RYE TN31 .... 85 F7
Coldharbour Rd HAIL BN27 .... 188 A1
RTON TN1 .... 17 F3
Coldthorn La HAIL BN27 .... 189 F8
Coldwaltham La BURH RH15 ..... 119 K2
Colebrooke Rd BEXW TN39 ...... 195 F8
Colebrook Rd BRI BN1 .... 177 J7
SBGH/RUST TN4 .... 20 A1
STHW BN42 .... 201 J4
Coleman Av HOVE BN3............. 202 D4
Colemans Hatch Rd FROW RH18 .. 36 B6
Coleman St ROTT BN2 .... 7 E2
Coleridge St HOVE BN3 .... 203 F3
Colgate Cl ROTT BN2 .... 205 G5
College Cl EGRIN RH19 .... 22 D2 🔟
PTSD BN41 .... 175 J8
College Dr RTWE/PEM TN2 .... 20 D7
College Gdns ROTT BN2............. 7 E6
College Gn EAST BN21 .... 10 A3
College La EGRIN RH19 .... 22 D2
HPPT/KEY BN6 .... 118 C6
College Pl HPPT/KEY BN6 .... 118 C5
ROTT BN2 .... 7 E6
College Rd BEX TN40 .... 195 K7
EAST BN21 .... 10 B5 🔟
ROTT BN2 .... 7 E6
SEAF BN25 .... 232 A1 🔟
College St ROTT BN2 .... 7 E6
College Ter ROTT BN2 .... 7 E5
Collier Cl LW/ROSE BN22 .... 230 C4 🔟
Collier Rd HAS TN34 .... 5 E4
PEV BN24 .... 218 A7
Collingford La RHWH RH17........ 49 F7
Collington Av BEXW TN39 .... 194 E8
Collington Cl EDN/EASTW BN20 .. 10 A6 🔟
Collington Gv BEXW TN39 .... 194 D7
Collington La East BEXW TN39 .. 194 D7
Collington La West BEXW TN39 .. 194 C8
Collington Park Crs BEXW TN39 .. 194 E7
Collington Ri BEXW TN39.......... 194 D7
Collingwood Av HTHF TN21 ...... 100 A4
Collingwood Cl EGRIN RH19 ...... 22 D4 🔟
LGNY BN23 .... 231 F5
PEAHV BN10 .... 222 D2
Collingwood Ct SHOR BN43 ...... 200 C5 🔟
Collingwood Ri HTHF TN21 ...... 100 A4
Collinstone Rd STLEO TN38 ...... 197 H4
Collinswood Dr STLEO TN38 ..... 197 H4

Colmer Ct BURH RH15 .... 88 E8
Colmer Pl BURH RH15 .... 88 E8 🔟
Colonade Rd LW/ROSE BN22 ..... 11 D4 🔟
Colonel's Wy SBGH/RUST TN4.... 20 A1
Coltstocks Rd
EDN/EASTW BN20 .... 236 D3 🔟
Columbus Dr LGNY BN23 .... 231 G5
Colvill Av SHOR BN43 .... 200 A3
Colwell La RHWH RH17............. 90 B2
Colwell Rd HWH RH16 .... 90 B1
Colwood Crs EDN/EASTW BN20 .. 229 G5
Combe End CROW TN6................ 53 H3
Combe La BAT TN33 .... 165 J5
EDN/EASTW BN20 .... 236 D4
Combe Ri EDN/EASTW BN20 .... 229 F1
Combermere Rd STLEO TN38 .... 197 J2
The Combe EDN/EASTW BN20 .. 229 F4
Commanders Wk RHAS TN35 .... 172 D7
Command Rd EDN/EASTW BN20 .. 229 G6
Commercial Rd BURH RH15 ...... 89 F8 🔟
EAST BN21 .... 10 C4
RTW TN1 .... 20 B6
Common La HPPT/KEY BN6 ..... 119 K6
POLE BN26 .... 212 D2
Common Vw SBGH/RUST TN4 ... 19 G8
Common Wood Ri CROW TN6..... 39 H7
Compasses La RBTBR TN32 ..... 107 J5
Comphurst La HAIL BN27 .... 163 J7
Compton Av BRI BN1 .... 6 B4
Compton Cl BEX TN40 .... 195 K6 🔟
Compton Dr EDN/EASTW BN20 .. 236 C1
Compton Place Rd
EDN/EASTW BN20 .... 229 J8
Compton Rd BRI BN1 .... 203 J2
Compton St EDN/EASTW BN20 .. 10 C6
Compton Ter HAIL BN27 .... 189 H5 🔟
The Compts PEAHV BN10 .... 222 A2 🔟
Concord Ct RTWE/PEM TN2 ...... 20 C7 🔟
Concorde Cl BEXW TN39 .... 194 E5
Condor Wy BURH RH15 .... 88 E8
Conduit Hl RYE TN31 .... 113 J5 🔟
Coneyburrow Gdns STLEO TN38 .. 169 F7 🔟
Coneyburrow La BEXW TN39 .... 193 J7
Coneyburrow Rd RTWE/PEM TN2 .. 20 E6
Coney Furlong PEAHV BN10 ..... 222 C2
Conghurst La HAWK TN18 .... 63 G6
Conifer Cl HAS TN34 .... 5 D1
The Conifers EAST BN21 .... 10 B3
Coniston Av SBGH/RUST TN4 .... 19 J7
Coniston Rd LGNY BN23 .... 216 D7 🔟
Connaught Av SHOR BN43........ 200 B3
Connaught Rd EAST BN21 .... 10 C5
HOVE BN3 .... 203 F5
SEAF BN25 .... 224 D8
Connaught Ter HOVE BN3 .... 203 G4
Connaught Wy SBGH/RUST TN4 .. 19 K6
Connell Dr ROTT BN2 .... 206 B4
Conqueror Rd STLEO TN38 .... 197 G4
Consort Wy BURH RH15............ 118 E1
Constable Rd LGNY BN23......... 230 E2
Constable Wy BEX TN40 .... 195 J5
Constitutional Hill Rd
SBGH/RUST TN4 .... 19 J2
Conway Pl HOVE BN3 .... 203 G3
Conway St HOVE BN3............... 203 G3
Cooden Cl BEXW TN39 .... 194 B8
Cook Av LGNY BN23 .... 231 F5 🔟
Cookham Dene BEX TN40 .... 195 H7 🔟
Cooksbridge Rd ROTT BN2 .... 205 F5
Cookstown Cl BAT TN33 .... 165 J5
Coolham Dr ROTT BN2 .... 205 F5
Coombe Cl HAIL BN27 .... 163 J6
Coombe Hill Rd EGRIN RH19 ..... 22 A5
Coombe La WADH TN5 .... 57 J4
Coombe Rd EDN/EASTW BN20 .. 229 H7
LEW BN7 .... 3 D3 🔟
ROTT BN2 .... 7 F1
Coombe Shaw BAT TN33 .... 165 K5
Coombe V ROTT BN2 .... 207 G8
Coombs Cl RYE TN31 .... 83 G6
Cooper Dr BEXW TN39 .... 195 F3
Cooper Ri STLEO TN58 .... 169 H6 🔟
Cooper Rd RYE TN31 .... 113 G6
Coopers Cl BURH RH15 .... 89 H6
Coopers Hl EDN/EASTW BN20 .. 229 G1
Coopers La CROW TN6 .... 39 F7
RRTW TN3 .... 18 A5
Coopers Wy HAIL BN27 .... 189 F5
Coopers Wd CROW TN6 .... 39 F7
Copestake Dr BURH RH15 .... 89 K8
Coplands Ri RYE TN31 .... 81 K4
Coppards Cl RHWH RH17 .... 90 E7 🔟
Coppards La RYE TN31 .... 82 A3
Copper Beeches SLVH TN37 ..... 169 K7 🔟
Coppice Av EDN/EASTW BN20 .. 215 F7
Coppice Cl EDN/EASTW BN20 .. 215 F7
The Coppice BAT TN33 .... 137 G8
HAS TN34 .... 5 D1
RTWE/PEM TN2 .... 21 K4
Coppice Vw HTHF TN21 .... 100 B5 🔟
Copse Cl EGRIN RH19 .... 12 D8
STLEO TN38 .... 168 E8
Copse Hl BRI BN1 .... 177 J6
Copse Rd BEXW TN39 .... 194 D7

Copthall Av HAWK TN18 .... **63** F2
Copwood Av UCK TN22 .... **95** H4
Copyhold Rd EGRIN RH19 .... **22** B3
Corbyn Crs SHOR BN43 .... **200** D4
Cordons LEW BN7 .... **181** G6
Cormorant CI LGNY BN23 .... **230** D1
Cornelius Av NEWHV BN9 .... **8** A5
Cornfield CI BEXW BN25 .... **225** C8 ◫
Cornfield La EAST BN21 .... **10** C5
Cornfield Rd EAST BN21 .... **10** C4
  SEAF BN25 .... **225** C8
Cornfield Ter EAST BN21 .... **10** C5 ◫
  SLVH TN37 .... **4** A3
Cornford CI BURH RH15 .... **88** E6
  CROW TN6 .... **53** J2
  PTSD BN41 .... **202** A1 ◫
  RTWE/PEM TN2 .... **21** H5 ◫
Cornford La RTWE/PEM TN2 .... **20** E7
Cornford Pk RTWE/PEM TN2 .... **21** J5
Cornish CI LGNY BN23 .... **216** C7
Cornmill Gdns POLE BN26 .... **214** D7
Cornwall Av PEAHV BN10 .... **222** D5
Cornwall Gdns BRI BN1 .... **177** K8
  EGRIN RH19 .... **22** D3 ◫
Cornwallis CI LGNY BN23 .... **231** C4 ◫
Cornwallis Gdns HAS TN34 .... **4** C4
Cornwallis St HAS TN34 .... **5** D4 ◫
Cornwallis Ter HAS TN34 .... **4** C4 ◫
Cornwall Rd BEXW TN39 .... **195** G8
Coronation Cottages RBTBR TN32 .... **78** C6
Coronation Gdns BAT TN33 .... **137** F6
  BUR/ETCH TN19 .... **61** K8
Coronation Rd EGRIN RH19 .... **22** C4
Coronation St ROTT BN2 .... **7** E3 ◫
Corseley Rd RRTW TN3 .... **27** J8
Corsica CI SEAF BN25 .... **232** B2
Corsica Rd SEAF BN25 .... **232** B2
Cotchford HI HRTF TN7 .... **37** K2
Cotchford La HRTF TN7 .... **37** H2
Cotswold CI HAS TN34 .... **170** E2
  LGNY BN23 .... **D1**
The Cotswolds STHW BN42 .... **201** H4 ◫
Cottage Bush CI PTSD BN41 .... **202** E1 ◫
Cottage CI NEWHV BN9 .... **9** D1 ◫
Cottage La BAT TN33 .... **138** A4
  PEV BN24 .... **215** K2
Coulstock Rd HPPT/KEY BN6 .... **88** C7
County Oak Av BRI BN1 .... **178** C5
The Course LEW BN7 .... **2** B5
Court CI BRI BN1 .... **177** K4
  EGRIN RH19 .... **22** D2
Court Crs EGRIN RH19 .... **22** E2
Court Farm CI NEWHV BN9 .... **209** H4
Court Farm Rd HOVE BN3 .... **202** E1
  NEWHV BN9 .... **8** C5
  ROTT BN2 .... **206** B8
Courthope Av WADH TN5 .... **44** B7
Courthope Dr BEXW TN39 .... **194** D6
Courthouse St HAS TN34 .... **5** F4 ◫
Courtland Rd PTSD BN41 .... **215** F6
Courtlands UCK TN22 .... **66** D1
Courtlands PI CROW TN6 .... **53** G2
Courtlands Rd LW/ROSE BN22 .... **10** C2
Court Meadow CROW TN6 .... **55** F3
Court Ord Rd ROTT BN2 .... **206** B8
Court Rd LEW BN7 .... **3** D5 ◫
  LW/ROSE BN22 .... **230** A1
  SBGH/RUST TN4 .... **19** J7
The Courtyard EGRIN RH19 .... **23** F2
Cousley Wood Rd WADH TN5 .... **44** C5
Coventry CI STLEO TN38 .... **169** H8
Coventry St BRI BN1 .... **6** C3
Coverdale Av BEXW TN39 .... **194** B8
The Covers SEAF BN25 .... **232** B1
Cowden CI HAWK TN18 .... **62** E3
Cowden Hall La HTHF TN21 .... **130** C6
Cowden La HAWK TN18 .... **62** E4
Cowden Ms EDEN TN8 .... **15** G6
Cowden Rd ROTT BN2 .... **221** G3
Cowdens CI HOVE BN3 .... **176** C7
Cowdray CI BEXW TN39 .... **194** C5
Cowdray Park Rd BEXW TN39 ...... **194** B5
Cowfold Rd ROTT BN2 .... **205** F6
Cowhurst La BEXW TN39 .... **195** H4
Cow La EDEN TN8 .... **15** K1
  POLE BN26 .... **226** C3
Cowley Dr ROTT BN2 .... **206** B5
Cowper St HOVE BN3 .... **203** F4
Cox Gv BURH RH15 .... **88** E5
Crabtree Av BRI BN1 .... **178** B6
Cradle Hill Rd SEAF BN25 .... **225** H5
Craig CI BAT TN33 .... **168** B5
Craignair Av BRI BN1 .... **178** A5
Cranborne Av EDN/EASTW BN20 ... **236** C3
Cranbrook Rd SLVH TN37 .... **4** A3 ◫
Cranedown LEW BN7 .... **2** A6
Cranfield Av ROTT BN2 .... **220** G2
Cranfield Rd BEXW TN39 .... **195** F7
Cranmer Av HOVE BN3 .... **202** E2
Cranmer CI LEW BN7 .... **3** D3 ◫
Cranston Av BEXW TN39 .... **194** E7
Cranston CI BEXW TN39 .... **194** E7
Cranston Ri BEXW TN39 .... **194** E7
Cranston Rd EGRIN RH19 .... **22** D1
Cranwell Rd SBGH/RUST TN4 .... **19** G7
Craven Rd ROTT BN2 .... **7** F4
Crawfurd Wy EGRIN RH19 .... **12** D8 ◫
Crawley Crs LW/ROSE BN22 .... **229** K1
Crawley Rd BRI BN1 .... **178** E5
Crayford Rd ROTT BN2 .... **7** F1
Crazy La BAT TN33 .... **138** A4
Crecy CI SLVH TN37 .... **169** G4
Crendon Pk SBGH/RUST TN4 .... **20** A7
Crescent Dr BURH RH15 .... **89** H8 ◫
  ROTT BN2 .... **206** B3
Crescent Dr North ROTT BN2 .... **206** B3
Crescent Dr South ROTT BN2 ...... **206** B5
Crescent PI ROTT BN2 .... **7** E6
Crescent Rd BURH RH15 .... **89** G8
  EGRIN RH19 .... **22** B2
  ROTT BN2 .... **7** D2
The Crescent EDN/EASTW BN20 ... **215** F8
  EDN/EASTW BN20 .... **229** G6
  EGRIN RH19 .... **12** A3
  HPPT/KEY BN6 .... **119** H8
  ROTT BN2 .... **205** F1
  SLVH TN37 .... **4** A1
  STHW BN42 .... **201** J3
Crescent Wy BURH RH15 .... **89** G8
Crespin Wy BRI BN1 .... **7** E1
Cresta CI POLE BN26 .... **215** F4
Cresta Rd NEWHV BN9 .... **8** A4
Crest Rd NEWHV BN9 .... **9** F1
Crest Wy PTSD BN41 .... **176** A8
The Crestway BRI BN1 .... **7** E1
Cricket Ct EGRIN RH19 .... **12** C8
Cricketers Fld RBTBR TN32 .... **108** A2
Cricketfield RING/NEW BN8 .... **93** H3
Cricketfield Rd SEAF BN25 .... **232** B1
Cricketing La HAIL BN27 .... **162** D7
Criers La MAYF TN20 .... **70** D4
Crink HI RING/NEW BN8 .... **123** K8
Cripps Av PEAHV BN10 .... **222** C2
Crisp Rd LEW BN7 .... **2** A2
Crockers La RYE TN31 .... **81** K3
Crocks Dean PEAHV BN10 .... **222** C1 ◫
Croft Av STHW BN42 .... **201** H4
Croft CI POLE BN26 .... **214** E7
Croft Ct SEAF BN25 .... **225** F8 ◫
Croft Dr PTSD BN41 .... **175** K8
Croft La SEAF BN25 .... **225** F8
Croft Rd BRI BN1 .... **177** J7
  CROW TN6 .... **53** H2
  HAS TN34 .... **5** E4
The Croft EDN/EASTW BN20 .... **229** G2
  HAS TN34 .... **5** E4
  HPPT/KEY BN6 .... **119** F6
Croft Works HAIL BN27 .... **189** G4
Croham Rd CROW TN6 .... **39** H8
Cromer Wy HAIL BN27 .... **189** F1
Cromleigh Wy STHW BN42 .... **201** H1 ◫
Cromwell PI EGRIN RH19 .... **22** D4 ◫
Cromwell Rd BURH RH15 .... **89** F8
  HOVE BN3 .... **203** H4
  RTWE/PEM TN2 .... **20** C8
Cromwell St ROTT BN2 .... **7** E3 ◫
Crooked La SEAF BN25 .... **232** B1
Crossbush Rd ROTT BN2 .... **205** F5
Cross Lane Gdns WADH TN5 .... **60** B2
Cross Levels Wy EAST BN21 .... **10** A1
Cross Rd STHW BN42 .... **201** J3
Crossroad CI STHW BN42 .... **201** G3 ◫
Cross St BRI BN1 .... **6** C3
  HOVE BN3 .... **203** A6
  POLE BN26 .... **215** F5
  SLVH TN37 .... **4** A5 ◫
Cross Wy LEW BN7 .... **2** A1
Crossways Av EGRIN RH19 .... **22** A2
The Crossways PEV BN24 .... **216** B6
The Crossway BRI BN1 .... **204** C1
  PTSD BN41 .... **201** K1 ◫
  SBGH/RUST TN4 .... **29** H1
Crouch CI EDN/EASTW BN20 .... **229** G2
Crouch La BAT TN33 .... **166** A7
  SEAF BN25 .... **232** A1
Crowborough HI CROW TN6 .... **54** A3
Crowborough Rd RHAS TN35 .... **171** G7
  ROTT BN2 .... **221** G3
  UCK TN22 .... **51** F5
Crowders La BAT TN33 .... **135** G8
Crowhurst CI LGNY BN23 .... **216** B7
Crowhurst Rd BAT TN33 .... **168** B8
  STLEO TN38 .... **196** F1
Crowmere Av BEX TN40 .... **195** H4
Crowmere Ter BEX TN40 .... **195** H6
Crown CI HAIL BN27 .... **189** F4
  UCK TN22 .... **95** J3
Crown HI SEAF BN25 .... **225** F5
Crown La HAS TN34 .... **5** F4 ◫
Crown Rd PTSD BN41 .... **201** K3
  SHOR BN43 .... **200** E3
Crown St BRI BN1 .... **6** B5 ◫
Croxden Wy LW/ROSE BN22 .... **215** J8 ◫
Crunden Rd EDN/EASTW BN20 ... **229** G7
Crundwell Rd SBGH/RUST TN4 .... **19** K2
Cubitt Wy STLEO TN38 .... **169** F7
Cuckfield CI BEX TN40 .... **196** B5
Cuckfield Rd BURH RH15 .... **88** E4

HPPT/KEY BN6 .... **118** A5
RHWH RH17 .... **88** B3
Cuckmere Dr PEV BN24 .... **216** B6
Cuckmere Ri HTHF TN21 .... **100** A4
Cuckmere Rd NEWHV BN9 .... **8** A5
  SEAF BN25 .... **232** D1
Cuckmere Wk LW/ROSE BN22 ...... **229** J2
Cuckmere Wy BRI BN1 .... **178** C6
Cuckoo Dr HTFW TN21 .... **100** A5
Cuckoo La STPH/PW TN12 .... **33** J1
Cuckoo Trail HAIL BN27 .... **189** C3
  HTHF TN21 .... **99** K7
  HTHF TN21 .... **100** A5
  POLE BN26 .... **215** F3
Culpepper CI BURH RH15 .... **88** E7
Culpepper CI ROTT BN2 .... **204** E1 ◫
Culver CI LGNY BN23 .... **216** C7
Culverden Av SBGH/RUST TN4 .... **19** K5
Culverden Down SBGH/RUST TN4 . **19** K6
Culverden Pk SBGH/RUST TN4 .... **19** K6
Culverden Park Rd
  SBGH/RUST TN4 .... **19** K5
Culverden Sq SBGH/RUST TN4 ...... **20** A6
Culverden St RTW TN1 .... **20** A7 ◫
Cumberland Dr BRI BN1 .... **203** K1 ◫
Cumberland Gdns STLEO TN38 .... **197** J3 ◫
Cumberland Rd BEXW TN39 .... **195** G4
  BRI BN1 .... **203** K1
Cumberland Yd RTW TN1 .... **30** A1 ◫
Cunningham CI SBGH/RUST TN4 ... **20** B4 ◫
Cunningham Dr LGNY BN23 .... **231** F4
Cunningham Rd SBGH/RUST TN4 .. **20** B4
Curlew Ct STLEO TN38 .... **169** F8 ◫
The Curlews SHOR BN43 .... **200** D3
Currie Rd SBGH/RUST TN4 .... **20** A5
Curwen PI BRI BN1 .... **177** K8
Cuthbert CI BEXW TN39 .... **195** F4
Cuthbert Rd ROTT BN2 .... **7** E4
Cutter La HAS TN34 .... **5** E5 ◫
The Cygnets SHOR BN43 .... **200** C3 ◫
Cypress CI SHOR BN43 .... **200** C2
  STLEO TN38 .... **197** K3
Cypress PI RYE TN31 .... **113** H6 ◫
Cyprus Rd BURH RH15 .... **89** G8

Dacre Rd EDN/EASTW BN20 .... **229** H7
  HAIL BN27 .... **163** F5
  NEWHV BN9 .... **9** D8 ◫
Dagg La RBTBR TN32 .... **80** A6
The Dakins EGRIN RH19 .... **22** C3 ◫
Dale Av BRI BN1 .... **178** A6
  HPPT/KEY BN6 .... **119** F8
Dale Crs BRI BN1 .... **178** A5
Dale Dr BRI BN1 .... **178** A5
Dale HI POY/PYE BN45 .... **149** F5
Dale Rd FROW RH18 .... **35** K2
  LEW BN7 .... **2** A5
Dales CI HAIL BN27 .... **163** J6
Dale St RTW TN1 .... **20** B7
Dale Vw HOVE BN3 .... **202** C1
Dale View Gdns HOVE BN3 .... **202** C1 ◫
Dalewood Gdns BURH RH15 .... **119** J1
Dallaway Dr PEV BN24 .... **216** C6
Dallaway Gdns EGRIN RH19 .... **22** C2
Dallington CI BEX TN40 .... **196** B5
Dallington Rd HOVE BN3 .... **202** D3
  LW/ROSE BN22 .... **230** A2
Dalmeny Rd BEXW TN39 .... **195** F6
Dalton Rd EDN/EASTW BN20 .... **236** E3
Damian Wy HPPT/KEY BN6 .... **119** H7
Damon CI PEAHV BN10 .... **222** B4
Dane Court CI BEXW TN39 .... **195** G5 ◫
Danehill La EDN/EASTW BN20 ..... **236** E4
Danehill Rd ROTT BN2 .... **205** G6
Dane Rd STLEO TN38 .... **4** A5
  STLEO TN38 .... **197** J3
Daniel Wy RYE TN31 .... **145** H1
Danum CI HAIL BN27 .... **161** H8
Danworth La HPPT/KEY BN6 .... **88** B3
Darby's La WADH TN5 .... **58** C1
Darcey Dr BRI BN1 .... **178** B5
Darent CI POLE BN26 .... **216** A6
Daresbury CI BEXW TN39 .... **195** F5
Darley Rd EDN/EASTW BN20 .... **236** D3
Dartmouth CI ROTT BN2 .... **205** G2
Dartmouth Crs ROTT BN2 .... **205** F2
Darvel Down BAT TN33 .... **135** F1
Darwall Dr SEAF BN25 .... **225** H8
Darwell CI STLEO TN38 .... **197** F2
Darwell Dr POLE BN26 .... **216** A6
Davey Dr BRI BN1 .... **7** D1
Davey's La LEW BN7 .... **3** E3
Davigdor Rd HOVE BN3 .... **203** J4
Davis CI BEXW TN39 .... **195** F4
Dawlish CI ROTT BN2 .... **205** F2
Dawson Ter ROTT BN2 .... **7** E4
Daynes Wy BURH RH15 .... **118** E2

Deacons Dr PTSD BN41 .... 202 A1
Deadmans La RYE TN31 .... 113 J5
Deadmantree HI RING/NEW BN8 .. 123 F8
Deal Av SEAF BN25 .... 225 K6
The Deals RYE TN31 .... 113 H6 ▣
Dean CI PTSD BN41 .... 202 B1
Dean Court Rd ROTT BN2 .... 220 D1
Deanery CI LEW BN7 .... 3 D2
Dean Gdns PTSD BN41 .... 202 B1
Dean Rd SEAF BN25 .... 232 D1
Deans CI BEXW TN39 .... 195 G4
    ROTT BN2 .... 206 B3
Deans Dr BEXW TN39 .... 195 F5
Deans Meadow RING/NEW BN8 .. 123 J6
Deans Rd POLE BN26 .... 212 C8
Dean St BRI BN1 .... 6 A5
Deanway HOVE BN3 .... 177 G8
Dean Wood CI LGNY BN23 .... 216 B7
De Cham Av SLVH TN37 .... 4 B4 ▣
De Cham Rd SLVH TN37 .... 4 A4 ▣
De Chardin Dr HAS TN34 .... 170 D6
De Courcel Rd ROTT BN2 .... 205 F8 ▣
Decoy Dr LW/ROSE BN22 .... 229 J3
Deepdene WADH TN5 .... 44 B5
Deepdene Gdns HAS TN34 .... 5 F1
Deerswood CI BEXW TN39 .... 194 D6
The Deeside BRI BN1 .... 178 B4
De Grey CI LEW BN7 .... 3 D3 ▣
Delaware Dr STLEO TN38 .... 169 G5
Delaware Rd LEW BN7 .... 2 A5
De La Warr Pde BEX TN40 .... 195 J8
De La Warr Rd BEX TN40 .... 195 J6
    EGRIN RH19 .... 22 D2
Dell CI STLEO TN38 .... 197 H1
Dell Dr RTWE/PEM TN2 .... 20 D7
The Dell EGRIN RH19 .... 23 F2
Delmonden Rd HAWK TN18 .... 62 C5
Delves Av RTWE/PEM TN2 .... 20 C2
Delves CI RING/NEW BN8 .... 155 J5
Delves Wy RING/NEW BN8 .... 155 J5
De Moleyns CI BEX TN40 .... 195 J7 ▣
De Montfort Rd LEW BN7 .... 2 B4
    ROTT BN2 .... 7 E3
Denbigh Rd SBGH/RUST TN4 .... 20 C4 ▣
Dencher Rd LEW BN7 .... 181 H8
Dene CI EDN/EASTW BN20 .... 235 F2
Dene Dr LW/ROSE BN22 .... 229 H2
Denehurst Gdns HAS TN34 .... 170 D6
Dene Pth UCK TN22 .... 95 K2
Deneside BRI BN1 .... 177 J6 ▣
Dene Side EDN/EASTW BN20 .... 235 F2
The Dene EDN/EASTW BN20 .... 229 F1
    HAS TN34 .... 170 D6
    HOVE BN3 .... 176 C8 ▣
Dene V BRI BN1 .... 177 J6
Dene Wy RRTW TN3 .... 18 E4
The Deneway BRI BN1 .... 177 J7
Denham CI STLEO TN38 .... 169 G7
Denham Rd BURH RH15 .... 88 D7
Denham Wy RYE TN31 .... 145 G1
Den HI EDN/EASTW BN20 .... 229 F7
Denmark Rd PTSD BN41 .... 202 B4
Denmark Ter BRI BN1 .... 6 A4
Denmark Vis HOVE BN3 .... 203 G4
Dennis Hobden CI ROTT BN2 .... 205 F2
Denton CI RYE TN31 .... 113 G5
Denton Dr BRI BN1 .... 178 B6
    NEWHV BN9 .... 9 E1
Denton Ri NEWHV BN9 .... 223 K1
Denton Rd EDN/EASTW BN20 .... 236 B5
    NEWHV BN9 .... 9 E1
The Dentons EDN/EASTW BN20 .... 236 B5
Derek Av HOVE BN3 .... 202 C5
Dern La HTHF TN21 .... 128 E7
De Roos Rd EAST BN21 .... 229 J7
Derwent CI HAIL BN27 .... 189 F2
Derwent Dr SBGH/RUST TN4 .... 19 J6
Derwent Rd EDN/EASTW BN20 .... 236 C5
Desmond Rd LW/ROSE BN22 .... 11 F2
Desmond Wy ROTT BN2 .... 205 G5
Devil's Dyke Rd HOVE BN3 .... 176 E5
    POY/PYE BN45 .... 176 A1
    PTSD BN41 .... 176 B2
Devonshire CI RTWE/PEM TN2 .... 29 K3 ▣
Devonshire PI EAST BN21 .... 10 C5
    ROTT BN2 .... 7 D5
Devonshire Rd BEX TN40 .... 195 H8
    HAS TN34 .... 5 D4
De Walden Ms
    EDN/EASTW BN20 .... 236 E3 ▣
De Warrenne Rd LEW BN7 .... 2 B4
Dewe Rd ROTT BN2 .... 7 E1
Dewhurst La WADH TN5 .... 43 H3
Dewlands HI MAYF TN20 .... 70 C2
Dew La RYE TN31 .... 112 A3
The Dewpond PEAHV BN10 .... 222 A2 ▣
Dexter Dr EGRIN RH19 .... 22 C3
Diana CI BEX TN40 .... 196 B5
Dickens CI EGRIN RH19 .... 22 A2
Dickens Wy HAWK TN18 .... 63 G2
    LGNY BN23 .... 217 F8
Dillingburgh Rd
    EDN/EASTW BN20 .... 229 H7
Dillon Wy RTWE/PEM TN2 .... 20 D5
Diplock CI POLE BN26 .... 214 E5 ▣

Diplocks Wy HAIL BN27 .... 189 F4
Dirty La EGRIN RH19 .... 23 J5
Ditchling Bostall HPPT/KEY BN6 .. 150 E4
Ditchling CI POLE BN26 .... 216 A7
Ditchling Crs BRI BN1 .... 178 D6
Ditchling Dr RHAS TN35 .... 171 H7
Ditchling Gdns BRI BN1 .... 6 C1
Ditchling Ri BRI BN1 .... 6 C2 ▣
Ditchling Rd BRI BN1 .... 178 D3
    ROTT BN2 .... 6 C1
Ditchling Wy HAIL BN27 .... 189 G5
Dittons Ms STLEO TN38 .... 197 F1 ▣
Dittons Rd EAST BN21 .... 10 A4
    POLE BN26 .... 215 H5
Dixter La RYE TN31 .... 81 J4
Dixter Rd RYE TN31 .... 81 J4
The Dock RING/NEW BN8 .... 184 D6
Dodshill CROW TN6 .... 53 J2
Dog Kennel La UCK TN22 .... 70 C5
Dogs Hill Rd WSEA TN36 .... 143 H6
Doleham La RHAS TN35 .... 139 J6
Dolphin Rd SHOR BN43 .... 200 E4
Dolphin Wy SHOR BN43 .... 200 E4
Donald Hall Rd ROTT BN2 .... 7 F5
Donald Wy WSEA TN36 .... 143 G6
Donkey Ms HOVE BN3 .... 203 J6 ▣
Donnington Rd ROTT BN2 .... 206 B5
Doon Brae SBGH/RUST TN4 .... 20 A1
Dordrecht Wy HAS TN34 .... 4 C3
Doric Av SBGH/RUST TN4 .... 19 K2
Doric CI SBGH/RUST TN4 .... 19 K2
Dorking Rd RTW TN1 .... 20 C5
Dormans Av LING RH7 .... 12 E1
Dorman's CI LING RH7 .... 12 E3
Dormans High St LING RH7 .... 12 E4
Dormans Park Rd EGRIN RH19 .... 12 D8
    EGRIN RH19 .... 12 C5
Dormans Rd LING RH7 .... 12 E1
Dormans Station Rd LING RH7 ...... 12 D4
Dornden Dr RRTW TN3 .... 18 E7
Dorothy Av PEAHV BN10 .... 222 B3
Dorothy Av North PEAHV BN10 ...... 222 B3
Dorothy Rd HOVE BN3 .... 202 C3
Dorset Av EGRIN RH19 .... 12 A8
Dorset Gdns EGRIN RH19 .... 12 A8
    ROTT BN2 .... 7 D5
Dorset PI HAS TN34 .... 4 C5 ▣
    ROTT BN2 .... 7 D5
Dorset Rd BEX TN40 .... 195 J2
    LEW BN7 .... 3 D5
    RTWE/PEM TN2 .... 30 D1
Dorset Rd South BEX TN40 .... 195 J7
Dorset St ROTT BN2 .... 6 C5 ▣
Doubledays BURH RH15 .... 119 H1
Doucegrove STLEO TN38 .... 197 H1
Douglas CI HAIL BN27 .... 189 G1
Douglas Rd CROW TN6 .... 55 H2
Dove CI UCK TN22 .... 95 J3
Dovedale Gdns LW/ROSE BN22 .... 230 A1 ▣
Dover CI SEAF BN25 .... 225 K6
Dover Rd BRI BN1 .... 204 B1
    POLE BN26 .... 215 G4
Dowding Wy RTWE/PEM TN2 .... 20 E2
Dower CI ROTT BN2 .... 206 A8
Downash CI ROTT BN2 .... 205 F5
Down Av RRTW TN3 .... 33 J8
Downey CI SLVH TN37 .... 169 J5
Downland Av PEAHV BN10 .... 222 D5
    STHW BN42 .... 201 G2
Downland CI ROTT BN2 .... 205 J3 ▣
    STHW BN42 .... 201 G2
Downland Copse UCK TN22 .... 95 J3
Downland Crs HOVE BN3 .... 176 E8
Downland Dr HOVE BN3 .... 176 E8
Downland Rd ROTT BN2 .... 205 J3
Downlands Av BEXW TN39 .... 195 G2
Downlands CI BEXW TN39 .... 195 F7 ▣
Downlands Wy
    EDN/EASTW BN20 .... 235 F2 ▣
Down La RRTW TN3 .... 42 C3
Downline CI HTHF TN21 .... 129 K4
Down Rd BEXW TN39 .... 195 F6
Downs Av EDN/EASTW BN20 .... 229 G5
Downs CI LEW BN7 .... 2 A3
Downscroft BURH RH15 .... 89 K6
Downside BRI BN1 .... 177 J6 ▣
    HOVE BN3 .... 177 G7
    LEW BN7 .... 2 A4
    SHOR BN43 .... 200 D2
Downside CI SHOR BN43 .... 200 C2
Downs Rd BURH RH15 .... 88 E7
    HAS TN34 .... 5 D1
    LW/ROSE BN22 .... 229 G1
    SEAF BN25 .... 225 H8
Down St UCK TN22 .... 66 C3
Downsvalley Rd
    EDN/EASTW BN20 .... 215 F7
Downs Valley Rd ROTT BN2 .... 206 B3
Downs Vw BAT TN33 .... 165 K6
Downsview HOVE BN3 .... 176 C8
    HTHF TN21 .... 100 B3
Downs Vw PEAHV BN10 .... 222 C1 ▣
Downsview Av ROTT BN2 .... 205 K2
Downs View CI EDN/EASTW BN20 .. 235 J3 ▣
    RING/NEW BN8 .... 92 C5

Downsview Crs UCK TN22 .... 95 K3
Downsview Dr RHWH RH17 .... 90 E7
Downs View La EDN/EASTW BN20 .. 235 G3
Downsview Rd
    EDN/EASTW BN20 .... 215 F8 ▣
Downs View Rd HPPT/KEY BN6 ...... 119 F8
Downsview Rd PTSD BN41 .... 201 K1
    SEAF BN25 .... 225 H8
Downsview Wy HAIL BN27 .... 189 G4 ▣
Downs Wk PEAHV BN10 .... 222 A1
Downsway ROTT BN2 .... 206 A3
    SHOR BN43 .... 200 C2
    STHW BN42 .... 201 J1
Down Ter ROTT BN2 .... 7 E4
The Down HOVE BN3 .... 176 B7
Draffin La RYE TN31 .... 115 F8
Drake Av LGNY BN23 .... 231 F4
Draper St SBGH/RUST TN4 .... 19 K1
Drapers Wy STLEO TN38 .... 197 H1
Draxmont Wy BRI BN1 .... 178 A8
Drayton Ri BEXW TN39 .... 194 C7
The Drive BURH RH15 .... 89 H7
    CROW TN6 .... 53 F1 ▣
    HAIL BN27 .... 189 G5
    HOVE BN3 .... 203 H4
    NEWHV BN9 .... 8 C5
    RTWE/PEM TN2 .... 30 A2
    SHOR BN43 .... 200 C3
    STHW BN42 .... 201 H2
    STLEO TN38 .... 197 G3
    UCK TN22 .... 67 G6
    UCK TN22 .... 95 J3
The Driveway SHOR BN43 .... 200 C3
Drockmill CI POLE BN26 .... 215 H5 ▣
Drove Av ROTT BN2 .... 206 A1
Drove Crs PTSD BN41 .... 201 K1
Drove Rd NEWHV BN9 .... 9 E2
    PTSD BN41 .... 201 K2
    ROTT BN2 .... 205 K2
Drovers CI PTSD BN41 .... 202 B1
Drovers Wy BURH RH15 .... 119 J1
The Drove BRI BN1 .... 179 K6
    BRI BN1 .... 203 J2
    NEWHV BN9 .... 9 E2
    RING/NEW BN8 .... 153 K6
The Droveway HOVE BN3 .... 203 H2
Duchess Dr SEAF BN25 .... 225 F5
Dudley Rd BRI BN1 .... 7 D1
    LW/ROSE BN22 .... 11 D3
    RHAS TN35 .... 139 J1
    RTW TN1 .... 20 A7 ▣
Dudwell Rd ROTT BN2 .... 206 B4
Duke Ms SLVH TN37 .... 197 J1 ▣
Duke Rd SLVH TN37 .... 197 J1
Dukes CI SEAF BN25 .... 224 E6
Duke's Dr EDN/EASTW BN20 ...... 236 D4
Dukes HI BAT TN33 .... 136 D5
Duke's Mound ROTT BN2 .... 7 F6
Dukes Rd RTW TN1 .... 20 C6
Duke St BEXW TN39 .... 194 E6
    BRI BN1 .... 6 B5
    SLVH TN37 .... 197 J1
Duke Ter SLVH TN37 .... 197 J1
Dulwich CI SEAF BN25 .... 225 J7 ▣
Dumbrells Court Rd
    HPPT/KEY BN6 .... 119 K7
Dumbrills CI BURH RH15 .... 89 G6
Dumb Woman's La RYE TN31 .... 112 D8
Dunbar Dr HAIL BN27 .... 189 F2
Dunclutcha Rd HAS TN34 .... 170 C7
Dundale Rd RRTW TN3 .... 32 A2
Dunes Av RYE TN31 .... 145 H1
Dunning's Rd EGRIN RH19 .... 22 C4
    EGRIN RH19 .... 22 C5
Dunstall Av BURH RH15 .... 88 E7
Dunstall Farm Rd BURH RH15 ...... 89 F7
Dunstan Gv SBGH/RUST TN4 .... 20 B6
Dunstan Rd SBGH/RUST TN4 .... 20 B5
Dunstans Cft MAYF TN20 .... 56 C8
Dunster CI BRI BN1 .... 7 D1
Dunvan CI LEW BN7 .... 2 C2
Durham CI ROTT BN2 .... 205 H2
Durkins Rd EGRIN RH19 .... 12 B8
Durrell CI LGNY BN23 .... 231 G1
Dursley Rd LW/ROSE BN22 .... 10 C3
Dutchells Wy LW/ROSE BN22 ...... 215 J7
Dyall CI BURH RH15 .... 88 E7
Dyke CI HOVE BN3 .... 177 G7
Dyke Rd BRI BN1 .... 6 B4
    HOVE BN3 .... 6 A3
Dyke Road Av HOVE BN3 .... 177 G7
Dyke Road Dr BRI BN1 .... 6 D8
Dyke Road PI HOVE BN3 .... 177 H8
Dymchurch CI POLE BN26 .... 215 H4
    SEAF BN25 .... 225 J6
Dymock CI SEAF BN25 .... 225 K7 ▣
The Dymock's HPPT/KEY BN6 ..... 119 K8 ▣
Dymond Rd STLEO TN38 .... 169 H8
Dynevor Rd SBGH/RUST TN4 ...... 20 C4

E

Eagle Cl UCK TN22 96 A6
Eagle Rd RYE TN31 113 J5
Earls Cl SEAF BN25 224 D6 1
Earl's Rd SBGH/RUST TN4 19 K7
Earl St HAS TN34 5 D4
East Albany Rd SEAF BN25 225 G7
East Ascent STLEO TN38 197 J5
Eastbank STHW BN42 201 J2
East Beach St HAS TN34 5 F4 3
East Beeches Rd CROW TN6 53 J1
Eastbourne Av PEV BN24 218 A6
Eastbourne La POLE BN26 228 B4
Eastbourne Rd EDN/EASTW BN20 229 G1
LGNY BN23 217 G7
LW/ROSE BN22 229 H2
PEV BN24 217 J8
POLE BN26 215 F6
RING/NEW BN8 126 E5
ROTT BN2 7 F1
SEAF BN25 225 K8
UCK TN22 126 B2
East Bourne St HAS TN34 5 F4 4
Eastbridge Rd NEWHV BN9 9 E3
Eastbrook Rd PTSD BN41 202 A4
Eastbrook Wy STHW BN42 201 K4
East Cliff RYE TN31 113 J6
East Cliff Rd SBGH/RUST TN4 20 A5
East Cl POLE BN26 215 G5
Eastdale Rd BURH RH15 89 J7
East Dean Ri SEAF BN25 225 H6
East Dean Rd EDN/EASTW BN20 235 H3
East Dr ROTT BN2 7 E5
East End La HPPT/KEY BN6 119 K8
Eastergate BEXW TN39 194 C6
Eastergate Rd ROTT BN2 179 F7
Eastern Av POLE BN26 215 G5
SHOR BN43 200 D4
Eastern Cl SHOR BN43 200 D4
Eastern Pl ROTT BN2 205 F7
Eastern Rd ROTT BN2 7 E6
ROTT BN2 205 F7 1
Eastern Ter ROTT BN2 7 F6 6
Eastern Terrace Ms ROTT BN2 7 F6 7
East Gdns HPPT/KEY BN6 119 K8
Eastgate St LEW BN7 3 D4
Eastgate Whf LEW BN7 3 D4 2
East Hl EGRIN RH19 12 C5
Easthill Dr PTSD BN41 202 A2
Easthill Wy PTSD BN41 202 A2
Eastlands Cl SBGH/RUST TN4 29 J3
Eastlands Rd SBGH/RUST TN4 29 J3 1
East Meadway SHOR BN43 200 D5
Eastport La LEW BN7 2 C5
East St BRI BN1 6 C5 5
BRI BN1 179 K5
HAS TN34 5 E5 2
LEW BN7 3 D4
MAYF TN20 56 C8
PTSD BN41 202 B5
RYE TN31 113 J6 2
SEAF BN25 225 F8
SHOR BN43 200 C4
East View Flds LEW BN7 121 G6
East View Ter BAT TN33 138 B2
Eastway BEXW TN39 194 B7
East Wy LEW BN7 181 J1
Eastwick Cl BRI BN1 178 C4
Eastwood Rd BEXW TN39 195 F7
Eatenden La BAT TN33 135 K1
Eaton Gdns HOVE BN3 203 H4
Eaton Gv HOVE BN3 203 H4 1
Eaton Pl ROTT BN2 7 F6
Eaton Rd HOVE BN3 203 H5
Eaton Vls HOVE BN3 203 G4
Eaton Wk BAT TN33 137 K2
Ebden's Hl BAT TN33 169 J2
Ebenezer Rd HAS TN34 5 F4 5
Ecmod Rd LW/ROSE BN22 11 E1
Edburton Av BRI BN1 6 C1
Edburton Gdns SHOR BN43 200 C2
Edenbridge Rd EDEN TN8 25 K1
HRTF TN7 25 K1
Eden Dr BEXW TN39 194 D7
Eden Rd RTW TN1 30 A1
Edensor Rd EDN/EASTW BN20 236 D4
Eden V EGRIN RH19 12 C7
Edgar Rd RHAS TN35 199 F1
Edgehill Cl HTHF TN21 99 K4
Edgehill Wy PTSD BN41 201 J1
Edinburgh Rd BEX TN40 195 H6 2
ROTT BN2 7 D2 3
SEAF BN25 224 E8
STLEO TN38 197 F4
Edinburgh Wy EGRIN RH19 22 D4
Edith Av PEAHV BN10 222 A4
Edith Av North PEAHV BN10 222 B3
Edith Rd RHAS TN35 171 G8
Edmond Cl LGNY BN23 231 F3
Edmonton Rd BEXW TN39 195 G4
Edmund Rd RHAS TN35 199 F1
Edward Av HOVE BN3 177 F8
ROTT BN2 207 G8
Edward Cl HOVE BN3 177 F8
SEAF BN25 224 B5 1
Edward Rd SLVH TN37 4 B5
Edward St LEW BN7 3 D4 3
ROTT BN2 7 D5
SBGH/RUST TN4 19 F7
SBGH/RUST TN4 19 K2
Edward Ter STLEO TN38 169 H7 2
Edwin Rd RHAS TN35 199 F1
Effingham Cl ROTT BN2 221 F1
Effingham Dr BEXW TN39 194 C8
Egerton Rd BEXW TN39 195 G8
Egginton Cl BRI BN1 179 H6
Egginton Rd ROTT BN2 179 G7
Egles Gv UCK TN22 95 H3
Egmont Rd HOVE BN3 202 C2
Egremont Pl HAS TN34 5 F2
ROTT BN2 7 D5 4
Eight Acre La RHAS TN35 171 G2
Eight Bells Cl UCK TN22 68 E7
Eileen Av ROTT BN2 220 E2
Eisenhower Dr STLEO TN38 169 G5
Elder Cl PTSD BN41 202 A1
Elder Pl BRI BN1 6 C3
Elderwood Cl BEXW TN39 195 H4
LW/ROSE BN22 229 J1
Eldon Rd EAST BN21 229 H6
Eldred Av BRI BN1 177 J6
Eleanor Cl SEAF BN25 224 E6 3
Eley Crs ROTT BN2 206 B8
Eley Dr ROTT BN2 206 B7
Elford St HAS TN34 5 D4 4
Elgar Wy LGNY BN23 217 F8
Elgin Gdns SEAF BN25 225 K7
Elim Court Gdns CROW TN6 39 G7
Elizabethan Cl BAT TN33 193 J1
Elizabeth Av HOVE BN3 177 F8
Elizabeth Cl HOVE BN3 177 F8 1
SEAF BN25 224 B5
Elizabeth Crs EGRIN RH19 12 D8
Elizabeth Rd SHOR BN43 201 F3
Ellenslea Rd SLVH TN37 4 A5 3
Ellen St HOVE BN3 203 G4
PTSD BN41 202 B4
Ellenwhorne La RBTBR TN32 108 C4
Ellerslie La BEXW TN39 194 E4
Elliots Wy HTHF TN21 100 A3
Ellison Cl CROW TN6 39 G7
Ellis Wy UCK TN22 95 G4
Elm Cl HOVE BN3 203 H1
RING/NEW BN8 157 K4
SEAF BN25 225 K8 3
SHOR BN43 200 C2
Elm Ct NEWHV BN9 8 B3
Elm Dr EGRIN RH19 22 E2
HOVE BN3 202 D2
Elm Gv LW/ROSE BN22 230 A2
ROTT BN2 7 E3
Elmhurst Av RTWE/PEM TN2 21 K3
Elmore Rd ROTT BN2 7 D4
Elm Rd PTSD BN41 202 A3
SBGH/RUST TN4 19 K2
Elms Av EAST BN21 11 D5
Elmsdown Pl HAIL BN27 189 H4
Elms La RHAS TN35 172 E2
Elms Lea Av BRI BN1 177 K8
Elmsmead RYE TN31 85 H7
Elms Rd EAST BN21 11 D5 3
Elmstead Rd BEX TN40 195 K6
The Elms RING/NEW BN8 155 H6
Elm Wy HTHF TN21 100 B5
Elmwood Cl LGNY BN23 216 D7 4
Elmwood Gdns LGNY BN23 216 D7 5
Elphick Pl CROW TN6 39 H8 1
Elphick Rd NEWHV BN9 8 C2
RING/NEW BN8 156 A4
Elphick's Pl RTWE/PEM TN2 30 B3 1
Elphinstone Av HAS TN34 5 D2
Elphinstone Gdns HAS TN34 5 D1
Elphinstone Rd HAS TN34 170 D7
Elrington Rd HOVE BN3 203 H2
Elsted Crs BRI BN1 178 D5
Elven La EDN/EASTW BN20 235 G2 1
Elvin Crs ROTT BN2 206 B7
Elwood Cl BURH RH15 119 F2
Emerald Quay SHOR BN43 200 D5
Emmanuel Rd HAS TN34 5 E3
Endwell Rd BEX TN40 195 H8
Engalee EGRIN RH19 22 A1
English Cl HOVE BN3 202 D3
Enys Rd EAST BN21 10 B3
Epsom Cl STLEO TN38 197 H3 2
Erica Cl LGNY BN23 230 C1
Eridge Cl BEXW TN39 194 E7
Eridge Dr CROW TN6 39 H8
Eridge Gdns CROW TN6 39 J8
Eridge Gn LEW BN7 2 B3
Eridge La CROW TN6 55 F1
Eridge Rd CROW TN6 40 A7
EAST BN21 229 H4
HOVE BN3 203 F1
RRTW TN3 28 B5
SBGH/RUST TN4 29 K1
Erin Wy BURH RH15 88 E8
Erringham Rd SHOR BN43 200 B2
Erroll Rd HOVE BN3 202 B5
Ersham Rd HAIL BN27 189 G6
Ersham Wy HAIL BN27 189 G5
Erskine Park Rd SBGH/RUST TN4 19 F7
Esher Cl SEAF BN25 225 G7 2
Eskbank Av BRI BN1 178 B4
Eskdale Cl LGNY BN23 216 C7 1
Esplanade SEAF BN25 232 B2
Esplanade Ms SEAF BN25 232 A1
The Esplanade PEAHV BN10 221 J4
Essenden Rd STLEO TN38 197 H5
Essex Cl RTWE/PEM TN2 29 K3
Essex Rd STLEO TN38 169 H7
Essex St ROTT BN2 7 E5
Estate Rd NEWHV BN9 9 E2 1
Estcots Dr EGRIN RH19 22 E2
Etchingham Rd LGNY BN23 231 F2
Ethelred Cl LGNY BN23 231 F3 1
Ethel St HOVE BN3 203 G4
Etherington Hl RRTW TN3 19 G3
Etherton Wy SEAF BN25 225 H7
Eton Cl SEAF BN25 225 H7
Evelyn Av NEWHV BN9 8 C3
Evelyn Rd LEW BN7 2 B3
Evelyn Ter ROTT BN2 7 E5
Eversfield Pl SLVH TN37 4 B6
Eversfield Rd EAST BN21 10 B3
Eversley Cl SLVH TN37 4 A2
Eversley Rd BEX TN40 195 H8
SLVH TN37 4 A2
Ewart St ROTT BN2 7 D4
Ewehurst La RRTW TN3 18 D5
Ewhurst Cl HAS TN34 170 C7
Ewhurst La RYE TN31 81 H7
Ewhurst Rd ROTT BN2 7 E2
Exceat Cl ROTT BN2 205 F5 1
Exeat Cl LGNY BN23 216 B7
Exeter Cl LW/ROSE BN22 229 G1
Exeter St BRI BN1 6 A2
Exmouth Pl HAS TN34 5 E4 5

F

Factory La HAIL BN27 189 F5
Fairbridge Wy BURH RH15 89 F6
Faircrouch La WADH TN5 43 H6
Fairdene STHW BN42 201 J2
Fairfax Av STLEO TN38 169 G4
Fairfield HAIL BN27 163 F5
Fairfield Av RTWE/PEM TN2 20 C6 2
Fairfield Cha BEXW TN39 194 E7
Fairfield Cl BURH RH15 89 F7
SHOR BN43 200 E2
Fairfield Crs HPPT/KEY BN6 118 A5
Fairfield Gdns PTSD BN41 202 A2
Fairfield Rd BURH RH15 89 F8
EDN/EASTW BN20 10 A6
EGRIN RH19 22 D3
SLVH TN37 169 K5
Fairglen Rd WADH TN5 43 H8
Fairholme Rd NEWHV BN9 9 F1
Fairisle Cl HAIL BN27 189 F1
Fair Isle Cl LGNY BN23 231 F3 2
Fair La RBTBR TN32 78 B7
Fairlawns SHOR BN43 200 D3
Fairlawns Dr HAIL BN27 163 F5
Fairlea Cl BURH RH15 89 F7
Fairlie Gdns BRI BN1 177 K8
Fairlight Av PEAHV BN10 221 J4
RHAS TN35 171 G8
Fairlight Cl BEX TN40 196 B6
POLE BN26 215 F5 2
SBGH/RUST TN4 20 A1
Fairlight Fld RING/NEW BN8 155 J6
Fairlight Gdns RHAS TN35 172 E7 1
Fairlight Pl ROTT BN2 7 E2 2
Fairlight Rd LW/ROSE BN22 11 E2
RHAS TN35 171 G8
Fair Meadow RYE TN31 113 J4
Fairmile Rd RTWE/PEM TN2 20 E6
Fairmount Rd BEX TN40 195 J6
Fair Oak Cl HTHF TN21 100 A4
Fairstone Cl RHAS TN35 171 H7
Fairview HAWK TN18 63 F1
Fairview La CROW TN6 39 G7
Fairview Ri BRI BN1 177 J6
Fairway Cl EDN/EASTW BN20 236 C1
Fairway Crs PTSD BN41 202 B1
Fairways Cl SEAF BN25 232 E1 1
Fairways Rd SEAF BN25 232 D1
The Fairways SBGH/RUST TN4 20 A4 1
The Fairway BEXW TN39 194 E5
NEWHV BN9 8 A4
STLEO TN38 197 G3
Falaise Rd HAS TN34 4 B5
NEWHV BN9 9 F1
Falconbury Dr BEXW TN39 194 C8
Falcon Cl SHOR BN43 201 F5
Falconer Dr BAT TN33 137 F7
Falcon Wy HAIL BN27 189 G1
Fallowfield Cl HOVE BN3 202 E1 1

Fallowfield Crs *HOVE* BN3 .... 202 D1
Falmer Av *ROTT* BN2 .... 206 E8
  ROTT BN2 .... 220 E1
Falmer Gdns *ROTT* BN2 .... 206 A3
Falmer House Rd *BRI* BN1 .... 179 K4
Falmer Rd *ROTT* BN2 .... 206 A1
Falmouth Cl *LGNY* BN23 .... 231 G3
Faraday Av *EGRIN* RH19 .... 22 D5
Farlaine Rd *EAST* BN21 .... 229 H5
Farley Bank *HAS* TN34 .... 5 F2
Farleys Wy *RYE* TN31 .... 112 B1
Farley Wy *RHAS* TN35 .... 172 D6
Farm Cl *EGRIN* RH19 .... 23 F3
  HPPT/KEY BN6 .... 118 E7
  PTSD BN41 .... 201 K1
  SEAF BN25 .... 225 J7
Farmcombe Cl *RTW* TN1 .... 30 B1
Farmcombe La *RTW* TN1 .... 30 B1
Farmcombe Rd *RTW* TN1 .... 30 B1
Farm Gdns *RYE* TN31 .... 112 C1
Farm Hl *ROTT* BN2 .... 205 K3
Farmlands Av *POLE* BN26 .... 214 E7
Farmlands Cl *POLE* BN26 .... 215 F7
  SLVH TN37 .... 169 K6
Farmlands Wy *POLE* BN26 .... 214 E6
Farmland Wy *HAIL* BN27 .... 189 H2
Farm La *HPPT/KEY* BN6 .... 120 A8
  RYE TN31 .... 115 F8
Farm Ms *HOVE* BN3 .... 203 J5
Farm Rd *HOVE* BN3 .... 203 J5
Farm Wy *BURH* RH15 .... 119 J2
  STHW BN42 .... 201 K4
Farmway Cl *HOVE* BN3 .... 202 C1
Farncombe Cl *RHWH* RH17 .... 91 F6
Farncombe Rd *LEW* BN7 .... 3 E4
Farne Cl *HAIL* BN27 .... 189 F1
Farnham Av *HPPT/KEY* BN6 .... 119 G6
Farnham Beeches *RRTW* TN3 .... 18 E7
Farnham Cl *RRTW* TN3 .... 18 E8
Farnham La *RRTW* TN3 .... 18 E7
Farnham Pl *RRTW* TN3 .... 18 E8
Farningham Rd *CROW* TN6 .... 54 A4
Farnlea Rd *BURH* RH15 .... 89 K6
Farriers Wy *UCK* TN22 .... 95 J5
Farthing Hl *WADH* TN5 .... 60 C2
Farthing La *HAIL* BN27 .... 133 G6
The Farthings *CROW* TN6 .... 39 J8
Fastnet Cl *LGNY* BN23 .... 231 F3
Faulkners Wy *BURH* RH15 .... 89 C6
Faversham Rd *LGNY* BN23 .... 230 E1
Faygate Cl *BEXW* TN39 .... 195 G3
Fayre Meadow *RBTBR* TN32 .... 78 B7
Fearon Rd *HAS* TN34 .... 5 D2
Felbridge Cl *EGRIN* RH19 .... 12 A3
Felcourt Rd *EGRIN* RH19 .... 12 A4
Fellows Rd *HAS* TN34 .... 5 E1
Fennell's Cl *EAST* BN21 .... 10 A2
Ferbies *RRTW* TN3 .... 18 E4
Ferguson Rd *LYDD* TN29 .... 147 G1
Fermor Rd *CROW* TN6 .... 53 H4
Fermor Wy *CROW* TN6 .... 53 H3
Fern Cl *LGNY* BN23 .... 216 D8
Ferndale *RTWE/PEM* TN2 .... 20 D6
Ferndale Cl *RTWE/PEM* TN2 .... 20 C7
  RTWE/PEM TN2 .... 20 C7
Ferndale Rd *BURH* RH15 .... 119 H2
  HOVE BN3 .... 203 J4
Fernhurst Cl *BRI* BN1 .... 178 D5
Fernhurst Crs *BRI* BN1 .... 178 C6
  SBGH/RUST TN4 .... 20 A1
Fernlea Cl *RHAS* TN35 .... 139 G7
Fern Rd *STLEO* TN38 .... 197 G2
Fernside Av *STLEO* TN38 .... 197 G3
The Ferns *RTW* TN1 .... 20 B7
Fernwood Rd *BRI* BN1 .... 177 J6
Ferrers Rd *LEW* BN7 .... 2 B3
Ferring Cl *RYE* TN31 .... 113 G5
Ferry Hl *WSEA* TN36 .... 142 E5
Ferry Rd *RYE* TN31 .... 113 H6
  SHOR BN43 .... 200 C5
Festival Gdns *BEXW* TN39 .... 195 H4
Feversham Cl *SHOR* BN43 .... 200 E5
Field Cl *BURH* RH15 .... 88 E7
  SEAF BN25 .... 232 D1
Field End *UCK* TN22 .... 67 G7
Fielden La *CROW* TN6 .... 53 F2
Fielden Rd *CROW* TN6 .... 52 E3
Fieldway *HPPT/KEY* BN6 .... 119 K8
  RYE TN31 .... 109 K6
Field Wy *STLEO* TN38 .... 197 F3
Fieldways *HAWK* TN18 .... 63 G2
Fiennes Rd *HAIL* BN27 .... 163 F5
Figg La *CROW* TN6 .... 53 H3
Filching Cl *POLE* BN26 .... 214 D8
Filching Rd *EDN/EASTW* BN20 .... 229 G6
Filder Cl *LW/ROSE* BN22 .... 10 C1
Filsham Dr *BEX* TN40 .... 196 B5
Filsham Rd *STLEO* TN38 .... 197 G4
Filsham Va *STLEO* TN38 .... 197 G4
The Finches *BEX* TN40 .... 196 A7
  SHOR BN43 .... 200 D4
  STLEO TN38 .... 169 H6
Findon Av *ROTT* BN2 .... 221 H2

Findon Cl *BEXW* TN39 .... 194 D8
  HOVE BN3 .... 176 E8
  SEAF BN25 .... 225 K8
Findon Rd *ROTT* BN2 .... 205 G6
Finisterre Av *LGNY* BN23 .... 231 G3
Finmere Cl *LW/ROSE* BN22 .... 11 E1
Finmere Rd *LW/ROSE* BN22 .... 11 E1
Finsbury Rd *ROTT* BN2 .... 7 D4
Fir Cl *ROTT* BN2 .... 206 C4
Fircroft Cl *BRI* BN1 .... 177 K8
Fir Grove Rd *HTHF* TN21 .... 99 F4
Firle Bostal *RING/NEW* BN8 .... 210 C1
Firle Cl *RHAS* TN35 .... 171 H7
  SEAF BN25 .... 225 F6
Firle Crs *LEW* BN7 .... 181 J1
Firle Dr *SEAF* BN25 .... 225 F6
Firle Gra *SEAF* BN25 .... 225 F6
Firle Rd *BEXW* TN39 .... 194 C7
  LW/ROSE BN22 .... 11 D3
  PEAHV BN10 .... 222 A2
  ROTT BN2 .... 7 F4
  SEAF BN25 .... 225 F6
First Av *BEX* TN40 .... 196 A6
  HOVE BN3 .... 203 H6
  NEWHV BN9 .... 8 C4
  RYE TN31 .... 145 H1
First St *RRTW* TN3 .... 18 D8
Firtoft Cl *BURH* RH15 .... 89 H8
Fir Toll Cl *MAYF* TN20 .... 71 K1
Fir Toll Rd *MAYF* TN20 .... 71 G1
Fir Tree Cl *BEXW* TN39 .... 194 B8
  HAIL BN27 .... 189 H1
Firtree Rd *HAS* TN34 .... 5 E2
Fir Tree Rd *SBGH/RUST* TN4 .... 29 K1
Fir Tree Wy *HPPT/KEY* BN6 .... 119 G7
Firwood Cl *HTHF* TN21 .... 100 A3
  LW/ROSE BN22 .... 229 K2
Firwood Ri *HTHF* TN21 .... 100 A3
Fisher Cl *LGNY* BN23 .... 231 G4
Fishergate Cl *PTSD* BN41 .... 201 K4
Fishermans Wk *SHOR* BN43 .... 200 A6
Fishersgate Ter *PTSD* BN41 .... 201 K4
Fisher St *LEW* BN7 .... 2 C4
Fishmarket Rd *RYE* TN31 .... 113 J6
Fishponds La *RHAS* TN35 .... 139 G8
Fitch Dr *ROTT* BN2 .... 205 F2
Fitzgerald Av *SEAF* BN25 .... 232 B1
Fitzgerald Cl *EDN/EASTW* BN20 .... 10 B6
Fitzgerald Pk *SEAF* BN25 .... 232 B1
Fitzgerald Rd *LEW* BN7 .... 3 D2
Fitzherbert Dr *ROTT* BN2 .... 7 F2
Fitzjohns Rd *LEW* BN7 .... 2 A3
Fitzmaurice Av *LW/ROSE* BN22 .... 11 D2
Fitzroy Rd *LEW* BN7 .... 2 A4
Five Chimneys La *UCK* TN22 .... 69 J6
Flag Sq *SHOR* BN43 .... 200 C5
Flamsteed Rd *HAIL* BN27 .... 191 H2
Flaxmore Pl *SBGH/RUST* TN4 .... 20 A1
Fleming Cl *LGNY* BN23 .... 231 C1
Fletcher Av *STLEO* TN38 .... 169 G4
Fletching Cl *ROTT* BN2 .... 205 C5
Fletching Rd *LW/ROSE* BN22 .... 230 B1
Fletching St *MAYF* TN20 .... 56 B8
Flimwell Cl *LGNY* BN23 .... 216 B7
  ROTT BN2 .... 205 F6
  STLEO TN38 .... 196 E1
  WADH TN5 .... 47 H7
Flint Cl *PTSD* BN41 .... 202 A1
  SEAF BN25 .... 225 F5
The Flints *LEW* BN7 .... 181 H6
Flitterbrook La *HTHF* TN21 .... 101 J6
  HTHF TN21 .... 131 K1
Florance La *RRTW* TN3 .... 27 K5
Florence Av *HOVE* BN3 .... 202 C3
Florence Pl *BRI* BN1 .... 7 D1
Florence Rd *BRI* BN1 .... 6 C2
Folders Cl *BURH* RH15 .... 119 K2
Folders La *BURH* RH15 .... 119 J2
Foley Cl *LGNY* BN23 .... 231 F4
Folkestone Cl *SEAF* BN25 .... 225 K6
Folkestone Rd *RYE* TN31 .... 86 E8
Folkington Gdns *SLVH* TN37 .... 169 K6
Folkington Rd *POLE* BN26 .... 214 C6
Fonthill Rd *HOVE* BN3 .... 203 G3
Fontridge La *BUR/ETCH* TN19 .... 76 B8
Fontwell Av *BEXW* TN39 .... 194 B6
Foords La *PEV* BN24 .... 216 C4
Foot's La *BUR/ETCH* TN19 .... 74 D8
Fordbrook Hl *CROW* TN6 .... 69 G1
Fordcombe Rd *RRTW* TN3 .... 18 B8
Ford Manor Rd *LING* RH7 .... 13 F1
Ford Rd *STLEO* TN38 .... 197 G1
Foredown Cl *EDN/EASTW* BN20 .... 236 C1
  PTSD BN41 .... 202 A1
Foredown Dr *PTSD* BN41 .... 202 A2
Foredown Rd *PTSD* BN41 .... 176 A8
  PTSD BN41 .... 202 A1
Forest Dene *CROW* TN6 .... 54 B2
Forest La *HTHF* TN21 .... 101 K6
Forest Pk *CROW* TN6 .... 53 F1
Forest Pl *HTHF* TN21 .... 98 D5
Forest Ri *CROW* TN6 .... 54 B2
Forest Rd *BRI* BN1 .... 179 F6
  FROW RH18 .... 36 B2
  RTWE/PEM TN2 .... 30 C2

Forest Vw *HAIL* BN27 .... 189 F3
  UCK TN22 .... 50 C8
Forest View Rd *EGRIN* RH19 .... 22 C5
Forest Wy *EGRIN* RH19 .... 23 F6
  HAS TN34 .... 4 C3
  HRTF TN7 .... 26 E5
  RTWE/PEM TN2 .... 21 K3
  RTWE/PEM TN2 .... 30 C2
Forewood La *BAT* TN33 .... 168 B3
Forewood Ri *BAT* TN33 .... 167 K5
Forge Cl *PTSD* BN41 .... 202 A1
  UCK TN22 .... 95 J5
Forge Fld *WADH* TN5 .... 59 H5
Forge La *RBTBR* TN32 .... 108 A2
Forge Ri *UCK* TN22 .... 95 J5
Forge Rd *RRTW* TN3 .... 27 K8
  SBGH/RUST TN4 .... 19 K2
Forge Wy *BURH* RH15 .... 89 F7
  SLVH TN37 .... 169 K6
Forstall *RRTW* TN3 .... 18 E7
Fort Hvn *SHOR* BN43 .... 201 F5
Fort La *LW/ROSE* BN22 .... 11 F1
Fort Ri *NEWHV* BN9 .... 9 D5
Fort Rd *LW/ROSE* BN22 .... 11 F1
  NEWHV BN9 .... 9 D5
Forward Cl *NEWHV* BN9 .... 223 K1
Foster Cl *SEAF* BN25 .... 225 F7
Foundry La *LEW* BN7 .... 3 E4
Foundry St *BRI* BN1 .... 6 C4
Fountains Cl *BRI* BN1 .... 204 C1
  LW/ROSE BN22 .... 215 K8
Founthill Av *ROTT* BN2 .... 220 E2
Founthill Rd *ROTT* BN2 .... 220 E2
Fourteen Acre La *RHAS* TN35 .... 140 B6
Fourth Av *ROTT* BN2 .... 203 G6
Fowey Cl *SHOR* BN43 .... 200 D5
Fowlers Cl *BEXW* TN39 .... 194 D6
Fowle La *UCK* TN22 .... 68 C4
Fox Cl *BURH* RH15 .... 119 F2
Foxcote *SLVH* TN37 .... 170 A7
Foxdown Rd *ROTT* BN2 .... 206 C4
Foxglove Cl *BURH* RH15 .... 88 D7
  RING/NEW BN8 .... 156 B3
Foxglove Rd *LGNY* BN23 .... 216 C8
Foxhill *BEXW* TN39 .... 194 D6
Fox Hl *HWH* RH16 .... 90 A2
Foxhill *PEAHV* BN10 .... 222 D2
Fox Hill *HWH* RH16 .... 90 A2
Fox Hill Village *HWH* RH16 .... 90 B3
Foxhole La *HAWK* TN18 .... 63 K3
  WADH TN5 .... 44 D8
Foxhunters Rd *PTSD* BN41 .... 175 J8
Fox Wy *PTSD* BN41 .... 175 K8
Framelle Mt *UCK* TN22 .... 96 D5
Framfield Cl *BRI* BN1 .... 179 F5
Framfield Rd *UCK* TN22 .... 68 D8
  UCK TN22 .... 95 K5
Framfield Wy *EAST* BN21 .... 229 J5
Francis St *BRI* BN1 .... 6 C3
Frankfield Ri *RTWE/PEM* TN2 .... 29 K2
Franklands Cl *BURH* RH15 .... 119 H2
Franklands Gdns *BURH* RH15 .... 119 G3
Franklands Wy *BURH* RH15 .... 119 G3
Franklin Rd *PTSD* BN41 .... 202 B4
  ROTT BN2 .... 7 E3
  SHOR BN43 .... 201 F3
Franklin St *ROTT* BN2 .... 7 E3
Frank's Hollow Rd *RRTW* TN3 .... 19 G2
Frant Av *BEXW* TN39 .... 194 B6
Frant Cl *BEXW* TN39 .... 194 B6
Frant Rd *HOVE* BN3 .... 203 F1
  RTWE/PEM TN2 .... 30 A4
Frary Wk *RTWE/PEM* TN2 .... 100 A8
Fraser Av *LGNY* BN23 .... 231 F4
Freckley Hollow *BAT* TN33 .... 166 A1
Frederick Pl *BRI* BN1 .... 6 C4
Frederick Rd *RHAS* TN35 .... 171 F8
Frederick St *BRI* BN1 .... 6 B4
Free Heath Rd *RRTW* TN3 .... 32 E8
Freehold St *SHOR* BN43 .... 200 B4
Freehold Ter *ROTT* BN2 .... 7 D2
Freek's La *BURH* RH15 .... 89 G5
Freeland Cl *SEAF* BN25 .... 224 C5
Freeman Av *LW/ROSE* BN22 .... 229 K2
Freemans Rd *PTSD* BN41 .... 201 K3
Freezeland La *BEXW* TN39 .... 194 E2
Fremlin Cl *SBGH/RUST* TN4 .... 19 F7
Frenches Farm Dr *HTHF* TN21 .... 100 A6
Frenchgate Cl *LW/ROSE* BN22 .... 230 A1
Frenchgate Rd *LW/ROSE* BN22 .... 230 A1
Freshfield Bank *FROW* RH18 .... 35 J1
Freshfield Cl *HAIL* BN27 .... 189 G5
Freshfield La *RHWH* RH17 .... 64 A3
Freshfield Pl *ROTT* BN2 .... 7 E5
Freshfield Rd *ROTT* BN2 .... 7 E5
Freshfield St *ROTT* BN2 .... 7 E4
Freshfield Wy *ROTT* BN2 .... 7 E5
Freshford Cl *LGNY* BN23 .... 230 E1
Freshway *LW/ROSE* BN22 .... 215 H8
Frewen Cl *RYE* TN31 .... 81 K4
Frewyn Cl *STLEO* TN38 .... 169 G2
Friar Cl *BRI* BN1 .... 178 B7
Friar Crs *BRI* BN1 .... 178 A8
Friar Rd *BRI* BN1 .... 178 B7
Friars' Av *PEAHV* BN10 .... 222 D5

Friars Bank *RHAS* TN35 .... 172 A4
Friars Cl *HPPT/KEY* BN6 .... 118 E7
Friars Hl *RHAS* TN35 .... 171 J4
Friars Oak Rd *HPPT/KEY* BN6 ...... 118 E6
Friars Rd *WSEA* TN36 .... 143 F4
Friars' Wk *LEW* BN7 .... 3 D4
Friar's Wy *TN34* 170 C7
   RTWE/PEM TN2 .... 20 D5
Friar Wk *BRI* BN1 .... 178 A7
Friday St *LGNY* BN23 .... 216 D7
Friezland Rd *SBGH/RUST* TN4 ...... 29 H2
Frimley Cl *ROTT* BN2 .... 206 B4
Friston Av *LW/ROSE* BN22 .... 229 H2
Friston Cl *EDN/EASTW* BN20 .... 234 E2
   ROTT BN2 .... 179 G7
   SEAF BN25 .... 224 D7
Friston Downs *EDN/EASTW* BN20 .. 235 H3
Frith Pk *EGRIN* RH19 .... 12 C8
Frith Rd *HOVE* BN3 .... 203 F3
Frobisher Cl *LGNY* BN23 .... 231 F4
Frog Hole La *MAYF* TN20 .... 71 F6
Frog La *RTW* TN1 .... 30 A1
Fryatts Wy *BEXW* TN39 .... 194 C5
Fry Crs *BURH* RH15 .... 88 E6
Fryman's La *RYE* TN31 .... 139 F1
Fulford Cl *STLEO* TN38 .... 197 H3
Fuller Cl *WADH* TN5 .... 44 A6
Fuller Rd *LEW* BN7 .... 2 A2
Fullers La *RYE* TN31 .... 81 K5
Fullwood Av *NEWHV* BN9 .... 8 B3
Fulmar Cl *HOVE* BN3 .... 203 J2
Fulmar Dr *EGRIN* RH19 .... 12 E8
The Furlongs *POLE* BN26 .... 212 C8
Furnace Av *RRTW* TN3 .... 33 H8
Furnace La *HTHF* TN21 .... 129 H3
   RRTW TN3 .... 33 F7
   RYE TN31 .... 109 K6
Furnace Wy *UCK* TN22 .... 96 A4 1
Furness Rd *EDN/EASTW* BN20 ...... 10 B5
Furzefield Av *RRTW* TN3 .... 18 E3
Furzefield Cha *EGRIN* RH19 .... 12 C5
Furzefield Rd *EGRIN* RH19 .... 12 B7
Furze Hl *HOVE* BN3 .... 203 J5
Fyning Pl *BEXW* TN39 .... 194 B6
Fyrsway *RHAS* TN35 .... 172 D8
Fysie La *BUR/ETCH* TN19 .... 61 H8

G

Gableson Av *BRI* BN1 .... 177 G7
Gage Rdg *FROW* RH18 .... 35 J2
The Gages *HAIL* BN27 .... 189 J4
Gainsborough Crs *LGNY* BN23 .... 230 E2 1
Gainsborough La *POLE* BN26 .... 214 C5
Gainsborough Rd *BEX* TN40 .... 195 K5 1
Galley Hill Vw *BEX* TN40 .... 195 K7
Galliers Cl *BRI* BN1 .... 178 C5
Gallipot Hl *HRTF* TN7 .... 25 J8
The Gallops *LEW* BN7 .... 2 A1
Gallows Cl *PEV* BN24 .... 217 F5
Gallows La *PEV* BN24 .... 217 F5
Galveston Cl *LGNY* BN23 .... 231 G4
Gammons Wy *BAT* TN33 .... 138 A2
Gander Cl *BURH* RH15 .... 89 G6 1
Garden Cl *BEX* TN40 .... 195 J7 1
   EGRIN RH19 .... 22 D4
   PTSD BN41 .... 202 B3
   SHOR BN43 .... 200 E2
Gardener St *PTSD* BN41 .... 201 K3
Garden House La *EGRIN* RH19 ...... 22 C7
Garden Rd *RTW* TN1 .... 20 B7 1
The Gardens *PTSD* BN41 .... 202 B3
   STHW BN42 .... 201 J4
Garden St *LEW* BN7 .... 2 C5
   RTW TN1 .... 20 B7 1
Garden Wood Rd *EGRIN* RH19 ...... 22 A2
Gardner Cl *LGNY* BN23 .... 231 F4 1
Gardner Rd *PTSD* BN41 .... 201 K4
Gardner's Hl *RYE* TN31 .... 85 H5
Gardner St *BRI* BN1 .... 6 C5 1
   HAIL BN27 .... 163 G5
Garfield Rd *HAIL* BN27 .... 189 G4
Garland Rd *EGRIN* RH19 .... 22 B2
Garlinge Rd *SBGH/RUST* TN4 .... 20 A1
Garnet Dr *EDN/EASTW* BN20 ...... 229 H4
Garston Pk *BUR/ETCH* TN19 .... 75 K5
Garth Cl *BEXW* TN39 .... 195 F6
Gatehouse La *BURH* RH15 .... 88 C7
   HPPT/KEY BN6 .... 88 B6
   UCK TN22 .... 96 E5
   UCK TN22 .... 97 G6
Gatelands Dr *BEXW* TN39 .... 195 F5
The Cattons *BURH* RH15 .... 88 E8
Gaudick Cl *EDN/EASTW* BN20 ..... 10 A6 1
Gaudick Rd *EDN/EASTW* BN20 .... 10 A5
Geering Rd *PEV* BN24 .... 216 C6
Geers Wd *HTHF* TN21 .... 99 K5
Gemma Cl *HAIL* BN27 .... 189 K4
Geneva Rd *NEWHV* BN9 .... 9 D4
Gensing Rd *STLEO* TN38 .... 4 A5
George Hl *RBTBR* TN32 .... 78 B8
George St *HAIL* BN27 .... 189 H4

HAS TN34 .... 5 E5
HOVE BN3 .... 203 G5
PTSD BN41 .... 201 K4
PTSD BN41 .... 202 B4 1
ROTT BN2 .... 7 D5 1
WADH TN5 .... 44 B6
Georgian Cl *BEX* TN40 .... 195 K5
Georgian Wk *STLEO* TN38 .... 197 G3
Gerald Cl *BURH* RH15 .... 89 K8
Gerald Rd *SEAF* BN25 .... 232 B2
Gerard St *BRI* BN1 .... 6 C2
German St *WSEA* TN36 .... 142 E4
Ghyll Rd *CROW* TN6 .... 39 F7
   HTHF TN21 .... 99 K5
Ghyllside *ROTT* BN2 .... 205 F2
Ghyllside Av *SLVH* TN37 .... 169 K7
Ghyllside Dr *HAS* TN34 .... 170 A7
Ghyll Side Rd *RYE* TN31 .... 81 K4
Ghyllside Wy *HAS* TN34 .... 170 A7
Gibb Cl *BEX* TN40 .... 196 A6
Gibbetts *RRTW* TN3 .... 18 D8
Gibbon Rd *NEWHV* BN9 .... 8 D4
Gibraltar Ri *HTHF* TN21 .... 100 A4
Giffards Cl *EGRIN* RH19 .... 22 D2 1
Gilbert Rd *LW/ROSE* BN22 .... 11 D3
   STLEO TN38 .... 197 J3
Gilberts Dr *EDN/EASTW* BN20 .... 235 F4
Gilbert Wy *HAIL* BN27 .... 189 G6
Gilda Crs *POLE* BN26 .... 215 F5
Gildredge Rd *EAST* BN21 .... 10 B4
   SEAF BN25 .... 225 G8
Gilham La *FROW* RH18 .... 35 J1
Gillham Wood Rd *BEXW* TN39 ... 194 C8
The Gilligans *BURH* RH15 .... 89 F6
Gillridge Gn *CROW* TN6 .... 39 H7 1
Gillsman's Dr *STLEO* TN38 .... 197 G3
Gillsman's Hl *STLEO* TN38 .... 197 H2
Gillsman's Pk *STLEO* TN38 .... 197 G2
Gimble Wy *RTWE/PEM* TN2 .... 21 K3
Gingerbread La *HAWK* TN18 .... 47 K8
Gipps Cross La *RRTW* TN3 .... 18 D8 1
Githa Rd *RHAS* TN35 .... 199 F1
The Glades *BEX* TN40 .... 195 K5
   EGRIN RH19 .... 23 F2
The Glade *HAIL* BN27 .... 188 E5
   MAYF TN20 .... 72 A1
   UCK TN22 .... 95 K4
Gladstone Av *LW/ROSE* BN22 .... 230 A2
Gladstone Pl *ROTT* BN2 .... 7 E2
Gladstone Rd *BURH* RH15 .... 89 J6
   CROW TN6 .... 53 H3
   HAS TN34 .... 5 E3 1
   PTSD BN41 .... 202 A4
   SBGH/RUST TN4 .... 19 F7 1
Gladys Av *PEAHV* BN10 .... 222 C5
Gladys Rd *HOVE* BN3 .... 202 C3
Glassenbury Dr *BEX* TN40 .... 196 A6
Glastonbury Rd *HOVE* BN3 .... 202 C5
Gleave Cl *EGRIN* RH19 .... 22 E1
Glebe Cl *BEXW* TN39 .... 194 C7
   EDN/EASTW BN20 .... 229 J8
   LEW BN7 .... 2 A5
   STHW BN42 .... 201 J4
Glebe Dr *SEAF* BN25 .... 225 F8
Glebelands Cl *SHOR* BN43 .... 200 E3 1
The Glebelands *CROW* TN6 .... 53 H1
The Glebe *HAS* TN34 .... 5 F3 1
   RTWE/PEM TN2 .... 21 K3
Glebe Vls *HOVE* BN3 .... 202 C4
Glen Cl *POLE* BN26 .... 214 E7
Glendale *EAST* BN21 .... 229 H5
Glendale Rd *BURH* RH15 .... 119 H1
   HOVE BN3 .... 203 J4
Glendor Rd *HOVE* BN3 .... 202 D5
Glendyke Rd *EGRIN* RH19 .... 22 E3
Glendyne Wy *EGRIN* RH19 .... 22 E3
Gleneagles Cl *BEX* TN40 .... 195 K6 1
   SEAF BN25 .... 224 B5
Gleneagles Dr *HAIL* BN27 .... 188 E3
   STLEO TN38 .... 197 G4
Glenfalls Av *BRI* BN1 .... 178 A4
Glengorse *BAT* TN33 .... 137 F8
Glenleigh Park Rd *BEXW* TN39 .. 195 F5
Glenleigh Wk *RBTBR* TN32 .... 78 A7
Glenmore Pk *RTWE/PEM* TN2 .... 29 K3
Glenmore Rd *CROW* TN6 .... 38 E8
Glenmore Rd East *CROW* TN6 .... 39 F8
Glen Ri *BRI* BN1 .... 177 G6
Glen Rise Cl *BRI* BN1 .... 177 G6
The Glen *UCK* TN22 .... 95 K2 1
Glenthorn Rd *BEXW* TN39 .... 195 F7
Glenview Cl *RHAS* TN35 .... 199 G2
Glen Vue *EGRIN* RH19 .... 22 C2
Glessing Rd *PEV* BN24 .... 216 C6
Gleton Av *HOVE* BN3 .... 202 C1
Gloucester Av *BEX* TN40 .... 196 B6
Gloucester Cl *LW/ROSE* BN22 .... 229 H1
Gloucester Pl *BRI* BN1 .... 6 C4
   ROTT BN2 .... 6 C4 1
Gloucester Rd *BRI* BN1 .... 6 B4
   HAS TN34 .... 89 F8
   WADH TN5 .... 44 B5
Gloucester St *BRI* BN1 .... 6 C4
Glovers La *BEX* TN40 .... 195 J4

BEXW TN39 .... 195 H4
Glynde Av *LW/ROSE* BN22 .... 229 K2
   ROTT BN2 .... 221 F1
Glyndebourne Av *ROTT* BN2 .... 221 F2
Glyndebourne Gdns *SLVH* TN37 .. 169 K6 1
Glynde Cl *NEWHV* BN9 .... 223 J1 1
Glynde Rd *ROTT* BN2 .... 7 F4
Glyne Ascent *BEX* TN40 .... 196 A6
Glyne Barn Cl *BEX* TN40 .... 196 B6
Glyne Dr *BEX* TN40 .... 196 B6
Glynleigh Dr *POLE* BN26 .... 215 H5
Glynleigh Rd *PEV* BN24 .... 215 K2
Glynn Ri *PEAHV* BN10 .... 222 A2
Glynn Rd *PEAHV* BN10 .... 222 B2
Goatham La *RYE* TN31 .... 109 C6
Godden Cl *RYE* TN31 .... 81 K3
Godden Rd *RING/NEW* BN8 .... 93 C4
Godfrey Cl *LEW* BN7 .... 2 C2
Godwin Rd *HOVE* BN3 .... 202 C3
   RHAS TN35 .... 199 F2
The Goffs *EAST* BN21 .... 10 A4
Goldbridge Rd *RING/NEW* BN8 ...... 93 J4
Coldcrest Dr *UCK* TN22 .... 95 K6
Golden Hl *BURH* RH15 .... 89 K8
Golden Miller La *POLE* BN26 .... 214 D5
Goldhurst Gn *WSEA* TN36 .... 141 J6
Golding Rd *LGNY* BN23 .... 231 C1
Gold La *PEAHV* BN10 .... 222 B1
Goldsmid Rd *HOVE* BN3 .... 6 A3
Goldsmith Cl *LGNY* BN23 .... 217 F8 2
Goldsmiths Av *CROW* TN6 .... 39 F8
Goldstone Cl *HOVE* BN3 .... 177 G8
Goldstone Crs *HOVE* BN3 .... 203 F1
Goldstone La *HOVE* BN3 .... 203 G3
Goldstone Rd *HOVE* BN3 .... 203 F4
Goldstone Vls *HOVE* BN3 .... 203 G4
Goldstone Wy *HOVE* BN3 .... 203 F1
Golf Dr *BRI* BN1 .... 178 C8
Goods Station Rd *RTW* TN1 .... 20 B7
Goodtrees La *EDEN* TN8 .... 25 H1
Goodwin Cl *HAIL* BN27 .... 188 E1
Goodwins Cl *EGRIN* RH19 .... 12 B8
The Goodwins *RTWE/PEM* TN2 .... 29 K2 2
Goodwood Cl *EDN/EASTW* BN20 .. 229 C1
Goodwood Wy *ROTT* BN2 .... 179 F8
Gooseberry La *RYE* TN31 .... 81 J8
Gordon Av *SHOR* BN43 .... 200 D4
Gordon Rd *BRI* BN1 .... 204 A1
   BURH RH15 .... 89 J7
   CROW TN6 .... 53 H1
   HAIL BN27 .... 189 C4
   HAS TN34 .... 5 E4 1
   PTSD BN41 .... 201 K4
   SBGH/RUST TN4 .... 20 C4
   SHOR BN43 .... 200 C4
   UCK TN22 .... 68 E8
Gore Park Av *EAST* BN21 .... 229 J7
Gore Park Rd *EAST* BN21 .... 229 J7
Goreham Av *ROTT* BN2 .... 220 D1
Gorham Cl *ROTT* BN2 .... 220 D1
Gorham Wy *PEAHV* BN10 .... 221 H3
Gorringe Cl *EDN/EASTW* BN20 ... 215 F8
   SHOR BN43 .... 201 G4
Gorringe Rd *LW/ROSE* BN22 .... 10 B2
Gorringe Valley Rd
   EDN/EASTW BN20 .... 215 F8
Gorse Cl *EDN/EASTW* BN20 .... 229 C6
   PTSD BN41 .... 175 J7
Gorse Dr *SEAF* BN25 .... 225 C5
Gorse Hl *HTHF* TN21 .... 100 E1
Gorselands *BAT* TN33 .... 138 A2
Gorse Rd *RTWE/PEM* TN2 .... 20 E6
Gorsethorn Wy *RHAS* TN35 .... 172 D7
The Gorseway *BEXW* TN39 .... 194 B6
Gosford Wy *POLE* BN26 .... 214 E5
Gote La *RING/NEW* BN8 .... 155 J7
Goudhurst Cl *LGNY* BN23 .... 230 E2 1
Gradwell End *RING/NEW* BN8 ...... 122 A4
Graffham Ct *ROTT* BN2 .... 205 F5
Grafton St *ROTT* BN2 .... 7 D6 1
Graham Av *BRI* BN1 .... 177 K7
   PTSD BN41 .... 175 J7
Graham Crs *PTSD* BN41 .... 175 J7
Grampian Cl *LGNY* BN23 .... 216 D8
   RTWE/PEM TN2 .... 20 D6
Grand Av *BEX* TN40 .... 196 A5
   HOVE BN3 .... 203 H5
   HPPT/KEY BN6 .... 119 F7
   SEAF BN25 .... 224 D6
Grand Crs *ROTT* BN2 .... 220 D2
Grand Junction Rd *BRI* BN1 .... 6 C6
Grand Pde *EAST* BN21 .... 10 C6
   POLE BN26 .... 214 E5 1
   ROTT BN2 .... 6 C5
   STLEO TN38 .... 4 A6
Grand Parade Ms *ROTT* BN2 .... 6 C5 1
Grange Av *SLVH* TN37 .... 169 K7
Grange Cl *BRI* BN1 .... 6 A1
   BURH RH15 .... 89 J6
   CROW TN6 .... 53 F2
   HTHF TN21 .... 129 K5
Grange Court Dr *BEXW* TN39 .... 195 C5
Grange Gdns *SBGH/RUST* TN4 .... 19 H7

Grange Rd *EAST* BN21 .... **10** B5
  HAS TN34 .... **170** B6
  HOVE BN3 .... **202** D4
  LEW BN7 .... **2** C5
  RING/NEW BN8 .... **123** H7
  SBGH/RUST TN4 .... **19** H7
  STHW BN42 .... **201** H4
  UCK TN22 .... **95** J4
The Grange *RING/NEW* BN8 .... **123** H7
Grangeways *BRI* BN1 .... **177** K6 🔲
Grantham Bank *RING/NEW* BN8 .... **123** J7
Grantham CI *RING/NEW* BN8 .... **122** C4 🔲
Grantham Rd *BRI* BN1 .... **6** C1
Grant St *ROTT* BN2 .... **7** D3
Granville Rd *EDN/EASTW* BN20 .... **10** B5
  HOVE BN3 .... **6** A3
  RTW TN1 .... **20** B6
Grasmere CI *LGNY* BN23 .... **216** C7
Grassington Rd *EDN/EASTW* BN20 .... **10** B6
Grassmere Av *PEAHV* BN10 .... **221** J3
Gravett Ct *BURH* RH15 .... **119** F1
Graycoats Dr *CROW* TN6 .... **53** H1 🔲
Graystone La *RHAS* TN35 .... **171** F8
Grazebrook CI *BEXW* TN39 .... **194** B8
Great Brooms Rd *SBGH/RUST* TN4... **20** B3
Great Cliffe Rd *LGNY* BN23 .... **231** F2
Great College St *ROTT* BN2 .... **7** E6
Great Courtlands *RRTW* TN3 .... **18** E8
Greater Paddock *RING/NEW* BN8 .. **155** K5
Great Oak *BUR/ETCH* TN19 .... **62** A8
Great Rough *RING/NEW* BN8 .... **92** E5
Great Wd *BAT* TN33............... **137** C7
Grecian Rd *RTW* TN1 .... **30** B1 🔲
Greenacres *PEAHV* BN10 .... **222** C1
  RHAS TN35 .... **139** C8
  SHOR BN43 .... **200** B3
Greenacres Dr *HAIL* BN27 .... **189** H3
  RING/NEW BN8............... **155** H7
Greenacres Wy *HAIL* BN27 .... **189** H3 🔲
Greenbank Av *ROTT* BN2 .... **221** F2
Green CI *RING/NEW* BN8 .... **155** K5
  STHW BN42 .... **201** H4 🔲
Greenfield CI *BRI* BN1 .... **178** B6
  SBGH/RUST TN4 .... **19** G6 🔲
Green Field CI *STHW* BN42 .... **201** H3 🔲
Greenfield Crs *BRI* BN1 .... **178** A6
Greenfield Dr *UCK* TN22............... **95** K7
Greenfield Rd *BUR/ETCH* TN19 .... **76** A4
  EAST BN21 .... **229** J8
Greenfields *HAIL* BN27 .... **189** F2
Greenfields CI *SLVH* TN37 .... **169** J5
Green Ga *PEAHV* BN10 .... **222** B2
Green Gv *HAIL* BN27 .... **189** G3
Green Hedges Av *EGRIN* RH19 .... **22** B1 🔲
Green Hedges CI *EGRIN* RH19 .... **22** B1
Greenhill Pk *HWH* RH16 .... **90** C1
Greenhill Wy *HWH* RH16 .... **90** C1
  PEAHV BN10............... **222** B1 🔲
Greenlands CI *BURH* RH15 .... **119** H3
Greenlands Dr *BURH* RH15 .... **119** H3
Green La *BEXW* TN39 .... **194** C6
  CROW TN6 .... **39** K8
  HTHF TN21 .... **100** B5
  LEW BN7 .... **2** C5
  POLE BN26 .... **228** B2
  RING/NEW BN8 .... **122** C4 🔲
  RING/NEW BN8 .... **122** C2
  RING/NEW BN8 .... **156** B2
  ROTT BN2 .... **206** B5
  SEAF BN25 .... **232** A1
Greenleaf Gdns *POLE* BN26 .... **215** F4
Greenleas *HOVE* BN3 .... **202** C1
  RTWE/PEM TN2 .... **21** J5
Green Pk Cnr *RHWH* RH17 .... **90** C7
Green Rdg *BRI* BN1 .... **177** G6
Green Rd *RHWH* RH17 .... **90** C6
Green Sq *WADH* TN5 .... **44** B6
Greenstede Av *EGRIN* RH19 .... **12** D8
Green St *EDN/EASTW* BN20 .... **229** H7
The Green *BAT* TN33 .... **138** A3
  BAT TN33 .... **165** K5
  HOVE BN3 .... **203** H1
  RING/NEW BN8 .... **93** H4
  ROTT BN2 .... **220** C1
  RRTW TN3 .... **18** C8
  STLEO TN38 .... **197** J2
  UCK TN22 .... **97** J5
Green Wk *HAIL* BN27 .... **189** H2
  SEAF BN25 .... **232** D1
Green Wy *EDN/EASTW* BN20 .... **229** G5
  RTWE/PEM TN2 .... **20** E3
Greenways *BEXW* TN39 .... **194** C6
  ROTT BN2 .... **206** A7
  STHW BN42 .... **201** J2
Greenways Crs *SHOR* BN43 .... **200** D2
Greenwell CI *SEAF* BN25 .... **225** J7
Greenwich Rd *HAIL* BN27 .... **189** J4
Greenwich Wy *PEAHV* BN10 .... **222** A4
Greggs Wood Rd *RTWE/PEM* TN2 ... **20** E4
Gregory La *PEV* BN24 .... **217** G6
Gregory Wk *BAT* TN33 .... **138** A3
Grenada CI *BEXW* TN39 .... **194** B8
Grenville Gdns *PEV* BN24 .... **217** K7
Grenville St *BRI* BN1 .... **6** B5

Gresham CI *EAST* BN21 .... **229** H5 🔲
Gresham Wy *STLEO* TN38 .... **197** H3
Greville Rd *RHAS* TN35 .... **171** F8
Greyfriars *HOVE* BN3 .... **203** J3
Greyfriars PI *WSEA* TN36 .... **143** H5 🔲
Greys Rd *EDN/EASTW* BN20 .... **229** J8
Grinstead La *EGRIN* RH19 .... **34** A3
Gromenfield *RRTW* TN3 .... **28** A4 🔲
Groombridge HI *RRTW* TN3 .... **28** A3
Groombridge Rd *RRTW* TN3 .... **27** J3
Grosvenor Br *SBGH/RUST* TN4 .... **20** B6
Grosvenor CI *POLE* BN26 .... **214** E6
Grosvenor Crs *STLEO* TN38 .... **197** G5
Grosvenor Gdns *STLEO* TN38 .... **197** G5
Grosvenor Pk *RTW* TN1 .... **20** A6
Grosvenor Rd *EGRIN* RH19 .... **22** B2
  SEAF BN25 .... **225** F7
Grosvenor St *ROTT* BN2 .... **7** D5 🔲
Grosvenor Wk *RTW* TN1 .... **20** A7 🔲
Grove Av *RTW* TN1 .... **30** A1 🔲
Grove HI *HAIL* BN27 .... **161** H6
  ROTT BN2 .... **7** D4
Grove HI Gdns *RTW* TN1 .... **30** B1
Grove Hill Rd *RTW* TN1 .... **20** A8
Grovelands CI *BURH* RH15 .... **119** F2 🔲
Grovelands Rd *HAIL* BN27 .... **189** F2
Grove La *RYE* TN31 .... **85** J7
Grovely La *HTHF* TN21 .... **132** D2
Grove Rd *BURH* RH15 .... **119** H1
  EAST BN21 .... **10** B5
  EDEN TN8 .... **7** G7
  RHAS TN35 .... **171** G7
  SEAF BN25 .... **225** G8
Grove St *ROTT* BN2 .... **7** D4
The Grove *BAT* TN33 .... **137** F8
  BEXW TN39 .... **194** D6
  CROW TN6 .... **53** G2
  EDN/EASTW BN20 .... **214** E8
  EDN/EASTW BN20 .... **229** G4
  HAIL BN27 .... **189** G5
  MAYF TN20 .... **72** A1
  NEWHV BN9 .... **223** K1
  RTWE/PEM TN2 .... **21** K3
  RYE TN31 .... **113** J5
Growers End *RING/NEW* BN8 .... **93** H4
Guardswell PI *SEAF* BN25 .... **225** F8
Guestling Rd *LW/ROSE* BN22 .... **11** F2
Guildford Rd *RTW* TN1 .... **20** B8 🔲
Guildford St *BRI* BN1 .... **6** B4 🔲
Guilford Rd *BRI* BN1 .... **6** B4
Guldeford La *RYE* TN31 .... **87** H8
Guldeford Rd *RYE* TN31 .... **114** A5
Gundreda Rd *LEW* BN7 .... **2** B3
Gun Rd *UCK* TN22 .... **97** J5
Gunter's La *BEXW* TN39 .... **195** F4
Gurth Rd *RHAS* TN35 .... **199** F2
Gwyneth Gv *BEX* TN40 .... **196** A4
Gwynne Gdns *EGRIN* RH19 .... **22** A1

H

Hackenden CI *EGRIN* RH19 .... **12** C8
Hackenden La *EGRIN* RH19 .... **12** C8
Hackhurst La *HAIL* BN27 .... **160** A6
Hackwood *RBTBR* TN32............... **77** J7
Haddington CI *HOVE* BN3 .... **203** G5
Haddington St *HOVE* BN3 .... **203** G4 🔲
Hadlow Av *LGNY* BN23 .... **216** B7
Hadlow CI *ROTT* BN2 .... **7** F4
Hadlow Down Rd *CROW* TN6 .... **69** H1
Hadrian Av *STHW* BN42 .... **201** J3
Hadrian St *STLEO* TN38 .... **169** H5 🔲
Haig Av *BRI* BN1 .... **178** E5
Hailsham Av *ROTT* BN2 .... **207** G8
Hailsham Rd *HAIL* BN27 .... **163** F6
  HTHF TN21 .... **100** A5
  POLE BN26 .... **214** E4
  POLE BN26 .... **216** A3
Hairpin Cft *PEAHV* BN10 .... **222** B2
Half Mile Dro *RING/NEW* BN8 .... **156** C5
Halland CI *LW/ROSE* BN22 .... **229** J2 🔲
Halland Rd *ROTT* BN2 .... **179** G7
Hallett Rd *ROTT* BN2 .... **7** F3
Halley Rd *HAIL* BN27 .... **191** J2
  HTHF TN21 .... **100** E3
Hall La *UCK* TN22 .... **70** A6
Hall's Hole Rd *RTWE/PEM* TN2 .... **20** E8
Hallyburton Rd *HOVE* BN3 .... **202** C3
Halsford Park Rd *EGRIN* RH19 .... **22** A1
Halton Crs *HAS* TN34 .... **5** F2
Halton PI *HAS* TN34............... **5** F2
Halton Rd *LW/ROSE* BN22 .... **11** E3 🔲
Halton Ter *HAS* TN34 .... **5** F2
Hamble Rd *POLE* BN26 .... **216** A6
Hambleton CI *LGNY* BN23 .... **216** E8
Hambrook *BURH* RH15 .... **119** J2 🔲
Hamelsham Ct *HAIL* BN27 .... **189** F3 🔲
Hamilton CI *PTSD* BN41 .... **175** K8
Hamilton Gdns *RHAS* TN35 .... **171** G5
Hamilton Rd *BRI* BN1 .... **6** B2
Hamilton Ter *BEXW* TN39 .... **195** F2
Hamlands La *LW/ROSE* BN22 .... **215** G8

Ham La *BUR/ETCH* TN19 .... **75** J4
  LEW BN7 .... **3** D5
  RING/NEW BN8............... **155** G5
Hammer La *HTHF* TN21 .... **131** F3
Hammerwood Rd *EGRIN* RH19 .... **23** J5
Hammonds *HAWK* TN18 .... **63** G1 🔲
Hammonds Gdns *BURH* RH15 .... **119** F2 🔲
Hammonds Rdg *BURH* RH15 .... **118** E2
Hammy CI *SHOR* BN43 .... **200** E3
Hammy La *SHOR* BN43 .... **200** E3
Hammy Wy *SHOR* BN43 .... **200** E3
Hampden Av *LW/ROSE* BN22 .... **230** A2
Hampden CI *BAT* TN33 .... **136** B7
Hampden Park Dr *LW/ROSE* BN22.. **229** K1
Hampden Rd *ROTT* BN2 .... **7** E3
Hampstead Rd *BRI* BN1 .... **203** J2
Hampton PI *BRI* BN1 .... **6** A5
Hampton St *BRI* BN1 .... **6** A5 🔲
Hampton Wy *EGRIN* RH19 .... **22** D4
Ham Rd *SHOR* BN43 .... **200** C4
Hamsey CI *EDN/EASTW* BN20 .... **229** G5
  ROTT BN2 .... **205** G6
Hamsey Crs *LEW* BN7 .... **2** A3
Hamsey La *RING/NEW* BN8 .... **153** K4
  SEAF BN25 .... **232** E1
Hamsey Rd *ROTT* BN2 .... **221** G3
Hamsland *RHWH* RH17 .... **48** A7
Hanging Birch La *HTHF* TN21 .... **99** H8
  HTHF TN21 .... **129** H1
Hangleton CI *HOVE* BN3 .... **202** C1
Hangleton Gdns *HOVE* BN3............... **202** C2
Hangleton La *HOVE* BN3 .... **202** B1
  PTSD BN41 .... **202** A1
Hangleton Manor CI *HOVE* BN3 ... **202** B1
Hangleton Rd *HOVE* BN3 .... **202** D1
Hangleton Valley Dr *HOVE* BN3 ... **178** B8
Hangleton Wy *HOVE* BN3............... **202** C1
Hankham Hall Rd *PEV* BN24 .... **216** D3
Hankham Rd *PEV* BN24............... **216** C5
Hankham St *PEV* BN24............... **216** C2
Hannington PI *HPPT/KEY* BN6 .... **118** A4
Hanover CI *BEX* TN40 .... **195** H6 🔲
  SEAF BN25............... **224** C5
Hanover Crs *ROTT* BN2 .... **7** D3 🔲
Hanover Ms *ROTT* BN2............... **7** D3
Hanover Rd *LW/ROSE* BN22 .... **11** E3
  RTW TN1 .... **20** A7 🔲
Hanover St *ROTT* BN2 .... **7** D3
Hanover Ter *ROTT* BN2 .... **7** D3
Hanson Rd *NEWHV* BN9............... **8** B4
Harbour Farm *WSEA* TN36 .... **143** H5
Harbour Rd *RYE* TN31 .... **113** J7
Harbour View CI *SEAF* BN25 .... **224** C5 🔲
Harbour View Rd *NEWHV* BN9 .... **8** B5
Harbour Wy *SHOR* BN43 .... **200** E5
  STLEO TN38 .... **169** F4
Harcourt CI *UCK* TN22 .... **95** K5
Harcourt Rd *UCK* TN22 .... **95** K5
Harding Av *LW/ROSE* BN22 .... **11** D1
Hardwicke Rd *HAS* TN34 .... **5** F3
Hardwick Rd *EAST* BN21 .... **10** C5
  HOVE BN3 .... **176** D8
Hardwick Wy *HOVE* BN3 .... **176** D7
Hardy Dr *SHOR* BN43 .... **200** C5 🔲
Hardy Dr *LGNY* BN23 .... **231** G5
Harebeating CI *HAIL* BN27 .... **189** H1 🔲
Harebeating Crs *HAIL* BN27............... **189** H1
Harebeating Dr *HAIL* BN27 .... **161** G8
Harebeating Gdns *HAIL* BN27 .... **189** H1 🔲
Harebeating La *HAIL* BN27 .... **189** H1
Harebell CI *LGNY* BN23 .... **216** D8 🔲
Harebell Dr *PTSD* BN41 .... **175** K8
Harecombe Ri *CROW* TN6 .... **53** G3
Harecombe Rd *CROW* TN6 .... **53** G3
Haremere HI *BUR/ETCH* TN19 .... **77** H2
Harescroft *RTWE/PEM* TN2 .... **29** K4 🔲
Hare Wy *SLVH* TN37 .... **169** K6
Harewood CI *BEXW* TN39 .... **194** T8
Harfield CI *NEWHV* BN9 .... **224** A1
Hargate CI *RTWE/PEM* TN2 .... **29** K4
Harison Rd *SEAF* BN25 .... **225** H7
Harkness Dr *HAS* TN34 .... **170** E6
Harlequin Gdns *SLVH* TN37 .... **169** H5
Harlequin La *CROW* TN6............... **53** G3
Harlequin PI *CROW* TN6 .... **53** G3
Harley La *HTHF* TN21 .... **100** A5
Harley Shute Rd *STLEO* TN38 .... **197** F4
Harley Wy *STLEO* TN38............... **197** F5
Harmans Md *EGRIN* RH19 .... **22** E2
Harmers Hay Rd *HAIL* BN27 .... **189** G2
Harmers HI *RING/NEW* BN8 .... **93** G4
Harmony St *SBGH/RUST* TN4 .... **19** H7
Harmsworth Crs *HOVE* BN3 .... **176** D8 🔲
Harold CI *BEX* TN40 .... **218** C4
Harold Dr *LGNY* BN23 .... **231** F3
Harold Ms *STLEO* TN38 .... **4** A6 🔲
Harold PI *HAS* TN34 .... **5** D5 🔲
Harold Rd *RHAS* TN35 .... **199** G1
Harpers Rd *NEWHV* BN9 .... **8** C3
Harrier La *BAT* TN33 .... **137** F8
Harries Rd *RTWE/PEM* TN2 .... **20** D4
Harrington PI *BRI* BN1 .... **204** C3
Harrington Rd *BRI* BN1 .... **203** K1
Harrington Vls *BRI* BN1 .... **204** C1
Harris Ct *EAST* BN21 .... **10** C4 🔲

Harrisons La RING/NEW BN8 ...... 155 K5
Harrow Cl SEAF BN25 .... 225 H7
Harrow La SLVH TN37 .... 169 J5
Hart Cl UCK TN22 .... 95 G4
Hartfield Av BRI BN1 .... 178 B7
Hartfield La EAST BN21 .... 10 B3
Hartfield Meadow STLEO TN38 ... 168 E8
Hartfield Rd EAST BN21 .... 10 B4
 EDEN TN8 .... 15 K8
 FROW RH18 .... 36 A1
 ROTT BN2 .... 221 G2
 SEAF BN25 .... 225 H8
Hartington Pl EAST BN21 .... 10 C5
 ROTT BN2 .... 7 E2
Hartington Rd ROTT BN2 .... 7 E2
Hartington Ter ROTT BN2 .... 7 E2
Hartington Vls HOVE BN3 .... 203 G3
Hartnokes HAWK TN18 .... 63 G1
Harvard Cl LEW BN7 .... 2 C2
Harvard Rd RING/NEW BN8 .... 155 J6
Harvest Cl PEAHV BN10 .... 222 A1
Harvesters HWH RH16 .... 89 K1
Harvest Hl EGRIN RH19 .... 22 C3
 RHWH RH17 .... 88 C1
Harvest Wy SLVH TN37 .... 169 K6
Harvey Cl STLEO TN38 .... 169 G7
Harvey's La RING/NEW BN8 ...... 125 H8
 UCK TN22 .... 126 B3
Harveys Wy LEW BN7 .... 3 E4
Harwood Cl LGNY BN23 .... 231 F4
Harwoods Cl BRI BN1 .... 22 D4
Harwood's La EGRIN RH19 .... 22 D3
 EGRIN RH19 .... 22 D5
Haslam Crs BEX TN40 .... 196 A5
Hasletts Cl SBGH/RUST TN4 ..... 20 B5
Hassocks Cl LW/ROSE BN22 ...... 216 A4
Hassocks Rd HPPT/KEY BN6 ...... 118 B6
Hastings Av SEAF BN25 .... 225 K6
Hastings Cl POLE BN26 .... 215 G4
Hastings Rd BAT TN33 .... 137 G8
 BEX TN40 .... 195 J6
 HAWK TN18 .... 62 E2
 ROTT BN2 .... 7 E2
 RTWE/PEM TN2 .... 21 K5
Hatch End FROW RH18 .... 35 K1
Hatherley Rd SLVH TN37 .... 4 A5
Havelock Rd BEXW TN39 .... 195 H5
 BRI BN1 .... 6 B1
 HAS TN34 .... 5 D4
 LW/ROSE BN22 .... 11 D3
Haven Brow SEAF BN25 .... 225 H7
Haven Cl LW/ROSE BN22 .... 215 G8
 PEV BN24 .... 218 B5
Haven Rd STLEO TN38 .... 196 E5
Havenside SHOR BN43 .... 200 A6
Havering Cl RTWE/PEM TN2 ...... 21 F5
Hawkenbury Cl RTWE/PEM TN2 ... 30 D1
Hawkenbury Md
 RTWE/PEM TN2 .... 30 D2
Hawkenbury Rd RTWE/PEM TN2 ... 30 E2
Hawkenbury Wy LEW BN7 .... 2 A4
Hawkhurst Cl LGNY BN23 .... 230 D1
Hawkhurst Rd BRI BN1 .... 177 G8
 BUR/ETCH TN19 .... 61 J1
Hawkins Cl SHOR BN43 .... 201 G2
Hawkins Crs SHOR BN43 .... 201 G1
Hawkins Rd SHOR BN43 .... 201 G2
Hawkins Wy HAIL BN27 .... 189 G1
Hawksbridge Cl LW/ROSE BN22 .. 215 G8
Hawks Farm Cl HAIL BN27 .... 189 G1
Hawks Rd HAIL BN27 .... 189 G1
Hawkstown Cl HAIL BN27 .... 161 G8
Hawks Town Crs HAIL BN27 ...... 161 G8
Hawkstown Gdns HAIL BN27 ...... 161 G8
Hawkstown Vw HAIL BN27 .... 161 G8
Hawkswood Dr HAIL BN27 .... 161 H8
Hawkswood Rd HAIL BN27 .... 161 G8
Hawth Cl SEAF BN25 .... 224 D7
Hawth Crs SEAF BN25 .... 224 D7
Hawth Gv SEAF BN25 .... 224 D6
Hawth Hl SEAF BN25 .... 224 C6
Hawthorn Av BEXW TN39 .... 194 C8
Hawthorn Cl BURH RH15 .... 89 K6
 ROTT BN2 .... 221 F4
Hawthorne Cl HTHF TN21 .... 100 B5
The Hawthorns RYE TN31 .... 109 J7
Hawthorn Ri NEWHV BN9 .... 8 B3
Hawthorn Rd RHAS TN35 .... 199 G1
The Hawthorns BURH RH15 .... 89 C6
 HAIL BN27 .... 189 F4
Hawthorn Wk RTWE/PEM TN2 ...... 20 E3
Hawthorn Wy PTSD BN41 .... 175 K8
Hawth Park Rd SEAF BN25 .... 224 D6
Hawth Ri SEAF BN25 .... 224 D6
Hawth Wy SEAF BN25 .... 224 E7
Hawthylands Crs HAIL BN27 ..... 189 G1
Hawthylands Dr HAIL BN27 ...... 189 G1
Hawthylands Rd HAIL BN27 ...... 189 G1
Haybourne Cl ROTT BN2 .... 205 F4
Haybourne Rd ROTT BN2 .... 205 F4
Hayes Cl PTSD BN41 .... 202 B3
 RING/NEW BN8 .... 155 J6
Hayes La RYE TN31 .... 111 F6
Hayes Plat RYE TN31 .... 82 A6
Haystoun Cl LW/ROSE BN22 ...... 229 H1

Haystoun Pk LW/ROSE BN22 ...... 229 H1
Hayward Rd LEW BN7 .... 2 A2
Haywards Rd BRI BN1 .... 178 B5
Hazelbank RRTW TN3 .... 18 D8
Hazel Cl NEWHV BN9 .... 8 B3
 PTSD BN41 .... 176 A8
Hazeldene SEAF BN25 .... 225 H8
Hazeldene Meads BRI BN1 .... 177 J8
 BRI BN1 .... 203 J1
Hazeledene La RING/NEW BN8 .... 92 D4
Hazel Gv BURH RH15 .... 119 H2
 EDN/EASTW BN20 .... 215 F8
Hazelwood Av LW/ROSE BN22 ..... 215 G8
Hazelwood Cl BEXW TN39 .... 194 A8
 RTWE/PEM TN2 .... 20 D3
Hazelwood Gdns HAS TN34 .... 170 A6
Headland Av SEAF BN25 .... 225 H8
Headlands Cl PEAHV BN10 .... 222 D4
Heansill La HAWK TN18 .... 62 E3
Heathdown Cl PEAHV BN10 .... 222 C1
Heather Cl LGNY BN23 .... 216 C8
Heatherdune Rd BEXW TN39 ...... 195 F6
Heather Wy RHAS TN35 .... 172 E7
Heathfield Av ROTT BN2 .... 221 G1
Heathfield Cl HAS TN34 .... 170 C6
Heathfield Crs PTSD BN41 ...... 175 J7
Heathfield Gdns RBTBR TN32 .... 78 B3
Heathfield Rd SEAF BN25 .... 225 G8
Heath Hill Av ROTT BN2 .... 205 G2
Heathlands RHAS TN35 .... 139 G8
Heathy Brow PEAHV BN10 .... 222 A2
Heavegate Rd CROW TN6 .... 52 E3
Hebe Rd SHOR BN43 .... 200 D3
Heighton Cl BRI BN1 .... 194 C8
Heighton Crs NEWHV BN9 .... 223 J1
Heighton Rd NEWHV BN9 .... 223 K1
The Heights BRI BN1 .... 177 G6
 RHAS TN35 .... 171 H7
Helena Cl PTSD BN41 .... 202 B2
Helena Rd ROTT BN2 .... 206 A2
Hellingly Cl ROTT BN2 .... 205 F6
Hempstead Gdns UCK TN22 .... 95 K4
Hempstead La HAIL BN27 .... 188 D3
 UCK TN22 .... 96 A3
Hempstead Ri UCK TN22 .... 95 J4
Hempstead Rd ROTT BN2 .... 221 G1
 UCK TN22 .... 95 J4
Henderson Cl HAS TN34 .... 5 D1
Hendon St ROTT BN2 .... 7 E5
Henfield Cl ROTT BN2 .... 205 G7
Henfield Rd LW/ROSE BN22 ...... 229 K1
Henfield Wy HOVE BN3 .... 176 B8
Henge Wy PTSD BN41 .... 202 A1
Hengist Cl LGNY BN23 .... 231 G3
Henley Cl RTWE/PEM TN2 .... 20 C7
 RYE TN31 .... 113 G5
Henley Rd ROTT BN2 .... 205 G7
Henley's Hl BAT TN33 .... 164 D2
Henry Burt Wy BURH RH15 .... 118 E2
Henwood Green Rd
 RTWE/PEM TN2 .... 21 K4
Henwoods Crs RTWE/PEM TN2 .... 21 K5
Herbert Rd BRI BN1 .... 204 A1
Herbrand Wk PEV BN24 .... 219 J2
Hereford St ROTT BN2 .... 7 D5
Hereward Rd LGNY BN23 .... 231 G2
Hereward Wy LEW BN7 .... 3 D3
Hermitage La EGRIN RH19 .... 22 D3
Hermitage Rd EGRIN RH19 .... 12 B8
Herne Down CROW TN6 .... 53 H4
Herne Rd CROW TN6 .... 53 H3
Heron Cl LGNY BN23 .... 230 D1
 STLEO TN38 .... 197 F3
 UCK TN22 .... 95 K6
Heron Pl EGRIN RH19 .... 22 D3
Heron Rdg POLE BN26 .... 215 G5
Heronsdale Rd ROTT BN2 .... 206 C3
Herontye Dr EGRIN RH19 .... 22 D3
Herring's La HTHF TN21 .... 133 G2
Hertford Cl STLEO TN38 .... 169 H7
Hertford Rd BRI BN1 .... 204 C1
Heston Av BRI BN1 .... 178 A4
Hever Cl LGNY BN23 .... 230 E1
Hever Crs BEXW TN39 .... 194 E6
Heyworth Cl ROTT BN2 .... 206 C3
Hickling Cl LGNY BN23 .... 216 C7
Hickman Wy SLVH TN37 .... 170 A7
Hide Hollow LGNY BN23 .... 216 E8
Higham Gdns RHAS TN35 .... 171 K3
Higham La RYE TN31 .... 81 J5
Highbank BRI BN1 .... 177 H6
High Bank RHAS TN35 .... 199 F1
High Bank Cl RHAS TN35 .... 199 F1
High Beech Cl STLEO TN38 ...... 169 G5
High Beeches RTWE/PEM TN2 .... 20 D5
High Branches BEXW TN39 .... 194 D7
Highbridge La LEW BN7 .... 121 K7
Highbrook Cl ROTT BN2 .... 204 E1
High Broom La CROW TN6 .... 53 G4
High Broom Rd CROW TN6 .... 53 G4
High Brooms Rd SBGH/RUST TN4 .. 20 C3
High Cl EDN/EASTW BN20 .... 201 K2
 PTSD BN41 .... 201 K2
Highcroft Crs HTHF TN21 .... 100 A4

Highcroft Vls BRI BN1 .... 6 A1
High Cross Flds CROW TN6 ...... 39 H8
Highdown STHW BN42 .... 201 J2
Highdown Cl STHW BN42 .... 201 J2
Highdown Rd HOVE BN3 .... 6 A3
 LEW BN7 .... 2 A3
Highfield Cl HAWK TN18 .... 63 C2
 RTWE/PEM TN2 .... 21 K5
Highfield Crs BRI BN1 .... 178 B6
Highfield Dr HPPT/KEY BN6 .... 118 B6
 STLEO TN38 .... 168 E8
Highfield Rd EGRIN RH19 .... 12 B8
 HTHF TN21 .... 100 E2
 HTHF TN21 .... 129 K4
 SBGH/RUST TN4 .... 20 C4
Highfields BRI BN1 .... 179 F6
 BUR/ETCH TN19 .... 75 J6
 FROW RH18 .... 35 K1
High Fords WSEA TN36 .... 141 G6
High Fords Cl WSEA TN36 .... 141 G5
Highgate Hl HAWK TN18 .... 63 F2
Highgate Rd FROW RH18 .... 35 K2
Highgrove BAT TN33 .... 136 B7
 RTWE/PEM TN2 .... 30 A3
High Hurst Cl RING/NEW BN8 ... 93 H4
Highlands Av UCK TN22 .... 95 K7
Highlands Cl BEXW TN39 .... 194 E4
 CROW TN6 .... 39 G8
 HPPT/KEY BN6 .... 119 G8
Highlands Dr BURH RH15 .... 89 G7
Highlands Gdns STLEO TN38 .... 197 J4
Highlands Rd PTSD BN41 .... 202 A2
 SEAF BN25 .... 225 G8
The Highlands BEXW TN39 .... 194 E3
Highlea Cl LGNY BN23 .... 169 K6
High Meadow RYE TN31 .... 81 J4
High Pk RYE TN31 .... 81 J4
High Park Av HOVE BN3 .... 176 D8
High Rocks La RRTW TN3 .... 29 G2
Highsted Pk PEAHV BN10 .... 222 C1
High St BAT TN33 .... 136 D6
 BAT TN33 .... 165 K5
 BUR/ETCH TN19 .... 75 J5
 BUR/ETCH TN19 .... 77 F3
 CROW TN6 .... 39 H8
 CROW TN6 .... 55 F3
 EAST BN21 .... 10 A4
 EDEN TN8 .... 15 C6
 EGRIN RH19 .... 22 D3
 HAIL BN27 .... 189 H4
 HAS TN34 .... 5 F4
 HAWK TN18 .... 62 D1
 HPPT/KEY BN6 .... 118 A6
 HPPT/KEY BN6 .... 119 K8
 HRTF TN7 .... 25 K7
 HTHF TN21 .... 100 A4
 LEW BN7 .... 3 D4
 MAYF TN20 .... 72 A1
 NEWHV BN9 .... 8 C3
 PEV BN24 .... 217 J5
 POLE BN26 .... 215 F4
 POLE BN26 .... 226 C1
 PTSD BN41 .... 201 K2
 RBTBR TN32 .... 78 B7
 RING/NEW BN8 .... 93 H4
 RING/NEW BN8 .... 123 H7
 RING/NEW BN8 .... 127 J6
 ROTT BN2 .... 7 D5
 ROTT BN2 .... 220 C2
 RRTW TN3 .... 30 C7
 RRTW TN3 .... 33 J7
 RTW TN1 .... 30 A1
 RTWE/PEM TN2 .... 21 J5
 RYE TN31 .... 113 J6
 SEAF BN25 .... 232 A1
 SHOR BN43 .... 200 A6
 UCK TN22 .... 50 C7
 UCK TN22 .... 67 H7
 UCK TN22 .... 68 E8
 UCK TN22 .... 95 J5
 WADH TN5 .... 44 A6
 WADH TN5 .... 47 H8
 WADH TN5 .... 59 F2
 WSEA TN36 .... 142 E4
Highview Av North BRI BN1 .... 177 K5
Highview Av South BRI BN1 .... 177 K6
Highview Cl HAIL BN27 .... 163 J6
 HAS TN34 .... 170 A6
Highview La UCK TN22 .... 95 K7
Highview Rd BRI BN1 .... 177 K5
 PEAHV BN10 .... 221 H4
Highview Wy BRI BN1 .... 177 K5
Highwater Vw BAT TN33 .... 169 F4
Highway Cl ROTT BN2 .... 204 E1
Highways PTSD BN41 .... 202 A1
The Highway PEAHV BN10 .... 222 E5
 ROTT BN2 .... 178 E8
 ROTT BN2 .... 204 E1
High Weald Landscape Trail
 CROW TN6 .... 38 E3
 EGRIN RH19 .... 22 B4
 EGRIN RH19 .... 24 C5
 HRTF TN7 .... 38 E1
High Weald Wk RRTW TN3 .... 19 F4
 RRTW TN3 .... 28 A4

RTWE/PEM TN2 .... 30 E3
SBGH/RUST TN4 .... 19 J2
SBGH/RUST TN4 .... 20 A1
SBGH/RUST TN4 .... 29 K1
High Wickham *RHAS* TN35 .... 5 F3
Highwoods Av *BEXW* TN39 .... 194 B5
High Woods La *RTWE/PEM* TN2 ..... 31 F1
Hiham Gn *WSEA* TN36 .... 142 E4
Hilary Cl *POLE* BN26 .... 214 E6
Hilbert Cl *RTW* TN1 .... 20 C6
Hilders Farm Cl *CROW* TN6 .... 53 K2
Hilgrove Rd *ROTT* BN2 .... 207 G8
Hillary Cl *EGRIN* RH19 .... 22 E1
Hillbank Cl *PTSD* BN41 .... 175 J8
Hillborough Cl *BEXW* TN39 ...... 194 C7
Hill Brow *HOVE* BN3 .... 177 G7
Hillbrow Rd *BRI* BN1 .... 177 H7
Hillbury Gdns *WADH* TN5 .... 60 B2
Hill Cl *CROW* TN6 .... 53 G2
Hill Crest *EGRIN* RH19 .... 12 C5
SBGH/RUST TN4 .... 20 B3
Hillcrest *BRI* BN1 .... 177 H6
RYE TN31 .... 113 H4
Hillcrest Av *BEXW* TN39 .... 195 F5
Hillcrest Cl *RHWH* RH17 .... 91 H1
Hillcrest Dr *RTWE/PEM* TN2 .... 20 D4
Hill Crest Rd *NEWHV* BN9 .... 8 C4
Hillcroft *PTSD* BN41 .... 201 J1
Hill Dr *HOVE* BN3 .... 177 G8
Hillgarth *SBGH/RUST* TN4 .... 20 A3
Hill Md *UCK* TN22 .... 50 C7
Hillrise *CROW* TN6 .... 53 K1
Hill Ri *NEWHV* BN9 .... 9 F1
SEAF BN25 .... 224 D6
Hill Rd *EDN/EASTW* BN20 .... 229 F6
LEW BN7 .... 2 A3
NEWHV BN9 .... 9 F1
RHAS TN35 .... 172 B7
ROTT BN2 .... 220 E2
Hill Side *NEWHV* BN9 .... 9 D3
Hillside *EDN/EASTW* BN20 .... 235 F2
PTSD BN41 .... 202 B2
ROTT BN3 .... 179 F8
ROTT BN2 .... 204 E1
STHW BN42 .... 201 J2
Hillside Av *SEAF* BN25 .... 225 J6
Hillside Cl *EGRIN* RH19 .... 12 C8
Hillside Dr *HTHF* TN21 .... 129 K4
Hillside Rd *BEX* TN40 .... 195 G6
HAS TN34 .... 4 C1
HAS TN34 .... 170 B5
Hillside Wy *BRI* BN1 .... 177 H7
Hill St *HAS* TN34 .... 5 E4
RTW TN1 .... 20 B6
Hill Top *BRI* BN1 .... 177 G6
Hill Top Cl *PTSD* BN41 .... 201 J1
Hilltop Dr *RYE* TN31 .... 113 H4
Hillview Rd *ROTT* BN2 .... 205 H3
Hill View Rd *SBGH/RUST* TN4 ..... 19 G7
Hillyfield *LEW* BN7 .... 2 B5
Hillyglen Cl *HAS* TN34 .... 4 C4
Hindover Crs *SEAF* BN25 .... 225 H7
Hindover Rd *SEAF* BN25 .... 225 H7
Hinton Cl *BRI* BN1 .... 204 D1
Hither Chantlers *RRTW* TN3 ...... 18 E8
Hoadleys La *CROW* TN6 .... 39 F6
Hoad Rd *LW/ROSE* BN22 .... 11 D3
Hoad's Wood Rd *HAS* TN34 .... 5 D1
Hoath Hl *RBTBR* TN32 .... 106 C1
Hobbs La *RYE* TN31 .... 83 H5
Hobney Ri *PEV* BN24 .... 217 G6
Hockington La *EDN/EASTW* BN20 ... 229 G2
Hodcombe Cl *LGNY* BN23 .... 216 C2
Hoddern Av *PEAHV* BN10 .... 222 A4
Hodshrove Rd *ROTT* BN2 .... 179 F8
The Hoe *SLVH* TN37 .... 169 J5
Hogarth Rd *HOVE* BN3 .... 202 E4
LGNY BN23 .... 230 E2
Hoghole La *RRTW* TN3 .... 45 G1
Hogtrough La *WSEA* TN36 .... 142 E4
Holbrook Cl *EDN/EASTW* BN20 .... 236 C3
Holden Cnr *SBGH/RUST* TN4 ...... 19 J2
Holden Park Rd *SBGH/RUST* TN4 ... 19 K3
Holden Rd *SBGH/RUST* TN4 .... 19 K2
The Holdings *BRI* BN1 .... 181 J6
Hole Farm Cl *HAS* TN34 .... 4 C2
Holland Av *BEXW* TN39 .... 194 B7
Holland Ms *HOVE* BN3 .... 203 J6
Holland Rd *HOVE* BN3 .... 203 J5
Holland St *ROTT* BN2 .... 7 D4
Hollands Wy *EGRIN* RH19 .... 12 E7
Hollier's Hl *BEX* TN40 .... 195 H6
Hollin Cl *SBGH/RUST* TN4 .... 19 K7
Hollingbury Copse *BRI* BN1 ..... 178 B7
Hollingbury Crs *BRI* BN1 .... 204 C1
Hollingbury Park Av *BRI* BN1 ... 204 B1
Hollingbury Pl *BRI* BN1 .... 204 C1
Hollingbury Ri *BRI* BN1 .... 178 C8
Hollingbury Ri West *BRI* BN1 ... 204 B1
Hollingbury Ter *BRI* BN1 .... 7 D1
Hollingbury Ter *BRI* BN1 ...... 204 B1
Hollingdean La *BRI* BN1 .... 7 D2
Hollingdean Rd *ROTT* BN2 .... 7 D2
Hollingdean St *BRI* BN1 .... 7 D1

Hollingdean Ter *BRI* BN1 .... 7 D1
Hollinghurst Cl *SLVH* TN37 ..... 169 J6
Hollinghurst Rd *SLVH* TN37 ..... 169 J7
Hollington Ct *STLEO* TN38 ...... 197 H3
Hollington Old La *STLEO* TN38 .. 169 H7
Hollington Park Cl *STLEO* TN38 . 197 H2
Hollington Park Rd *STLEO* TN38 . 197 H2
Hollow La *LING* RH7 .... 13 F3
UCK TN22 .... 97 J7
Hollybank Gdns *STLEO* TN38 .... 197 J2
Holly Cl *BEXW* TN39 .... 194 B5
BRI BN1 .... 177 K8
HAIL BN27 .... 189 G5
HTHF TN21 .... 100 A5
Holly Ct *CROW* TN6 .... 53 G1
Hollydene Rd *WADH* TN5 .... 44 B5
Holly Pl *HTHF* TN21 .... 100 A5
Holly Pl *LW/ROSE* BN22 .... 215 K8
Hollyshaw Cl *RTWE/PEM* TN2 ..... 30 C1
Holmbush Cl *HWH* RH16 .... 90 A1
SHOR BN43 .... 201 G2
Holmbush Wy *STHW* BN42 .... 201 G2
Holmdale Rd *NEWHV* BN9 .... 9 F1
Holmes Av *HOVE* BN3 .... 202 E1
Holmes Cl *SEAF* BN25 .... 224 B5
Holmesdale Cl *WADH* TN5 .... 44 A6
Holmesdale Gdns *HAS* TN34 .... 4 C4
Holmesdale Rd *BEXW* TN39 ...... 195 F5
BURH RH15 .... 119 F2
Holmewood Rdg *RRTW* TN3 .... 18 D8
Holmwood Rd *SBGH/RUST* TN4 ..... 20 C4
Holmhurst Rd *SBGH/RUST* TN4 .... 19 K7
Holmhurst La *SLVH* TN37 .... 169 J5
Holm Oak Cl *BEXW* TN39 .... 194 D8
Holters Wy *SEAF* BN25 .... 225 G6
Holton Hl *ROTT* BN2 .... 206 B4
The Holt *BURH* RH15 .... 119 J1
HAIL BN27 .... 189 F5
SEAF BN25 .... 225 G6
Holtview Rd *ROTT* BN2 .... 205 J3
Holtye Av *EGRIN* RH19 .... 12 D8
Holtye Rd *EGRIN* RH19 .... 13 J8
EGRIN RH19 .... 22 D1
Holyhead Cl *HAIL* BN27 .... 189 F2
Holywell Cl *EDN/EASTW* BN20 ... 236 E4
Holywell Rd *EDN/EASTW* BN20 ... 236 E4
Homebush Av *ROTT* BN2 .... 207 J8
ROTT BN2 .... 221 G2
Home Farm La *RTWE/PEM* TN2 ..... 20 E3
Home Farm Rd *BRI* BN1 .... 178 B3
Homefield Cl *SEAF* BN25 .... 225 G7
Homefield Rd *SEAF* BN25 .... 225 G7
Homelands Cl *BEXW* TN39 .... 195 F5
Home Rd *BRI* BN1 .... 203 K1
Homestall Rd *EGRIN* RH19 .... 23 J3
Homestead La *BURH* RH15 .... 89 J5
The Homestead *RRTW* TN3 .... 28 A4
Homewood Cl *LW/ROSE* BN22 ...... 11 D1
Homewood Rd *RRTW* TN3 .... 18 D8
Honeycrag Cl *POLE* BN26 .... 214 E4
Honey Cft *HOVE* BN3 .... 176 C7
Honey La *RING/NEW* BN8 .... 186 A4
Honeypot La *RING/NEW* BN8 ..... 121 K4
Honeysuckle Cl *HAIL* BN27 ..... 189 G6
LGNY BN23 .... 216 C8
SLVH TN37 .... 170 A6
Honeyway Cl *POLE* BN26 .... 214 E8
Hood Cl *LGNY* BN23 .... 231 F4
Hoo Gdns *EDN/EASTW* BN20 ...... 229 G2
Hook Hl *WADH* TN5 .... 45 J5
Hook La *LYDD* TN29 .... 87 K5
Hookswood Cl *CROW* TN6 .... 39 J3
Hoopers Cl *LEW* BN7 .... 2 C2
Hoover Cl *STLEO* TN38 .... 169 G4
Hopfield Gdns *UCK* TN22 .... 96 A3
Hop Gdn *UCK* TN22 .... 67 J1
Hopgarden Cl *HAS* TN34 .... 4 C4
Hoppers Croft La *BUR/ETCH* TN19 . 75 K5
Hopwood Gdns *SBGH/RUST* TN4 .... 20 A5
Horam Park Cl *HTHF* TN21 ...... 129 K4
Horebeech La *HTHF* TN21 .... 129 K4
Horizon Cl *SBGH/RUST* TN4 ...... 20 B3
Horleigh Green Rd *MAYF* TN20 ... 71 G2
Horley Pl *ROTT* BN2 .... 205 F5
Hornbeam *BUR/ETCH* TN19 .... 75 K4
Hornbeam Av *RTWE/PEM* TN2 ...... 20 D4
Hornbuckles Cl *RING/NEW* BN8 .. 122 C4
Hornby Rd *ROTT* BN2 .... 205 G2
Horning Cl *LGNY* BN23 .... 216 C7
Hornshurst Rd *CROW* TN6 .... 55 F3
Horns Rd *HAWK* TN18 .... 62 D3
Horntye Rd *SLVH* TN37 .... 4 A3
Horse Br *BAT* TN33 .... 192 C4
Horsegrove Av *WADH* TN5 .... 60 D2
Horsegrove La *CROW* TN6 .... 55 F3
Horseshoe Cl *STLEO* TN38 ...... 197 J1
Horseshoe La *RYE* TN31 .... 82 D8
Horsewalk *HAIL* BN27 .... 192 C4
Horsfield Rd *LEW* BN7 .... 2 B2
Horsham Av *PEAHV* BN10 .... 222 B3
Horsham Av North *PEAHV* BN10 .. 222 B3
Horsham Cl *ROTT* BN2 .... 205 G5
Horsted La *RHWH* RH17 .... 48 D7
UCK TN22 .... 124 E4
Horsted Pond La *UCK* TN22 ...... 95 G7

Horsye Rd *LW/ROSE* BN22 .... 230 C4
Horton Rd *BRI* BN1 .... 7 D1
Hoskins Pl *EGRIN* RH19 .... 12 D7
Hosmers Fld *CROW* TN6 .... 55 H2
Hospital Vls *HWH* RH16 .... 90 B1
Houghton Green La *RYE* TN31 ... 113 K1
Houghton La *RYE* TN31 .... 85 J8
Houndean Cl *LEW* BN7 .... 2 A5
Houndean Ri *LEW* BN7 .... 2 A5
LEW BN7 .... 181 J3
Hova Vls *HOVE* BN3 .... 203 G5
Hove Park Gdns *HOVE* BN3 ...... 203 G3
Hove Park Rd *HOVE* BN3 .... 203 H2
Hove Park Vls *HOVE* BN3 .... 203 G3
Hove Park Wy *HOVE* BN3 .... 203 H2
Hove Pl *HOVE* BN3 .... 203 G6
Hove St *HOVE* BN3 .... 203 F5
Howard Av *BURH* RH15 .... 88 E7
Howard Cl *HAIL* BN27 .... 189 J5
Howard Pl *BRI* BN1 .... 6 B3
Howard Rd *ROTT* BN2 .... 7 E3
Howards Crs *BEXW* TN39 .... 194 B5
Howard Sq *EAST* BN21 .... 10 C6
Howard Ter *BRI* BN1 .... 6 B3
Howbourne La *UCK* TN22 .... 69 G6
Howey Cl *NEWHV* BN9 .... 9 F1
Howlett Cl *STLEO* TN38 .... 169 G7
Howlett Dr *HAIL* BN27 .... 189 G1
Howletts Cl *LW/ROSE* BN22 ..... 230 A2
How's Cl *RYE* TN31 .... 109 K6
Hoyle Rd *PEAHV* BN10 .... 222 B4
Hudson Cl *LGNY* BN23 .... 231 H4
Huggett's La *LW/ROSE* BN22 .... 215 G8
Hughenden Pl *HAS* TN34 .... 5 D2
Hughenden Rd *HAS* TN34 .... 5 D2
Hughes Rd *ROTT* BN2 .... 7 D2
Hughes Wy *UCK* TN22 .... 95 J3
Huggletts La *HTHF* TN21 .... 101 G5
Humboldt Ct *RTWE/PEM* TN2 ...... 20 D6
Humphrey's Gap *SHOR* BN43 .... 200 D5
Hundred Acre La *HPPT/KEY* BN6 . 120 D2
Hundredhouse La *RYE* TN31 ..... 110 D8
Hungershall Pk *SBGH/RUST* TN4 .. 29 J1
Hunloke Av *LW/ROSE* BN22 .... 11 D1
Hunston Cl *ROTT* BN2 .... 206 C1
Hunters Wy *RTWE/PEM* TN2 .... 29 K2
UCK TN22 .... 95 H3
Hunting Cl *BEX* TN40 .... 195 H6
Huntingdon Wy *BURH* RH15 .... 89 K6
Huntley Mill Rd *WADH* TN5 ...... 46 B8
Huntleys Pk *SBGH/RUST* TN4 ..... 19 K5
Hurdis Rd *SEAF* BN25 .... 224 B5
Hurrell Rd *HAS* TN34 .... 5 F2
Hurst Crs *PTSD* BN41 .... 202 A3
Hurst Farm Rd *EGRIN* RH19 ...... 22 B3
Hurstfield Cl *HWH* RH16 .... 90 C1
Hurst Hl *BRI* BN1 .... 178 D6
Hurst La *BAT* TN33 .... 108 A8
EAST BN21 .... 229 J7
HAIL BN27 .... 163 J6
Hurst Rd *EAST* BN21 .... 229 J6
HPPT/KEY BN6 .... 118 D7
The Hurst *RTWE/PEM* TN2 .... 20 E4
Hurstwood Cl *BEX* TN40 .... 196 C6
Hurstwood La *HWH* RH16 .... 90 B3
RHWH RH17 .... 48 B2
SBGH/RUST TN4 .... 19 J8
Hurstwood Pk *SBGH/RUST* TN4 .... 19 J8
Hurstwood Rd *UCK* TN22 .... 68 C5
Hurtis Hl *CROW* TN6 .... 53 G4
Hutton Rd *BRI* BN1 .... 178 C8
Hyde Cl *LEW* BN7 .... 181 H6
Hyde Gdns *EAST* BN21 .... 10 C5
Hydehurst Cl *CROW* TN6 .... 53 H2
Hyde Rd *EAST* BN21 .... 10 B5
The Hyde *ROTT* BN2 .... 205 G2
Hyde Tynings Cl
EDN/EASTW BN20 .... 236 C3
The Hydneye *LW/ROSE* BN22 ..... 230 A2
Hylden Cl *ROTT* BN2 .... 205 J3
Hyperion Av *POLE* BN26 .... 214 D5
Hythe Av *STLEO* TN38 .... 196 C6
Hythe Cl *POLE* BN26 .... 215 H4
SBGH/RUST TN4 .... 20 A2
SEAF BN25 .... 225 K6
Hythe Crs *SEAF* BN25 .... 225 K7
Hythe Rd *BRI* BN1 .... 204 B1
Hythe Vw *SEAF* BN25 .... 225 K7

I

Ian Cl *BEX* TN40 .... 196 A4
Icklesham Dr *STLEO* TN38 ...... 168 E8
Iden Cl *ROTT* BN2 .... 205 F6
Iden Hurst *HPPT/KEY* BN6 ...... 118 A4
Iden Rd *RYE* TN31 .... 85 H8
Iden's La *HTHF* TN21 .... 100 D3
Iden St *LW/ROSE* BN22 .... 230 B1
Ifield Cl *ROTT* BN2 .... 221 H1
Ifield Mill Cl *PEV* BN24 ...... 216 C6
Iford Cl *NEWHV* BN9 .... 223 J1
Impala Gdns *SBGH/RUST* TN4 ..... 20 B5

Ingham Dr *BRI* BN1.................... 178 E5
Ingleside Cl *STLEO* TN38.............. 169 F7
Ingleside Dr *CROW* TN6................ 53 G1
Inglewood Gdns *STLEO* TN38............ 169 F7
Ingram Crs *HOVE* BN3................. 202 D4 🔢
Ingram Crs East *HOVE* BN3............ 202 D4
Ingram Crs West *HOVE* BN3........... 202 D4
Ingrams Av *BEXW* TN39............... 195 H4
Ingrams Wy *HAIL* BN27............... 189 H6
Inholmes Cl *BURH* RH15.............. 119 H1
Inholmes Park Rd *BURH* RH15......... 89 H8
Inkpen La *FROW* RH18................. 35 K2
Innham's Wd *CROW* TN6............... 39 F7
Innings Dr *PEV* BN24................ 217 K7
Innovation Dr *HPPT/KEY* BN6......... 118 C1
Inverness Rd *ROTT* BN2.............. 7 E2 🔢
Inwood Crs *BRI* BN1................. 203 J2
Irelands La *LEW* BN7................ 2 B4 🔢
Ironlatch Av *STLEO* TN38............ 197 G2
Ironlatch Cl *STLEO* TN38............ 197 G1
Ironstones *RRTW* TN3................ 19 F8 🔢
Ironstone Wy *UCK* TN22.............. 96 A4 🔢
Isaac's La *BURH* RH15............... 89 F5
Isabel Cl *SEAF* BN25................ 225 F6
Isabel Crs *HOVE* BN3................ 202 D3
Isfield Rd *BRI* BN1................. 204 D1
  UCK TN22.............. 124 E7
Islingword Pl *ROTT* BN2............. 7 E4
Islingword Rd *ROTT* BN2............. 7 D3
Islingword St *ROTT* BN2............. 7 D4
Iveagh Crs *NEWHV* BN9............... 9 D1
Ivor Rd *ROTT* BN2................... 205 G2
Ivors La *RING/NEW* BN8.............. 154 A6
Ivory Pl *ROTT* BN2.................. 7 D4
Ivy Dene La *EGRIN* RH19............. 23 H5
Ivyhouse La *HAS* TN34............... 170 E6
  RHAS TN35............. 170 E3
Ivy Pl *HOVE* BN3.................... 203 J6 🔢
Ivy Ter *EAST* BN21.................. 10 B4 🔢

J

The Jackdaws *UCK* TN22.............. 96 A7 🔢
Jackies La *RING/NEW* BN8............ 93 F4
Jack O'dandy Cl *EAST* BN21.......... 229 H4 🔢
Jacks Hl *HRTF* TN7.................. 37 K1
Jackson Ms *NEWHV* BN9............... 8 C3 🔢
Jackson St *ROTT* BN2................ 7 D3
Jacobs Acre *BEX* TN40............... 195 H6 🔢
Jamaica Wy *LGNY* BN23............... 231 G3
James Av *HAIL* BN27................. 163 F5
Jameson Crs *STLEO* TN38............. 169 H8
Jameson Rd *BEX* TN40................ 195 J8
Jane Murray Wy *BURH* RH15........... 118 E2
  HPPT/KEY BN6.......... 118 C1
Janes Cl *BURH* RH15................. 89 J6
Janes La *BURH* RH15................. 89 J6
Japonica Cl *BEXW* BN43.............. 200 E2
Jardine Ct *CROW* TN6................ 53 F1
Jarvisbrook Cl *BEXW* TN39........... 194 C8
Jason Cl *PEAHV* BN10................ 222 B4
Jay Cl *LGNY* BN23................... 230 D1
Jay Rd *PEAHV* BN10.................. 222 D5
The Jays *BURH* RH15................. 89 K7 🔢
  UCK TN22............. 95 K7 🔢
Jefferies *RHWH* RH17................ 48 A7
Jefferies Wy *CROW* TN6.............. 39 H7
Jellicoe Cl *LGNY* BN23.............. 231 G5
Jenner's La *RHAS* TN35.............. 171 H5
Jephson Cl *BRI* BN20................ 237 F3 🔢
Jerome Cl *LGNY* BN23................ 231 F1
Jersey St *ROTT* BN2................. 7 D4
Jervis Av *LGNY* BN23................ 231 F5
Jesmond Rd *HOVE* BN3................ 202 D4
Jesters *BURH* RH15.................. 89 J4
Jevington Dr *ROTT* BN2.............. 7 F1
  SEAF BN25............. 224 D7
Jevington Gdns *EDN/EASTW* BN20...... 10 B6
Jevington Rd *POLE* BN26............. 228 B3
Jew St *BRI* BN1..................... 6 C5 🔢
Job's La *HPPT/KEY* BN6.............. 88 A5
Joe's La *HAIL* BN27................. 163 J6
John Dann Cl *UCK* TN22.............. 97 J5
John Macadam Wy *SLVH* TN37.......... 169 H5
Johns Cl *PEAHV* BN10................ 222 B1
John's Cross Rd *RBTBR* TN32......... 78 B3
  RBTBR TN32........... 106 B2
Johnson Cl *STLEO* TN38.............. 169 G5
Johnson Dr *BURH* RH15............... 89 K8
John St *ROTT* BN2................... 7 D4
  SBGH/RUST TN4........ 20 A6
  SHOR BN43............ 200 D4
Jonas Dr *WADH* TN5.................. 44 A6
Jonas La *WADH* TN5.................. 44 A6
Jordans La East *LW/ROSE* BN22....... 215 J3
Jordans La West *LW/ROSE* BN22....... 215 H8
The Jordans *EGRIN* RH19............. 22 C3
Jubilee Gdns *SEAF* BN25............. 225 H6 🔢
Jubilee Rd *BEXW* TN39............... 195 F4
  BURH RH15........... 118 C1
  PTSD BN41............ 201 K3
Judge's Ter *EGRIN* RH19............. 22 C3 🔢

Juggs Cl *LEW* BN7................... 2 B5 🔢
Juggs Rd *LEW* BN7................... 2 A6
  LEW BN7.............. 2 B5 🔢
Julian Rd *HOVE* BN3................. 6 A3
Junction Rd *BURH* RH15.............. 119 H1
  EAST BN21........... 10 C4 🔢
  RBTBR TN32.......... 79 G1
  RBTBR TN32.......... 107 K6
  SLVH TN37........... 169 J4
Junction St *POLE* BN26.............. 215 G5
Juniper Cl *PTSD* BN41............... 176 A8 🔢
  RTWE/PEM TN2........ 20 D2
  SEAF BN25........... 225 K8
  STLEO TN38.......... 169 H8
Jury's Gap Rd *LYDD* TN29............ 117 J7

K

Kammond Av *SEAF* BN25............... 225 J6
Katherine Wy *SEAF* BN25............. 224 E6
Keats Cl *STLEO* TN38................ 197 G5
Keats Pl *EGRIN* RH19................ 22 B2 🔢
Kedale Rd *SEAF* BN25................ 225 F7
Keel Gdns *SBGH/RUST* TN4............ 19 J3
Keere St *LEW* BN7................... 2 C5 🔢
Keld Av *UCK* TN22................... 95 K5
Keld Cl *UCK* TN22................... 95 K5
Keld Dr *UCK* TN22................... 95 K5
Kelly Rd *HOVE* BN3.................. 203 J2
Kemble Ct *RTWE/PEM* TN2............. 20 D4
Kemps Farm Rd *CROW* TN6............. 53 K2 🔢
Kemp St *BRI* BN1.................... 6 C4
Kemp Town Pl *ROTT* BN2.............. 7 F6 🔢
Kendal Pk *SBGH/RUST* TN4............ 19 J6
Kendal Rd *HOVE* BN3................. 202 E3
Kenilworth Cl *ROTT* BN2............. 205 H1
Kenilworth Rd *STLEO* TN38........... 197 J4
Kenmure Av *BRI* BN1................. 178 B4
Kennedy Av *EGRIN* RH19.............. 12 B8
Kennedy Cl *HTHF* TN21............... 100 B5
Kennedy Rd *BEX* TN40................ 195 K7
Kennedy Wy *NEWHV* BN9............... 8 B5
Kennel La *BEXW* TN39................ 194 B7
Kennett Cl *POLE* BN26............... 216 A6
Kensington Gdns *BRI* BN1............ 6 C4 🔢
Kensington Pl *BRI* BN1.............. 6 C4
Kensington St *BRI* BN1.............. 6 C4 🔢
Kent Cl *BEX* TN40................... 196 B6
  SHOR BN43........... 201 F4
  WSEA TN36........... 142 E4
Kent Flds *LEW* BN7.................. 181 H6
Kentfield Gdns *RTWE/PEM* TN2........ 29 J5
Kent La *RBTBR* TN32................. 104 E4
Kenton Cl *BEXW* TN39................ 195 F6
Kenton Rd *HOVE* BN3................. 202 C4
Kent Rd *SBGH/RUST* TN4.............. 20 A5 🔢
  STLEO TN38.......... 169 G7
Kent's La *HPPT/KEY* BN6............. 120 C4
Kent St *BAT* TN33................... 138 B7
Kenwards *BRI* BN1................... 178 A3
Kenwood Cl *HAS* TN34................ 170 E7 🔢
Keppel Rd *HAS* TN34................. 5 D2
Kerrara Ter *NEWHV* BN22............. 11 D2
Kestrel Cl *BEX* TN40................ 195 K7
  HOVE BN3............ 203 J3
The Kestrels *STLEO* TN38............ 169 G6 🔢
Ketche's La *RHWH* RH17.............. 64 C4
  UCK TN22............ 64 E5
Kevin Gdns *ROTT* BN2................ 206 B3
Kewhurst Av *BEXW* TN39.............. 194 B8
Kew St *BRI* BN1..................... 6 B4 🔢
Keymer Av *PEAHV* BN10............... 222 C5
Keymer Cl *LGNY* BN23................ 231 F2
  STLEO TN38.......... 197 F5
Keymer Ct *BURH* RH15................ 119 H1 🔢
Keymer Gdns *BURH* RH15.............. 119 H2
Keymer Pde *BURH* RH15............... 119 H1 🔢
Keymer Pk *HPPT/KEY* BN6............. 119 H8
Keymer Rd *BRI* BN1.................. 178 C5
  BURH RH15........... 119 H3
  HPPT/KEY BN6........ 119 F8 🔢
Key West *LGNY* BN23................. 231 G4
Kibbles La *SBGH/RUST* TN4........... 19 J3
Kidd's Hl *HRTF* TN7................. 37 F6
Kildare Cl *HAS* TN34................ 170 E7
Kilda St *LW/ROSE* BN22.............. 11 D3
Kilnbarn Wy *HWH* RH16............... 89 K1
Kiln Cl *UCK* TN22................... 95 K7 🔢
Kiln Dr *RYE* TN31................... 113 H3
Kiln La *BAT* TN33................... 192 E4
  UCK TN22............ 124 E6
Kiln Rd *RING/NEW* BN8............... 156 B5
The Kiln *BURH* RH15................. 89 J8
Kilnwood La *RING/NEW* BN8........... 122 C4
Kilpatrick Cl *LGNY* BN23............ 216 E8
Kimberley Rd *ROTT* BN2.............. 7 F2
  SEAF BN25........... 224 D7
Kindersley Cl *EGRIN* RH19........... 13 F8 🔢
Kinfauns Av *LW/ROSE* BN22........... 11 D1
King Edward Av *SLVH* TN37........... 169 K7
King Edward Cl *SLVH* TN37........... 4 A1 🔢

King Edward's Pde
  EDN/EASTW BN20...... 236 E4
Kingfisher Cl *UCK* TN22............. 96 A6
Kingfisher Dr *LGNY* BN23............ 230 D1
Kingfisher Ri *EGRIN* RH19........... 22 D3
King George Av *EGRIN* RH19.......... 12 A8
King George V Hl *RTW* TN1........... 20 C6
King George Rd *SHOR* BN43........... 201 F3
King George Vi Av *HOVE* BN3......... 176 C8
King George Vi Dr *HOVE* BN3......... 177 F8
King Henry's Rd *LEW* BN7............ 2 B3
King Offa Wy *BEX* TN40.............. 195 H6
King Pl *BRI* BN1.................... 6 C5 🔢
King's Av *EAST* BN21................ 10 A2
  NEWHV BN9........... 9 E1
  RYE TN31............ 113 K5
King's Bank La *RYE* TN31............ 110 D1
Kingsbury Rd *BRI* BN1............... 6 C3 🔢
Kingsbury St *BRI* BN1............... 6 C3 🔢
Kings Cha *CROW* TN6................. 39 F8
Kings Cl *BEX* TN40.................. 195 H7
  EAST BN21........... 10 A2
  PEAHV BN10.......... 222 A2 🔢
Kings Copse *EGRIN* RH19............. 22 D3 🔢
Kingscott Cl *BEXW* TN39............. 195 F3
Kings Dr *SHOR* BN43................. 200 A6
Kingsdale Cl *BAT* TN33.............. 137 F8
  SLVH TN37........... 169 K5
King's Dr *EAST* BN21................ 10 A1
  EAST BN21........... 229 H3
  HPPT/KEY BN6........ 119 F7
  SHOR BN43........... 200 A5
King's Esp *HOVE* BN3................ 203 F6
King's Gap *SHOR* BN43............... 200 A6
King's Gdns *HOVE* BN3............... 203 G6
King's Hill Rd *BUR/ETCH* TN19....... 75 K7
Kingsland Cl *SHOR* BN43............. 201 F4
Kingsley Cl *SLVH* TN37.............. 169 H6
Kingsley Rd *BRI* BN1................ 203 J2
  LEW BN7............. 2 B3
Kingsmead *SEAF* BN25................ 224 E6 🔢
Kingsmead Cl *SEAF* BN25............. 225 F7 🔢
King's Mead La *SEAF* BN25........... 224 E7
Kingsmead Wk *SEAF* BN25............. 225 F7
Kingsmead Wy *SEAF* BN25............. 225 F7
Kingsmere Wy *LGNY* BN23............. 231 F3
Kings Ms *HOVE* BN3.................. 203 G5 🔢
Kings Ride *BURH* RH15............... 119 K2
  POLE BN26........... 226 C1
  SEAF BN25........... 224 E7
King's Rd *BRI* BN1.................. 6 C6 🔢
  BRI BN1............. 6 A5
  HWH RH16............ 90 B1
  SLVH TN37........... 4 A5
  STHW BN42........... 201 G2
Kings Standing Wy
  RTWE/PEM TN2........ 21 F1
Kingsthorpe Rd *HOVE* BN3............ 202 D3
Kingston Av *SEAF* BN25.............. 225 J8
Kingston Bay Rd *SHOR* BN43.......... 201 F5
Kingston Broadway *SHOR* BN43........ 201 F2
Kingston Cl *BRI* BN1................ 179 F5
  HOVE BN3............ 202 D1
  SEAF BN25........... 225 J8
  SHOR BN43........... 201 F3
Kingston Gn *SEAF* BN25.............. 225 J8
Kingston La *SHOR* BN43.............. 201 G4
Kingston Rdg *LEW* BN7............... 181 G5
Kingston Rd *LEW* BN7................ 2 B6
  LW/ROSE BN22........ 230 A1
Kingston Wy *SEAF* BN25.............. 225 K8
  SEAF BN25........... 232 D1
  SHOR BN43........... 201 F3
King St *BRI* BN1.................... 6 C5 🔢
Kings Wk *SHOR* BN43................. 200 A6
Kings Wy *BURH* RH15................. 119 J2
Kingsway *HOVE* BN3.................. 202 E5
  SEAF BN25........... 224 E7
Kingswood Av *BEXW* TN39............. 194 E5
Kingswood Rd *RTWE/PEM* TN2.......... 20 C8
Kingswood St *ROTT* BN2.............. 6 C5 🔢
King Wood Hl *RYE* TN31.............. 109 H3
Kinnibrugh Dr *LING* RH7............. 12 E2
Kinver La *BEX* TN40................. 196 B5
Kipling Av *ROTT* BN2................ 206 D3
Kipling Wy *EGRIN* RH19.............. 22 A2
Kirby Dr *PEAHV* BN10................ 221 K2
Kirdford Cl *BURH* RH15.............. 119 J2 🔢
Kirkdale Rd *RTW* TN1................ 20 B7
Kirkstall Cl *LW/ROSE* BN22.......... 215 K8
Kirk Wy *EDN/EASTW* BN20............. 229 G6
Kitchenour La *RYE* TN31............. 83 J6
Kite Cl *STLEO* TN38................. 197 F3
Knebworth Rd *BEXW* TN39............. 194 E6
Knelle Rd *RBTBR* TN32............... 77 K7
Knepp Cl *ROTT* BN2.................. 205 G1
Knightsbridge Cl *SBGH/RUST* TN4..... 19 K6
Knights Cl *RTWE/PEM* TN2............ 21 K4
Knights Gdn *HAIL* BN27.............. 189 G5
Knights Meadow *UCK* TN22............ 96 A3 🔢
Knights Pk *RTWE/PEM* TN2............ 21 F2
Knight's Rd *RTWE/PEM* TN2........... 21 K4 🔢
Knight's Rdg *RTWE/PEM* TN2.......... 21 F3
Knight's Wy *RTWE/PEM* TN2........... 21 F3
Knock Hl *TENT* TN30................. 86 C1
Knole Gv *EGRIN* RH19................ 12 A8

Knole Rd BEX TN40 .... 195 J8
  ROTT BN2 .... 220 D2
Knoll Cl HOVE BN3.................... 202 C2
Knoll Ri STLEO TN38.................... 197 H4
Knoll Rd LW/ROSE BN22.................... 230 B1
Knowle Av RHAS TN35 .... 172 D6
Knowle Cl CROW TN6 .... 54 A3
  RRTW TN3 .... 18 C6
Knowle Hl MAYF TN20 .... 72 A2
Knowle Pk CROW TN6 .... 53 F1
Knowle Park La MAYF TN20 .... 72 A1
Knowle Rd RHAS TN35 .... 172 D6
Knoyle Rd BRI BN1 .... 203 K1
Kymer Gdns HPPT/KEY BN6 .... 119 G8

L

Laburnum Av HOVE BN3 .... 202 D2
Laburnum Gdns BEX TN40 .... 196 A5
Lacys Hl RING/NEW BN8.................... 183 K3
Ladbroke Hurst LING RH7 .... 12 E2
Ladies Mile RRTW TN3 .... 27 F7
Ladies Mile Cl BRI BN1 .... 178 A5
Ladies' Mile Rd BRI BN1 .... 177 K5
Ladycross Cl SEAF BN25 .... 225 K8
Ladymead BURH RH15 .... 89 J6
Lady Oak La CRBK TN17 .... 47 G5
Lady's Gift Rd SBGH/RUST TN4.................... 19 K5
Ladysmith Rd ROTT BN2 .... 7 F2
Lagwood Cl HPPT/KEY BN6.................... 118 E8
Laine Cl BRI BN1 .... 177 K8
Lake Dr PEAHV BN10 .... 222 A3
Lake House Cl EAST TN39.................... 194 C7
Lakehurst La BAT TN33 .... 133 H3
Lakelands Cl LW/ROSE BN22.................... 230 B1
Lakelands Dr BEXW TN39.................... 194 C7
Lake Rd SBGH/RUST TN4 .... 19 J7
Lakeside Cl RTWE/PEM TN2 .... 20 E3
Lake St CROW TN6 .... 56 A2
  MAYF TN20 .... 56 C3
Lake View Rd EGRIN RH19.................... 12 D6
Laleham Cl EAST BN21 .... 10 A3
  SLVH TN37.................... 169 K6
Lambersart Cl RTWE/PEM TN2 .... 20 D2
Lambert Pl LEW BN7 .... 3 D2
Lambert Rd LGNY BN23 .... 217 F8
Lamberts Rd RTWE/PEM TN2 .... 20 D3
Lambourn Cl EGRIN RH19 .... 12 C8
Lambourne Cl BRI BN1 .... 204 D1
Lambourne Rd BRI BN1 .... 204 D1
Lambourn Wy RTWE/PEM TN2 .... 30 D2
Lampington Rw RRTW TN3 .... 18 C8
Lancaster Dr EGRIN RH19 .... 12 E8
Lancaster Rd BRI BN1 .... 6 B3
  STLEO TN38.................... 169 G6
Lancaster St LEW BN7 .... 2 C4
Lancing Cl HAS TN34 .... 4 B1
Lancing Wy POLE BN26 .... 214 E7
Landgate RYE TN31 .... 113 J5
Landport Rd LEW BN7 .... 2 C3
Landsdowne Rd SEAF BN25 .... 225 H2
Landseer Rd HOVE BN3 .... 203 F3
The Lane RRTW TN3 .... 18 A6
Langdale Cl LGNY BN23 .... 216 D7
Langdale Gdns HOVE BN3 .... 202 E5
Langdale Rd HOVE BN3 .... 202 E5
Langham Cl HAS TN34 .... 170 C7
  RING/NEW BN8 .... 155 J6
Langham Rd HAS TN34 .... 170 C7
  RBTBR TN32 .... 77 K7
Langholm Rd RRTW TN3 .... 18 D8
Langley Cl BEXW TN39 .... 195 G3
Langley Crs ROTT BN2 .... 206 A2
Langney Gn LGNY BN23 .... 231 F3
Langney Ri LGNY BN23.................... 230 E1
Langney Rd EAST BN21 .... 11 D4
Langridge Dr EGRIN RH19 .... 22 C3
  PTSD BN41.................... 202 A1
Langridge Wy BURH RH15.................... 88 E6
Langton Cl BAT TN33 .... 136 E7
Langton Rd RRTW TN3 .... 18 D8
  RRTW TN3 .... 18 E4
Langtye La RING/NEW BN8 .... 186 B5
Lansdowne Crs HAIL BN27 .... 189 F1
Lansdowne Dr HAIL BN27 .... 189 F1
Lansdowne Gdns HAIL BN27 .... 189 C1
Lansdowne Ms HOVE BN3 .... 203 J5
Lansdowne Pl HOVE BN3 .... 203 J6
Lansdowne Rd HAIL BN27 .... 189 F1
  HOVE BN3.................... 203 J5
  RTW TN1 .... 20 C7
Lansdowne Sq HOVE BN3 .... 203 J6
  RTW TN1 .... 20 B7
Lansdowne St HOVE BN3 .... 203 J5
Lansdowne Wy HAIL BN27 .... 161 F8
Lansdown Pl LEW BN7 .... 3 D5
Lapierre Rd NEWHV BN9 .... 8 B3
Lapwing Cl LGNY BN23 .... 230 D1
Larch Cl HTHF TN21 .... 100 B6
  ROTT BN2 .... 206 C4
  STLEO TN38.................... 197 H2

Larch Gdns LW/ROSE BN22 .... 215 J8
Larke Cl SHOR BN43 .... 201 F4
Larkfield Cl STLEO TN38 .... 169 H8
Larkfield Wy BRI BN1 .... 178 B7
Larkhill BEX TN40 .... 195 H7
Lark Hl HOVE BN3 .... 176 D8
Larkspur Dr LGNY BN23 .... 216 C8
Larnach Cl UCK TN22 .... 95 K3
Lascelles Ter EAST BN21 .... 10 C6
Lashbrooks Rd UCK TN22 .... 95 H4
Latimer Rd LW/ROSE BN22 .... 11 E2
Laton Rd HAS TN34 .... 4 C2
Laughton Cl LW/ROSE BN22 .... 216 B7
Laughton Rd RING/NEW BN8 .... 156 E5
  RING/NEW BN8 .... 157 K4
  ROTT BN2 .... 206 C3
Laundry La RHWH RH17 .... 49 H3
Laurel Bank SBGH/RUST TN4 .... 20 B5
Laurel Cl BURH RH15 .... 89 K6
Laurel Dene EGRIN RH19 .... 22 D2
Laurel La WSEA TN36 .... 141 K6
Laurel Rd RTWE/PEM TN2 .... 20 D4
The Laurels UCK TN22 .... 96 A3
Lauriston Rd BRI BN1 .... 203 K1
Lavant Cl BEXW TN39 .... 194 B5
Lavender Cl LGNY BN23 .... 216 C8
Lavender Gdns WADH TN5 .... 60 C2
Lavender Hl SHOR BN43 .... 200 E2
Lavender St ROTT BN2 .... 7 D6
Lawes Av NEWHV BN9 .... 8 C3
Lawns Av EAST BN21 .... 229 J7
The Lawn STLEO TN38 .... 4 A5
Lawrence Cl LGNY BN23 .... 230 E2
Lawrence Rd HOVE BN3 .... 202 E4
Laylands Rd PTSD BN41 .... 201 K4
Lea Av RYE TN31 .... 113 G5
Leaf Hall Rd LW/ROSE BN22 .... 11 D4
Leaf Rd EAST BN21 .... 11 D4
Leahurst Court Rd BRI BN1 .... 177 K8
Lealands Cl RRTW TN3 .... 28 A4
Lealands Dr UCK TN22 .... 95 J3
Lea Rd PEAHV BN10 .... 222 A3
Leasam La RYE TN31 .... 113 H3
Leasingham Gdns BEXW TN39 .... 195 F6
The Leas PEAHV BN10 .... 222 E6
  WADH TN5.................... 44 C5
Le Brun Rd EAST BN21 .... 10 B2
Ledsham Av SLVH TN37 .... 169 J6
Ledsham Cl SLVH TN37 .... 169 J6
Ledsham Pk SLVH TN37 .... 169 J6
Ledsham Wy SLVH TN37 .... 169 J6
Leeds Av LGNY BN23 .... 230 E3
Leeds Cl RHAS TN35 .... 171 G8
Leeds La MAYF TN20 .... 71 G5
Lee Rd LEW BN7 .... 2 B3
Leeves Cl HTHF TN21 .... 100 A5
Leeves Wy HTHF TN21 .... 99 K5
Leeward Quay LGNY BN23 .... 231 G3
Lee Wy NEWHV BN9 .... 8 B2
Leggs' La RRTW TN3 .... 18 C6
Legsheath La EGRIN RH19 .... 34 D4
Leicester Dr RTWE/PEM TN2 .... 29 K3
Leicester Rd LEW BN7 .... 2 B4
Leicester St ROTT BN2 .... 7 D5
Leicester Vls HOVE BN3 .... 202 C4
Leighton Dr RTWE/PEM TN2 .... 29 J3
Leighton Rd HOVE BN3 .... 203 F3
  RHWH RH17.................... 48 A6
Leneda Dr RTWE/PEM TN2 .... 29 J3
Lenham Av ROTT BN2 .... 220 E2
Lenham Rd East ROTT BN2 .... 220 E2
Lenham Rd West ROTT BN2 .... 220 D2
Lennox Cl EDN/EASTW BN20 .... 229 G6
Lennox Rd HOVE BN3 .... 202 E3
  SHOR BN43.................... 200 C3
Lennox St ROTT BN2 .... 7 D5
Leopold Rd BEXW TN39 .... 195 G7
  BRI BN1 .... 6 B4
Lepeland HAIL BN27 .... 189 F2
Lesley Cl BEX TN40 .... 196 A4
Leslie St LW/ROSE BN22 .... 11 D3
Lesser Foxholes SHOR BN43 .... 200 A2
Leveller Rd RING/NEW BN8 .... 93 H4
Levett Av POLE BN26 .... 215 H4
Levett Rd POLE BN26 .... 215 H5
Levetts La RBTBR TN32 .... 79 K7
Levett Wy POLE BN26 .... 215 H5
Lewes Av BEXW TN39 .... 195 F5
  ROTT BN2 .... 221 H2
Lewes Crs ROTT BN2 .... 205 F7
Lewes Rd BRI BN1 .... 179 H5
  EAST BN21 .... 10 B3
  EGRIN RH19.................... 22 D3
  FROW RH18.................... 23 J8
  HPPT/KEY BN6.................... 151 F1
  NEWHV BN9.................... 8 B2
  POLE BN26.................... 214 A5
  RHWH RH17.................... 48 A7
  RING/NEW BN8.................... 155 J6
  ROTT BN2 .... 7 D3
  UCK TN22.................... 124 E5
Lewes St ROTT BN2.................... 7 D4
Lewis Cl NEWHV BN9 .... 224 A1

Lewis Rd STLEO TN38 .... 169 H8
Lewry Cl NEWHV BN9 .... 8 B3
Lexden Ct SEAF BN25 .... 225 H7
Lexden Dr SEAF BN25.................... 225 G6
Lexden Rd SEAF BN25.................... 225 G6
Leybourne Cl ROTT BN2 .... 205 H2
Leybourne Gdns SLVH TN37 .... 169 K7
Leybourne Rd ROTT BN2 .... 205 H1
Leyland Rd PEV BN24 .... 218 A7
Leylands Pk BURH RH15 .... 89 H6
Leylands Rd BURH RH15 .... 89 G7
Library Wy UCK TN22 .... 95 J4
Lilac Cl LW/ROSE BN22 .... 229 J1
Lillywhite Cl BURH RH15 .... 89 F6
Limden Cl WADH TN5 .... 59 H5
Lime Cl RRTW TN3 .... 30 B8
  STLEO TN38.................... 197 J2
  UCK TN22.................... 95 K3
Lime Hill Rd RTW TN1 .... 20 A7
Limekiln Ct CROW TN6 .... 39 K8
Limes La UCK TN22 .... 69 F8
Limetree Av LW/ROSE BN22 .... 215 J8
Lime Tree Av UCK TN22 .... 95 K4
Lime Wy HTHF TN21 .... 100 B5
Limney Rd ROTT BN2 .... 205 F4
Linchmere Av ROTT BN2 .... 221 F2
Lincoln Av PEAHV BN10 .... 221 K4
Lincoln Av South PEAHV BN10 .... 221 K4
Lincoln Cl EDN/EASTW BN20 .... 236 C3
  STLEO TN38.................... 169 G7
Lincoln Cottages ROTT BN2 .... 7 D4
Lincoln Rd PTSD BN41 .... 202 A4
Lincoln St ROTT BN2 .... 7 D4
Lincoln Wy CROW TN6 .... 53 J3
Linden Av EGRIN RH19 .... 22 A1
Linden Cha UCK TN22 .... 95 J4
Linden Cl LW/ROSE BN22 .... 215 K8
  RTWE/PEM TN2 .... 29 K1
Linden Ct UCK TN22 .... 95 J4
Linden Gdns RTWE/PEM TN2 .... 29 K1
Linden Gv HAIL BN27 .... 161 H8
Linden Park Rd RTWE/PEM TN2 .... 29 K2
Linden Rd BEX TN40 .... 195 K8
Lindfield Av SEAF BN25 .... 232 E1
Lindfield Cl ROTT BN2 .... 220 E1
Lindfield Dr HAIL BN27 .... 189 C4
Lindfield Rd LW/ROSE BN22 .... 229 J2
Lindon Cl EDN/EASTW BN20 .... 235 F2
Lindsay Cl EDN/EASTW BN20 .... 236 C1
Lingfield Rd EGRIN RH19 .... 12 B8
Link Rd EDN/EASTW BN20 .... 236 D2
Links Av NEWHV BN9 .... 8 A3
Links Cl CROW TN6 .... 53 F2
  PTSD BN41.................... 202 B3
  SEAF BN25.................... 225 H8
Links Dr BEX TN40 .... 195 K7
Links Rd PTSD BN41 .... 202 B3
  SEAF BN25.................... 232 C1
The Links STLEO TN38.................... 197 G3
Links Wy RYE TN31 .... 115 G1
The Link EDN/EASTW BN20 .... 235 G1
  RYE TN31.................... 113 G6
Linkway EDN/EASTW BN20 .... 229 F4
Link Wy RTWE/PEM TN2 .... 20 E3
The Linkway BRI BN1 .... 7 D1
Linley Cl BEX TN40 .... 195 J7
  HAS TN34.................... 5 E2
Linley Dr HAS TN34 .... 5 E1
Linnet Cl LGNY BN23 .... 230 D1
Linnet Gn UCK TN22 .... 95 K6
Linthouse Cl PEAHV BN10 .... 222 C1
Linton Crs HAS TN34 .... 4 C4
Linton Rd HAS TN34 .... 4 C4
  HOVE BN3.................... 202 E3
Lionel Rd BEX TN40 .... 195 K8
Lion Hl PEV BN24 .... 216 C6
Lion La LW/ROSE BN22 .... 11 D4
Lions Pl SEAF BN25 .... 232 E1
Lion St RYE TN31 .... 113 J6
Liphook Cl BRI BN1 .... 7 E1
Lipscombe Rd RTWE/PEM TN2 .... 20 D5
Liptraps La RTWE/PEM TN2 .... 20 D4
Lismore Rd EAST BN21 .... 10 C5
Lister Av EGRIN RH19 .... 22 C5
Little Common Rd BEXW TN39 .... 194 C7
Little Copse Rd HPPT/KEY BN6 .... 118 E6
Little Crs ROTT BN2 .... 220 E2
Little East St LEW BN7 .... 3 D4
Little Footway RRTW TN3 .... 18 D8
Little High St SHOR BN43 .... 200 B4
Little King St EGRIN RH19 .... 22 C1
Little London Rd HTHF TN21 .... 129 J3
Little Mallett RRTW TN3 .... 18 D8
Little Md RING/NEW BN8 .... 153 K4
Little Mount Sion RTW TN1 .... 30 A1
Little Paddock CROW TN6 .... 53 G2
  RING/NEW BN8.................... 155 K5
Little Pk WADH TN5 .... 44 A6
Little Preston St BRI BN1 .... 6 A5
Little Ridge Av SLVH TN37 .... 169 J5
Little Sunnyside CROW TN6 .... 53 K6
Little Trogers La MAYF TN20 .... 56 B7
Little Twitten BEXW TN39 .... 194 B8
Little Western St BRI BN1 .... 6 A5
Littlewood La UCK TN22 .... 68 C7

Littleworth CI *ROTT* BN2 .... 206 C4
Livingstone Rd *BURH* RH15 .... 89 F8
  HOVE BN3 .... 203 C4
Livingstone St *ROTT* BN2 .... 7 F5 ⑤
Lloyd CI *HOVE* BN3 .... 203 H3
Lloyd Rd *HOVE* BN3 .... 203 H3
Lockitt Wy *LEW* BN7 .... 181 H6
Locks Crs *PTSD* BN41 .... 202 A3
Locks HI *PTSD* BN41 .... 202 A2
Locks Meadow *LING* RH7 .... 12 E2 ②
Lockwood CI *ROTT* BN2 .... 206 B4
Lockwood Crs *ROTT* BN2 .... 206 B4
Loder PI *BRI* BN1 .... 204 A1
Loder Rd *BRI* BN1 .... 204 A1
Lodge Av *LW/ROSE* BN22 .... 229 H1
Lodge CI *EGRIN* RH19 .... 22 A2
  LEW BN7 .... 2 A5
  PTSD BN41 .... 201 J1 ②
Lodge Ct *SHOR* BN43 .... 200 B2
Lodge Hill La *HPPT/KEY* BN6 .... 119 J7
Lodge La *HPPT/KEY* BN6 .... 119 C8
Lodge Rd *RHAS* TN35 .... 199 F2 ②
Lodsworth CI *ROTT* BN2 .... 205 C4
Lomond Av *BRI* BN1 .... 178 B4
London Rd *BAT* TN33 .... 136 C1
  BEXW TN39 .... 195 G6
  BRI BN1 .... 6 C3
  BRI BN1 .... 177 J3
  BUR/ETCH TN19 .... 62 A8 ②
  BURH RH15 .... 89 F8 ②
  CROW TN6 .... 39 C7
  EGRIN RH19 .... 22 C2
  FROW RH18 .... 23 J7
  HAIL BN27 .... 189 G3
  HPPT/KEY BN6 .... 118 E6
  HPPT/KEY BN6 .... 148 C1
  RBTBR TN32 .... 78 B5
  RBTBR TN32 .... 106 D6
  RHWH RH17 .... 48 E7
  RING/NEW BN8 .... 127 H6
  SBGH/RUST TN4 .... 20 A8
  STLEO TN38 .... 4 A4
  UCK TN22 .... 67 H7
  WADH TN5 .... 47 H8
London Ter *BRI* BN1 .... 6 C3
Long Acre CI *EAST* BN21 .... 229 J6
Longacre CI *SLVH* TN37 .... 169 K5
Long Av *BEX* TN40 .... 196 B5
Longbury *UCK* TN22 .... 95 C5
Longfield Rd *RTWE/PEM* TN2 .... 20 E3
Longhill CI *ROTT* BN2 .... 206 B7
Longhill Rd *ROTT* BN2 .... 206 A7
Longhurst *BURH* RH15 .... 119 K1
Longland Rd *EDN/EASTW* BN20 ...... 229 H7
Long La *BAT* TN33 .... 138 A2
Long Meads *RTW* TN3 .... 19 F8
Long Park Cnr *HPPT/KEY* BN6 .... 150 E1
Longridge Av *ROTT* BN2 .... 221 F3
Long Slip *RRTW* TN3 .... 18 E8
Longstone Rd *EAST* BN21 .... 10 C4
Longview *HTHF* TN21 .... 100 A6
Longview Wy *RTWE/PEM* TN2 .... 20 D3
Lonsdale Gdns *RTW* TN1 .... 20 A8 ②
The Lookout *PEAHV* BN10 .... 208 B8
Lordine La *RBTBR* TN32 .... 80 D7
Lordslaine CI *EDN/EASTW* BN20 .... 236 C3
Lords La *RHAS* TN35 .... 171 G8
The Lords *SEAF* BN25 .... 225 F5
Lordswell La *CROW* TN6 .... 53 G3
Lorna Rd *HOVE* BN3 .... 203 J4
Lorne Rd *BRI* BN1 .... 6 C2
Lorraine Rd *NEWHV* BN9 .... 9 D3 ②
Lottbridge Dro *LW/ROSE* BN22 ..... 11 F1
  LW/ROSE BN22 .... 230 A2
Love La *MAYF* TN20 .... 71 K1
  RYE TN31 .... 113 H5
Lover's Wk *BRI* BN1 .... 6 B2
Lowdells CI *EGRIN* RH19 .... 12 A7
Lowdells Dr *EGRIN* RH19 .... 12 B7
Lowdells La *EGRIN* RH19 .... 12 A8
Lower Beach Rd *SHOR* BN43 .... 200 C5
Lower Bevendean Av *ROTT* BN2 .... 205 F2
Lower Chalvington PI
  ROTT BN2 .... 205 F6 ②
Lower Church Rd *BURH* RH15 .... 89 F8
Lower Dene *EGRIN* RH19 .... 22 E2
Lower Dr *SEAF* BN25 .... 225 G6
  STHW BN42 .... 201 H2
Lower Glen Rd *SLVH* TN37 .... 169 J7
Lower Green Rd *RRTW* TN3 .... 19 C6
  RTWE/PEM TN2 .... 21 K5
  SBGH/RUST TN4 .... 19 G7
Lower Hazelhurst *WADH* TN5 .... 45 K8
Lower High St *WADH* TN5 .... 44 C8
Lower Lake *BAT* TN33 .... 136 E7
Lower Market St *HOVE* BN3 .... 203 J6 ②
Lower Mere *EGRIN* RH19 .... 22 D3
Lower Park Rd *HAS* TN34 .... 4 C3
Lower PI *NEWHV* BN9 .... 8 C3 ②
Lower Platts *WADH* TN5 .... 60 C2
Lower Rd *EAST* BN21 .... 229 J7
  HAIL BN27 .... 162 E8
Lower Rock Gdns *ROTT* BN2 .... 7 D6 ②
Lower Saxonbury *CROW* TN6 .... 53 H1 ②
Lower South Rd *SLVH* TN37 .... 4 A3 ②

Lower Station Rd *RING/NEW* BN8 .. 92 E5
Lower Stoneham *RING/NEW* BN8 .. 3 E1
Lower St *BAT* TN33 .... 166 A7
  EDN/EASTW BN20 .... 235 F3
Lower Waites La *RHAS* TN35 .... 172 E7
Lowlands Rd *BURH* RH15 .... 89 H6
The Lowlands *HAIL* BN27 .... 189 F2
Lowther CI *LGNY* BN23 .... 216 E8
Lowther Rd *BRI* BN1 .... 204 B1
Loxfield CI *MAYF* TN20 .... 72 A1
Loxwood CI *BEXW* TN39 .... 194 B6
  LW/ROSE BN22 .... 229 H2
Lucas RHWH RH17 .... 48 B6
Lucas CI *EGRIN* RH19 .... 22 D2 ②
Lucas Shadwell Wy *RYE* TN31 ..... 144 B1
Lucerne CI *PTSD* BN41 .... 202 A2
Lucerne Rd *BRI* BN1 .... 6 B1
Lucinda Wy *SEAF* BN25 .... 225 G6
Lucraft Rd *ROTT* BN2 .... 179 G6
Ludley HI *RYE* TN31 .... 110 E5
Ludlow Ri *ROTT* BN2 .... 205 H2
Ludpit La *BUR/ETCH* TN19 .... 77 G5
Lulham CI *PEAHV* BN10 .... 222 A2 ②
Lullington Av *HOVE* BN3 .... 202 E3
Lullington CI *BEX* TN40 .... 196 B5
  EAST BN21 .... 229 H4
  SEAF BN25 .... 232 D1
Lullington Gdns *SLVH* TN37 .... 169 K6 ②
Lunce's HI *RHWH* RH17 .... 90 B3
Lundy Wk *HAIL* BN27 .... 188 E1 ①
Lurgashall *BURH* RH15 .... 119 J2 ②
Lushington CI *EAST* BN21 .... 10 C5
Lushington Rd *EAST* BN21 .... 10 C5
Lustrells CI *ROTT* BN2 .... 220 E1
Lustrells Crs *ROTT* BN2 .... 220 E1
Lustrells V *ROTT* BN2 .... 220 E1
Luther St *ROTT* BN2 .... 7 E3
Luton CI *EAST* BN21 .... 229 H5
Luxford CI *CROW* TN6 .... 53 J3
Luxford La *CROW* TN6 .... 53 J3
Luxford Rd *CROW* TN6 .... 53 J4
Luxfords La *EGRIN* RH19 .... 23 F6
  EGRIN RH19 .... 23 F6
Lychgates CI *BEX* TN40 .... 195 J6
Lydd CI *LGNY* BN23 .... 230 E1 ②
Lydd Rd *RYE* TN31 .... 145 G1
Lymden La *WADH* TN5 .... 59 J4
Lyminster Av *BRI* BN1 .... 178 B6
Lynchet CI *BRI* BN1 .... 204 D1
Lynchet Down *BRI* BN1 .... 204 D1
Lynchets Crs *HOVE* BN3 .... 176 C8
The Lynchets *LEW* BN7 .... 3 E2
Lynchet Wk *BRI* BN1 .... 204 D1
Lyndhurst Av *HAS* TN34 .... 170 D7
Lyndhurst Rd *HOVE* BN3 .... 203 J4
Lynholm Rd *POLE* BN26 .... 215 G5
Lynton CI *HPPT/KEY* BN6 .... 118 B6
Lynton Park Av *EGRIN* RH19 .... 22 E1
  SEAF BN25 .... 7 E3
Lynwood *RRTW* TN3 .... 28 A5
Lynwood CI *HAS* TN34 .... 170 A6
Lynwood Rd *ROTT* BN2 .... 221 F3
Lyon CI *HOVE* BN3 .... 203 J4
Lytham CI *STLEO* TN38 .... 197 G3

M

Maberley Rd *BEX* TN40 .... 195 H5 ②
Mackerel HI *RYE* TN31 .... 83 K6
Mackerel's Rocks *RING/NEW* BN8 . 93 K8
Mackie Av *BRI* BN1 .... 178 A5
  HPPT/KEY BN6 .... 119 G6
Macmichaels Wy
  BUR/ETCH TN19 .... 62 A8 ②
Macmillan Dr *EAST* BN21 .... 229 H6
Madehurst CI *ROTT* BN2 .... 7 E5
Madeira Dr *ROTT* BN2 .... 7 D6
Madeira PI *RTW* TN1 .... 30 B1 ②
Madeira PI *ROTT* BN2 .... 7 D6 ②
Maderia Dr *SLVH* TN37 .... 4 A1
Mafeking Rd *ROTT* BN2 .... 7 E2
Magdalen CI *LGNY* BN23 .... 216 D8 ②
Magdalen Rd *BEX* TN40 .... 195 J7
  SLVH TN37 .... 4 B5
Magellan Wy *LGNY* BN23 .... 231 H5
Magnolia CI *HTHF* TN21 .... 100 B6
Magnolia Dr *LW/ROSE* BN22 .... 229 J1
Magpie CI *BEXW* TN39 .... 194 B5
  STLEO TN38 .... 197 F3
Magpie Rd *LGNY* BN23 .... 216 D8
Magreed La *HTHF* TN21 .... 100 E1
Maidstone Rd *RTWE/PEM* TN2 .... 21 J3
Main Rd *RHAS* TN35 .... 139 G7
  RHAS TN35 .... 141 F7
Mainstone Rd *HOVE* BN3 .... 202 E4 ②
Main St *RYE* TN31 .... 81 K5
  RYE TN31 .... 85 H8
  RYE TN31 .... 112 B1
Maitland CI *HAS* TN34 .... 170 B5
Major CI *BRI* BN1 .... 7 D1
Major York's Rd *SBGH/RUST* TN4 . 19 K8

Malcolm Gdns *POLE* BN26 .... 215 F4
Maldon Rd *BRI* BN1 .... 203 J1
Malines Av *PEAHV* BN10 .... 222 A4
Malines Av South *PEAHV* BN10 ... 221 K4
Mallard CI *LW/ROSE* BN22 .... 230 A2
Mallard Dr *UCK* TN22 .... 95 K6
Mallard PI *EGRIN* RH19 .... 22 D5
Mallett CI *SEAF* BN25 .... 232 A1 ②
Malling CI *LEW* BN7 .... 3 D2 ②
Malling Down *LEW* BN7 .... 3 E2
Malling HI *LEW* BN7 .... 3 E2
Malling St *LEW* BN7 .... 3 E4
Mallory Rd *HOVE* BN3 .... 203 H1
Malthouse La *HPPT/KEY* BN6 ...... 88 C8
  ROTT BN2 .... 7 D4
  RYE TN31 .... 112 B1
Malthouse Wy *RING/NEW* BN8 .... 153 K4
The Maltings *BURH* RH15 .... 88 D7
Malton Wy *RTWE/PEM* TN2 .... 21 F5
Malvern St *HOVE* BN3 .... 203 G4 ②
Malvern Wy *HAS* TN34 .... 5 F1
Manchester Rd *BAT* TN33 .... 165 K5
Manchester St *ROTT* BN2 .... 6 C6 ②
Manifold Rd *LW/ROSE* BN22 .... 11 D5
Manning CI *EGRIN* RH19 .... 22 B1
Mann St *HAS* TN34 .... 5 D4
Manor Av *HPPT/KEY* BN6 .... 119 C6
Manor CI *BURH* RH15 .... 89 K7
  EDN/EASTW BN20 .... 229 F1
  HTHF TN21 .... 129 K3
  RING/NEW BN8 .... 156 A4 ②
  ROTT BN2 .... 205 F6
  SBGH/RUST TN4 .... 19 J7
  SEAF BN25 .... 225 J8
  STHW BN42 .... 201 K3
  UCK TN22 .... 95 J3
  WSEA TN36 .... 141 K6
Manor Dr *PEAHV* BN10 .... 222 A2
Manor End *UCK* TN22 .... 95 J3
Manor Gdns *ROTT* BN2 .... 205 F6
Manor Gn *ROTT* BN2 .... 205 F6
Manor Hall Rd *STHW* BN42 .... 201 H3
Manor HI *ROTT* BN2 .... 205 F6
Manor Paddock *ROTT* BN2 .... 205 F7
Manor Pk *SBGH/RUST* TN4 .... 19 J8
Manor Park Rd *HAIL* BN27 .... 161 F8
Manor PI *ROTT* BN2 .... 205 F7
Manor Rd *BEX* TN40 .... 195 J7
  BURH RH15 .... 89 J7
  EGRIN RH19 .... 22 A1
  HAS TN34 .... 5 E3
  HTHF TN21 .... 129 K3
  LW/ROSE BN22 .... 230 B3
  PTSD BN41 .... 202 A2
  ROTT BN2 .... 205 F7
  SBGH/RUST TN4 .... 19 G7
  SBGH/RUST TN4 .... 19 J2
  SEAF BN25 .... 225 J8
Manor Rd North *SEAF* BN25 .... 225 J8
Manor Wy *CROW* TN6 .... 53 G3
  EDN/EASTW BN20 .... 229 G3
  POLE BN26 .... 215 F5
  ROTT BN2 .... 205 F6
  UCK TN22 .... 95 J3
Mansell CI *BEXW* TN39 .... 194 B7
Mansell Rd *SHOR* BN43 .... 200 E3
Mansers La *HAIL* BN27 .... 160 B8
Mansfield Rd *HOVE* BN3 .... 202 D4
Mansion CI *BURH* RH15 .... 89 K8
Manston Wy *HAS* TN34 .... 4 C2
Mantell CI *LEW* BN7 .... 2 C1
Manton Rd *ROTT* BN2 .... 205 F2
Manvers Rd *EDN/EASTW* BN20 .... 229 G8
Maple Av *BEXW* TN39 .... 194 B8
Maple CI *BEXW* TN39 .... 194 B8
  BURH RH15 .... 89 H6
  ROTT BN2 .... 206 B4
  UCK TN22 .... 67 G7 ②
Maple Ct *HAIL* BN27 .... 189 F3
Maple Dr *BURH* RH15 .... 89 G6
  EGRIN RH19 .... 22 E2
Maple Gdns *HOVE* BN3 .... 202 D2
Maple Hts *SLVH* TN37 .... 169 J4
Maplehurst CI *SLVH* TN37 .... 169 J4
Maplehurst Dr *SLVH* TN37 .... 169 K5
Maplehurst Ri *SLVH* TN37 .... 169 J4 ②
Maplehurst Rd *LW/ROSE* BN22 .... 229 J1
  PTSD BN41 .... 201 K2
Maple Leaf CI *NEWHV* BN9 .... 8 B3
Mapleleaf Gdns *POLE* BN26 .... 215 F3 ②
Maple Wk *BEXW* TN39 .... 194 B8
Marbles Rd *RING/NEW* BN8 .... 93 H4
Marchants CI *HPPT/KEY* BN6 ...... 118 A5
Marchants Dr *RYE* TN31 .... 145 C1
Marchants Rd *HPPT/KEY* BN6 ..... 118 A5
Marchants Wy *BURH* RH15 .... 89 F6
Marcia CI *EDN/EASTW* BN20 .... 229 F3
Marcus Gdns *STLEO* TN38 .... 169 H6
Marden's HI *CROW* TN6 .... 38 D5
Mardyke *SHOR* BN43 .... 200 A5
Mare Bay CI *STLEO* TN38 .... 169 F4
Maresfield Dr *PEV* BN24 .... 218 B5
Maresfield Rd *ROTT* BN2 .... 205 F6
Margaret St *ROTT* BN2 .... 7 D6 ②
Margery Rd *HOVE* BN3 .... 202 C3

Marina *BEX* TN40............................ **195** H8
　STLEO TN38................................ **197** H5
Marina Court Av *BEX* TN40.......... **195** H8
Marina Wk *LGNY* BN23................ **231** F3
Marine Av *HOVE* BN3.................... **202** C5
Marine Cl *PEV* BN24...................... **218** C5
　ROTT BN2..................................... **220** E2
Marine Crs *SEAF* BN25................. **232** A1
Marine Dr *ROTT* BN2.................... **205** G8
　ROTT BN2..................................... **220** C2
　SEAF BN25.................................... **224** B5
Marine Gdns *ROTT* BN2................. **7** D6 [2]
Marine Pde *LW/ROSE* BN22........ **11** D5
　ROTT BN2....................................... **7** E6
　SEAF BN25.................................. **224** C7
Marine Rd *LW/ROSE* BN22......... **11** D4 [1]
　PEV BN24..................................... **218** A6
Mariners Cl *SHOR* BN43.............. **200** A6 [1]
Marine Sq *ROTT* BN2....................... **7** E6
Marine Terrace Ms *ROTT* BN2..... **7** E6 [1]
Marine Vw *ROTT* BN2...................... **7** D5
Marjoram Pl *SHOR* BN43............ **200** E2 [2]
Mark Cl *SEAF* BN25...................... **232** E1 [1]
Market La *LEW* BN7......................... **3** D4 [1]
Market Pl *HAIL* BN27.................... **189** H4
Market Rd *BAT* TN33................... **136** C6
　RYE TN31...................................... **113** J6 [3]
Market St *BRI* BN1........................... **6** C5 [13]
　LEW BN7.. **3** D4
　RTWE/PEM TN2........................... **30** A1 [1]
　RYE TN31...................................... **113** J6 [2]
　STLEO TN38.................................... **4** A6 [2]
Markland Wy *UCK* TN22............... **95** G4
Mark La *EAST* BN21...................... **10** C5
Marklye La *HTHF* TN21................ **101** J8
　HTHF TN21................................... **101** J8
Markstakes Cnr *RING/NEW* BN8.. **122** C2
Markstakes La *RING/NEW* BN8.... **122** C2
Markwick Ter *STLEO* TN38........ **197** J3
Marlborough Cl *LGNY* BN23....... **216** E8 [1]
　SBGH/RUST TN4........................... **19** J7
　STLEO TN38.................................. **197** J2
Marlborough Dr *BURH* RH15...... **89** J8
Marlborough Ms *BRI* BN1.............. **6** B5 [9]
Marlborough Pl *BRI* BN1................. **6** C5 [13]
Marlborough St *BRI* BN1................. **6** B5 [7]
Marle Av *BURH* RH15.................... **89** G7 [1]
Marley Cl *BAT* TN33.................... **137** F7
Marley Gdns *BAT* TN33.............. **137** F7
Marley La *BAT* TN33.................... **137** F7
Marley Ri *BAT* TN33.................... **137** F7
Marley Rd *RYE* TN31................... **113** C5
Marline Av *STLEO* TN38.............. **169** H4
Marline Rd *STLEO* TN38.............. **169** H7
The Marlinspike *SHOR* BN43...... **200** D5
Marlow Av *LW/ROSE* BN22......... **11** D1
Marlow Dr *SLVH* TN37................. **169** J6
Marlow Rd *ROTT* BN2.................. **205** C7
Marlpit Cl *EGRIN* RH19............... **12** C8
Marlpits La *BAT* TN33................. **165** K4
The Marlpit *WADH* TN5................. **44** A6
Marmion Rd *HOVE* BN3............... **202** E4
Marsden Rd *LGNY* BN23............. **231** F2
Marshalls Rw *BRI* BN1................... **6** C5 [2]
Marshall Wy *HOVE* BN3............... **202** E2
Marshfoot La *HAIL* BN27............ **189** H3
Marshlands La *HTHF* TN21........ **100** A3
Martello Rd *LW/ROSE* BN22....... **11** F1
　SEAF BN25................................... **232** A1
Martha Gunn Rd *ROTT* BN2......... **7** F1
Martineau La *RHAS* TN35........... **171** J6
Martingale Cl *SLVH* TN37........... **169** K6 [2]
Martin Rd *HOVE* BN3.................. **202** C2
The Martins *PEAHV* BN10........... **222** A2 [3]
Martlets *BEX* TN40...................... **195** K6 [3]
The Martlets *CROW* TN6................ **53** H2
　LEW BN7... **3** D2 [3]
　RYE TN31..................................... **110** A7
　SHOR BN43................................. **200** C3
The Martlet *HOVE* BN3................ **203** J3
The Martletts *RING/NEW* BN8... **155** K5 [3]
Martyn's Cl *ROTT* BN2................ **206** B7
Martyns Pl *EGRIN* RH19.............. **22** E3
Martyns Wy *BEX* TN40................ **196** B6
Maryan Ct *HAIL* BN27................. **189** G3
Maryland Rd *RTWE/PEM* TN2..... **30** C1
Mary Stamford Gn *RYE* TN31.... **114** C8 [1]
Maskelyne Rd *HAIL* BN27........... **191** H5
Mason Cl *EGRIN* RH19................. **22** C1
Mason Rd *RYE* TN31.................... **113** C6
　SEAF BN25................................... **225** C7
Matlock Rd *BRI* BN1.................... **203** J2
　EDN/EASTW BN20....................... **236** D3
Maurice Rd *SEAF* BN25............... **232** B2
Maxfield Cl *EDN/EASTW* BN20... **229** G6 [1]
Maxfield La *RHAS* TN35.............. **171** G1
May Av *SEAF* BN25...................... **225** J8
Mayfair Cl *POLE* BN26................ **214** E7
Mayfield *LINC* RH7........................ **12** E2
Mayfield Av *PEAHV* BN10........... **222** C5
Mayfield Crs *BRI* BN1................. **178** A6
Mayfield Flat *HTHF* TN21............ **98** E3
Mayfield La *STLEO* TN38............ **196** E1

　WADH TN5....................................... **43** J7
Mayfield Pk *WADH* TN5................ **43** K6
Mayfield Pl *LW/ROSE* BN22........ **10** C3
Mayfield Rd *CROW* TN6................ **56** A1
　SBGH/RUST TN4........................... **19** K7
Mayfield Wy *BEX* TN40.............. **195** K6
Mayhew Wy *LEW* BN7.................... **3** D2
Mayhouse Rd *BURH* RH15.......... **119** F2 [3]
Mayne Waye *HAS* TN34............... **170** D7
Mayo La *BEXW* TN39.................. **195** F3
Mayo Ri *BEXW* TN39................... **195** F3
Mayo Rd *ROTT* BN2........................ **7** D2
Maypole Cottages *UCK* TN22..... **68** D3
Maypole Rd *EGRIN* RH19............ **22** B1
　EGRIN RH19................................... **23** J5
May Rd *ROTT* BN2........................... **7** F3
May Tree Cdns *BEX* TN40.......... **196** A5
Maytree Wk *HOVE* BN3............... **202** D2
Maywood Av *LW/ROSE* BN22..... **229** J1
Mcindoe Rd *EGRIN* RH19............ **12** B8
Mcwilliam Rd *ROTT* BN2............ **205** K2
Meades Cl *LINC* RH7.................... **12** E2 [3]
The Meades *LINC* RH7................... **13** F2
Meadow Cl *HAIL* BN27................ **189** G2
　HOVE BN3................................... **177** G8
　PTSD BN41................................... **202** A1 [3]
　ROTT BN2..................................... **206** B8
　STLEO TN38................................ **169** H7 [1]
Meadow Crs *BEXW* TN39............ **195** H4
Meadowcroft Cl *EGRIN* RH19..... **22** A1
Meadow Hill Rd *RTW* TN1.......... **20** B8 [2]
Meadowlands Av *LW/ROSE* BN22.. **229** J1
Meadow La *BAT* TN33................. **137** K2
　BURH RH15.................................. **119** F2
Meadow Pde *ROTT* BN2.............. **206** C8
Meadow Rd *HAIL* BN27............... **189** F5
　RRTW TN3...................................... **27** K4
　SBGH/RUST TN4........................... **19** C7
　SBGH/RUST TN4........................... **19** K2
Meadows *HPPT/KEY* BN6............. **118** E6
Meadows Rd *LW/ROSE* BN22..... **229** C1
The Meadows *HOVE* BN3............. **176** B8
　LEW BN7... **3** E2
　SLVH TN37.................................. **169** K5
The Meadow *RTWE/PEM* TN2..... **21** K3
Meadow Vw *CROW* TN6................ **54** E4
Meadowview *ROTT* BN2.............. **205** F2
Meadow Wy *HTHF* TN21............. **100** A6
　RHAS TN35.................................. **172** D7
　SEAF BN25................................... **225** H8
Meads Av *BEXW* TN39................ **194** B7
　HOVE BN3................................... **176** B8
Meads Brow *EDN/EASTW* BN20. **236** D3 [2]
Meads Cl *HOVE* BN3.................. **176** B8 [1]
Meads Rd *BEXW* TN39................ **194** B7
　EDN/EASTW BN20....................... **10** A6
　SEAF BN25................................... **225** C8
Meads St *EDN/EASTW* BN20...... **236** E5
The Meads *BRI* BN1.................... **178** K6
　EGRIN RH19................................... **22** C4
　RTWE/PEM TN2........................... **30** C1
The Mead *BEXW* TN39................ **194** C7
Meadway Ct *STHW* BN42............ **201** G3
Meadway Crs *HOVE* BN3............ **202** E1
The Meadway *ROTT* BN2............ **205** C6
　SHOR BN43................................. **200** C5
Mealla Cl *LEW* BN7........................ **2** C2 [3]
Medina Dr *PEV* BN24.................. **216** C6
Medina Pl *HOVE* BN3................. **202** E4
Medina Ter *HOVE* BN3................ **203** G6 [1]
Medina Vls *HOVE* BN3................ **203** G6
Medmerry Hl *ROTT* BN2............. **205** F1
Medway *CROW* TN6........................ **54** A2
　HAIL BN27................................... **189** F1
Medway Dr *EGRIN* RH19............. **22** B5
　FROW RH18.................................... **36** A1
Medway Rd *RTW* TN1.................. **20** B6 [3]
Medway Wy *HAIL* BN27............... **189** F1
Meeching Ri *NEWHV* BN9............. **8** C5
Meeching Rd *NEWHV* BN9............ **9** D5
Meeds Rd *BURH* RH15................ **119** G1
Meeting House La *BRI* BN1........... **6** C5 [14]
Melbourne Rd *LW/ROSE* BN22... **11** D3
Melbourne St *ROTT* BN2............... **7** E2
Melfort Rd *CROW* TN6................... **53** F7
Melrose Av *PTSD* BN41............... **201** K2
Melrose Cl *BRI* BN1..................... **204** D1
　HAIL BN27.................................. **189** F3
Melville Rd *HOVE* BN3................... **6** A3
Melvill La *EDN/EASTW* BN20..... **229** G3
Mendip Av *LGNY* BN23............... **216** D8
Mendip Gdns *HAS* TN34............... **5** F1
Menzies Rd *SLVH* TN37.............. **169** J8 [1]
Meon Cl *PEV* BN24...................... **216** B6
Mercatoria *STLEO* TN38................ **4** A6 [3]
Mercers *HAWK* TN18..................... **63** C2
　RRTW TN3...................................... **18** E8
Mercer St *RTW* TN1..................... **20** B6 [3]
Mercread Rd *SEAF* BN25............ **225** C8
Meres La *MAYF* TN20.................... **71** F8
　MAYF TN20..................................... **71** H3
Merevale *BRI* BN1........................ **204** C1
Mereworth Rd *SBGH/RUST* TN4... **20** A5
Meridian Rd *LEW* BN7.................... **2** B5
Meridian Wy *EGRIN* RH19........... **12** D8

Merlin Cl *HOVE* BN3................... **203** J3
Merlin Wy *EGRIN* RH19................ **12** E8
Mermaid St *RYE* TN31................ **113** H6
Merriemede Cl *STLEO* TN38....... **197** H4
Merriments La *BUR/ETCH* TN19.. **62** A7
Merrion Cl *SBGH/RUST* TN4........ **20** B4
Merrion Wy *SBGH/RUST* TN4...... **20** B4
Merston Cl *ROTT* BN2................. **206** B5
Metcalfe Av *NEWHV* BN9............... **8** B2
Mews Ct *EGRIN* RH19.................. **22** C5
Mews Rd *STLEO* TN38.................... **4** A6 [1]
The Mews *RING/NEW* BN8.......... **127** J6
　RTWE/PEM TN2............................. **21** J5
Meyners Cl *HOVE* BN3................ **176** B8 [2]
Michael Flds *FROW* RH18............ **35** J1
Micheldore Cl *BURH* RH15......... **118** E2 [1]
Michel Cl *EDN/EASTW* BN20...... **235** F2
Michel Dene Cl
　EDN/EASTW BN20...................... **235** G2 [2]
Michel Dene Rd
　EDN/EASTW BN20...................... **235** G2 [3]
Michele Cl *STLEO* TN38............. **197** J2 [1]
Michel Gv *EAST* BN21................. **10** A3
Michelham Cl *LGNY* BN23.......... **216** B3
Michelham Rd *UCK* TN22............ **96** A2
Michelson Cl *STLEO* TN38......... **169** G7
Middle Dr *UCK* TN22.................... **67** G5
Middle Furlong *SEAF* BN25....... **225** C8
Middleham Cl *RING/NEW* BN8.... **155** H7
Middleham Wy *LGNY* BN23........ **216** D2 [2]
Middle Rd *BRI* BN1......................... **6** A1
　RHAS TN35.................................. **171** C8
　RRTW TN3...................................... **31** C6
　SHOR BN43.................................. **200** E4
Middlesex Rd *BEX* TN40............. **195** J8
Middle St *BRI* BN1.......................... **6** B5 [3]
　BRI BN1....................................... **179** K5
　HAS TN34... **5** D4 [3]
　PTSD BN41................................... **202** A5
　SHOR BN43.................................. **200** C4
Middleton Av *HOVE* BN3............ **202** C5
Middleton Dr *LGNY* BN23........... **231** F4 [1]
Middleton Ri *BRI* BN1................. **179** F6
Middle Wk *RTWE/PEM* TN2......... **20** E3
Middle Wy *BURH* RH15................ **89** H8
Middleway *HAIL* BN27................ **163** J6
Middle Wy *LEW* BN7....................... **2** A4
Midfields Cl *BURH* RH15............. **89** H7 [1]
Midfields Dr *BURH* RH15............ **89** H8
Midfields Wk *BURH* RH15........... **89** H7 [2]
Midhurst Ri *BRI* BN1................... **178** C5
Midhurst Rd *LW/ROSE* BN22...... **230** A1
Midhurst Wk *HOVE* BN3.............. **176** E8 [2]
Midway Rd *ROTT* BN2................. **205** K3
The Midway *SBGH/RUST* TN4...... **29** H1
Midline Cl *HTHF* TN21.................... **7** D5 [2]
Milcote Av *HOVE* BN3................. **202** E3
Mildenhall Dr *SLVH* TN37.......... **169** K6 [1]
Mildmay Cl *RING/NEW* BN8....... **155** J5
Mildmay Rd *LEW* BN7..................... **2** A4
Mile Oak Crs *STHW* BN42........... **201** J2
Mile Oak Gdns *PTSD* BN41....... **201** K2
Mile Oak Rd *PTSD* BN41............ **201** K2
Milfoil Dr *LGNY* BN23................ **216** D8 [3]
Military Rd *RYE* TN31................. **113** K2
Milland Cl *BEX* TN40.................. **195** K5
Milland Rd *HAIL* BN27................ **189** G2
Mill Av *SHOR* BN43..................... **200** C2 [1]
Millbank *BURH* RH15................... **89** H7
Millberg Rd *SEAF* BN25............. **225** J7
Millbrook Cl *HTHF* TN21............ **130** A4
Millbrook Gdns *EDN/EASTW* BN20.. **229** G5
Millbrook Rd *CROW* TN6.............. **39** J8
Mill Brooks *RING/NEW* BN8...... **122** B4
Mill Cl *EDN/EASTW* BN20........... **234** E2
　EGRIN RH19................................... **22** C4
　HTHF TN21..................................... **99** K4
　POLE BN26................................... **214** A2
　POY/PYE BN45............................ **148** B6
　PTSD BN41................................... **202** B2
　RBTBR TN32................................. **108** A1
　RHAS TN35.................................. **139** G6
　RHAS TN35.................................. **171** H7
Mill Crs *CROW* TN6....................... **39** J8 [3]
Millcroft *BRI* BN1........................ **177** H6
Millcroft Av *STHW* BN42............ **201** H2
Millcroft Gdns *STHW* BN42....... **201** H2
Millcross Rd *PTSD* BN41............ **202** A2
Milldown Rd *SEAF* BN25............ **225** G7
Mill Dr *CROW* TN6......................... **53** H1
　HOVE BN3................................... **177** F8
　SEAF BN25................................... **225** H8
Mill Dro *SEAF* BN25....................... **9** F5
　UCK TN22.. **95** J5
Miller Rd *BRI* BN1........................... **6** A1
Miller's Hill Cottage La *RHAS* TN35.. **139** F4
Millers Ri *HAIL* BN27................... **189** F5
Millers Rd *BRI* BN1......................... **6** A1 [3]
Millers Wy *BURH* RH15................ **89** G7
Millfield *BAT* TN33...................... **165** K5
Millfield Cl *RING/NEW* BN8......... **93** G4
　SEAF BN25................................... **225** H7
Millfield Cottages *ROTT* BN2....... **7** F6 [3]
Millfield Ri *BEX* TN40................. **195** H7
Mill Gap Rd *EAST* BN21.............. **10** B2

Mill Gdns *HTHF* TN21.................... 100 A6
  RING/NEW BN8............................ 155 J6
Millham Cl *BEXW* TN39................. 194 E6
Mill Hi *SHOR* BN43........................ 174 B6
Mill Hill Cl *SHOR* BN43................. 200 B2
Mill Hill Dr *SHOR* BN43................. 200 B2
Mill Hill Gdns *SHOR* BN43........... 200 B2
Mill La *BAT* TN33........................... 193 J1
  CROW TN6.................................... 53 G1
  HAIL BN27.................................... 161 F6
  HPPT/KEY BN6............................ 88 A8
  HPPT/KEY BN6............................ 149 K4
  LEW BN7...................................... 208 B4
  LING RH7...................................... 12 D1
  POY/PYE BN45............................ 148 B6
  PTSD BN41.................................. 202 A1
  RHAS TN35.................................. 139 G6
  RHAS TN35.................................. 171 H6
  RING/NEW BN8............................ 122 D4
  RING/NEW BN8............................ 127 J6
  RING/NEW BN8............................ 154 C1
  RYE TN31.................................... 83 K8
  SHOR BN43................................. 200 B3
  UCK TN22..................................... 95 J5
Mill Md *RING/NEW* BN8................. 155 J6
Mill Race *HPPT/KEY* BN6.............. 118 E3
The Millrace *POLE* BN26.............. 214 E7
Mill Ri *BRI* BN1............................. 177 H6
  RBTBR TN32................................. 78 A8
Mill Rd *BRI* BN1............................. 177 H5
  BURH RH15.................................. 89 H7
  EAST BN21.................................. 10 A2
  EAST BN21.................................. 229 J6
  HAIL BN27................................... 189 H4
  HTHF TN21................................... 99 K4
  LEW BN7...................................... 3 E2
  PTSD BN41.................................. 202 A4
  RING/NEW BN8............................ 113 J4
  RYE TN31.................................... 113 J4
  WSEA TN36.................................. 142 E3
Millstream Cl *RRTW* TN3............. 27 F1 🔟
Millstream Gdns *POLE* BN26....... 214 E7
Mill St *BRI* BN1............................. 179 H4
Mill Vw *RING/NEW* BN8................. 155 H7
Mill View Cl *PEV* BN24................. 216 E5
Mill View Rd *BEXW* TN39............. 195 G4
Millward *PEV* BN24...................... 217 K8
Mill Wy *EGRIN* RH19..................... 22 C4
  POLE BN26.................................. 214 D8
Mill Wd *BURH* RH15..................... 89 H8
Millwood *UCK* TN22..................... 67 K7
Millwood La *UCK* TN22................. 67 J7
Millwood *BEXW* TN39................... 195 F3
Millyard Crs *ROTT* BN2................ 206 A4
Milner Rd *ROTT* BN2..................... 7 E1
Milnthorpe Rd *EDN/EASTW* BN20... 236 E3
  HOVE BN3.................................... 202 E3
Milton Crs *EAST* BN21................. 229 H7
  EGRIN RH19................................. 22 A2
Mitton Dr *RTWE/PEM* TN2........... 20 D4
  STHW BN42.................................. 201 J3
Milton Rd *EAST* BN21................... 229 H7
  ROTT BN2.................................... 7 D3
Milton St *PEV* BN24...................... 216 E5
Milward Crs *HAS* TN34................. 5 E4
Milward Rd *HAS* TN34................... 5 E4
Mimosa Cl *POLE* BN26................. 215 F4 🔟
Mimram Rd *POLE* BN26................. 216 B6
Mindleheim Av *EGRIN* RH19......... 23 F1
The Minnels *HPPT/KEY* BN6......... 119 F8
Minster Cl *POLE* BN26................. 215 F4 🔟
The Mint *RYE* TN31...................... 113 H6 🔟
Mistley Cl *BEX* TN40..................... 196 B5
Mitchelldean *PEAHV* BN10.......... 222 C2
Mitten Rd *BEX* TN40..................... 195 H7
Moat Croft Rd *EAST* BN21........... 10 A4
Moat Farm *RTWE/PEM* TN2......... 30 A4
Moat La *BAT* TN33........................ 169 J1
  EDEN TN8.................................... 15 K4
  HTHF TN21................................... 128 B2
Moat Rd *EGRIN* RH19................... 22 C3 🔟
Mocatta Wy *BURH* RH15.............. 88 D6
Modena Rd *HOVE* BN3................. 202 E4
Molesworth St *HOVE* BN3........... 202 E3
Molyneux Park Rd
  SBGH/RUST TN4.......................... 19 K7
Monarch Gdns *LGNY* BN23.......... 231 J5 🔟
  SEAF BN25.................................. 225 H6 🔟
Monarchs Wy *BRI* BN1................. 6 A5
  HOVE BN3.................................... 203 H4
  PTSD BN41.................................. 176 C5
  SHOR BN43................................. 174 D4
  STHW BN42.................................. 175 H8
Mona Rd *LW/ROSE* BN22............. 11 D2
Monceux Rd *EDN/EASTW* BN20.... 229 H7
  HAIL BN27................................... 163 F5
Monckton Wy *LEW* BN7................ 181 J5
Monger's Md *RING/NEW* BN8....... 123 J7
Monk Cl *BRI* BN1.......................... 179 F5
Monks La *WADH* TN5.................... 44 D4
Monks' Wk *WSEA* TN36................ 142 E5
Monks Wy *RYE* TN31.................... 81 K3
Monmouth St *HOVE* BN3............. 203 G4 🔟
Monson Rd *RTW* TN1.................... 20 B7 🔟
Monson Wy *RTW* TN1................... 20 B7 🔟

Montacute Gdns
  RTWE/PEM TN2........................... 29 K1 🔟
Montacute Rd *LEW* BN7............... 2 A5
  LEW BN7...................................... 181 J3
  RTWE/PEM TN2........................... 30 A2
Montacute Wy *UCK* TN22............. 95 K5 🔟
Montague Cl *SHOR* BN43............ 201 G4 🔟
Montague Pl *ROTT* BN2............... 7 E6
Montague St *BRI* BN1.................. 7 E6
Montague Wy *PEV* BN24.............. 217 G6
Montargis Wy *CROW* TN6............ 53 H2
Montefiore Rd *HOVE* BN3........... 6 A3
Monteith Cl *RRTW* TN3................ 18 E3
Monterey Gdns *BEXW* TN39........ 194 C8
Montford Cl *SHOR* BN43.............. 201 G3
Montfort Cl *PEV* BN24................. 217 G5
Montfort Rd *RHAS* TN35.............. 171 G6
Montgomery Rd *RHAS* TN35....... 171 G6
  SBGH/RUST TN4.......................... 20 B4
Montgomery St *HOVE* BN3.......... 202 E4
Montpelier Crs *BRI* BN1.............. 6 A4
Montpelier Pl *BRI* BN1................. 6 A4
Montpelier Rd *BRI* BN1................ 6 A5
Montpelier St *BRI* BN1................. 6 A4
Montpelier Ter *BRI* BN1............... 6 A4
Montpelier Vls *BRI* BN1............... 6 A4
Montreal Rd *ROTT* BN2................ 7 D4
Monument Vw *ROTT* BN2............. 7 F4
Moons Hi *BAT* TN33...................... 166 A5
Moon's La *EGRIN* RH19................ 13 H4
Moore's La *RYE* TN31................... 110 C4
Moor Hall Dr *BAT* TN33................ 165 J5
Moor Hi *HAWK* TN18..................... 63 F3
The Moorings *SHOR* BN43........... 201 F5
Moor La *RHAS* TN35...................... 139 G8
  RING/NEW BN8............................ 156 B8
Moor Pl *EGRIN* RH19................... 22 B1
Moor Rd *RHAS* TN35..................... 139 G7
The Moor *HAWK* TN18................... 63 F3
Morecambe Rd *BRI* BN1.............. 178 B5
Morestead *PEAHV* BN10.............. 222 C2
Morgan Cl *BEXW* TN39................. 195 G3 🔟
Morgay Wood La *RHAS* TN35....... 171 H1
Morlais Pl *WSEA* TN36................. 143 H5
Morlais Rdg *WSEA* TN36.............. 143 H5
Morland Dr *RRTW* TN3.................. 33 K6
Morlands Cl *BAT* TN33................. 166 A6 🔟
Morley Cl *BRI* BN1........................ 2 B6
Morley St *ROTT* BN2..................... 6 C4
Morningside Cl *SEAF* BN25......... 225 G7
Mornington Crs *HOVE* BN3.......... 202 C4 🔟
Morris Rd *LEW* BN7...................... 3 E4 🔟
Mortain Rd *PEV* BN24.................. 217 G5
Mortimer Gdns *POLE* BN26......... 214 E7
Mortimer Rd *HOVE* BN3............... 202 E3
  LW/ROSE BN22.......................... 10 C1
Morton Rd *EGRIN* RH19................ 22 C4
Moscow Rd *RHAS* TN35............... 171 F8
Motcombe La *EAST* BN21............ 229 J7
Motcombe Rd *EAST* BN21........... 229 J7
Motte Fld *HRTF* TN7..................... 26 A7
Mottins Hi *CROW* TN6.................. 54 B3
Moulsecoomb Wy *ROTT* BN2...... 179 F8
Mountain Ash Cl *HAIL* BN27........ 189 H5
Mountbatten Cl *RHAS* TN35........ 171 G6
Mountbatten Dr *LGNY* BN23........ 231 K4
Mount Caburn Crs *PEAHV* BN10.. 222 B1 🔟
Mount Cl *NEWHV* BN9................... 9 F2
Mount Dr *ROTT* BN2..................... 221 G1
Mount Edgcumbe Rd
  SBGH/RUST TN4.......................... 20 A8
Mount Ephraim *RTW* TN1............. 20 A7
Mount Ephraim Rd *RTW* TN1....... 20 A7 🔟
Mountfield Gdns *RTWE/PEM* TN2.. 20 B8
Mountfield La *RBTBR* TN32......... 105 F4
Mountfield Rd *LEW* BN7............... 3 D5
  RTWE/PEM TN2........................... 20 B8
Mountfields *BRI* BN1.................... 204 D3
Mount Harry Rd *LEW* BN7............ 2 A3
Mount Idol Vw *BEXW* TN39.......... 194 C3
Mount Joy *BAT* TN33.................... 136 D6
Mountney Dr *PEV* BN24................ 218 C5
Mountney Rd *EAST* BN21............. 229 H7
Mount Pl *LEW* BN7....................... 2 C4
Mount Pleasant *CROW* TN6......... 54 A4
  ROTT BN2.................................... 7 D5 🔟
  UCK TN22..................................... 97 J5
  WADH TN5.................................... 44 A6 🔟
Mount Pleasant Av
  RTWE/PEM TN2........................... 20 B8 🔟
Mount Pleasant La *RRTW* TN3..... 33 H5
Mount Pleasant Rd *HAS* TN34..... 5 D2
  RTW TN1...................................... 20 A8
Mountread *MAYF* TN20................ 71 F4
Mount Rd *EDN/EASTW* BN20....... 237 F3
  NEWHV BN9................................. 9 F2
  RHAS TN35.................................. 199 F1
Mount Sion *RTW* TN1................... 30 A1
Mount St *BAT* TN33...................... 136 D6
The Mount *HAIL* BN27.................. 189 H5
  UCK TN22..................................... 95 J5
Mount View Ter *HAIL* BN27.......... 189 H5 🔟
Mount Zion Pl *BRI* BN1................ 6 B4 🔟
Moy Av *LW/ROSE* BN22................ 10 C3

Moyne Cl *HOVE* BN3.................... 202 D2
Muirfield Ri *STLEO* TN38............. 197 G4
Mulberry Cl *BEXW* TN39.............. 194 B7
  BRI BN1....................................... 178 A8 🔟
  LW/ROSE BN22.......................... 215 K8
  RTWE/PEM TN2........................... 20 D2
  SHOR BN43................................. 201 G2
Mulberry La *HPPT/KEY* BN6........ 119 K8
Mulberry Wk *SLVH* TN37............. 170 A6
Mulberry Wy *HTHF* TN21.............. 100 B6
Munns Dr *BURH* RH15.................. 89 H7
Munster Gn *RING/NEW* BN8......... 123 J7 🔟
Murray Av *NEWHV* BN9................ 8 C3 🔟
Murton-neale Cl *HAWK* TN18...... 63 G1 🔟
Musgrave Av *EGRIN* RH19........... 22 C4
Mushroom Fld *LEW* BN7.............. 181 H6
Mutton Hall Hi *HTHF* TN21........... 100 A3
Mutton Hall La *HTHF* TN21.......... 100 A5
Mutton Hl *LING* RH7..................... 12 E4
Myrtle Rd *CROW* TN6................... 53 H2
  LW/ROSE BN22.......................... 11 F1

N

Namrik Ms *HOVE* BN3................... 203 F5
Nanson Rd *BRI* BN1...................... 178 E5
Nan Tucks La *UCK* TN22............... 68 E8
Naomi Cl *EDN/EASTW* BN20........ 10 A6 🔟
Napier Rd *RTWE/PEM* TN2........... 30 D1
  STLEO TN38................................ 169 F6
Natal Rd *ROTT* BN2...................... 7 F1
  ROTT BN2.................................... 204 D1
Neath Rd *LYDD* TN29................... 146 D2
Neaves La *RING/NEW* BN8.......... 156 B7
Neill's Cl *NEWHV* BN9.................. 8 C3 🔟
Neills Rd *RRTW* TN3..................... 45 F1
Nellington Rd *RRTW* TN3............. 19 F7
Nelson Dr *LGNY* BN23.................. 231 F5 🔟
Nelson Rd *HAS* TN34.................... 5 E3
  RTWE/PEM TN2........................... 30 D1
Nelson Rw *ROTT* BN2................... 7 D5 🔟
Nesbitt Rd *ROTT* BN2................... 7 F1
Netherfield Av *LGNY* BN23.......... 231 G1
Netherfield Gn *ROTT* BN2........... 206 C3
Netherfield Hi *BAT* TN33.............. 136 B4
Netherfield Rd *BAT* TN33............. 136 B4
Netherfield Wy *BAT* TN33............ 135 J1
Nether La *UCK* TN22.................... 50 C8
Netherwood Cl *HAS* TN34............ 170 B6
Nevill Av *HOVE* BN3..................... 202 E2
  LW/ROSE BN22.......................... 229 K2
Nevill Cl *HOVE* BN3...................... 203 F1
  LW/ROSE BN22.......................... 11 D3 🔟
Nevill Crs *LEW* BN7..................... 2 A4
Neville Rd *LW/ROSE* BN22.......... 11 D3 🔟
  PEAHV BN10............................... 222 C5
Nevill Gdns *HOVE* BN3................. 203 F1
Nevill Ga *RTWE/PEM* TN2........... 30 B2
Nevill Pk *SBGH/RUST* TN4.......... 19 J8
Nevill Pl *HOVE* BN3...................... 203 F1
Nevill Rdg *SBGH/RUST* TN4........ 19 H8
Nevill Rd *CROW* TN6.................... 39 H8
  HOVE BN3.................................... 203 F1
  LEW BN7...................................... 2 A3
  ROTT BN2.................................... 220 C2
  UCK TN22..................................... 95 K2
Nevill St *RTWE/PEM* TN2............. 30 A1
Nevill Ter *RTWE/PEM* TN2........... 29 K1 🔟
Nevill Wy *HOVE* BN3.................... 203 F1
Newark Pl *ROTT* BN2.................... 7 D4
New Barn Cl *HAIL* BN27............... 189 H5
  PTSD BN41.................................. 202 A1
  SHOR BN43................................. 200 E2 🔟
New Barn La *UCK* TN22............... 95 J6
New Barn Rd *ROTT* BN2.............. 206 B3
  SHOR BN43................................. 200 E2
Newbury La *WADH* TN5................ 44 E3
New Church Rd *HOVE* BN3........... 202 C4
Newcomen Rd *SBGH/RUST* TN4.. 20 A6
New Cut *RBTBR* TN32................... 106 C6
  RHAS TN35.................................. 139 G7
New Dorset St *BRI* BN1................ 6 B4
Newells Cl *ROTT* BN2................... 206 B2
New England La *BAT* TN33........... 138 A6
New England Ri *PTSD* BN41......... 175 K7
New England Rd *BRI* BN1............. 6 B3
  SBGH/RUST TN4.......................... 20 A4
New England St *BRI* BN1.............. 6 C3 🔟
New Farthingdale *LING* RH7........ 12 E4
Newfield La *NEWHV* BN9............. 8 C3 🔟
Newfield Rd *NEWHV* BN9............. 8 C3 🔟
Newgate Rd *SLVH* TN37............... 4 A3
Newhache *LING* RH7.................... 12 E2
Newhaven Rd *SEAF* BN25............ 224 B6
Newhaven St *ROTT* BN2.............. 7 D4
Newick Cl *SEAF* BN25.................. 232 E1 🔟
Newick Dr *RING/NEW* BN8........... 93 G4
Newick Hi *RING/NEW* BN8........... 93 G3
Newick La *MAYF* TN20................. 72 A3
Newick Rd *BRI* BN1...................... 179 F7
  EDN/EASTW BN20....................... 229 H5 🔟
Newlands *RRTW* TN3.................... 18 E7
Newlands Av *BEXW* TN39............. 195 F6

Newlands Cl HAS TN34 .... 170 B6
  HPPT/KEY BN6 .... 119 C8
Newlands Crs EGRIN RH19 .... 22 B1
Newlands Ri BURH RH15 .... 20 A5
Newlands Rd ROTT BN2 .... 220 D2
  SBGH/RUST TN4 .... 20 B5
Newlands Wy SBGH/RUST TN4 .... 20 B4
New Lydd Rd RYE TN31 .... 115 F8
Newmans Wy RHAS TN35 .... 171 C7
Newmarket Rd ROTT BN2 .... 7 E2
New Moorsite RHAS TN35 .... 139 H8
Newnham Rd HTHF TN21 .... 100 A5
Newnham Wy HTHF TN21 .... 100 A4
New Park Av BEX TN40 .... 195 H7
New Pl EAST BN21 .... 229 J8
  UCK TN22 .... 95 J6
New Pond Hl HTHF TN21 .... 99 H5
Newport Rd BURH RH15 .... 89 F8
Newport St ROTT BN2 .... 7 D3
New Rd BRI BN1 .... 6 C5
  CROW TN6 .... 39 H8
  CROW TN6 .... 55 F3
  HAIL BN27 .... 161 H7
  HPPT/KEY BN6 .... 150 A2
  LEW BN7 .... 2 C4
  LW/ROSE BN22 .... 11 D4
  NEWHV BN9 .... 9 D1
  POLE BN26 .... 215 G5
  RHAS TN35 .... 172 C7
  RHAS TN35 .... 199 G1
  RING/NEW BN8 .... 155 J8
  RTON TN11 .... 17 J2
  RYE TN31 .... 81 J8
  RYE TN31 .... 113 K5
  SHOR BN43 .... 200 C4
  UCK TN22 .... 95 K8
New Steine ROTT BN2 .... 7 D6
  ROTT BN2 .... 7 D6
Newtimber Dr PTSD BN41 .... 201 K2
Newtimber Gdns SHOR BN43 .... 200 C2
Newton Av EGRIN RH19 .... 22 D5
Newton Cl LEW BN7 .... 2 B3
  PEAHV BN10 .... 222 B4
  RTW TN1 .... 20 E7
Newton Willows RRTW TN3 .... 28 A4
Newtown Rd HOVE BN3 .... 203 J3
New Upperton Rd EAST BN21 .... 10 A3
New Way La HPPT/KEY BN6 .... 149 G1
New Winchelsea Rd RYE TN31 .... 143 H1
Nicolson Dr SHOR BN43 .... 200 C3
Nightingale Cl EGRIN RH19 .... 22 B4
  LGNY BN23 .... 230 D1
Nightingale La BURH RH15 .... 119 F3
Nightingale Ri UCK TN22 .... 95 K7
Nile St BRI BN1 .... 6 C5
Ninfield Pl ROTT BN2 .... 205 F4
Ninfield Rd BEXW TN39 .... 194 D2
Nizells Av HOVE BN3 .... 203 J4
Nodes La HAIL BN27 .... 162 A7
Noel Gn BURH RH15 .... 89 H7
Noel Ri BURH RH15 .... 89 H7
Nolan Rd ROTT BN2 .... 206 B4
Nook Cl RHAS TN35 .... 171 G8
The Nook UCK TN22 .... 95 K7
Norbury Cl CROW TN6 .... 39 C7
Nore Rd NEWHV BN9 .... 8 B4
Norfolk Buildings BRI BN1 .... 6 A5
Norfolk Cl BEXW TN39 .... 195 G4
Norfolk Dr STLEO TN38 .... 169 C7
Norfolk Ms BRI BN1 .... 6 A5
Norfolk Rd BRI BN1 .... 6 A5
  RTW TN1 .... 30 B3
Norfolk Sq BRI BN1 .... 6 A5
Norfolk St BRI BN1 .... 203 J6
Norfolk Ter BRI BN1 .... 6 A4
Norlington Ct RING/NEW BN8 .... 155 J5
Norlington Flds RING/NEW BN8 .... 155 H4
Norlington La RING/NEW BN8 .... 155 J3
Norman Cl BAT TN33 .... 137 F7
  SEAF BN25 .... 224 C5
Norman Crs SHOR BN43 .... 200 C2
Normandale BEXW TN39 .... 194 E8
Normandy Cl EGRIN RH19 .... 22 D3
Normandy Rd SLVH TN37 .... 4 A1
Norman Rd BURH RH15 .... 89 F8
  HOVE BN3 .... 202 D5
  NEWHV BN9 .... 8 C5
  PEV BN24 .... 218 A7
  RTW TN1 .... 20 B6
  STLEO TN38 .... 4 A6
Normansal Cl SEAF BN25 .... 225 H5
Normansal Park Av SEAF BN25 .... 225 G6
Normansland UCK TN22 .... 67 H1
Normanton St ROTT BN2 .... 7 E3
Norstead Gdns SBGH/RUST TN4 .... 20 B4
Northampton Wy STLEO TN38 .... 169 H7
North Av EDN/EASTW BN20 .... 229 G6
North Bank BRI BN1 .... 118 E7
North Barnes La LEW BN7 .... 121 H6
North Beeches Rd CROW TN6 .... 53 J1
Northbourne Cl SHOR BN43 .... 200 C3
Northbourne Rd LW/ROSE BN22 .... 230 C4
Northbridge St RBTBR TN32 .... 78 B6
North Camp La SEAF BN25 .... 225 G6
Northcliffe SEAF BN25 .... 225 G7

North Cl POLE BN26 .... 215 G4
  PTSD BN41 .... 201 K1
North Common Rd RHWH RH17 .... 91 F6
Northcote La PEAHV BN10 .... 221 K2
North Ct HPPT/KEY BN6 .... 118 E7
  LEW BN7 .... 3 E4
Northdown Cl NEWHV BN9 .... 8 C4
Northdown Rd NEWHV BN9 .... 8 B4
North Dr ROTT BN2 .... 7 E4
Northease Cl HOVE BN3 .... 202 C1
Northease Dr HOVE BN3 .... 202 C1
Northease Gdns HOVE BN3 .... 176 D8
North End HPPT/KEY BN6 .... 119 K7
Northern Av POLE BN26 .... 215 G4
North Farm La RTWE/PEM TN2 .... 20 D3
North Farm Rd SBGH/RUST TN4 .... 20 C4
Northfield POLE BN26 .... 214 E6
Northfield Cl SEAF BN25 .... 225 G6
Northfield Ri HOVE BN3 .... 176 C7
  ROTT BN2 .... 220 D7
Northfields RRTW TN3 .... 18 E3
Northfield Wy BRI BN1 .... 178 B7
North Gdns BRI BN1 .... 6 B4
Northgate Cl ROTT BN2 .... 220 C1
Northgrove Rd HAWK TN18 .... 63 F1
North Heath Cl HAIL BN27 .... 189 H1
North Hill Rd HAWK TN18 .... 62 C2
Northiam Ri STLEO TN38 .... 196 E1
Northiam Rd EDN/EASTW BN20 .... 229 H7
  RYE TN31 .... 109 J4
North La PTSD BN41 .... 201 K1
  RHAS TN35 .... 140 C6
North Pl BRI BN1 .... 6 C5
North Quay Rd NEWHV BN9 .... 9 D1
Northridge RYE TN31 .... 81 J5
North Rd BEXW TN39 .... 195 H4
  BRI BN1 .... 6 B4
  BRI BN1 .... 6 A1
  HAIL BN27 .... 163 K1
  PEV BN24 .... 218 A7
  POLE BN26 .... 212 B8
  PTSD BN41 .... 201 K1
  RING/NEW BN8 .... 155 J5
  STLEO TN38 .... 4 A3
North Rw UCK TN22 .... 95 J3
North Salts RYE TN31 .... 113 J5
North St BRI BN1 .... 6 C5
  CROW TN6 .... 55 F3
  EAST BN21 .... 10 C4
  EDEN TN8 .... 15 G5
  HAIL BN27 .... 160 E7
  HAIL BN27 .... 189 G3
  HTHF TN21 .... 98 D6
  HTHF TN21 .... 101 K6
  LEW BN7 .... 2 C3
  MAYF TN20 .... 56 B8
  POLE BN26 .... 212 D8
  PTSD BN41 .... 202 A4
  RTWE/PEM TN2 .... 20 C8
  SHOR BN43 .... 200 B4
  STLEO TN38 .... 4 A5
  WSEA TN36 .... 142 E3
North Ter HAS TN34 .... 5 F2
North Trade Rd BAT TN33 .... 135 K7
Northway BURH RH15 .... 89 J7
North Wy LEW BN7 .... 2 A3
  NEWHV BN9 .... 8 C3
  SEAF BN25 .... 225 G6
Northwood Av ROTT BN2 .... 221 H2
Norton Cl HOVE BN3 .... 203 G5
Norton Dr ROTT BN2 .... 206 A2
Norton Rd HOVE BN3 .... 203 G5
  NEWHV BN9 .... 9 E3
  SBGH/RUST TN4 .... 20 A2
Norton Ter NEWHV BN9 .... 9 E3
Norway Rd LW/ROSE BN22 .... 11 F1
Norway St PTSD BN41 .... 202 B4
Norwich Cl LGNY BN23 .... 205 H1
Norwich Dr ROTT BN2 .... 205 H1
Nottidge Rd SBGH/RUST TN4 .... 29 H2
Novington La LEW BN7 .... 152 D2
Nunnery La RTON TN11 .... 17 H5
Nunnery Stable LEW BN7 .... 2 B4
Nursery Cl HAIL BN27 .... 189 H3
  POLE BN26 .... 215 G5
  PTSD BN41 .... 175 H7
  SHOR BN43 .... 200 C3
  WADH TN5 .... 47 F8
Nursery Fld UCK TN22 .... 68 D7
Nursery La HAIL BN27 .... 163 J6
  UCK TN22 .... 50 C7
  UCK TN22 .... 67 H6
  UCK TN22 .... 95 K7
  UCK TN22 .... 98 C2
Nursery Rd SBGH/RUST TN4 .... 20 B3
The Nursery BURH RH15 .... 89 J7
Nursery Wy HTHF TN21 .... 99 J4
Nuthatch Rd LGNY BN23 .... 216 D8
Nuthurst Cl ROTT BN2 .... 205 G5
Nuthurst Pl ROTT BN2 .... 205 G6
Nutley Av ROTT BN2 .... 221 G3
Nutley Cl HOVE BN3 .... 176 E8
  RYE TN31 .... 113 G3
Nutley Mill Rd PEV BN24 .... 216 C6
Nye Cl CROW TN6 .... 53 H2

Nye La HPPT/KEY BN6 .... 150 E3
Nye Rd BURH RH15 .... 89 H8
Nyetimber Hl ROTT BN2 .... 205 F1

O

Oakapple Rd STHW BN42 .... 201 G1
Oak Cl BRI BN1 .... 177 K8
Oak Cft EGRIN RH19 .... 22 E3
Oakdale Rd SBGH/RUST TN4 .... 19 K7
Oakdene Av PTSD BN41 .... 175 H8
Oakdene Cl PTSD BN41 .... 175 H8
Oakdene Crs PTSD BN41 .... 175 H8
Oakdene Gdns PTSD BN41 .... 175 H8
Oakdene Ri PTSD BN41 .... 175 H7
Oakdene Wy PTSD BN41 .... 175 H8
Oak End Cl SBGH/RUST TN4 .... 20 A1
Oakenden La EDEN TN8 .... 16 D2
Oakenfield BURH RH15 .... 89 F6
Oakfield HAWK TN18 .... 63 F1
Oakfield Court Rd
  RTWE/PEM TN2 .... 20 C8
Oakfield Rd RHAS TN35 .... 171 F8
The Oak Fld RHAS TN35 .... 172 C2
The Oakfield RYE TN31 .... 113 H3
Oakfield Wy BEXW TN39 .... 194 B5
  EGRIN RH19 .... 12 D3
Oak Hall Pk BURH RH15 .... 119 H2
Oakhill Dr RYE TN31 .... 109 K6
Oakhurst Cl HAS TN34 .... 170 B6
Oakhurst Dr CROW TN6 .... 39 J8
Oakhurst Gdns EGRIN RH19 .... 22 A1
Oakhurst Rd BAT TN33 .... 136 D5
Oakland Dr RBTBR TN32 .... 77 H7
Oaklands PEV BN24 .... 216 E5
Oaklands Av ROTT BN2 .... 221 F2
Oaklands Cl POLE BN26 .... 215 G5
Oaklands Cl HAWK TN18 .... 63 F2
  RRTW TN3 .... 27 K5
Oaklands Wy HAIL BN27 .... 189 F5
Oaklea Cl SLVH TN37 .... 169 K7
Oakleaf Dr POLE BN26 .... 215 F4
Oaklea Wy UCK TN22 .... 95 H4
Oakleigh Dr HTHF TN21 .... 100 B5
Oakleigh Rd BEXW TN39 .... 194 B7
Oakley Cl EGRIN RH19 .... 23 F4
Oakmead Rd BURH RH15 .... 119 F2
Oakmede Wy RING/NEW BN8 .... 155 H6
Oak Rd RTWE/PEM TN2 .... 20 D4
Oakroyd Cl BURH RH15 .... 89 J6
Oaks Cl BUR/ETCH TN19 .... 77 F2
The Oaks BRI BN1 .... 88 C7
  EGRIN RH19 .... 22 E3
  HTHF TN21 .... 100 B5
  SLVH TN37 .... 170 A6
Oaktree RING/NEW BN8 .... 123 J7
Oak Tree Av UCK TN22 .... 95 J7
Oak Tree Ct UCK TN22 .... 95 K3
Oak Tree La LGNY BN23 .... 216 D7
Oak Tree Wy HAIL BN27 .... 189 H1
Oakwood Av BEXW TN39 .... 195 G4
Oakwood Cl BURH RH15 .... 119 H1
  HAS TN34 .... 5 D1
Oakwood Dr UCK TN22 .... 96 A3
Oakwood Pk UCK TN22 .... 50 C6
Oakwood Ri RTWE/PEM TN2 .... 20 E4
Oakwood Rd BURH RH15 .... 119 H1
Oast Cl RTWE/PEM TN2 .... 20 D4
Oasthouse Cl HAS TN34 .... 170 A6
Oast House Dr RYE TN31 .... 113 F7
Oast House Fld WSEA TN36 .... 142 C6
Oast House Rd WSEA TN36 .... 141 K6
Oban Rd SLVH TN37 .... 169 J8
Observatory Vw HAIL BN27 .... 189 J5
Ochiltree Cl HAS TN34 .... 170 D7
Ochiltree Rd HAS TN34 .... 170 D7
Ockenden Wy HPPT/KEY BN6 .... 118 E8
Ockley La BURH RH15 .... 119 H4
  HPPT/KEY BN6 .... 119 G7
Ockley Rd HAWK TN18 .... 63 G1
Ockley Wy HPPT/KEY BN6 .... 119 G7
Ocklynge Cl BEXW TN39 .... 194 C6
Ocklynge Rd EAST BN21 .... 229 J7
Ockman La RYE TN31 .... 113 J6
Offa Rd RHAS TN35 .... 171 G3
Offham Cl LW/ROSE BN22 .... 216 A7
  SEAF BN25 .... 225 G6
Offham Rd LEW BN7 .... 2 A5
Okehurst Rd EAST BN21 .... 229 H8
Oldaker Rd RING/NEW BN8 .... 93 H4
Old Barn Cl EDN/EASTW BN20 .... 229 G2
Old Barn Wy STHW BN42 .... 201 K4
Old Boat Wk BRI BN1 .... 178 C4
Old Camp Rd EDN/EASTW BN20 .... 236 C1
Old Church Rd RTWE/PEM TN2 .... 21 K2
  STLEO TN38 .... 169 F7
Old Court Cl BRI BN1 .... 178 A7
Old Dr POLE BN26 .... 214 E6
Old Dro LGNY BN23 .... 216 D8
Olde Place Ms ROTT BN2 .... 220 C2
Old Farm Rd BEXW TN39 .... 195 G5

BRI BN1 .... 178 A6
Oldfield Av EDN/EASTW BN20 ...... 215 F8
Oldfield Crs HAIL BN27 .... 189 G2
  STHW BN42 .... 201 G4
Oldfield Rd EDN/EASTW BN20 ...... 215 F7
Old Forest La CROW TN6 .... 54 C5
Old Forewood La BAT TN33 .... 168 A4
Old Forge La UCK TN22 .... 67 F3
Old Fort Rd SHOR BN43 .... 200 D5
Old Gardens CI RTWE/PEM TN2 ..... 30 B3
Old Ghyll Rd HTHF TN21 .... 100 A6
Old Harrow Rd SLVH TN37 .... 169 J7
Old Heath CI RING/NEW BN8 .... 126 E5
The Old Hop Gdn RYE TN31 .... 112 C1
Old House Gdns TN34 .... 170 C7
Old House La RRTW TN3 .... 18 B6
Oldlands Av HPPT/KEY BN6 .... 119 G7
Oldlands HI UCK TN22 .... 67 J1
Old La CROW TN6 .... 39 F8
  CROW TN6 .... 53 K2
  MAYF TN20 .... 71 K1
Old London Rd BRI BN1 .... 177 K6
  RHAS TN35 .... 171 G7 🔲
Old Lydd Rd RYE TN31 .... 145 G1
Old Malling Wy LEW BN7 .... 2 C2
Old Manor CI BEX TN40 .... 195 J7
Old Mansion CI EDN/EASTW BN20 .. 229 F5
Old Mill CI BRI BN1 .... 177 K6
  HAIL BN27 .... 161 F8 🔲
Old Mill La POLE BN26 .... 214 D8
Old Mill Pk BEXW TN39 .... 195 F5
Old Motcombe Ms EAST BN21 ...... 229 J7 🔲
Old Orchard Pl HAIL BN27 .... 189 G4
Old Orchard Rd EAST BN21 .... 10 B5
Old Parish La ROTT BN2 .... 206 A3
Old Patcham Ms BRI BN1 .... 177 K5
Old Rectory Gdns STHW BN42 ...... 201 G4
Old River Wy WSEA TN36 .... 143 H4
Old Rd EGRIN RH19 .... 22 D3
  HAIL BN27 .... 162 A7
Old Roar Rd SLVH TN37 .... 169 K7
Old School CI RING/NEW BN8 ..... 155 K5 🔲
Old School La POLE BN26 .... 215 F4 🔲
Old School Pl BURH RH15 .... 119 F1
Old Shoreham Rd BRI BN1 .... 6 A3
  HOVE BN3 .... 203 H3
  STHW BN42 .... 201 J3
Old Station Rd WADH TN5 .... 44 A5
Old Steine ROTT BN2 .... 6 C5 🔲
Old Swan La HAIL BN27 .... 189 J6
Old Timbers La UCK TN22 .... 95 J5
Old Top Rd RHAS TN35 .... 171 G7
Old Wardsdown WADH TN5 .... 47 F5
Old Willingdon Rd
  EDN/EASTW BN20 .... 234 B2
Old Wish Rd EAST BN21 .... 10 B6 🔲
Oliver CI CROW TN6 .... 53 J2
  ROTT BN2 .... 7 E5
Olive Rd HOVE BN3 .... 202 D3
Olives Meadow UCK TN22 .... 95 K4
Onslow Rd HOVE BN3 .... 203 H2
Orange Rw BRI BN1 .... 6 C5 🔲🔲
Orchard Av HOVE BN3 .... 203 G2
Orchard CI HAS TN34 .... 5 D1
  RTWE/PEM TN2 .... 20 D4
  SHOR BN43 .... 200 B3
  STHW BN42 .... 201 J3
Orchard Gdns HOVE BN3 .... 203 G2
Orchard La HPPT/KEY BN6 .... 119 J7
  HPPT/KEY BN6 .... 119 F7
Orchard Ms NEWHV BN9 .... 224 A1
Orchard Ri BEX RRTW TN3 .... 27 K4
Orchard Rd BEX TN40 .... 195 H5
  BURH RH15 .... 88 E8
  HOVE BN3 .... 203 F2
  LEW BN7 .... 3 E3
The Orchard BUR/ETCH TN19 .... 77 G2
  RYE TN31 .... 109 K2
  UCK TN22 .... 50 C7
Orchard Wy BURH RH15 .... 89 F8 🔲
  EGRIN RH19 .... 22 C2
  RYE TN31 .... 112 C2
Orchid CI LGNY BN23 .... 216 C8
Orchidhurst RTWE/PEM TN2 .... 20 D4 🔲
Orchid Vw BRI BN1 .... 178 D5
Oriental PI BRI BN1 .... 6 A5
Orion CI HAIL BN27 .... 189 J3
Ormerod Av STLEO TN38 .... 169 H7
Ormonde Wy SHOR BN43 .... 200 A5
Orpen Rd HOVE BN3 .... 203 J2
Osbern CI BEXW TN39 .... 194 B8
Osborne CI HAS TN34 .... 4 C2
Osborne HI CROW TN6 .... 54 A3
Osborne Rd BRI BN1 .... 204 A1
  CROW TN6 .... 54 A2 🔲
  EDN/EASTW BN20 .... 229 G7
Osborne Vls HOVE BN3 .... 203 G6
Osmers HI WADH TN5 .... 44 B4
Osmond Rd HOVE BN3 .... 6 A3
Osmunda Bank EGRIN RH19 .... 12 C5
Osprey Dr UCK TN22 .... 96 A6
Ospringe Pl RTWE/PEM TN2 .... 21 F5
Otham Court La POLE BN26 .... 215 F3
Otham Rd LW/ROSE BN22 .... 230 B1
Otteham CI POLE BN26 .... 215 G5

Oulton CI LGNY BN23 .... 216 C8
Ousedale CI LEW BN7 .... 2 B4
Outlook Av PEAHV BN10 .... 222 E5
The Outlook EDN/EASTW BN20 .... 234 E2
Oval CI PEAHV BN10 .... 222 B1
Overdown Ri PTSD BN41 .... 175 J7
Overhill STHW BN42 .... 201 H2
Overhill Dr BRI BN1 .... 177 K6
Overhill Gdns BRI BN1 .... 177 K6
Overhill Wy BRI BN1 .... 177 K5
Overmead SHOR BN43 .... 200 B3
Over St BRI BN1 .... 6 C4
Overton Shaw EGRIN RH19 .... 12 C8
Ovingdean CI ROTT BN2 .... 206 A6
Ovingdean Rd ROTT BN2 .... 206 A7
Owen CI BURH RH15 .... 119 F2
Oxbottom CI RING/NEW BN8 .... 93 F5
Oxen Av SHOR BN43 .... 200 C3
Oxenbridge La BUR/ETCH TN19 .... 77 F3
Oxendean Gdns LW/ROSE BN22 .. 215 J2
Oxford Ct BRI BN1 .... 6 C3 🔲
Oxford Ms HOVE BN3 .... 203 H4
Oxford Pl BRI BN1 .... 6 C3 🔲
Oxford Rd LW/ROSE BN22 .... 11 D3 🔲
  STLEO TN38 .... 169 H8
Oxford St BRI BN1 .... 6 C3
Ox Lea RRTW TN3 .... 18 E8
Oyster Creek RYE TN31 .... 114 B8

P

Packham Wy BURH RH15 .... 89 F7 🔲
Paddock CI RRTW TN3 .... 17 K6
Paddock Gdns EGRIN RH19 .... 22 C4
  POLE BN26 .... 214 E7
Paddock La LEW BN7 .... 2 C4
Paddock Rd LEW BN7 .... 2 C4 🔲
The Paddocks EDEN TN8 .... 15 H4
  HAIL BN27 .... 189 F1
  LEW BN7 .... 121 G5 🔲
  LEW BN7 .... 208 C3
The Paddock HOVE BN3 .... 203 H2
  LW/ROSE BN22 .... 230 A1
  RTWE/PEM TN2 .... 21 J5
  RYE TN31 .... 81 K4
  SHOR BN43 .... 200 A2
  UCK TN22 .... 67 G7
Padgham La HTHF TN21 .... 133 F3
Pages Av BEXW TN39 .... 194 E8
Pages CI HTHF TN21 .... 99 J3
Pages HI HTHF TN21 .... 99 J4
Pages La BEXW TN39 .... 194 D8
The Pagets RING/NEW BN8 .... 93 H4
Pagham CI PEV BN24 .... 216 C7
Pain's Flat RHWH RH17 .... 88 D3
Palace PI BRI BN1 .... 6 C5 🔲
Palesgate Rd CROW TN6 .... 54 C3
Palliser CI LGNY BN23 .... 231 F5 🔲
Palma CI POLE BN26 .... 215 F4
Palmeira Av HOVE BN3 .... 203 H5
Palmeira Sq HOVE BN3 .... 203 H5
Palmerston Rd NEWHV BN9 .... 9 F1
Pangdean La HPPT/KEY BN6 .... 88 C7
Pangdene CI BURH RH15 .... 118 E2
Pankhurst Av ROTT BN2 .... 7 E4
Pankhurst Av BEXW TN39 .... 195 F3 🔲
Pankhurst Ri BEXW TN39 .... 195 F3
Pannel La RHAS TN35 .... 172 E1
Pannell CI EGRIN RH19 .... 22 B2
Pannett BURH RH15 .... 88 E7 🔲
The Pantiles RTWE/PEM TN2 .... 30 A7 🔲
The Parade PEV BN24 .... 218 B6
Paradise CI EDN/EASTW BN20 ..... 236 D1
Paradise Dr EAST BN21 .... 10 A5
  EDN/EASTW BN20 .... 236 D2
The Paragon EDN/EASTW BN20 ... 214 E8
Parham CI ROTT BN2 .... 7 F5
Park Av BEXW TN39 .... 195 G8
  EAST BN21 .... 229 H4
  HAS TN34 .... 4 B1
  HOVE BN3 .... 202 D4
  HPPT/KEY BN6 .... 150 B1
  PEAHV BN10 .... 221 K3
  SHOR BN43 .... 200 D5
Park CI BRI BN1 .... 179 F6
  BURH RH15 .... 89 F8
  EDN/EASTW BN20 .... 229 J8 🔲
  HAIL BN27 .... 189 C1
  HAS TN34 .... 4 B1
  HOVE BN3 .... 176 D8
  PTSD BN41 .... 202 A2
  SBGH/RUST TN4 .... 29 J1
Park Crs ROTT BN2 .... 7 F5
Park Crescent PI ROTT BN2 .... 7 D5
Park Crescent Rd ROTT BN2 .... 7 D5
Park Crescent Ter ROTT BN2 .... 7 D5
Park Cft POLE BN26 .... 215 F7
Park Dr HAS TN34 .... 4 B2

Park Drive CI NEWHV BN9 .... 224 A1
Parker CI EAST BN21 .... 10 A2
Parker Rd HAS TN34 .... 5 E2
Park Farm CI BUR/ETCH TN19 .... 77 F3
Parkfield Av LW/ROSE BN22 .... 229 J2
Park Ga HAIL BN27 .... 161 J8
Park HI ROTT BN2 .... 7 D5
Park House Gdns SBGH/RUST TN4 . 20 A2
Parkhurst Rd BEXW TN39 .... 195 H8
Parklands SHOR BN43 .... 200 D3
  UCK TN22 .... 67 G6
Parklands Rd HPPT/KEY BN6 .... 119 F8
Park La BAT TN33 .... 136 D7
  BEXW TN39 .... 195 F5
  EAST BN21 .... 229 H3
  RBTBR TN32 .... 107 G6
  RING/NEW BN8 .... 158 B5
  STHW BN42 .... 201 G4
Parkmore Ter BRI BN1 .... 6 B2
Park Ri HOVE BN3 .... 176 D8
Park Rd BEXW TN39 .... 195 G8
  BRI BN1 .... 179 F6
  BURH RH15 .... 89 F8
  CROW TN6 .... 53 H8
  EGRIN RH19 .... 12 C5
  EGRIN RH19 .... 22 B2
  FROW RH18 .... 36 A1
  HAIL BN27 .... 161 G8
  HTHF TN21 .... 100 B4
  LEW BN7 .... 2 C4
  PEAHV BN10 .... 222 B2
  ROTT BN2 .... 220 C2
  SBGH/RUST TN4 .... 20 B6
  SBGH/RUST TN4 .... 20 A1
  SEAF BN25 .... 224 E8
  SHOR BN43 .... 200 D3
Park Road Ter BRI BN2 .... 7 D5
Park Shaw BAT TN33 .... 138 A2
Parkside EGRIN RH19 .... 22 A2
  HPPT/KEY BN6 .... 119 G8
  HTHF TN21 .... 100 B5
  SHOR BN43 .... 200 D2
Parkside Rd SEAF BN25 .... 225 G7
The Parks PTSD BN41 .... 176 A8 🔲
Parkstone Rd HAS TN34 .... 170 A7
Park St BRI BN1 .... 179 K5
  ROTT BN2 .... 7 D5
  RTWE/PEM TN2 .... 20 C8 🔲
The Park CROW TN6 .... 53 H1
  ROTT BN2 .... 220 D2
Park Vw HAS TN34 .... 4 B1
  RYE TN31 .... 81 J5
  RYE TN31 .... 112 B1
  UCK TN22 .... 68 E7
Park View CI PEAHV BN10 .... 221 K2 🔲
Park View Ri PEAHV BN10 .... 221 K3 🔲
Park View Rd HOVE BN3 .... 203 C4
Parkview Rd UCK TN22 .... 95 K2
Parkway EDN/EASTW BN20 .... 229 G3
Park Wy HAS TN34 .... 4 B1
  STHW BN42 .... 201 J3
Park Way CI STHW BN42 .... 201 J3
Parkwood RYE TN31 .... 85 H7
Parkwood CI RTWE/PEM TN2 .... 20 C5
Park Wood Rd HAS TN34 .... 170 C5
Parrock La HRTF TN7 .... 36 D1
Parry CI LGNY BN23 .... 217 F8
Parsonage CI SBGH/RUST TN4 ..... 19 F6 🔲
Parsonage La RHAS TN35 .... 138 E7
  RRTW TN3 .... 33 K5
  WSEA TN36 .... 141 K5
Parsonage Rd EAST BN21 .... 229 J7
  SBGH/RUST TN4 .... 19 F6
Parsons CI STLEO TN38 .... 169 G7
Pashley Rd EDN/EASTW BN20 ..... 236 B1
Paston PI ROTT BN2 .... 7 F6
Patcham By-pass BRI BN1 .... 177 K6
Patcham Gra BRI BN1 .... 177 K6
Patcham Mill Rd PEV BN24 .... 216 C6
Patchdean BRI BN1 .... 178 A6
Paton Rd BEXW TN39 .... 194 E3
Paul CI HAIL BN27 .... 161 F8
Pavilion Buildings BRI BN1 .... 6 C5 🔲🔲
Pavilion CI HPPT/KEY BN6 .... 118 E6
Pavilion Pde ROTT BN2 .... 6 C5 🔲🔲
Pavilion St ROTT BN2 .... 6 C5 🔲🔲
Pavilion Wy EGRIN RH19 .... 22 C3
Paxhill CI STLEO TN38 .... 169 F7
Paygate Rd BAT TN33 .... 138 A4
Payne Av HOVE BN3 .... 202 E3
Paynsbridge Wy HTHF TN21 .... 129 K4
Paynters Wy RING/NEW BN8 .... 93 G4
Paynton Rd SLVH TN37 .... 169 J8
Paythorne CI STHW BN42 .... 201 G2 🔲
Payton Dr BURH RH15 .... 119 F1
Peace CI BRI BN1 .... 7 E1
Peacock La BRI BN1 .... 177 K7
Peakdean CI EDN/EASTW BN20 ... 235 F1
Peakdean La EDN/EASTW BN20 ... 235 F1
Pearse PI RRTW TN3 .... 33 J6
Peartree CI BURH RH15 .... 88 E8
Peartree Fld WSEA TN36 .... 141 K5 🔲
Peartree HI WADH TN5 .... 59 F8
Peartree La BEXW TN39 .... 194 C6
Pebble Rd PEV BN24 .... 218 B6

Pebsham Dr *BEX* TN40 .... **196** B5
Pebsham La *BEX* TN40 .... **196** A5
Peckham Cl *LEW* BN7 .... 2 C2 🔟
Peelings La *PEV* BN24 .... **216** C5
Peel Rd *ROTT* BN2 .... **205** G2
Pegasus Wy *EGRIN* RH19 .... 12 E8
Pegler Av *NEWHV* BN9 .... 8 B4
Pegwell Cl *HAS* TN34 .... 4 C2
Pelham Cl *PEAHV* BN10 .... **222** C1
  PEV BN24 .... **217** G6
Pelham Crs *HAIL* BN27 .... **189** H5
  HAS TN34 .... 5 E5 🔟
Pelham Pl *HAS* TN34 .... 5 D5
Pelham Ri *PEAHV* BN10 .... **222** B2
Pelham Rd *SEAF* BN25 .... **232** A1
Pelham Sq *BRI* BN1 .... 6 C4 🔟
Pelham St *BRI* BN1 .... 6 C4
Pelham Ter *LEW* BN7 .... 2 C3
Pelham Yd *SEAF* BN25 .... **232** A1 🔟
Pellbrook Rd *LEW* BN7 .... A2
Pell Cl *WADH* TN5 .... 44 C5
Pellings Farm Cl *CROW* TN6 ...... 53 K1
Pellings Ri *CROW* TN6 .... 53 K1
Pelwood Rd *RYE* TN31 .... **145** J1
Pembroke Av *HOVE* BN3 .... **203** F5
Pembroke Cl *HAIL* BN27 .... **161** H8 🔟
Pembroke Crs *HOVE* BN3 .... **203** F4
Pembroke Gdns *HOVE* BN3 .... **203** F5
Pembury Cl *RTWE/PEM* TN2 ...... 21 K4 🔟
Pembury Gra *RTWE/PEM* TN2 ... 21 C5
Pembury Gv *BEXW* TN39 .... **195** F4
Pembury Rd *LGNY* BN23 .... **230** E2
  RTWE/PEM TN2 .... 20 C8
Pembury Wks *RTON* TN11 .... 21 H1
Pendean *BURH* RH15 .... **119** J2 🔟
Penhale Dr *BEX* TN40 .... **196** A5
Penhale La *BAT* TN33 .... **134** C6
Penhurst Dr *BEX* TN40 .... **196** A5
Penhurst Pl *ROTT* BN2 .... **205** G5
Penland Rd *BEX* TN40 .... **195** K6
Penn Crs *RING/NEW* BN8 .... **155** J6
Pennine Ri *HAS* TN34 .... **170** E7
Pennine Wy *LGNY* BN23 .... **216** E7 🔟
Pennington Pl *SBGH/RUST* TN4 .. 20 B1
Pennington Rd *SBGH/RUST* TN4 .. 20 A1
Penns Yd *UCK* TN22 .... 21 J5
Pennybridge La *MAYF* TN20 ...... 56 D5
Penny La *BEX* TN40 .... **196** B6
Penrith Wy *LGNY* BN23 .... **216** D7
Pensford Dr *LGNY* BN23 .... **230** E1
Penshurst Rd *RTON* TN11 .... 18 B1
Pentland Cl *LGNY* BN23 .... **216** E8 🔟
  SLVH TN37 .... **169** K6 🔟
Peppercombe Rd
  EDN/EASTW BN20 .... **229** G7
Pepper Dr *BURH* RH15 .... **118** E1 🔟
  BURH RH15 .... **119** F2 🔟
Perch La *RRTW* TN3 .... 33 F2
Percival Crs *LW/ROSE* BN22 ...... **216** A8
Percival Rd *LW/ROSE* BN22 .... **216** A8
Percival Ter *ROTT* BN2 .... 7 F6 🔟
Percy Av *EGRIN* RH19 .... 12 C8
Perryfields *BURH* RH15 .... 88 E7
Perry Hl *ROTT* BN2 .... **221** F1
Perryman's La *RHWH* RH17 .... 49 H8
Perth Cl *SEAF* BN25 .... **225** K8
Perth Rd *SLVH* TN37 .... **169** J8
Peter James Cl *RYE* TN31 .... **145** G1 🔟
Peter James La *RHAS* TN35 .... **172** B4
Pett Cl *ROTT* BN2 .... **205** G5 🔟
Pett La *WSEA* TN36 .... **142** B7
Pett Level Rd *RHAS* TN35 .... **172** E5
  WSEA TN36 .... **143** C8
Pett Rd *RHAS* TN35 .... **171** K4
  RHAS TN35 .... **173** C4
Petworth Dr *BURH* RH15 .... 89 G7
Petworth Pl *LW/ROSE* BN22 ..... **229** K1 🔟
Petworth Rd *BRI* BN1 .... **178** C5
Pevensey Bay Rd *LGNY* BN23 .... **231** F3
Pevensey Cl *SEAF* BN25 .... **225** J7
Pevensey Park Rd *PEV* BN24 ...... **217** C5
Pevensey Rd *EAST* BN21 .... 11 D4 🔟
  NEWHV BN9 .... 8 A5
  POLE BN26 .... **215** G5
  ROTT BN2 .... 7 E2 🔟
  STLEO TN38 .... 4 A5
The Peverells *SEAF* BN25 .... **225** H6 🔟
Peyton Cl *LGNY* BN23 .... **231** G4
Phoenix Cswy *LEW* BN7 .... 3 D4
Phoenix Crs *STHW* BN42 .... **201** G3
Phoenix La *EGRIN* RH19 .... 23 J5
Phoenix Pl *LEW* BN7 .... 3 D4 🔟
  ROTT BN2 .... 7 D4 🔟
  ROTT BN2 .... 7 D4 🔟
Phoenix Ri *ROTT* BN2 .... 7 D4
Phoenix Wy *STHW* BN42 .... **201** G3
Phyllis Av *PEAHV* BN10 .... **222** A4
Picardy La *BAT* TN33 .... **136** E7
Piccadilly La *MAYF* TN20 .... 72 D2
Picketts La *UCK* TN22 .... 66 C4
Pickforde La *WADH* TN5 .... 60 C2
Picton St *ROTT* BN2 .... 7 E3
Piddinghoe Av *PEAHV* BN10 ..... **222** C5
Piddinghoe Cl *PEAHV* BN10 ...... **222** C4

Piddinghoe Md *NEWHV* BN9 .... 8 B2 🔟
Pilmer Rd *CROW* TN6 .... 39 H8
Pilot Rd *HAS* TN34 .... **170** D7
Piltdown Cl *BEXW* TN39 .... **195** G7
  HAS TN34 .... 4 C3 🔟
Piltdown Ri *UCK* TN22 .... 95 K3
Piltdown Rd *ROTT* BN2 .... **205** G5
Piltdown Wy *LW/ROSE* BN22 .... **216** B7
Pinders Rd *RHAS* TN35 .... **199** G1
Pine Av *HAS* TN34 .... 5 F1
Pine Gv *CROW* TN6 .... 53 G1
Pinehurst *BURH* RH15 .... **119** G2
Pine Tree Cl *HPPT/KEY* BN6 ...... **118** A6
Pine Tree Rd *HTHF* TN21 .... **100** A6
Pine Wk *UCK* TN22 .... 95 K3
Pine Wy *HAIL* BN27 .... **189** F4
Pine Way *EGRIN* RH19 .... 22 C4
Pinewood Cha *CROW* TN6 .... 39 F8
Pinewood Gdns *SBGH/RUST* TN4 .. 20 A2
Pinewood Rd *RTWE/PEM* TN2 ... 20 D6 🔟
Pinewoods *BEXW* TN39 .... **194** D7
Pinewood Wy *HWH* RH16 .... 89 K1 🔟
  STLEO TN38 .... **169** F8
Pinfold Cl *UCK* TN22 .... 95 K7
Pinton Hl *WADH* TN5 .... 45 K8
Pinwell Rd *LEW* BN7 .... 3 D5
Pipers Cl *BEX* TN40 .... **195** H6 🔟
  HOVE BN3 .... **176** B8
  WADH TN5 .... 44 C7
Pipers Fld *UCK* TN22 .... 95 K7
Piper's Ga *UCK* TN22 .... 95 K7
Pipit Meadow *UCK* TN22 .... 95 K6
Pitreavie Dr *HAIL* BN27 .... **189** F3
Pit Rd *HPPT/KEY* BN6 .... **118** A6
Pitt Dr *SEAF* BN25 .... **225** H6
Pitt Gdns *ROTT* BN2 .... **206** A3
Place La *SEAF* BN25 .... **225** F8
Plainfields Av *BRI* BN1 .... **178** B4
Plaistow Cl *ROTT* BN2 .... **205** G5
The Plat *RYE* TN31 .... 81 K5
The Platt *LING* RH7 .... 12 E5
Plaw Hatch La *EGRIN* RH19 .... 34 C6
Playden Cl *ROTT* BN2 .... **205** F7
Playden Gdns *HAS* TN34 .... **170** E7
Playden La *RYE* TN31 .... 85 H8
Pleasant View Rd *CROW* TN6 .... 39 G7
Plemont Gdns *BEXW* TN39 .... **195** F5
Pleyden Ri *BEXW* TN39 .... **193** J7
Plough La *SLVH* TN37 .... **169** J6
Plough Rd *LING* RH7 .... 12 E1
Plover Cl *LGNY* BN23 .... **230** D1
Plover Ct *STLEO* TN38 .... **169** F8
Plumpton Bostall *LEW* BN7 .... **152** A5
Plumpton Cl *BEX* TN40 .... **195** H5
  LW/ROSE BN22 .... **216** B7
Plumpton La *LEW* BN7 .... **152** B3
Plumpton Rd *ROTT* BN2 .... 7 F4
Plymouth Av *ROTT* BN2 .... **205** G2
Plymouth Cl *LGNY* BN23 .... **231** G3 🔟
Plynlimmon Rd *HAS* TN34 .... 4 D4
Pocock's Ga *EAST* BN21 .... **229** J6
Polegate By-pass *POLE* BN26 ... **214** E4
Polesden Rd *RTWE/PEM* TN2 .... 30 D1 🔟
Polley Cl *RTWE/PEM* TN2 .... 21 K4
Pollington Pl *CROW* TN6 .... 53 H1 🔟
Pomper La *HPPT/KEY* BN6 .... **118** A1
Pond Cl *RYE* TN31 .... **109** K6
Pond Rd *SHOR* BN43 .... **200** C4
Pond Wy *EGRIN* RH19 .... 23 F2
Ponswood Rd *STLEO* TN38 .... **197** J1 🔟
Pont Cl *HTHF* TN21 .... **101** J5
Pook Reed La *HTHF* TN21 .... 99 J5
Pool Va *BRI* BN1 .... 6 C6
Poona Rd *RTWE/PEM* TN2 .... 30 B1
Poplar Av *HOVE* BN3 .... **176** B4
Poplar Cl *BRI* BN1 .... **204** A1
  HOVE BN3 .... **176** D8
The Poplars *HPPT/KEY* BN6 ...... **119** G8 🔟
Poppinghole La *RBTBR* TN32 .... **106** D2
Popps La *BEXW* TN39 .... **194** D8
Porters Wy *POLE* BN26 .... **215** F5
Portfield Av *BRI* BN1 .... **178** B5
Portfield Cl *BEX* TN40 .... **195** K6
Port Hall Av *BRI* BN1 .... 6 A2 🔟
Port Hall Ms *BRI* BN1 .... 6 A2 🔟
Port Hall Pl *BRI* BN1 .... 6 A2
Port Hall Rd *HOVE* BN3 .... 6 A2
Port Hall St *BRI* BN1 .... 6 A2
Portland Av *HOVE* BN3 .... **202** D4
Portland Cl *HAIL* BN27 .... **189** F2
Portland Pl *HAS* TN34 .... 5 D4 🔟
  ROTT BN2 .... 7 E6
Portland Rd *BURH* RH15 .... 89 F8
  EGRIN RH19 .... 22 C3
  HOVE BN3 .... **202** C4
The Portlands *LGNY* BN23 .... **231** G4
Portland St *BRI* BN1 .... 6 B5 🔟
Portland Vls *HOVE* BN3 .... **202** C4
Port Rd *LW/ROSE* BN22 .... **230** B2
Portsdown Wy *EDN/EASTW* BN20 .. **229** G1
Port Vw *NEWHV* BN9 .... **223** K1
Possingworth Cl *HTHF* TN21 ..... 98 D3
Post Horn La *FROW* RH18 .... 36 A3

Post Office Rd *HAWK* TN18 .... 63 F1 🔟
Potato La *RING/NEW* BN8 .... **155** K6
Potman's La *BEXW* TN39 .... **194** D1
Pottens Mill La *MAYF* TN20 .... 73 F7
The Potteries *UCK* TN22 .... 95 K7
Potters Fld *RING/NEW* BN8 .... **155** J5
Potters La *BURH* RH15 .... **119** F2
  LEW BN7 .... 2 C5 🔟
Pottery Cl *RYE* TN31 .... **139** H1
Pottery La *RYE* TN31 .... **139** H1
Pottingfield Rd *RYE* TN31 .... **113** G5
Pound Cl *LGNY* BN23 .... **231** G5 🔟
Poundfield Rd *CROW* TN6 .... 53 K1
Pound La *RING/NEW* BN8 .... **157** K4
  UCK TN22 .... 97 F5
Poundsbridge Hl *RRTW* TN3 ...... 18 B5
The Pound *BURH* RH15 .... 89 F7
Poveys Cl *BURH* RH15 .... 88 D8
Powdermill Cl *RTWE/PEM* TN2 .. 20 C5 🔟
Powdermill La *BAT* TN33 .... **166** D3
  RYE TN31 .... 144 B2
Powder Mill La *SBGH/RUST* TN4 .. 20 B4
Powell Gdns *NEWHV* BN9 .... 9 E1 🔟
Powell Rd *RING/NEW* BN8 .... 93 H4
Powis Gv *BRI* BN1 .... 6 A4
Powis Rd *BRI* BN1 .... 6 A4
Powis Sq *BRI* BN1 .... 6 A4
Powis Vls *BRI* BN1 .... 6 A4
Poynings Cl *SEAF* BN25 .... **232** E1 🔟
Poynings Dr *HOVE* BN3 .... **176** C8
Poynter Rd *HOVE* BN3 .... **203** F3
Pratt's Folly La *CROW* TN6 .... 53 G2 🔟
Precincts Castle *LEW* BN7 .... 2 C4 🔟
Preemans La *UCK* TN22 .... 68 A1
Preston Dro *BRI* BN1 .... **204** A1
Preston Gv *UCK* TN22 .... 96 D5
Preston Park Av *BRI* BN1 .... 6 B1
Preston Rd *BEXW* TN39 .... **195** G4
  BRI BN1 .... 6 A1
  BRI BN1 .... **203** K1
Preston St *BRI* BN1 .... 6 A5
Prestonville Rd *BRI* BN1 .... 6 B5
Prideaux Rd *EAST* BN21 .... 10 A2
Primrose Cl *BURH* RH15 .... 88 D7
  LGNY BN23 .... **216** C8
Primrose Hl *BEXW* TN39 .... **194** E5
  HAS TN35 .... **172** E6
Primrose La *FROW* RH18 .... 36 A2
Prince Albert St *BRI* BN1 .... 6 C5 🔟
Prince Charles Cl *STHW* BN42 ... **201** J2
Prince Charles Rd *LEW* BN7 .... 3 E2
Prince Edward's Rd *LEW* BN7 .... 2 B4
Prince Regent's Cl *ROTT* BN2 .... **205** F7
Princes Av *HOVE* BN3 .... **203** F5
Princes Cl *SEAF* BN25 .... **225** F7
  UCK TN22 .... 95 G4
Princes Crs *HOVE* BN3 .... **203** F5
  ROTT BN2 .... 7 D2
Prince's Pl *BRI* BN1 .... 6 C5 🔟
Princes Rd *LGNY* BN23 .... **231** F4
  ROTT BN2 .... 7 D2
  SLVH TN37 .... 4 B5 🔟
Princess Dr *SEAF* BN25 .... **224** E6 🔟
Princes Sq *HOVE* BN3 .... **203** F5
Prince's St *ROTT* BN2 .... 6 C5 🔟
  RTWE/PEM TN2 .... 20 C8 🔟
Prince's Ter *ROTT* BN2 .... **205** F7
Prince William Pde *LGNY* BN23 .. **231** F5
Prinkle La *HAIL* BN27 .... **163** K2
Prinsep Rd *HOVE* BN3 .... **203** F3
Prior's Wy *EDEN* TN8 .... 15 G5 🔟
Priory Av *HAS* TN34 .... 4 C3
Priory Cl *HAS* TN34 .... 4 C3
  PEV BN24 .... **218** A6
Priory Crs *LEW* BN7 .... 2 C5
Priory Hts *EDN/EASTW* BN20 .... **229** F6
Priory La *LGNY* BN23 .... **217** F8
Priory Orch *LGNY* BN23 .... **231** F3
Priory Rd *BURH* RH15 .... **119** G2
  FROW RH18 .... 34 E5
  HAS TN34 .... 5 E4
  HPPT/KEY BN6 .... **118** E6
  LGNY BN23 .... **217** F8
Priory St *HAS* TN34 .... 4 C4
  LEW BN7 .... 2 C5
Promenade *PEAHV* BN10 .... **221** K5
The Promenade *PEV* BN24 .... **218** A4
Prospect Gdns *EAST* BN21 .... **229** J7 🔟
Prospect Pk *SBGH/RUST* TN4 .... 19 K2
Prospect Pl *HAS* TN34 .... 4 C5 🔟
Prospect Rd *HTHF* TN21 .... **100** B5
  RTWE/PEM TN2 .... 20 B8
  SBGH/RUST TN4 .... 19 K2
Providence Pl *BRI* BN1 .... 6 C3
Prowting Md *BEXW* TN39 .... **194** B7
Pudding Cake La *UCK* TN22 ...... 95 J4 🔟
Pulborough Av *LW/ROSE* BN22 .. **229** K2
Pulborough Cl *ROTT* BN2 .... **205** G4 🔟
Pump La *UCK* TN22 .... **127** F1
Purbeck Cl *LGNY* BN23 .... **216** D8
Pyecombe St *POY/PYE* BN45 .... **149** F5

Q

Quadrant *BRI* BN1 .... 6 B5
The Quadrant *EAST* BN21 .... 10 A3 ☑
  HPPT/KEY BN6 .... 119 G7
Quantock Cl *LGNY* BN23 .... 216 E8 ☑
  RTWE/PEM TN2 .... 20 D6
Quantock Gdns *HAS* TN34 .... 5 F5
Quarry Bank Rd *BRI* BN1 .... 204 C1 ☑
Quarry Cl *BURH* RH15 .... 89 K8
Quarry Crs *HAS* TN34 .... 5 E3
Quarry Hl *STLEO* TN38 .... 197 J4
Quarry La *SEAF* BN25 .... 225 H6
Quarry Ri *EGRIN* RH19 .... 12 E8
Quarry Rd *HAS* TN34 .... 5 D3
  NEWHV BN9 .... 8 C5
  RTW TN1 .... 20 B6
Quebec Cl *BEXW* TN39 .... 195 F6
  LGNY BN23 .... 231 G4
Quebec Rd *STLEO* TN38 .... 169 H7
Quebec St *ROTT* BN2 .... 7 D4
Queen Alexandra Av *HOVE* BN3 .... 177 F8
Queen Anne's Cl *LEW* BN7 .... 2 C4 ☑
Queen Caroline Cl *HOVE* BN3 .... 177 F8 ☑
Queen Elizabeth Av *BURH* RH15 ... 119 F1
Queen Mary Av *HOVE* BN3 .... 177 F8
Queens Ap *UCK* TN22 .... 95 K2 ☑
Queensbury Ms *BRI* BN1 .... 6 A5 ☑
  EAST BN21 .... 11 D4 ☑
Queen's Colonnade Gdns
  EAST BN21 .... 11 D4 ☑
Queens Cottages *WADH* TN5 .... 44 A6
Queens Ct *HAWK* TN18 .... 63 C1
Queens Crs *BURH* RH15 .... 119 J2
  LGNY BN23 .... 230 E4
Queensdown School Rd *BRI* BN1 .. 178 D8
Queens Dr *HPPT/KEY* BN6 .... 119 F7
  UCK TN22 .... 67 F7
Queen's Gdns *BRI* BN1 .... 6 C4
  HOVE BN3 .... 203 H6
  SBGH/RUST TN4 .... 20 B5
Queensmount *MAYF* TN20 .... 71 F4
Queens Park Gdns *SEAF* BN25 .... 224 D7
Queen's Park Ri *ROTT* BN2 .... 7 E4
Queen's Park Rd *ROTT* BN2 .... 7 D5
Queen's Park Ter *ROTT* BN2 .... 7 D5
Queen's Pl *BRI* BN1 .... 6 C3 ☑
  HOVE BN3 .... 203 H5
  SHOR BN43 .... 200 C4
Queen Sq *BRI* BN1 .... 6 B5
Queen's Rd *BRI* BN1 .... 6 B4
  CROW TN6 .... 53 H3
  EGRIN RH19 .... 22 C3
  HAIL BN27 .... 163 F6
  HAS TN34 .... 5 D5 ☑
  HAWK TN18 .... 63 C1
  LEW BN7 .... 3 D2
  LGNY BN23 .... 230 E4
  SBGH/RUST TN4 .... 20 B5
  STHW BN42 .... 201 H2
Queensway *EGRIN* RH19 .... 22 C3
  ROTT BN2 .... 7 F4
  SEAF BN25 .... 225 H6
  STLEO TN38 .... 169 F6
Queen Victoria Av *HOVE* BN3 ...... 177 F8
Quermby Cl *SHOR* BN43 .... 201 G4 ☑
Quickbourne La *RYE* TN31 .... 82 A4
Quinnell Dr *HAIL* BN27 .... 189 G1
Quintin Cl *HAIL* BN27 .... 189 F6 ☑

R

Radcliffe Cl *SLVH* TN37 .... 4 A1
Radinden Dr *HOVE* BN3 .... 203 J2
Radinden Manor Rd *HOVE* BN3 .... 203 H5
Radnor Ms *STLEO* TN38 .... 197 F1 ☑
Ragged Dog La *HTHF* TN21 .... 99 F8
Railway Ap *EGRIN* RH19 .... 22 B2
  NEWHV BN9 .... 9 D3
Railway La *LEW* BN7 .... 3 D4
Railway Rd *NEWHV* BN9 .... 9 D3
Railway St *BRI* BN1 .... 6 B4 ☑
Raleigh Cl *LGNY* BN23 .... 231 F4
  SHOR BN43 .... 200 B5
Ramsay Wy *LGNY* BN23 .... 231 F4
Ramslye Rd *SBGH/RUST* TN4 .... 29 H2
Randolph La *RYE* TN31 .... 85 G8
Ranelagh Vls *HOVE* BN3 .... 203 G3
Rangemore Dr *EAST* BN21 .... 229 J4
Rankine Rd *RTWE/PEM* TN2 .... 20 B5
Ranmore Cl *HAS* TN34 .... 170 B5
Rannoch Rd *CROW* TN6 .... 53 F1
Rannoch Rd West *CROW* TN6 ...... 53 F1 ☑
Ranscombe Hl *RING/NEW* BN8 .... 183 J5
Ranscombe La *RING/NEW* BN8 .... 183 G5
Ranworth Cl *LGNY* BN23 .... 216 C7 ☑
Raphael Rd *HOVE* BN3 .... 202 E4
Rapson's Rd *EDN/EASTW* BN20 ... 214 E8
Rastrick Cl *BURH* RH15 .... 119 F2
Rattle Rd *PEV* BN24 .... 216 E6
Ratton Dr *EDN/EASTW* BN20 ...... 229 G4

Ratton Rd *EAST* BN21 .... 10 A3
Raven Ct *BAT* TN33 .... 137 F7 ☑
  STLEO TN38 .... 169 F8
Ravensbourne Av *SHOR* BN43 ..... 200 C2
Ravensbourne Cl *SHOR* BN43 ..... 200 C2 ☑
Ravens Cl *BEXW* TN39 .... 194 B8
Ravens Cft *EDN/EASTW* BN20 ..... 237 F3 ☑
Raven's Rd *SLVH* TN37 .... 200 C4
Ravenswood Av *RTW* TN1 .... 20 C5
Ravenswood Dr *ROTT* BN2 .... 206 C5
Ravenswood Rd *BURH* RH15 .... 89 H8
Ravine Cl *HAS* TN34 .... 5 E1
Rayford Cl *PEAHV* BN10 .... 222 B4 ☑
Raymond Cl *SEAF* BN25 .... 225 H6
Readers La *RYE* TN31 .... 85 F6
Reading Rd *ROTT* BN2 .... 205 G7
Rectory Cl *BUR/ETCH* TN19 .... 75 K5
  EDN/EASTW BN20 .... 229 J8
  NEWHV BN9 .... 8 C4
  RING/NEW BN8 .... 127 J6
  SHOR BN43 .... 201 G4
  STLEO TN38 .... 197 J2 ☑
Rectory Fld *HRTF* TN7 .... 26 A7
Rectory La *RYE* TN31 .... 82 D6
  RYE TN31 .... 113 H3
  WSEA TN36 .... 142 E5
Rectory Rd *NEWHV* BN9 .... 223 K1
  SHOR BN43 .... 201 F4
Rectory Wy *BEX* TN40 .... 195 J6
Redbridge La *CROW* TN6 .... 53 F6
Redbrook La *UCK* TN22 .... 69 F7
Redcross St *BRI* BN1 .... 6 C4
Redford Cl *LGNY* BN23 .... 231 F2 ☑
Redgeland Ri *STLEO* TN38 .... 197 G1
Redgill La *RING/NEW* BN8 .... 93 F2
Redhill Cl *BRI* BN1 .... 177 H6
Redhill Dr *BRI* BN1 .... 177 H7
Red Lake Ter *RHAS* TN35 .... 171 G3 ☑
Redleaf Cl *RTWE/PEM* TN2 .... 20 D5
Red Oak *HAWK* TN18 .... 62 E3
Redoubt Rd *LW/ROSE* BN22 .... 11 E3
Redvers Rd *ROTT* BN2 .... 7 F1
Redwell Av *BEXW* TN39 .... 195 G3 ☑
Redwings La *RTWE/PEM* TN2 .... 21 K1
Redwood Dr *HWH* RH16 .... 89 K1
Reedham Rd *LGNY* BN23 .... 216 C7 ☑
Reedswood Rd *RYE* TN31 .... 109 K7
  STLEO TN38 .... 197 F3
Reeves Hl *BRI* BN1 .... 178 E6
Reeves Ter *WADH* TN5 .... 60 C2 ☑
Regal Dr *EGRIN* RH19 .... 22 D3
Regency Cl *UCK* TN22 .... 95 J4
Regency Gdns *STLEO* TN38 .... 197 H3
Regency Ms *BRI* BN1 .... 6 A5
  EDN/EASTW BN20 .... 10 C6 ☑
Regency Rd *BRI* BN1 .... 6 B5
Regency Sq *BRI* BN1 .... 6 A5
Regent Hl *BRI* BN1 .... 6 A5
Regent Pl *STLEO* TN38 .... 169 G4
Regent Rw *BRI* BN1 .... 6 B5 ☑
Regents Cl *SEAF* BN25 .... 225 H6
Regent St *BRI* BN1 .... 6 C5 ☑
Reginald Rd *BEXW* TN39 .... 195 G7
Regnum Cl *LW/ROSE* BN22 .... 215 K7
Reigate Rd *BRI* BN1 .... 203 J2
Resting Oak Hl *RING/NEW* BN8 ... 122 D7
Reynolds Dr *BEX* TN40 .... 195 K6
Reynolds Rd *SBGH/RUST* TN4 ...... 19 K5
Reynolds Rd *HOVE* BN3 .... 202 E4
  LGNY BN23 .... 230 E2
Reynoldstown La *POLE* BN26 ...... 214 E5 ☑
Riccards La *BAT* TN33 .... 137 G5
Rices Hl *EGRIN* RH19 .... 22 C2
Richardson Rd *HOVE* BN3 .... 202 E4
  SBGH/RUST TN4 .... 20 A5
Richborough Cl *HAS* TN34 .... 170 A7 ☑
Richington Wy *SEAF* BN25 .... 225 J6
Richland Cl *RHAS* TN35 .... 171 G7
Richmead Gdns *MAYF* TN20 .... 72 B1
Richmond Av *BEXW* TN39 .... 194 E8
Richmond Cl *BEXW* TN39 .... 195 F8
Richmond Pde *ROTT* BN2 .... 7 D4 ☑
Richmond Pl *ROTT* BN2 .... 6 C4
Richmond Rd *BEXW* TN39 .... 194 E8
  ROTT BN2 .... 7 D2
  SEAF BN25 .... 224 E8
Richmond St *HAS* TN34 .... 199 F1 ☑
  ROTT BN2 .... 7 D4
Richmond Ter *SEAF* BN25 .... 225 F8 ☑
Richmond Wy *EGRIN* RH19 .... 22 D3
Riddens Cl *LEW* BN7 .... 121 G6
Riddens La *LEW* BN7 .... 121 G5
Riddlesdale Av *SBGH/RUST* TN4 ... 20 A5
Riders Bolt *BEXW* TN39 .... 194 D6
The Ride *BRI* BN1 .... 6 B1
Ridge Cl *PTSD* BN41 .... 175 K7 ☑
  UCK TN22 .... 50 C5
Ridge Lands Cl
  EDN/EASTW BN20 .... 229 H8 ☑
Ridge Rd *BRI* BN1 .... 179 K3
Ridgeside Av *BRI* BN1 .... 177 K6
The Ridge *HAS* TN34 .... 170 E7
  SLVH TN37 .... 169 K5
  WSEA TN36 .... 143 H6
Ridge Vw *BRI* BN1 .... 179 F6

Ridge Wy *HWH* RH16 .... 90 D1
Ridgeway *BUR/ETCH* TN19 .... 61 K8
  EGRIN RH19 .... 22 C4
  PTSD BN41 .... 201 J2 ☑
  RTWE/PEM TN2 .... 21 K4
Ridgeway Cl *HTHF* TN21 .... 100 A3
  STHW BN42 .... 201 J2
The Ridgeway *SBGH/RUST* TN4 .... 20 A2
Ridgeway Gdns *ROTT* BN2 .... 206 B4 ☑
The Ridgeway *BURH* RH15 .... 89 H7 ☑
  EDN/EASTW BN20 .... 234 C2
  HAIL BN27 .... 163 F5
  SEAF BN25 .... 225 G7
The Ridge West *SLVH* TN37 .... 169 H4
Ridgewood Av *ROTT* BN2 .... 207 F8
Ridgewood Cl *UCK* TN22 .... 95 K7 ☑
Ridgewood Gdns *BEX* TN40 .... 196 A7
  HAS TN34 .... 170 B6
Ridgway Cl *ROTT* BN2 .... 206 A3
Ridgway Paddock *LEW* BN7 .... 181 G5
The Ridgway *ROTT* BN2 .... 206 A3
The Ridings *BEXW* TN39 .... 194 E4
  BURH RH15 .... 119 J2
  PEAHV BN10 .... 222 A2
  RING/NEW BN8 .... 93 C4
  RTWE/PEM TN2 .... 21 F5
  SEAF BN25 .... 225 J7
  SLVH TN37 .... 169 K6 🔟
Rigden Rd *HOVE* BN3 .... 203 H3
Riley Rd *ROTT* BN2 .... 7 E1
Rill Wk *EGRIN* RH19 .... 23 F2
Ringmer Cl *BRI* BN1 .... 179 F7
Ringmer Rd *BRI* BN1 .... 179 G7
  NEWHV BN9 .... 8 B4
  SEAF BN25 .... 232 A1
Ringmer Wy *LGNY* BN23 .... 216 B7 ☑
Ringwood Cl *LW/ROSE* BN22 .... 11 D2
Ringwood Rd *BEXW* TN39 .... 195 H4
  LW/ROSE BN22 .... 11 D2
Ripe La *RING/NEW* BN8 .... 158 C8
Risden La *HAWK* TN18 .... 63 J4
Riseden Rd *WADH* TN5 .... 57 J3
Rise Park Gdns *LGNY* BN23 .... 230 E1
The Rise *EGRIN* RH19 .... 22 D5
  PTSD BN41 .... 201 J1
The Rising *LGNY* BN23 .... 230 C1
River Cl *SHOR* BN43 .... 200 B5
Riverdale *LEW* BN7 .... 2 C3
River La *POLE* BN26 .... 212 D8
Riverside *FROW* RH18 .... 23 J8
  NEWHV BN9 .... 9 D3
  PTSD BN41 .... 201 H5
  SHOR BN43 .... 200 C4
  UCK TN22 .... 98 B2
Riverside Gdns *CROW* TN6 .... 54 A3
Riverside Rd *SHOR* BN43 .... 200 C5
River Wy *UCK* TN22 .... 95 J4
Rixons Cl *RHWH* RH17 .... 48 A6
Rixons Orch *RHWH* RH17 .... 48 A6
Roadean Cl *SEAF* BN25 .... 225 H7 ☑
Robert's Hl *WSEA* TN36 .... 142 E4
Robertson Pas *HAS* TN34 .... 5 D5 ☑
Robertson Rd *BRI* BN1 .... 203 J1
Robertsons Hl *HAS* TN34 .... 5 F2 ☑
Robertson St *HAS* TN34 .... 4 C5 ☑
Robertson Ter *HAS* TN34 .... 5 D5 ☑
Robert St *BRI* BN1 .... 6 C4 ☑
Robert Tressell Cl *HAS* TN34 .... 4 C3
Robian Cl *UCK* TN22 .... 67 G7
Robin Cl *EGRIN* RH19 .... 22 C1
  LGNY BN23 .... 230 D1 ☑
Robin Davis Cl *ROTT* BN2 .... 205 F3
Robin Dene *ROTT* BN2 .... 205 F7
Robin Hl *BEXW* TN39 .... 194 C7
Robin Post La *POLE* BN26 .... 214 A2
Robin Rd *HPPT/KEY* BN6 .... 118 D1
Robinson Rd *NEWHV* BN9 .... 8 C3
Roborough Cl *LW/ROSE* BN22 ..... 10 C3
Robsack Av *STLEO* TN38 .... 197 F1
Rochdale Rd *RTW* TN1 .... 20 C5
Rochester Cl *EDN/EASTW* BN20 ... 236 C3
Rochester Gdns *HOVE* BN3 .... 203 J5
Rochester Rd *SLVH* TN37 .... 197 J1 ☑
Rochester St *ROTT* BN2 .... 7 F5
Rochester Wy *CROW* TN6 .... 54 A2 ☑
Rochford Wy *SEAF* BN25 .... 224 C5
Rochmans Wy *CROW* TN6 .... 53 J3
Rockall Av *LGNY* BN23 .... 231 G3 ☑
Rockall Dr *HAIL* BN27 .... 189 F1
Rock-a-nore Pde *RHAS* TN35 ...... 199 F3 ☑
Rock-a-nore Rd *HAS* TN34 .... 5 F5
Rock Channel *RYE* TN31 .... 113 J6
Rock Cl *RHAS* TN35 .... 171 G7
Rock Gv *ROTT* BN2 .... 7 F6
Rockhurst Dr *EDN/EASTW* BN20 ... 229 C5
Rockington Wy *CROW* TN6 .... 53 K3
Rocklands La *RHAS* TN35 .... 199 F2 ☑
Rocks La *RHAS* TN35 .... 171 G3
Rockmead Rd *RHAS* TN35 .... 172 E7
Rock Pl *ROTT* BN2 .... 7 D6
Rocks Hl *RBTBR* TN32 .... 78 D5
Rocks La *UCK* TN22 .... 68 B4
Rocks Park Rd *UCK* TN22 .... 95 H4
The Rocks *EGRIN* RH19 .... 23 G5
Rock St *ROTT* BN2 .... 205 F7

Rock Villa Rd *RTW* TN1 .... 20 A7 🄳
Rocky La *HWH* RH16 .... 89 J2
Roderick Av *PEAHV* BN10 .... 222 B2
Roderick Av North *PEAHV* BN10.... 222 B1
Rodmell Av *ROTT* BN2 .... 221 G2
Rodmell Dr *RTWE/PEM* TN2 .... 30 A2 🄳
   SEAF BN25 .... 232 D1
Rodmill Dr *EAST* BN21 .... 229 J6
Rodmill Rd *EAST* BN21 .... 229 J6
Rodney Cl *LGNY* BN23 .... 231 G4 🄳
Rodwell *CROW* TN6 .... 54 A2 🄳
Roebuck St *HAS* TN34 .... 5 F4 🄳
Roedale Rd *BRI* BN1 .... 7 D1
Roedean Cl *BEXW* TN39 .... 195 F6
Roedean Crs *ROTT* BN2 .... 205 H7
Roedean Hts *ROTT* BN2 .... 205 H7
Roedean Pth *ROTT* BN2 .... 205 J8
Roedean Rd *ROTT* BN2 .... 205 H8
   RTWE/PEM TN2 .... 30 A2
Roedean V *ROTT* BN2 .... 205 J8
Roffrey Av *LW/ROSE* BN22 .... 229 J2
Rolfe Dr *BURH* RH15 .... 89 K6
Romaine Cl *BURH* RH15 .... 89 K6
Roman Cl *SEAF* BN25 .... 224 C5 🄳
Roman Crs *STHW* BN42 .... 201 H3
Roman Rd *HOVE* BN3 .... 202 C5
   STHW BN42 .... 201 H3
Romans Wy *WSEA* TN36 .... 143 F4
Roman Wy *PEV* BN24 .... 217 F5
Roman Wy *STHW* BN42 .... 201 H3
   UCK TN22 .... 96 A4
Romany Cl *PTSD* BN41 .... 202 A3
Romany Rd *SEAF* BN25 .... 225 K8 🄳
Romney Rd *POLE* BN26 .... 215 G5
   ROTT BN2 .... 220 D2
Romney St *LW/ROSE* BN22 .... 11 E2 🄳
Romsey Cl *BRI* BN1 .... 204 C1
Rookery Cl *BRI* BN1 .... 6 A1
   NEWHV BN9 .... 223 K1 🄳
Rookery La *WSEA* TN36 .... 143 F4
Rookery Wy *HWH* RH16 .... 90 A2
   NEWHV BN9 .... 224 A1
   SEAF BN25 .... 224 C6
Rookhurst Rd *BEX* TN40 .... 196 A6
Rookley Cl *RTWE/PEM* TN2 .... 30 D1 🄳
Rookwood Cl *UCK* TN22 .... 96 A3 🄳
Roopers *RRTW* TN3 .... 18 E4
Ropetackle *SHOR* BN43 .... 200 B4
Rope Wk *HAIL* BN27 .... 189 G3
   RYE TN31 .... 113 J5
   SHOR BN43 .... 200 B4
Rosebarn Cl *BURH* RH15 .... 119 J2
Rosebery Av *LW/ROSE* BN22 .... 229 K2
   ROTT BN2 .... 205 K3
Rosedale Pl *LW/ROSE* BN22 .... 215 J8 🄳
Rosedene Cl *ROTT* BN2 .... 206 B5
Rose Hl *ROTT* BN2 .... 7 D3
Rose Hill Cl *BRI* BN1 .... 6 C3
Rose Hill Ter *BRI* BN1 .... 6 C3
Rosehill Wk *RTW* TN1 .... 20 A8 🄳
Roselands *BEXW* TN39 .... 194 E5 🄳
Roselands Av *LW/ROSE* BN22 ...... 11 D1
   MAYF TN20 .... 71 K2
Roselands Cl *LW/ROSE* BN22 .... 11 E2 🄳
Rosemary Av *PEAHV* BN10 .... 222 B5
Rosemary Dr *SHOR* BN43 .... 200 E2
Rosemary La *MAYF* TN20 .... 172 D5
   WADH TN5 .... 46 E6
Rosemount Cl *SEAF* BN25 .... 224 E5
Rosetti Rd *PEV* BN24 .... 217 K7
Roseveare Rd *LW/ROSE* BN22 ...... 11 E1 🄳
Rose Wk *SEAF* BN25 .... 225 G7
Rose Walk Cl *NEWHV* BN9 .... 8 B3
The Rose Wk *NEWHV* BN9 .... 8 C3
Rossdale *RTWE/PEM* TN2 .... 20 C6
Rosslyn Av *SHOR* BN43 .... 200 C4
Rosslyn Ct *SHOR* BN43 .... 200 C3
Rosslyn Rd *SHOR* BN43 .... 200 C4
Rothbury Rd *HOVE* BN3 .... 202 C4
Rother Av *POLE* BN26 .... 216 A6
Rother Cl *BUR/ETCH* TN19 .... 75 K5
   CROW TN6 .... 53 J4
Rotherfield Av *BEX* TN40 .... 195 J7
   LW/ROSE BN22 .... 216 B7
Rotherfield Cl *BRI* BN1 .... 178 C5
Rotherfield Crs *BRI* BN1 .... 178 C6
Rotherfield La *MAYF* TN20 .... 55 K7
Rotherfield Rd *CROW* TN6 .... 54 C3
Rotherhill Rd *CROW* TN6 .... 53 J3
Rotherhurst La *CROW* TN6 .... 54 E5
Rothermead *MAYF* TN20 .... 71 K2
Rother Rd *SEAF* BN25 .... 232 C1
Rother Vw *BUR/ETCH* TN19 .... 75 K4
Rotherview *RBTBR* TN32 .... 78 C5
Rothsay Rd *STLEO* TN38 .... 4 A5 🄳
Rothwell Ct *NEWHV* BN9 .... 8 A3
Rotten Rw *LEW* BN7 .... 2 B5
Rotunda Rd *LGNY* BN23 .... 230 E3
The Rotyngs *ROTT* BN2 .... 220 C1
Rough Brow *SEAF* BN25 .... 225 H7
Rough Fld *EGRIN* RH19 .... 12 B7 🄳
The Rough *RING/NEW* BN8 .... 93 G4
Roundacres Wy *BEX* TN40 .... 195 K5
The Roundel *SLVH* TN37 .... 170 A6
Roundhay Av *PEAHV* BN10 .... 222 D3 🄳
Roundhill Crs *ROTT* BN2 .... 7 D2

Round Hill Rd *ROTT* BN2 .... 7 D2 🄳
Roundhill Rd *RTWE/PEM* TN2 ...... 30 D2
Round Hill St *ROTT* BN2 .... 7 D2 🄳
Roundway *BRI* BN1 .... 179 F6
Roundwood Rd *SLVH* TN37 .... 169 J6
Rowan Av *HOVE* BN3 .... 202 D2
   LW/ROSE BN22 .... 215 J8
Rowan Cl *HAS* TN34 .... 170 A5
   HTHF TN21 .... 100 A6
   PTSD BN41 .... 201 J2
   SEAF BN25 .... 225 K8 🄳
Rowan Gdns *BEX* TN40 .... 196 A5
Rowan Tree Rd *RTWE/PEM* TN2 ... 29 J2 🄳
Rowan Wy *ROTT* BN2 .... 206 B8
Rowbarns *BAT* TN33 .... 136 C5
Rowe Av *PEAHV* BN10 .... 222 A3
Rowley Hl *RTWE/PEM* TN2 .... 21 K2
Rowsley Rd *EDN/EASTW* BN20 ... 236 D4
Royal Cha *SBGH/RUST* TN4 .... 19 K7
Royal Crs *ROTT* BN2 .... 7 E6
Royal Crescent Ms *ROTT* BN2 .... 7 E6 🄳
Royal Dr *SEAF* BN25 .... 225 F5
Royal George Pde *SHOR* BN43 ... 200 E2
Royal George Rd *BURH* RH15 .... 88 E8
Royal Military Canal Pth
   TENT TN30 .... 86 C3
Royal Military Rd *WSEA* TN36 .... 143 G3
Royal Oak La *UCK* TN22 .... 68 D2
Royal Pde *LW/ROSE* BN22 .... 11 F2
Royal Sovereign Vw
   LGNY BN23 .... 231 G5 🄳
Royal Sussex Crs
   EDN/EASTW BN20 .... 229 G6
Royles Cl *ROTT* BN2 .... 220 D1
Royston Cl *EDN/EASTW* BN20 ..... 234 E2
Royston Gdns *BEX* TN40 .... 196 A6
Rudyard Cl *ROTT* BN2 .... 206 B3
Rudyard Rd *ROTT* BN2 .... 206 B3
Rue De Bayeux *BAT* TN33 .... 136 D6 🄳
Rufus Cl *LEW* BN7 .... 2 C4
Rugby Cl *SEAF* BN25 .... 225 J7
Rugby Pl *ROTT* BN2 .... 205 F7
Rugby Rd *BRI* BN1 .... 6 C1
Rumbolds La *HWH* RH16 .... 89 K1
Runbridge La *LEW* BN7 .... 3 E4 🄳
Ruscombe Cl *SBGH/RUST* TN4 ..... 19 K1 🄳
Rushetts *RRTW* TN3 .... 18 D7
Rushey Cl *RING/NEW* BN8 .... 155 K6
Rushlake Cl *BRI* BN1 .... 179 F5
Rushlake Crs *EAST* BN21 .... 229 J5
Rushlake Rd *BRI* BN1 .... 179 F5
Rushlye Cl *RRTW* TN3 .... 31 F6
Rushmere Ri *STLEO* TN38 .... 197 F2
Ruskin Rd *EDN/EASTW* BN20 .... 229 G2
   HOVE BN3 .... 202 C3
Rusper Rd *BRI* BN1 .... 178 C5
   EDN/EASTW BN20 .... 229 G5
Ruspers *BURH* RH15 .... 119 K1
Russell Crs *BRI* BN1 .... 6 B3 🄳
Russell Pl *BRI* BN1 .... 6 B5 🄳
Russell Rd *BRI* BN1 .... 6 B5 🄳
Russell Sq *BRI* BN1 .... 6 A5
Russell St *HAS* TN34 .... 5 D5
Russet Cl *POLE* BN26 .... 215 H5
Rusthall Gra *SBGH/RUST* TN4 ..... 19 H7 🄳
Rusthall High St *SBGH/RUST* TN4 .. 19 F7
Rusthall Pk *SBGH/RUST* TN4 .... 19 H7
Rusthall Rd *SBGH/RUST* TN4 .... 19 H8
Rustic Cl *PEAHV* BN10 .... 222 A2
Rustic Rd *PEAHV* BN10 .... 222 A1
Rustington Rd *BRI* BN1 .... 178 B6
Rustwick *SBGH/RUST* TN4 .... 19 H7
Rutland Cl *EAST* BN21 .... 229 J5
Rutland Gdns *HOVE* BN3 .... 202 E4
Rutland Rd *HOVE* BN3 .... 203 F4
Rydal Cl *SBGH/RUST* TN4 .... 19 J6
Rydal Dr *SBGH/RUST* TN4 .... 19 J6
Rydal Wy *LGNY* BN23 .... 216 C2 🄳
Ryde Rd *ROTT* BN2 .... 7 F3
Ryders *RRTW* TN3 .... 18 E3
Rye Cl *POLE* BN26 .... 215 H4
   ROTT BN2 .... 221 H1
   SEAF BN25 .... 225 K7
Ryefield Cl *EAST* BN21 .... 229 H4
Ryelands Dr *ROTT* BN2 .... 178 E8
Rye Rd *HAWK* TN18 .... 63 K3
   RHAS TN35 .... 171 G2
   RYE TN31 .... 113 F1
   TENT TN30 .... 85 G1
Rye St *LW/ROSE* BN22 .... 11 E1
Rylstone Rd *LW/ROSE* BN22 .... 11 E3
Rymers Cl *RTWE/PEM* TN2 .... 20 D4
Rymill Rd *STLEO* TN38 .... 169 H8
Ryst Wood Rd *FROW* RH18 .... 36 B1

HOVE BN3 .... 203 F5
   LW/ROSE BN22 .... 230 A1
Saddlers Cl *BURH* RH15 .... 119 K2
Saddler's Wall La *LYDD* TN29 ...... 87 K2
Sadlers Wy *RING/NEW* BN8 .... 155 J7
Sadler Wy *ROTT* BN2 .... 205 G5
Saffron Cl *SHOR* BN43 .... 201 F2
Saffron Gdns *POLE* BN26 .... 212 C8
Saffrons Pk *EDN/EASTW* BN20 .... 10 A6
Saffrons Rd *EAST* BN21 .... 10 A4
The Saffrons *BURH* RH15 .... 88 E6
St Agnes Rd *EGRIN* RH19 .... 22 C1
St Andrews Cl *HAIL* BN27 .... 189 F2
St Andrews Ct *SBGH/RUST* TN4 ... 20 A2 🄳
St Andrew's Dr *SEAF* BN25 .... 224 B5
St Andrew's La *LEW* BN7 .... 3 D5 🄳
   LEW BN7 .... 3 D4 🄳
St Andrews Park Rd
   SBGH/RUST TN4 .... 20 A2
St Andrew's Rd *BEX* TN40 .... 195 H6
   BRI BN1 .... 6 C1 🄳
   BURH RH15 .... 89 K8 🄳
   PTSD BN41 .... 202 A4
St Anne's Crs *LEW* BN7 .... 2 B4 🄳
St Anne's Rd *EAST* BN21 .... 10 A3
   LW/ROSE BN22 .... 215 G8
St Anthony's Av *LGNY* BN23 .... 230 E4
St Aubyns *HOVE* BN3 .... 203 F5
St Aubyn's Crs *PTSD* BN41 .... 202 A4 🄳
St Aubyn's Md *ROTT* BN2 .... 220 D2
St Aubyn's Rd *LW/ROSE* BN22 ... 11 D4 🄳
   PTSD BN41 .... 201 K4
St Aubyns South *HOVE* BN3 .... 203 F6 🄳
St Augustine's Cl *BEXW* TN39 ... 194 E8 🄳
St Barnabas' Cl *RTW* TN1 .... 20 B6 🄳
St Boswells Cl *HAIL* BN27 .... 188 E3
St Catherine's Cl *SLVH* TN37 .... 4 B4 🄳
St Crispians *SEAF* BN25 .... 224 E8
St Cuthmans Cl *ROTT* BN2 .... 205 F5
St David's Av *BEX* TN40 .... 195 H6
St Davids Cl *LW/ROSE* BN22 .... 215 J7
St David's Rd *SBGH/RUST* TN4 .... 20 B5
St Edward's Cl *EGRIN* RH19 .... 22 A2
St Francis Cha *BEXW* TN39 .... 195 F6
St Francis Cl *HWH* RH16 .... 90 A1
St George's La *HPPT/KEY* BN6 ... 118 B6
St George's Ms *BRI* BN1 .... 6 C4 🄳
St George's Pk *RTWE/PEM* TN2 ... 29 K3
St George's Pl *BRI* BN1 .... 6 C4 🄳
   HPPT/KEY BN6 .... 118 B6
St George's Rd *BEXW* TN39 .... 195 H6
   HAS TN34 .... 5 E3
   LW/ROSE BN22 .... 11 D3 🄳
   ROTT BN2 .... 7 E6
St George's Ter *ROTT* BN2 .... 7 E6
St Giles Cl *SHOR* BN43 .... 200 E3
   WSEA TN36 .... 142 E4
St Gregory Cl *EDN/EASTW* BN20 .. 236 E3
St Helen's Av *HAS* TN34 .... 4 C1
St Helen's Crs *HAS* TN34 .... 4 C2
   HOVE BN3 .... 176 C8
St Helen's Down *HAS* TN34 .... 5 E1
St Helen's Park Rd *HAS* TN34 .... 5 D1
St Helen's Rd *ROTT* BN2 .... 7 F3
   SLVH TN37 .... 4 B1
St Helen's Wood Rd *HAS* TN34 .. 170 B6
St Heliers Av *HOVE* BN3 .... 202 D4
St James' Av *BEX* TN40 .... 195 J5
St James' Crs *BEX* TN40 .... 195 J4
St James' Pk *RTW* TN1 .... 20 C6
   RTWE/PEM TN2 .... 20 C6
St James' Rd *BEX* TN40 .... 195 H5
   LW/ROSE BN22 .... 11 E3 🄳
   RTW TN1 .... 20 C6
Stjames' Rd *RTW* TN1 .... 20 C7
St James's Av *ROTT* BN2 .... 7 D6
St James's Rd *EGRIN* RH19 .... 22 B2
   HAS TN34 .... 5 D3
St James's St *ROTT* BN2 .... 6 C5 🄳🄳
St James's Street Ms *ROTT* BN2 .. 7 D5 🄳🄳
St James St *LEW* BN7 .... 2 C5
St John Bank *RING/NEW* BN8 .... 122 B3
St John's Av *BURH* RH15 .... 89 F8
St John's Cl *CROW* TN6 .... 39 G8
   EGRIN RH19 .... 22 C1
St John's Dr *PEV* BN24 .... 217 F5
St John's Hl *LEW* BN7 .... 2 C4
St John's Pk *SBGH/RUST* TN4 ...... 20 A3
St John's Pl *HOVE* BN3 .... 203 H5 🄳
   ROTT BN2 .... 7 D5 🄳🄳
St John's Rd *BEX* TN40 .... 195 H5
   BURH RH15 .... 89 G8
   CROW TN6 .... 38 E6
   EDN/EASTW BN20 .... 236 E3
   EGRIN RH19 .... 22 C1
   HOVE BN3 .... 203 H6
   POLE BN26 .... 215 F5
   SBGH/RUST TN4 .... 20 A4
   SEAF BN25 .... 232 A1
   SLVH TN37 .... 4 A5
St John's Ter *LEW* BN7 .... 2 C4
St John St *LEW* BN7 .... 3 D4
St Joseph's Cl *HOVE* BN3 .... 203 F3
St Julians Cl *SHOR* BN43 .... 201 F4

Sackville Cl *EGRIN* RH19 .... 12 A8
   LEW BN7 .... 2 C4 🄳
Sackville Gdns *HOVE* BN3 .... 202 E5
Sackville Rd *BEXW* TN39 .... 195 G8
   HAIL BN27 .... 189 H5

St Julian's La *SHOR* BN43 .... 201 F4
St Keyna Av *HOVE* BN3 .... 202 C5
St Laurence Cl *PEAHV* BN10 .... 221 K2
St Lawrence Rd *BEXW* TN39 .... 195 G4
St Lawrence Wy *HPPT/KEY* BN6 .... 118 A4
St Leonard's Av *HOVE* BN3 .... 202 B5
St Leonards Cl *NEWHV* BN9 .... 224 A1
St Leonard's Gdns *HOVE* BN3 .... 202 C5
St Leonard's Pl *EDN/EASTW* BN20 .. 229 H8
St Leonard's Rd *EAST* BN21 .... 10 C4
 HOVE BN3 .... 202 B5
 NEWHV BN9 .... 224 A1
 ROTT BN2 .... 7 E2
St Leonards Ter *POLE* BN26 .... 214 E4
St Louie Cl *STHW* BN42 .... 201 K3
St Luke's Rd *ROTT* BN2 .... 7 E4
 SBGH/RUST TN4 .... 20 B5
St Luke's Ter *ROTT* BN2 .... 7 E4
St Margaret's Av *EGRIN* RH19 .... 12 C5
St Margaret's Pl *BRI* BN1 .... 6 B5
St Margaret's Ri *SEAF* BN25 .... 224 B5
St Margaret's Rd *EGRIN* RH19 .... 12 D8
 SLVH TN37 .... 4 B5
St Marks Cl *BEXW* TN39 .... 194 C7
St Marks Fld *UCK* TN22 .... 69 K6
St Mark's Rd *RTWE/PEM* TN2 .... 29 K4
St Mark's St *ROTT* BN2 .... 205 F7
St Martins Crs *NEWHV* BN9 .... 9 D1
St Martin's Pl *ROTT* BN2 .... 7 D3
St Martin's Rd *LW/ROSE* BN22 ..... 215 J8
St Martin's St *ROTT* BN2 .... 7 D3
St Mary-in-the-Fields *MAYF* TN20 .. 72 B1
St Mary Magdalene St *ROTT* BN2 ... 7 D2
St Marys Av *HAIL* BN27 .... 189 H4
St Mary's Cl *LW/ROSE* BN22 .... 229 G1
 RYE TN31 .... 139 J1
 SHOR BN43 .... 200 C4
 WADH TN5 .... 60 B2
St Mary's Cottages
 EDN/EASTW BN20 .... 229 J8
Saint Marys Garth *UCK* TN22 .... 68 E7
St Mary's La *BEXW* TN39 .... 194 C7
 RRTW TN3 .... 18 E3
 WADH TN5 .... 60 B2
St Mary's Pl *ROTT* BN2 .... 7 D5
St Mary's Rd *EAST* BN21 .... 229 J7
 HAS TN34 .... 5 E3
 SHOR BN43 .... 200 C4
St Mary's Rd West *BURH* RH15 .... 88 E7
St Mary's Sq *ROTT* BN2 .... 7 F6
St Mary's Ter *HAS* TN34 .... 5 E3
St Matthew's Gdns *STLEO* TN38 ... 197 J2
St Matthew's Rd *STLEO* TN38 ...... 197 J2
St Mellion Cl *HAIL* BN27 .... 188 E3
St Michaels La *CROW* TN6 .... 53 K3
 PEV BN24 .... 216 B5
St Michael's Pl *BRI* BN1 .... 6 A4
St Michaels Rd *EGRIN* RH19 .... 22 C1
 PTSD BN41 .... 202 A4
 SBGH/RUST TN4 .... 20 B4
St Michael's Ter *LEW* BN7 .... 3 D3
St Nicholas La *LEW* BN7 .... 3 D4
St Nicholas Rd *BRI* BN1 .... 6 B4
 PTSD BN41 .... 202 A4
St Nicolas Cl *PEV* BN24 .... 217 J5
St Nicolas La *SHOR* BN43 .... 200 A3
St Olive's Cl *HTHF* TN21 .... 99 G4
St Pancras Gdns *LEW* BN7 .... 2 B5
St Pancras Gn *LEW* BN7 .... 181 G6
St Pancras Rd *LEW* BN7 .... 2 B5
St Patrick's Crs *BEX* TN40 .... 195 H6
St Patrick's Rd *HOVE* BN3 .... 203 F4
St Pauls Cl *LW/ROSE* BN22 .... 215 J8
St Paul's Pl *SLVH* TN37 .... 4 B5
St Paul's Rd *SLVH* TN37 .... 4 A4
St Paul's St *ROTT* BN2 .... 7 D2
 SBGH/RUST TN4 .... 19 G7
St Peters Av *PEAHV* BN10 .... 221 K3
St Peter's Cl *HOVE* BN3 .... 202 E1
 SEAF BN25 .... 225 F6
St Peter's Crs *BEX* TN40 .... 195 J6
St Peters Pl *LEW* BN7 .... 2 C5
 LEW BN7 .... 2 C4
St Peters Rd *BURH* RH15 .... 89 G7
 PTSD BN41 .... 202 A4
 SEAF BN25 .... 225 F6
 SLVH TN37 .... 4 A4
St Peters Rw *RRTW* TN3 .... 17 K6
St Peter's St *BRI* BN1 .... 6 C3
 RTWE/PEM TN2 .... 20 C8
St Philip's Av *LW/ROSE* BN22 ...... 11 D2
St Philips Ms *HOVE* BN3 .... 202 E4
St Richards Rd *CROW* TN6 .... 53 J4
 PTSD BN41 .... 202 A4
St Saviour's Rd *STLEO* TN38 .... 197 F5
Saints Hl *RTON* TN11 .... 17 J2
St Stephens Ct *RTW* TN1 .... 20 B6
St Swithun's Cl *EGRIN* RH19 .... 22 D2
St Swithun's Ter *LEW* BN7 .... 2 C5
St Thomas's St *WSEA* TN36 .... 143 F4
St Vincents Pl *EDN/EASTW* BN20 .. 10 A6
St Vincents Rd *STLEO* TN38 .... 197 G4
St Wilfred's Pl *SEAF* BN25 .... 232 D1
St Wilfreds Rd *BURH* RH15 .... 89 H7
St Wilfrid's Gn *HAIL* BN27 .... 189 G3

Salcey Cl *STLEO* TN38 .... 197 F1
Salehurst Gdns *STLEO* TN38 ...... 196 E1
Salehurst Rd *EAST* BN21 .... 229 H8
Salisbury Cl *LW/ROSE* BN22 .... 229 H1
Salisbury Rd *BEXW* TN59 .... 195 G6
 EDN/EASTW BN20 .... 236 C3
 HOVE BN3 .... 203 H5
 RRTW TN3 .... 18 D8
 SBGH/RUST TN4 .... 20 C3
 SEAF BN25 .... 225 F8
 SLVH TN37 .... 4 A3
Saltcote St *RYE* TN31 .... 113 J3
Saltdean Cl *BEXW* TN39 .... 194 D8
Saltdean Dr *ROTT* BN2 .... 220 E2
Saltdean Park Rd *ROTT* BN2 .... 221 F2
Saltdean V *ROTT* BN2 .... 207 G8
 ROTT BN2 .... 221 F1
Saltdean Wy *BEXW* TN39 .... 194 C8
Saltwood Rd *SEAF* BN25 .... 225 K7
Salvador Cl *LGNY* BN23 .... 231 G4
Salvington Crs *BEXW* TN59 .... 194 E7
Sancroft Rd *EDN/EASTW* BN20 ... 229 G8
The Sanctuary
 EDN/EASTW BN20 .... 229 G7
Sandbanks Cl *HAIL* BN27 .... 189 F6
Sandbanks Gdns *HAIL* BN27 .... 189 G6
Sandbanks Gv *HAIL* BN27 .... 189 G5
Sandbanks Rd *HAIL* BN27 .... 189 F5
Sandbanks Wy *HAIL* BN27 .... 189 G5
Sandfield Rd *RTON* TN11 .... 17 H4
Sandgate Cl *SEAF* BN25 .... 225 K6
Sandgate Rd *BRI* BN1 .... 204 B1
Sandhawes Hl *EGRIN* RH19 .... 12 E7
Sandhill La *CROW* TN6 .... 40 C4
 HAIL BN27 .... 132 C6
Sand Hill La *RING/NEW* BN8 .... 126 C5
 UCK TN22 .... 126 E2
Sandhurst Av *ROTT* BN2 .... 206 A2
Sandhurst Cl *RTWE/PEM* TN2 ...... 20 C4
Sandhurst Gdns *HAS* TN34 .... 170 C5
Sandhurst La *BEXW* TN39 .... 193 K7
Sandhurst Pk *RTWE/PEM* TN2 ..... 20 D5
Sandhurst Rd *RTWE/PEM* TN2 ..... 20 D4
Sandore Cl *SEAF* BN25 .... 225 H7
Sandore Rd *SEAF* BN25 .... 225 H7
Sandown Cl *LGNY* BN23 .... 216 C7
 RTWE/PEM TN2 .... 21 F5
Sandown Gv *RTWE/PEM* TN2 ...... 21 F5
Sandown Pk *RTWE/PEM* TN2 ...... 21 F6
Sandown Rd *RHAS* TN35 .... 171 F8
 ROTT BN2 .... 7 F3
 STHW BN42 .... 201 G3
Sandown Wy *BEX* TN40 .... 195 K5
Sandridge *CROW* TN6 .... 53 H2
Sandringham Cl *HOVE* BN3 .... 177 F8
 SEAF BN25 .... 225 H2
Sandringham Dr *HOVE* BN3 .... 177 F8
Sandringham Hts *STLEO* TN38 ... 168 E8
Sand Rd *RRTW* TN3 .... 33 J7
Sandrock Hl *BAT* TN33 .... 168 B7
Sandrock Pk *HAS* TN34 .... 170 C6
Sandrock Rd *RTWE/PEM* TN2 .... 20 C7
Sandrocks Wy *HWH* RH16 .... 90 A1
Sandwich Dr *STLEO* TN38 .... 197 G4
Sandwich St *LW/ROSE* BN22 .... 11 E1
Sandy Cl *SLVH* TN37 .... 169 J6
Sandy Cross La *HTHF* TN21 .... 100 B6
Sandy La *EGRIN* RH19 .... 23 F6
 HRTF TN7 .... 36 D5
 HTHF TN21 .... 129 J2
 RHWH RH17 .... 49 G3
 UCK TN22 .... 96 B4
Sandy V *HWH* RH16 .... 89 K1
San Feliu Ct *EGRIN* RH19 .... 23 F1
Santa Cruz Dr *LGNY* BN23 .... 231 G4
Sanyhils Av *BRI* BN1 .... 178 A4
Saunders Cl *HAS* TN34 .... 5 E3
 UCK TN22 .... 95 G3
Saunders Hl *BRI* BN1 .... 178 E4
Saunders Park Vw *ROTT* BN2 .... 7 E1
Saunders Rd *SBGH/RUST* TN4 ..... 29 J2
Saunders Wy *RYE* TN31 .... 145 J1
Sawyers Cl *BURH* RH15 .... 119 K2
Saxby Cl *LGNY* BN23 .... 231 F2
Saxby Rd *BEXW* TN39 .... 195 F7
 BURH RH15 .... 88 D7
Saxonbury Cl *CROW* TN6 .... 53 H1
Saxon Cl *EAST* BN21 .... 229 H5
 ROTT BN2 .... 221 F1
Saxon La *SEAF* BN25 .... 232 A1
Saxon Ri *BEX* TN40 .... 195 K7
Saxon Rd *HOVE* BN3 .... 202 C5
 NEWHV BN9 .... 8 C3
 RHAS TN35 .... 171 G8
Saxons *SHOR* BN43 .... 200 C4
Saxon Shore Wy *HAS* TN34 .... 5 F4
 RHAS TN35 .... 173 H3
 RHAS TN35 .... 199 G2
 RYE TN31 .... 114 A3
 WSEA TN36 .... 143 F5
Saxon St *SLVH* TN37 .... 4 A6
Saxonwood Rd *BAT* TN33 .... 136 C6
Sayerland La *POLE* BN26 .... 215 F3
Sayerland Rd *POLE* BN26 .... 214 E4

The Sayers *EGRIN* RH19 .... 22 A2
Scanlon Cl *EDN/EASTW* BN20 .... 215 F8
Scarborough Rd *BRI* BN1 .... 203 J2
Scarletts Cl *UCK* TN22 .... 95 H4
Schofield Wy *LGNY* BN23 .... 231 G4
School Cl *BURH* RH15 .... 119 F1
 STHW BN42 .... 201 H4
School Fld *RING/NEW* BN8 .... 123 J7
School Gdns *RING/NEW* BN8 ...... 123 H7
School Hl *RING/NEW* BN8 .... 123 J7
 RRTW TN3 .... 33 K5
 WSEA TN36 .... 142 E3
School La *CROW* TN6 .... 38 E7
 EGRIN RH19 .... 23 H5
 FROW RH18 .... 35 K1
 POLE BN26 .... 215 F4
 POY/PYE BN45 .... 149 H5
 RHWH RH17 .... 48 E7
 RYE TN31 .... 112 A2
 RYE TN31 .... 113 J2
 UCK TN22 .... 50 C6
 UCK TN22 .... 69 K5
 UCK TN22 .... 97 J5
School Pl *BEX* TN40 .... 196 B6
School Ri *ROTT* BN2 .... 205 F5
 RTWE/PEM TN2 .... 29 K2
School Rd *HOVE* BN3 .... 202 E4
 RHAS TN35 .... 171 F8
School Ter *HAWK* TN18 .... 63 F1
Schwerte Wy *SLVH* TN37 .... 4 C5
Scotland St *ROTT* BN2 .... 7 D4
Scotsford Hl *MAYF* TN20 .... 72 E1
Scotsford Rd *HTHF* TN21 .... 101 F2
Scott Rd *HOVE* BN3 .... 202 E4
Scotts Acre *RYE* TN31 .... 115 G8
Scotts Wy *RTWE/PEM* TN2 .... 29 J3
Scraper's Hl *RING/NEW* BN8 ...... 159 J3
Scutes Cl *HAS* TN34 .... 5 D1
Seabeach La *LW/ROSE* BN22 ...... 11 E2
Seabourne Rd *BEX* TN40 .... 196 A5
Seafield Cl *SEAF* BN25 .... 225 J6
Seafield Rd *HOVE* BN3 .... 203 G6
Seaford Rd *HOVE* BN3 .... 202 B5
 LW/ROSE BN22 .... 11 E2
 NEWHV BN9 .... 9 F3
Seagrave Cl *SEAF* BN25 .... 224 B5
Seagrove Wy *SEAF* BN25 .... 225 G6
Seahaven Gdns *SHOR* BN43 ...... 200 A6
Searle Av *PEAHV* BN10 .... 222 D5
Sea Rd *BEX* TN40 .... 195 J8
 PEV BN24 .... 218 A6
 RHAS TN35 .... 173 F6
 RYE TN31 .... 145 H1
 STLEO TN38 .... 197 G5
 WSEA TN36 .... 143 F3
Seasaw Wy *ROTT* BN2 .... 205 G4
Seaside *LW/ROSE* BN22 .... 11 E2
Seaside Rd *EAST* BN21 .... 11 D5
 STLEO TN38 .... 197 G5
Seaside Wy *STLEO* TN38 .... 197 G5
Seaview Av *PEAHV* BN10 .... 222 D5
Seaview Rd *NEWHV* BN9 .... 9 F1
 PEAHV BN10 .... 222 D6
 ROTT BN2 .... 205 G4
Seaville Dr *LGNY* BN23 .... 230 E3
 PEV BN24 .... 218 A6
Second Av *BEX* TN40 .... 196 A6
 HOVE BN3 .... 203 H6
 NEWHV BN9 .... 8 C4
 RYE TN31 .... 145 H1
Second Rd *PEAHV* BN10 .... 221 K4
Sedgebrook Gdns *HAS* TN34 .... 4 C2
Sedgewick Rd *BEXW* TN39 .... 195 H5
 BRI BN1 .... 178 D5
Sedlescombe Gdns *STLEO* TN38 . 197 J2
Sedlescombe Rd North *BAT* TN33 137 H1
 SLVH TN37 .... 4 A2
Sedlescombe Rd South
 STLEO TN38 .... 197 J2
Sefton Cha *CROW* TN6 .... 39 J8
Sefton Rd *PTSD* BN41 .... 175 J8
Sefton Wy *CROW* TN6 .... 39 J8
Segrave Cl *LEW* BN7 .... 2 B3
Selba Dr *ROTT* BN2 .... 205 F1
Selborne Pl *HOVE* BN3 .... 203 H4
Selborne Rd *HOVE* BN3 .... 203 H4
Selby Gdns *UCK* TN22 .... 95 K6
Selby Ri *UCK* TN22 .... 95 K6
Selby Rd *EAST* BN21 .... 229 J6
 UCK TN22 .... 95 K5
Selham Cl *BRI* BN1 .... 179 F1
Selham Dr *BRI* BN1 .... 178 E5
Selhurst Rd *ROTT* BN2 .... 206 D5
Sellbourne Pk *RRTW* TN3 .... 30 C7
Selmeston Cl *HAS* TN34 .... 4 B3
Selmestone Rd *ROTT* BN2 .... 205 G6
Selmeston Pl *ROTT* BN2 .... 205 G5
Selmeston Rd *EAST* BN21 .... 229 H4
Selsey Cl *BRI* BN1 .... 179 F5
Selsfield Cl *EAST* BN21 .... 229 J5
Selsfield Dr *ROTT* BN2 .... 178 E8
Selwyn Dr *EAST* BN21 .... 10 A3
Selwyn Rd *EAST* BN21 .... 10 A3
Semley Rd *BRI* BN1 .... 6 C1
 HPPT/KEY BN6 .... 118 E7

Sempstead La *RBTBR* TN32 .... 80 E8
Senlac St *NEWHV* BN3 .... 9 D5 ⊡
Senlac Wy *SLVH* TN37 .... 169 K6
Setfords Fld *RING/NEW* BN8 .... 122 C2
Sevelands Cl *ROTT* BN2 .... 205 G4 ⊡
Seven Acre Cl *SLVH* TN37 .... 169 H6
Sevenoaks Rd *LGNY* BN23 .... 230 E2
Seven Sisters Rd *LW/ROSE* BN22 ... 215 G8
Seville St *ROTT* BN2 .... 7 E5
Sewell Av *BEX* TN40 .... 195 H6
Seymour Sq *ROTT* BN2 .... 7 F6 ⊡
Seymour St *ROTT* BN2 .... 7 F6 ⊡
Shaftesbury Pl *BRI* BN1 .... 6 C2
Shaftesbury Rd *BRI* BN1 .... 6 C2
 SBGH/RUST TN4 .... 20 A5
Shakespeare St *HOVE* BN3 .... 203 F3
Shalesbrook La *FROW* RH18 .... 35 K2
Shalfleet Cl *LGNY* BN23 .... 216 C8
Shandon Cl *RTWE/PEM* TN2 .... 20 C7
Shanklin Cl *LGNY* BN23 .... 216 C7
Shanklin Rd *ROTT* BN2 .... 7 E2
Shannon Cl *PEAHV* BN10 .... 221 K2
Shannon Wy *LGNY* BN23 .... 231 G3
Sharpthorne Crs *PTSD* BN41 .... 202 B1
Shawfield *CROW* TN6 .... 53 K2 ⊡
The Shaw *RTWE/PEM* TN2 .... 30 C1
Sheddingdean Cl *BURH* RH15 .... 89 G7 ⊡
Sheen Rd *LW/ROSE* BN22 .... 11 D3 ⊡
Sheepbell Cl *PTSD* BN41 .... 176 A8
Sheepfair *LEW* BN7 .... 2 A3 ⊡
Sheep Pen La *SEAF* BN25 .... 225 H8
Sheep Pln *CROW* TN6 .... 53 F4
Sheepsetting La *HTHF* TN21 .... 99 J4
Sheepstreet La *BUR/ETCH* TN19 ... 60 C7
Sheep Wk *ROTT* BN2 .... 220 C2
Sheepwash La *UCK* TN22 .... 98 A3
Sheerwater Crs *HAS* TN34 .... 170 A7
Sheffield Br *UCK* TN22 .... 65 F7
Sheffield Mill La *UCK* TN22 .... 65 G5
Sheffield Park Wy *LW/ROSE* BN22... 216 B7
Sheffield Rd *SBGH/RUST* TN4 .... 19 K1
Sheiling Rd *CROW* TN6 .... 39 G8
Shelldale Av *PTSD* BN41 .... 202 A4
Shelldale Crs *PTSD* BN41 .... 202 A4
Shelldale Rd *PTSD* BN41 .... 201 K3
Shelley Cl *LEW* BN7 .... 2 B4 ⊡
Shelley Rd *EGRIN* RH19 .... 22 B2 ⊡
 HOVE BN3 .... 202 E4
 RING/NEW BN8 .... 155 J6
Shell La *HAS* TN34 .... 5 E5 ⊡
Shenfield Wy *BRI* BN1 .... 204 C1
Shepham Av *ROTT* BN2 .... 221 F2
Shepham La *POLE* BN26 .... 215 H4
Shepherd's Cl *BEXW* TN39 .... 194 B7
 NEWHV BN9 .... 223 G1 ⊡
 POLE BN26 .... 216 A8 ⊡
 RING/NEW BN8 .... 155 K6 ⊡
Shepherds Cft *PEAHV* BN10 .... 222 C1 ⊡
Shepherds Cft *BRI* BN1 .... 177 H8
Shepherdsgrove La *EGRIN* RH19 ... 13 K6
Shepherd's Hl *HRTF* TN7 .... 36 D2
Shepherds Md *BURH* RH15 .... 89 F7 ⊡
Shepherd St *STLEO* TN38 .... 4 A6 ⊡
Shepherds Wk *CROW* TN6 .... 54 A2 ⊡
 HPPT/KEY BN6 .... 118 E6
 RTWE/PEM TN2 .... 20 D7 ⊡
Shepherds Wy *RHAS* TN35 .... 172 D7
 RING/NEW BN8 .... 122 A4
 RING/NEW BN8 .... 155 K6
 UCK TN22 .... 95 J2
Sheppard St *PTSD* BN41 .... 175 K8
Sheppeys *HWH* RH16 .... 89 K1
Sheppey Wk *HAIL* BN27 .... 161 F8
The Shepway *SEAF* BN25 .... 225 J7
Sheraton Cl *EAST* BN21 .... 10 B5 ⊡
Sherbourne Cl *HOVE* BN3 .... 176 C8
Sherbourne Rd *HOVE* BN3 .... 176 C8
Sherbourne Wy *HOVE* BN3 .... 176 C8
Sheridan Cl *EGRIN* RH19 .... 22 A2
Sheridan Ter *HOVE* BN3 .... 203 F3
Sheriff's La *CROW* TN6 .... 55 G5
Sheringham La *RBTBR* TN32 .... 108 A1
Sherman Br *POLE* BN26 .... 213 F4
Sherrington Rd *ROTT* BN2 .... 206 C3
Sherwood Cl *HAS* TN34 .... 5 D3
Sherwood Gn *HAIL* BN27 .... 189 G5 ⊡
Sherwood Pl *RRTW* TN3 .... 18 C8 ⊡
Sherwood Ri *SEAF* BN25 .... 225 G7
Sherwood Rd *RTWE/PEM* TN2 ..... 20 D7 ⊡
 RTWE/PEM TN2 .... 20 E6
 SEAF BN25 .... 225 G7
Sherwood Wy *RTWE/PEM* TN2 ..... 20 D5
Shinewater La *LGNY* BN23 .... 216 C8
Shingle Cl *STLEO* TN38 .... 169 F4
Shingle Rd *SHOR* BN43 .... 200 D5
Shipley La *BEXW* TN39 .... 194 C8
Shipley Mill Cl *PEV* BN24 .... 216 C6
Shipley Rd *ROTT* BN2 .... 206 B4
Ship St *BRI* BN1 .... 6 B5 ⊡
 EGRIN RH19 .... 22 C3
 NEWHV BN9 .... 8 C2 ⊡
 SHOR BN43 .... 200 B4
Shirlea Vw *BAT* TN33 .... 136 E7
Shirley Av *HOVE* BN3 .... 203 G1
Shirley Cl *SHOR* BN43 .... 201 F3

Shirley Dr *HOVE* BN3 .... 203 H2
 SLVH TN37 .... 169 J7
Shirley Gdns *SBGH/RUST* TN4 ...... 19 G7 ⊡
Shirley Gv *SBGH/RUST* TN4 .... 19 H6
Shirley Rd *HOVE* BN3 .... 203 H3
Shirleys *HPPT/KEY* BN6 .... 151 F1
Shirley St *HOVE* BN3 .... 203 G4
Short Brow *SEAF* BN25 .... 225 H7
Short Brow Cl *LW/ROSE* BN22 ..... 215 G8 ⊡
Shortdean Pl *EAST* BN21 .... 229 J7 ⊡
Shortgate La *RING/NEW* BN8 ...... 157 H1
Shortgate Rd *ROTT* BN2 .... 179 G7
Shortlands Cl *LW/ROSE* BN22 ..... 229 H2 ⊡
Shovelstrode La *EGRIN* RH19 .... 23 J1
The Shrublands *BEXW* TN39 .... 194 D8
Shrub La *WADH* TN5 .... 59 K6
Sicklehatch La *HTHF* TN21 .... 130 A1
Sidcup Cl *LGNY* BN23 .... 230 E1 ⊡
Sidehill Dr *PTSD* BN41 .... 201 J1
Sidley Gn *BEXW* TN39 .... 195 H4
Sidley Rd *LW/ROSE* BN22 .... 11 E2
Sidley St *BEXW* TN39 .... 195 G4
Sidney Cl *RTWE/PEM* TN2 .... 29 J3
Silchester Rd *STLEO* TN38 .... 4 A5
Sillwood Pl *BRI* BN1 .... 6 A5 ⊡
Sillwood Rd *BRI* BN1 .... 6 A5 ⊡
Sillwood St *BRI* BN1 .... 6 A5
Silva Cl *BEX* TN40 .... 196 B5
Silvan Rd *STLEO* TN38 .... 169 F8 ⊡
Silverdale *HPPT/KEY* BN6 .... 119 H8
Silverdale Av *HOVE* BN3 .... 203 J4
Silverdale La *SBGH/RUST* TN4 .... 20 B5
Silverdale Rd *BURH* RH15 .... 119 H1
 EDN/EASTW BN20 .... 10 B6
 HOVE BN3 .... 203 J4
 SBGH/RUST TN4 .... 20 B5
Silverhill Av *SLVH* TN37 .... 169 K7
Silverlands Rd *SLVH* TN37 .... 197 J1
Silvester Rd *BEX* TN40 .... 195 H6
Silwood Cl *RTWE/PEM* TN2 .... 20 E4
Simons Cl *CROW* TN6 .... 53 J2 ⊡
Singleton Mill Rd *PEV* BN24 .... 216 D6
Singleton Rd *BRI* BN1 .... 178 B5
Singleton Wy *BURH* RH15 .... 119 J2
Sir David's Pk *SBGH/RUST* TN4 .... 19 J2
Six Bells Ms *RYE* TN31 .... 82 A6
Skinner's La *BAT* TN33 .... 166 B4
Skyline Vw *PEAHV* BN10 .... 222 C2
The Slade *RRTW* TN3 .... 33 J8
Sleepers Stile Rd *WADH* TN5 .... 44 E2
Slider's La *UCK* TN22 .... 64 E4
The Slides *STLEO* TN38 .... 169 G8
Slimbridge Rd *BURH* RH15 .... 89 F8
Slindon Av *PEAHV* BN10 .... 222 C5
Slindon Crs *LGNY* BN23 .... 231 F2 ⊡
Slinford Cl *ROTT* BN2 .... 7 F5
Slip Mill Rd *HAWK* TN18 .... 62 E1
Sliverick's La *HTHF* TN21 .... 133 H4
Sloe La *POLE* BN26 .... 213 D8
Slonk Hill Rd *SHOR* BN43 .... 200 D1
Slugwash La *RHWH* RH17 .... 90 D6
Smarts Hl *RTON* TN11 .... 17 J2
Smeatons La *WSEA* TN36 .... 143 H6
Smith Cl *BAT* TN33 .... 137 G8
Smithy's Cl *SLVH* TN37 .... 169 K6 ⊡
The Smithy *UCK* TN22 .... 95 H5
Smolletts *EGRIN* RH19 .... 22 A3 ⊡
Smugglers Cl *POLE* BN26 .... 212 C8
Smugglers La *CROW* TN6 .... 39 F6
Smugglers Ms *HAWK* TN18 .... 63 G2
Smugglers Wy *RHAS* TN35 .... 172 E7
Snape La *WADH* TN5 .... 58 A2
Snape Vw *WADH* TN5 .... 44 B7
Snatt's Rd *UCK* TN22 .... 95 J2
Snednore *LEW* BN7 .... 181 J6
Snowdon Cl *LGNY* BN23 .... 216 E8
Solomon's La *RBTBR* TN32 .... 106 C7
Solway *HAIL* BN27 .... 189 F1
Solway Av *BRI* BN1 .... 178 A4
Somerhill Av *HOVE* BN3 .... 203 J4
Somerhill Rd *HOVE* BN3 .... 203 J5
Somerset Cl *SBGH/RUST* TN4 ...... 20 A5
Somerset St *ROTT* BN2 .... 7 E5
Somerville Ct *LGNY* BN23 .... 231 H4 ⊡
Somerville Gdns *SBGH/RUST* TN4... 19 K7
Sompting Cl *ROTT* BN2 .... 205 G3 ⊡
Sorrel Cl *LGNY* BN23 .... 216 D8 ⊡
Sorrel Dr *LGNY* BN23 .... 216 D8
Southall Av *ROTT* BN2 .... 7 F1
Southampton Cl *LGNY* BN23 .... 231 G3 ⊡
Southampton St *ROTT* BN2 .... 7 D4
South Av *EDN/EASTW* BN20 .... 229 G6
 HPPT/KEY BN6 .... 118 A6
 ROTT BN2 .... 7 E5
South Bank *HPPT/KEY* BN6 .... 118 C7
Southbourne Rd *LW/ROSE* BN22 ... 11 E1
South Brooks Rd *LYDD* TN29 ...... 147 J3
South Cliff *EDN/EASTW* BN20 .... 237 F3
South Cliff Av *EDN/EASTW* BN20... 10 B6 ⊡
South Cl *BURH* RH15 .... 88 E8
 HAIL BN27 .... 189 G5
 PEV BN24 .... 218 C5
South Coast Rd *PEAHV* BN10 ..... 221 H3
 ROTT BN2 .... 221 G3

Southcourt Av *BEXW* TN39 .... 194 E8
Southdown Av *BRI* BN1 .... 6 C1
 EDN/EASTW BN20 .... 215 F8
 HAS TN34 .... 5 D4
 LEW BN7 .... 2 A5
 PEAHV BN10 .... 222 D5
 PTSD BN41 .... 202 B3 ⊡
Southdown Cl *HWH* RH16 .... 89 K1
 NEWHV BN9 .... 8 B4
Southdown Pl *BRI* BN1 .... 6 C1 ⊡
Southdown Rd *BRI* BN1 .... 6 C1
 EDN/EASTW BN20 .... 229 G4
 NEWHV BN9 .... 8 B4
 PTSD BN41 .... 201 K1
 SEAF BN25 .... 232 C2
 SHOR BN43 .... 200 C4
 STHW BN42 .... 201 H4
South Downs *LEW* BN7 .... 121 H6 ⊡
South Downs Rd *LEW* BN7 .... 3 D3
South Downs Wy
 EDN/EASTW BN20 .... 236 B2
 HFD BN5 .... 175 J3
 HPPT/KEY BN6 .... 150 D4
 LEW BN7 .... 180 D3
 LEW BN7 .... 207 H1
 POLE BN26 .... 213 H8
 POY/PYE BN45 .... 149 K5
 RING/NEW BN8 .... 209 J3
 RING/NEW BN8 .... 211 K6
 SEAF BN25 .... 226 D8
 SHOR BN43 .... 174 E1
South Dr *BURH* RH15 .... 88 E8
Southerden Cl *HAIL* BN27 .... 189 H4
Southern Av *POLE* BN26 .... 215 G5
Southern Rd *LW/ROSE* BN22 ...... 230 A1
Southfield *POLE* BN26 .... 214 E6
Southfield Rd *SBGH/RUST* TN4 ... 20 A5
Southfields *RRTW* TN3 .... 44 B5
 WADH TN5 .... 44 B5
Southfields Rd *EAST* BN21 .... 10 A4
Southfields Wy *SBGH/RUST* TN4 ... 20 B3
South Gv *RTW* TN1 .... 30 A1 ⊡
Southlands *EGRIN* RH19 .... 22 C4
Southlands Av *BEXW* TN39 .... 195 F4
Southlands Rd *BEXW* TN39 .... 195 F4
South La *HTHF* TN21 .... 133 C1
 NEWHV BN9 .... 9 D3 ⊡
South Lodge Cl *BURH* RH15 .... 89 F7 ⊡
South Lynn Dr *EAST* BN21 .... 10 B3
Southmead Cl *MAYF* TN20 .... 56 D8
Southmount *ROTT* BN2 .... 7 D1
Southon Cl *PTSD* BN41 .... 175 J8
Southover High St *LEW* BN7 .... 2 C5 ⊡
Southover Pl *ROTT* BN2 .... 7 D3
Southover Rd *LEW* BN7 .... 2 C5
Southover St *ROTT* BN2 .... 7 D4
Southridge Ri *CROW* TN6 .... 53 G3
Southridge Rd *CROW* TN6 .... 53 G5
South Rd *BRI* BN1 .... 6 A1
 HAIL BN27 .... 189 F5 ⊡
 NEWHV BN9 .... 9 D3 ⊡
 RHWH RH17 .... 90 E7
South Rough *RING/NEW* BN8 ...... 93 G5
South Rw *BRI* BN1 .... 6 B5
 BRI BN1 .... 179 K5
 CROW TN6 .... 53 H2
 CROW TN6 .... 55 F4
 EAST BN21 .... 10 B5 ⊡
 HPPT/KEY BN6 .... 119 K8
 LEW BN7 .... 3 E4
 MAYF TN20 .... 72 B1
 PTSD BN41 .... 201 K2
 RING/NEW BN8 .... 127 H7
 SEAF BN25 .... 232 A1
 SLVH TN37 .... 4 A5
South Ter *HAS* TN34 .... 5 D4
South Undercliff *RYE* TN31 .... 113 J6
South Vw *HPPT/KEY* BN6 .... 119 K6
South Vw *BUR/ETCH* TN19 .... 61 K8
Southview Cl *CROW* TN6 .... 53 G2 ⊡
 SHOR BN43 .... 201 F4
 STHW BN42 .... 201 H2 ⊡
Southview Dr *UCK* TN22 .... 95 J3
South View Rd *CROW* TN6 .... 53 G2
Southview Rd *PEAHV* BN10 .... 222 B3
South View Rd *SBGH/RUST* TN4 ... 20 B3
South View Wd *WADH* TN5 .... 44 B7
Southview Rd *STHW* BN42 .... 201 H3
Southwater Cl *ROTT* BN2 .... 7 F4
Southwater Rd *SLVH* TN37 .... 4 A4
Southway *BURH* RH15 .... 88 D8
South Wy *LEW* BN7 .... 2 A4
 NEWHV BN9 .... 9 D3 ⊡
 SEAF BN25 .... 232 E2
Southwick Cl *EGRIN* RH19 .... 22 B1
Southwick Sq *STHW* BN42 .... 201 H4
Southwick St *STHW* BN42 .... 201 H4
Southwood Av *SBGH/RUST* TN4 ... 20 B3
Southwood Cl *STLEO* TN38 .... 197 J2 ⊡
South Woodlands *BRI* BN1 .... 177 K7
Southwood Rd *SBGH/RUST* TN4 ... 19 F6
Sovereign Cl *HAS* TN34 .... 170 D7
 SEAF BN25 .... 225 H6 ⊡
The Spaldings *STLEO* TN38 .... 197 F2
The Sparrows *PEAHV* BN10 .... 222 C2 ⊡

Sparrow Wy *HPPT/KEY* BN6 .... 88 D8
Spatham La *HPPT/KEY* BN6 .... 120 B8
Speldhurst Hl *RRTW* TN3 .... 19 F5
Speldhurst Rd *RRTW* TN3 .... 18 D6
   SBGH/RUST TN4 .... 19 K5
Spencer Av *HOVE* BN3 .... 176 C8
Spencer Rd *EAST* BN21 .... 10 C5
Spences Fld *LEW* BN7 .... 3 E3
Spences La *LEW* BN7 .... 3 D3
Spicers Cl *BURH* RH15 .... 89 F6 🄳
Spindlewood Dr *BEXW* TN39 .... 194 B7
Spinnals Gv *STHW* BN42 .... 201 G4
Spinney La *HPPT/KEY* BN6 .... 118 C6
The Spinneys *HTHF* TN21 .... 100 B5 🄳
   LEW BN7 .... 3 E3
The Spinney *BAT* TN33 .... 137 F8
   BEXW TN39 .... 194 C8
   HAS TN34 .... 4 C3
   HOVE BN3 .... 177 H8
   HPPT/KEY BN6 .... 119 F6
   RBTBR TN32 .... 77 K8
Spital Rd *LEW* BN7 .... 2 B4
Spithurst Rd *RING/NEW* BN8 ..... 123 J4
Spode La *EDEN* TN8 .... 15 G3
Spotted Cow La *UCK* TN22 .... 69 G6
Spout Hl *CROW* TN6 .... 55 H2
Spray Hl *RRTW* TN3 .... 33 K7
Spray's La *BAT* TN33 .... 138 D7
Springate Rd *STHW* BN42 .... 201 J3
Spring Cl *EDN/EASTW* BN20 ...... 229 G2
Springett Av *RING/NEW* BN8 ..... 155 J6
Springfield *EGRIN* RH19 .... 12 B7
Springfield Av *PEAHV* BN10 ...... 221 J3
Springfield Cl *CROW* TN6 .... 53 K1 🄳
   PEV BN24 .... 217 G5
Springfield Rd *BEX* TN40 .... 195 H5
   BRI BN1 .... 6 C2
   LW/ROSE BN22 .... 11 D3 🄳
   RRTW TN3 .... 28 A4
   SBGH/RUST TN4 .... 19 K2
   STLEO TN38 .... 197 J2
Springfields *WADH* TN5 .... 60 C2
Springfield Valley Rd *STLEO* TN38 .. 197 J2
Spring Gdns *BRI* BN1 .... 6 C5
   LEW BN7 .... 3 D4 🄳
Springhead *RTWE/PEM* TN2 ...... 20 D6
Springhead Wy *CROW* TN6 .... 53 G3
Spring Hl *RTON* TN11 .... 17 J5
   RYE TN31 .... 81 K4
Spring La *BEXW* TN39 .... 194 B6
   BUR/ETCH TN19 .... 74 E3
   HPPT/KEY BN6 .... 149 K3
   UCK TN22 .... 70 D6
Spring Lodge Cl *LGNY* BN23 .... 231 F1 🄳
Spring Meadow *FROW* RH18 .... 35 K2
Springside Wk *STLEO* TN38 .... 197 G2
Spring St *BRI* BN1 .... 6 A5 🄳
   SLVH TN37 .... 4 A3 🄳
Spring Wy *EGRIN* RH19 .... 12 E7
Springwood Rd *HTHF* TN21 .... 99 K3
Spruce Cl *LW/ROSE* BN22 .... 229 J1
Spur Rd *POLE* BN26 .... 215 G6
Spurway Pk *POLE* BN26 .... 215 G6
Squab La *HAIL* BN27 .... 162 B7
The Square *RTWE/PEM* TN2 ...... 218 C5
Squirrel Cl *BEXW* TN39 .... 194 D6
Squirrel Wy *RTWE/PEM* TN2 ...... 20 E6
Stabledene Wy *RTWE/PEM* TN2 .. 21 K5 🄳
Stablefield *RHAS* TN35 .... 139 G7 🄳
Stables La *EAST* BN21 .... 10 C4 🄳
Stafford Rd *BRI* BN1 .... 6 A2
   RTWE/PEM TN2 .... 20 E7
   SEAF BN25 .... 225 G8
Stafford Wy *HPPT/KEY* BN6 ..... 119 G8
Stag Rd *RTWE/PEM* TN2 .... 20 D2
Stalkers La *RING/NEW* BN8 ...... 128 B5
Standard Hill Cl *BAT* TN33 .... 165 J5
Standean Cl *BRI* BN1 .... 178 E5
Standen St *SBGH/RUST* TN4 ...... 20 A6
Stanford Av *BRI* BN1 .... 6 B2
   HPPT/KEY BN6 .... 118 E7
Stanford Cl *HOVE* BN3 .... 203 H2
   HPPT/KEY BN6 .... 118 E7 🄳
Stanford Rd *BRI* BN1 .... 6 A2
Stanhope Pl *STLEO* TN38 .... 4 A6 🄳
Stanhope Rd *RTW* TN1 .... 20 C6 🄳
Stanley Av *PTSD* BN41 .... 175 J7
Stanley Rd *BRI* BN1 .... 6 C3
   HAS TN34 .... 4 C4
   LW/ROSE BN22 .... 11 D3 🄳🄳
   PEAHV BN10 .... 222 A2
   PTSD BN41 .... 201 K3
   RTW TN1 .... 20 B6
Stanley St *ROTT* BN2 .... 7 D5
Stanmer Av *ROTT* BN2 .... 207 G8
Stanmer Dr *LW/ROSE* BN22 ...... 229 J2
Stanmer Park Rd *BRI* BN1 .... 204 B3
Stanmer St *BRI* BN1 .... 204 C1 🄳
Stanmer Vls *BRI* BN1 .... 178 C8
Stansfield Rd *LEW* BN7 .... 2 B3
Stanstead Crs *ROTT* BN2 .... 206 C5
Stansted Rd *LW/ROSE* BN22 ...... 10 C3
Staplefield Dr *ROTT* BN2 .... 179 G8
Stapley Rd *HOVE* BN3 .... 202 C3
Starfield *CROW* TN6 .... 53 G2

Star La *MAYF* TN20 .... 72 B1 🄳
   POLE BN26 .... 212 C8
   UCK TN22 .... 97 K5
Starling Cl *HPPT/KEY* BN6 .... 88 C8
Star Rd *EAST* BN21 .... 10 A4
Starr's Green La *BAT* TN33 .... 137 F8
Starrs Md *BAT* TN33 .... 137 F8
Starvecrow La *RYE* TN31 .... 111 F5
Starwell Cl *HAS* TN34 .... 4 B1
Station Ap *BAT* TN33 .... 136 E8
   BRI BN1 .... 179 J5
   BUR/ETCH TN19 .... 77 G2 🄳
   HAS TN34 .... 4 C4 🄳
   HPPT/KEY BN6 .... 118 E7 🄳
   HTHF TN21 .... 100 A4
   LW/ROSE BN22 .... 230 A2
   MAYF TN20 .... 71 K1
   RYE TN31 .... 113 H5 🄳
   SEAF BN25 .... 225 F8
   SLVH TN37 .... 4 A5 🄳
Station Cl *CROW* TN6 .... 55 G2
   LEW BN7 .... 121 G6 🄳
Station Rd *BAT* TN33 .... 168 A6
   BEX TN40 .... 195 H7
   BRI BN1 .... 177 J8
   BUR/ETCH TN19 .... 61 K8
   BURH RH15 .... 119 F1
   CROW TN6 .... 55 G2
   EGRIN RH19 .... 22 B2
   FROW RH18 .... 23 K8
   HAIL BN27 .... 161 F6
   HAIL BN27 .... 189 G4
   HAS TN34 .... 5 D4 🄳
   HRTF TN7 .... 26 D6
   HTHF TN21 .... 100 A4
   LEW BN7 .... 3 D5 🄳
   LEW BN7 .... 121 G5
   MAYF TN20 .... 71 K1
   NEWHV BN9 .... 9 F1
   POLE BN26 .... 215 F5
   RBTBR TN32 .... 78 A8
   RHWH RH17 .... 48 A6
   RING/NEW BN8 .... 92 C4
   RING/NEW BN8 .... 28 A4
   RYE TN31 .... 81 K3
   SEAF BN25 .... 224 C7
   STHW BN42 .... 201 H4
   UCK TN22 .... 124 D3
   WADH TN5 .... 43 J5
   WADH TN5 .... 59 G6
   WSEA TN36 .... 142 E2
Station St *BRI* BN1 .... 6 C4 🄳🄳
   EAST BN21 .... 10 C4 🄳
Staveley Rd *EDN/EASTW* BN20 .. 236 E3
Steellands Ri *WADH* TN5 .... 60 C2
Steep Hill Brede La *RYE* TN31 ... 139 F1
Steep Rd *CROW* TN6 .... 54 A5
Steine Gdns *ROTT* BN2 .... 6 C5 🄳🄳
Steine La *BRI* BN1 .... 6 C5 🄳🄳
Steine St *ROTT* BN2 .... 6 C6
The Stennings *EGRIN* RH19 .... 12 A8
Stephens Cl *RING/NEW* BN8 ... 155 J6 🄳
Stephenson Dr *EGRIN* RH19 .... 22 D5
Stephens Rd *BRI* BN1 .... 204 C1
   SBGH/RUST TN4 .... 20 A6
Stevens Cl *BEXW* TN39 .... 195 H4
Stevenson Cl *LGNY* BN23 .... 217 F8 🄳
Stevenson Rd *ROTT* BN2 .... 7 E5
   SLVH TN37 .... 169 J8 🄳
Stewards Inn La *LEW* BN7 .... 2 C5 🄳
Stewart Rd *SBGH/RUST* TN4 .... 20 C4
Steyne Cl *SEAF* BN25 .... 232 B1 🄳
Steyne Rd *SEAF* BN25 .... 232 A1
Steyning Av *HOVE* BN3 .... 176 E8
   PEAHV BN10 .... 222 B4
Steyning Cl *SEAF* BN25 .... 232 E1 🄳
Steyning Rd *ROTT* BN2 .... 220 C2
   SEAF BN25 .... 232 E1
The Stiles *HAIL* BN27 .... 189 H4
Still La *SBGH/RUST* TN4 .... 19 K1 🄳
Stirling Av *SEAF* BN25 .... 225 K7
Stirling Cl *BURH* RH15 .... 89 J7
Stirling Court Rd *BURH* RH15 ..... 89 J7
Stirling Pl *HOVE* BN3 .... 203 F5 🄳
Stirling Rd *EGRIN* RH19 .... 13 F9
Stock Di *RHAS* TN35 .... 172 E7
Stockland Green Rd *RRTW* TN3 .. 19 G3
Stockland La *UCK* TN22 .... 69 K5
Stockleigh Rd *STLEO* TN38 .... 4 A5
Stocks Meadow *BAT* TN33 .... 166 A6
Stockwell Rd *EGRIN* RH19 .... 22 C5
Stoddards La *RYE* TN31 .... 82 C6
Stoke Cl *SEAF* BN25 .... 225 J8
Stoke Manor Cl *SEAF* BN25 ..... 225 J8
Stonebeach Ri *STLEO* TN38 ..... 169 G4
Stone Br *TENT* TN30 .... 86 D1
Stonebridge La *UCK* TN22 .... 97 H6
Stonecott Cl *CROW* TN6 .... 53 H3
Stonecroft Cl *HOVE* BN3 .... 176 D7
Stone Cross Rd *CROW* TN6 .... 53 H5
Stonecross Rd *ROTT* BN2 .... 179 G7
Stone Cross Rd *WADH* TN5 .... 44 C8
Stonedene Cl *FROW* RH18 .... 36 B1
Stonefield Pl *HAS* TN34 .... 5 D4 🄳

Stonefield Rd *HAS* TN34 .... 5 D4
Stonefield Wy *BURH* RH15 .... 89 F6
Stonegate Cl *LW/ROSE* BN22 .. 216 E7 🄳
Stonegate Rd *WADH* TN5 .... 58 E2
Stonegate Wy *HTHF* TN21 .... 100 B3 🄳
Stoneham Cl *BRI* BN1 .... 2 C2
Stoneham Rd *HOVE* BN3 .... 202 E4
Stonehouse Dr *BAT* TN33 .... 169 G2
   STLEO TN38 .... 197 H1
Stonehurst Ct *ROTT* BN2 .... 7 E4 🄳
Stonehurst La *MAYF* TN20 .... 70 E3
   UCK TN22 .... 70 A5
Stoneleigh Av *BRI* BN1 .... 178 A5
Stoneleigh Cl *BRI* BN1 .... 178 A5
   EGRIN RH19 .... 22 D1 🄳
Stonelink Cl *STLEO* TN38 .... 169 G4
Stonepark Dr *FROW* RH18 .... 36 A1
Stonepound Rd *HPPT/KEY* BN6 .. 118 E7
Stone Quarry Rd *RHWH* RH17 ..... 49 H4
Stonery Cl *PTSD* BN41 .... 201 K1
Stonery Rd *PTSD* BN41 .... 201 K1
Stonestile La *RHAS* TN55 .... 139 G8
Stone St *BRI* BN1 .... 6 A5
   HAS TN34 .... 5 D4 🄳
   RTW TN1 .... 20 B7
Stonewall Park Rd *RRTW* TN3 ..... 18 D8
Stonewood Cl *SEAF* BN25 ...... 225 K7 🄳
Stoney La *SHOR* BN43 .... 201 F3
Stonhouse Dr *STLEO* TN38 .... 169 J8
Storrington Dr *HOVE* BN3 .... 202 D1 🄳
Straight Half Mile *UCK* TN22 ...... 67 H6
Strand *RYE* TN31 .... 113 H6
Strand Hl *WSEA* TN36 .... 143 F4
Strand Meadow *BUR/ETCH* TN19 . 75 K4
The Strand *ROTT* BN2 .... 205 H8
Stratford St *RTW* TN1 .... 20 C6
Strawberry Cl *RRTW* TN3 .... 29 J3
Strawberry Flds *RYE* TN31 .... 81 J4
Stream La *BAT* TN33 .... 137 H1
   HAWK TN18 .... 63 F4
   RHAS TN55 .... 173 F5
Streamside Cl *HAS* TN34 .... 4 C1
Streat Bostall *HPPT/KEY* BN6 ... 115 K4
Streatfield Gdns *HTHF* TN21 .... 99 K3
Streatfield Rd *HTHF* TN21 .... 99 K3
   UCK TN22 .... 95 H4
Streat La *HPPT/KEY* BN6 .... 120 E3
   HPPT/KEY BN6 .... 151 K2
Streele La *UCK* TN22 .... 97 F2
Streele Vw *UCK* TN22 .... 100 C3
Street End La *HTHF* TN21 .... 100 D3
   MAYF TN20 .... 73 F7
Streetlands *BAT* TN33 .... 138 A2
The Street *BAT* TN33 .... 138 A3
   HPPT/KEY BN6 .... 151 C3
   LEW BN7 .... 181 H6
   RING/NEW BN8 .... 184 C7
   SHOR BN43 .... 200 A2
   TENT TN30 .... 84 D1
   UCK TN22 .... 96 D6
Stringer Wy *BRI* BN1 .... 178 A8
The Stringwalk *HAIL* BN27 .... 189 H4
Stroma Gdns *HAIL* BN27 .... 188 E1
Strood Ga *RHWH* RH17 .... 90 E6
Strood Rd *SLVH* TN37 .... 4 A4
Stuart Av *EAST* BN21 .... 229 H5
Stuart Cl *RTWE/PEM* TN2 .... 29 K3
Stuart Wy *EGRIN* RH19 .... 22 D3
Stubb La *RYE* TN31 .... 139 K2
Studdens La *HAIL* BN27 .... 162 E2
Sturdee Cl *LGNY* BN23 .... 231 G4
Sudeley Pl *ROTT* BN2 .... 7 F6
Sudeley St *ROTT* BN2 .... 7 F6
Sudeley Ter *ROTT* BN2 .... 7 F6 🄳🄳
Suffolk Rd *BEXW* TN39 .... 195 H4
Suffolk St *HOVE* BN3 .... 202 E3
Sullington Cl *ROTT* BN2 .... 179 G7
Sullington Wy *SHOR* BN43 .... 200 D3
Sumach Cl *LW/ROSE* BN22 .... 229 K1
Summer Cl *PTSD* BN41 .... 201 K4
Summercourt *HAIL* BN27 .... 189 G3 🄳
Summerdale Rd *HOVE* BN3 ...... 202 C1
Summerdown Cl
   EDN/EASTW BN20 .... 229 J8
Summerdown La
   EDN/EASTW BN20 .... 235 G2
Summerdown Rd
   EDN/EASTW BN20 .... 229 H8
Summerfields *SLVH* TN37 .... 4 B4 🄳
Summerfields Av *HAIL* BN27 ..... 189 F5
Summerheath Rd *HAIL* BN27 ... 189 G3
Summer Hl *STLEO* TN38 .... 169 J8
Summerhill Av *SBGH/RUST* TN4 . 19 K2 🄳
Summer Hill Rd *BEXW* TN39 .... 194 E5
Summerlands Rd *LW/ROSE* BN22.. 229 G1
Summersdeane *STHW* BN42 ..... 201 J2
Summervale Rd *SBGH/RUST* TN4.. 29 H2
Sun La *HAS* TN34 .... 5 E5 🄳
Sunningdale Av *BEX* TN40 .... 195 K6
   HAIL BN27 .... 189 F2
   SEAF BN25 .... 232 C1 🄳
Sunningdale Dr *STLEO* TN38 .... 197 G4
Sunninghill Av *HOVE* BN3 .... 202 D1
Sunninghill Cl *HOVE* BN3 .... 202 D1 🄳
Sunnybrooke Cl *UCK* TN22 ...... 95 K4 🄳

Sunnycroft Cl *RHWH* RH17 .... 91 G1
Sunnydale Av *BRI* BN1 .... 178 E5
Sunnydale Cl *BRI* BN1 .... 178 E5
Sunnyside Rd *SBGH/RUST* TN4 ...... 19 F7
Sunset *PEAHV* BN10 .... 222 A2 ②
 PEV BN24 .... 218 B5
Sunstar La *POLE* BN26 .... 214 C5
Sun St *LEW* BN7 .... 2 C4
Sunview Av *PEAHV* BN10 .... 222 C5
Surrenden Cl *BRI* BN1 .... 178 A7
Surrenden Crs *BRI* BN1 .... 177 K8
Surrenden Holt *BRI* BN1 .... 178 A8
Surrenden Pk *BRI* BN1 .... 178 B7
Surrenden Rd *BRI* BN1 .... 178 A8
Surrey Cl *RTWE/PEM* TN2 .... 29 K3
Surrey Rd *SEAF* BN25 .... 224 D7
Surrey St *BRI* BN1 .... 6 B4 ②
Surry St *SHOR* BN43 .... 200 C4
Susans Cl *RING/NEW* BN8 .... 127 J6
Susan's Rd *EAST* BN21 .... 10 C4 ②
Sussex Av *HAIL* BN27 .... 189 G3
Sussex Border Pth *BRI* BN1 .... 176 E1
 EDEN TN8 .... 14 C3
 EGRIN RH19 .... 22 E6
 HAWK TN18 .... 63 G5
 PTSD BN41 .... 175 H5
 RHWH RH17 .... 48 B3
 RRTW TN3 .... 17 F7
 TENT TN30 .... 84 D4
 WADH TN5 .... 43 K3
 WADH TN5 .... 46 E2
Sussex Cl *BEXW* TN39 .... 194 E6
 HAIL BN27 .... 189 G3
 RTWE/PEM TN2 .... 30 C2
Sussex Gdns *EDN/EASTW* BN20 ..... 235 G2
Sussex Ms *RTWE/PEM* TN2 .... 30 A1 ②
Sussex Pl *ROTT* BN2 .... 7 D4 ②
Sussex Rd *HOVE* BN3 .... 203 C6 ②
 STLEO TN38 .... 197 H5
Sussex Sq *ROTT* BN2 .... 205 F7
Sussex St *ROTT* BN2 .... 7 D5
Sussex Wy *BURH* RH15 .... 88 C6
 PEAHV BN10 .... 221 J4
Sutherland Av *BEXW* TN39 .... 195 F8
Sutherland Cl *BEXW* TN39 .... 194 E7
Sutherland Rd *ROTT* BN2 .... 7 B1
 RTW TN1 .... 30 D1
Sutton Av *PEAHV* BN10 .... 222 A4
 SEAF BN25 .... 232 C1
Sutton Av North *PEAHV* BN10 ...... 222 A3
Sutton Cl *ROTT* BN2 .... 206 B2
Sutton Croft La *SEAF* BN25 ...... 225 F8 ②
Sutton Dro *SEAF* BN25 .... 225 G7
Sutton Park Rd *SEAF* BN25 ...... 225 G7
Sutton Pl *BEX* TN40 .... 195 K7
Sutton Rd *EAST* BN21 .... 10 C4 ②
 SEAF BN25 .... 225 G8
The Suttons *RYE* TN31 .... 145 H2 ②
 STLEO TN38 .... 197 C1
Swaines Wy *HTHF* TN21 .... 100 A5
Swainham La *BAT* TN33 .... 168 B8
Swallow Bank *STLEO* TN38 ...... 197 G1
Swallow Cl *LGNY* BN23 .... 230 C1
Swallow Dr *UCK* TN22 .... 95 K6 ②
Swallow Dr *BAT* TN33 .... 137 F7 ②
 RTWE/PEM TN2 .... 21 F5
Swallowfield *LING* RH7 .... 12 E1 ①
The Swallows *PEAHV* BN10 ...... 222 A2 ①
Swanborough Dr *ROTT* BN2 ...... 205 G4
Swanborough Dro *LEW* BN7 ...... 181 J8
Swanborough Hollow *LEW* BN7 .... 181 K7
Swanborough Pl *ROTT* BN2 ...... 205 G4 ②
Swan Cl *RING/NEW* BN8 .... 122 C4
Swanley Cl *LGNY* BN23 .... 230 D1
Swann Cl *BURH* RH15 .... 89 K8
Swannee Cl *PEAHV* BN10 .... 222 C2 ②
Swan Rd *HAIL* BN27 .... 189 H5
Swansbrook La *HTHF* TN21 .... 160 C2
Swans Ghyll *FROW* RH18 .... 23 J8
Swan Ter *HAS* TN34 .... 5 E4 ①
Swaylands Av *CROW* TN6 .... 53 H4
Sweeps Hill Cl *RTWE/PEM* TN2 .... 21 K4 ②
Sweethaws La *CROW* TN6 .... 52 E5
Sweetings La *RRTW* TN3 .... 45 F2
Sweetlands *HPPT/KEY* BN6 ...... 119 H6 ①
Swife La *HTHF* TN21 .... 73 J8
Swift Cl *CROW* TN6 .... 53 F2
 HPPT/KEY BN6 .... 88 D8
 UCK TN22 .... 95 K6
Swinburne Av *LW/ROSE* BN22 .... 215 G8
Swiss Gdns *SHOR* BN43 .... 200 B4
Swissland Hi *EGRIN* RH19 .... 12 C5
Swynford Dr *STLEO* TN38 .... 169 G6
Sybron Wy *CROW* TN6 .... 54 B3
Sycamore Cl *BEXW* TN39 .... 194 B6
 HTHF TN21 .... 100 B5
 LW/ROSE BN22 .... 215 J8 ②
 PTSD BN41 .... 176 B8 ②
 ROTT BN2 .... 206 B3
 SEAF BN25 .... 225 K8 ②
 STLEO TN38 .... 197 H2 ②
Sycamore Ct *UCK* TN22 .... 95 K3
Sycamore Dr *EGRIN* RH19 .... 22 E2
 HAIL BN27 .... 189 G5
The Sycamores *PEAHV* BN10 ...... 222 C2 ②

Sydney Cl *STLEO* TN38 .... 169 J8
Sydney Little Rd *STLEO* TN38 ...... 168 E7
Sydney Rd *LW/ROSE* BN22 .... 11 D4
Sydney St *BRI* BN1 .... 6 C4
Sylvester Wy *HOVE* BN3 .... 176 B8
Symbister Rd *PTSD* BN41 .... 202 B4 ②

T

Tackleway *HAS* TN34 .... 5 F4
Taddington Rd *LW/ROSE* BN22 ...... 11 E3 ①
Tainter's Brook *UCK* TN22 .... 96 A3
Talbot Crs *BRI* BN1 .... 178 E5
Talbot Pk *RTWE/PEM* TN2 .... 20 D6
Talbot Rd *HAWK* TN18 .... 63 F3
Talbot Ter *LEW* BN7 .... 2 C4
Tall Ash Dr *SLVH* TN37 .... 169 K7
Tamarack Cl *LW/ROSE* BN22 ...... 229 J1
Tamar Cl *PEV* BN24 .... 216 B6
Tamplin Ter *ROTT* BN2 .... 7 D4
Tamworth Rd *HOVE* BN3 .... 202 E4
Tanbridge Rd *LGNY* BN23 .... 231 G2
Tandridge Rd *HOVE* BN3 .... 202 D5
Tangier La *RRTW* TN3 .... 30 B5
Tanglewood Coppice
 BEXW TN39 .... 194 D8 ①
Tangmere Cl *BEXW* TN39 .... 194 D8 ②
Tangmere Rd *BRI* BN1 .... 178 B5
Tanhouse La *RYE* TN31 .... 111 K1
Tanners Brook *LEW* BN7 .... 3 D5 ②
Tanners Fld *RHWH* RH17 .... 90 C6
Tanners Wy *CROW* TN6 .... 53 J2 ②
Tanyard Av *EGRIN* RH19 .... 22 E3
Tanyard La *RHWH* RH17 .... 49 G7
 SBGH/RUST TN4 .... 19 K2
 WSEA TN36 .... 142 E3
Tapsell's La *WADH* TN5 .... 43 J6
Tarmount La *SHOR* BN43 .... 200 C4
Tarner Rd *ROTT* BN2 .... 7 D4
Tarragon Wy *SHOR* BN43 .... 201 F2
Tarring Cl *NEWHV* BN9 .... 223 J1 ①
Tas Combe Wy *EDN/EASTW* BN20 .. 229 G1
Tate Crs *BURH* RH15 .... 89 F6 ②
Tates *HAWK* TN18 .... 63 G2
Taunton Rd *ROTT* BN2 .... 205 G2
Taunton Wy *ROTT* BN2 .... 205 H2 ②
Tavistock Down *BRI* BN1 .... 204 D1
Taylor Cl *STLEO* TN38 .... 169 G7
Taylor St *SBGH/RUST* TN4 .... 19 K3
Tea Garden La *RRTW* TN3 .... 29 F2
Teal Cl *STLEO* TN38 .... 169 F8
Tedder Rd *SBGH/RUST* TN4 .... 20 B4
Teg Cl *PTSD* BN41 .... 202 B1
Telegraph St *ROTT* BN2 .... 7 E6 ②
Telford Rd *STLEO* TN38 .... 169 H6
Telham Cl *HAS* TN34 .... 170 D6
Telham La *BAT* TN33 .... 167 K2
Telscombe Cliffs Wy *PEAHV* BN10 .. 221 J4
Telscombe Pk *PEAHV* BN10 ...... 222 B1 ③
Telscombe Rd *LGNY* BN23 ...... 231 C1
 PEAHV BN10 .... 222 B1
Temple Gdns *HOVE* BN3 .... 6 A4
Temple Gv *BURH* RH15 .... 88 D7
Temple St *BRI* BN1 .... 6 A5
Tenantry Down Rd *ROTT* BN2 .... 205 F4
Tenantry Rd *ROTT* BN2 .... 7 F2
Tennis Cl *HAIL* BN27 .... 189 C4
Tennis Rd *HOVE* BN3 .... 202 D5
Tennyson Ri *EGRIN* RH19 .... 22 A2
Tenterden Cl *LGNY* BN23 .... 230 E1
Tenterden Ri *HAS* TN34 .... 4 B1
Terminus Av *BEXW* TN39 .... 194 E8
Terminus Pl *BRI* BN1 .... 6 B3 ②
Terminus Rd *BEXW* TN39 .... 195 F8
 BRI BN1 .... 6 B3 ②
 EAST BN21 .... 10 B4
Terminus St *BRI* BN1 .... 6 B4 ②
Terrace Rd *SLVH* TN37 .... 4 A5 ②
Thackeray Cl *LGNY* BN23 .... 217 F8
Thakeham Cl *BEX* TN40 .... 196 B5
Thames Cl *ROTT* BN2 .... 7 D5
Thanet Wy *HAS* TN34 .... 4 C2
Thatchers Cl *BURH* RH15 .... 119 K2
The Thatchings *POLE* BN26 ...... 215 F6
Theobalds *HAWK* TN18 .... 63 F1
Theobalds Gn *HTHF* TN21 ...... 100 A6
Theobalds Rd *BURH* RH15 .... 89 J5
Theodore Cl *RTWE/PEM* TN2 ...... 20 E4
Third Av *HOVE* BN3 .... 203 C6
 NEWHV BN9 .... 8 C4
Third Rd *PEAHV* BN10 .... 221 K4 ③
Third St *RRTW* TN3 .... 18 D8
Thirlmere Rd *SBGH/RUST* TN4 ...... 19 H6
Thomas Brassey Cl *SLVH* TN37 ...... 169 J2 ③
Thomas St *LEW* BN7 .... 3 E4 ②
 SBGH/RUST TN4 .... 20 A6
Thomas Turner Dr
 RING/NEW BN8 .... 127 J6
Thompson Rd *BRI* BN1 .... 7 E1
 NEWHV BN9 .... 224 A1
Thornbank Crs *BEXW* TN39 .... 194 E8
Thornbush Crs *PTSD* BN41 .... 176 A8

Thorndean Rd *ROTT* BN2 .... 178 E8
Thorne Crs *BEXW* TN39 .... 194 D2
Thornfield Gdns *RTWE/PEM* TN2 .... 21 F6
Thornhill Av *BRI* BN1 .... 178 B4
Thornhill Cl *HOVE* BN3 .... 202 D1 ②
Thornhill Ri *PTSD* BN41 .... 175 K7
Thornhill Wy *PTSD* BN41 .... 175 K8
The Thorns *RHAS* TN35 .... 171 K3
Thornwell Rd *POLE* BN26 .... 213 J4
Thornwood Cl *LW/ROSE* BN22 ...... 229 K1 ③
Thorny Cl *HTHF* TN21 .... 100 A4
Three Leg Cross Rd *WADH* TN5 ...... 46 B8
Three Oaks La *WADH* TN5 .... 43 J4
Thurrock Cl *EDN/EASTW* BN20 .. 215 G7 ③
Thyme Cl *SHOR* BN43 .... 201 F2 ③
Thyssel La *RYE* TN31 .... 81 K5
Tibbs Mill La *UCK* TN22 .... 69 G2
Ticehurst Av *BEXW* TN39 .... 193 J6
Ticehurst Rd *ROTT* BN2 .... 205 G6
Tichborne St *BRI* BN1 .... 6 C5 ③②
Tickerage La *UCK* TN22 .... 97 H5
Tidebrook Gdns *LGNY* BN23 ...... 231 G1
Tideswell Rd *EAST* BN21 .... 10 C4 ②
Tidy St *BRI* BN1 .... 6 C4
Tilbury Pl *ROTT* BN2 .... 7 D5 ①②
Tilbury Wy *ROTT* BN2 .... 7 D4
Tile Barn Cl *UCK* TN22 .... 124 D3
Tile Barn Rd *STLEO* TN38 .... 169 G7
Tilehurst Dr *HAIL* BN27 .... 189 F3
Tilekiln La *RHAS* TN35 .... 171 H7
Tilers Cl *BURH* RH15 .... 89 K8 ②
Tilgate Cl *EAST* BN21 .... 229 J4
 ROTT BN2 .... 7 F4
Tilgate Dr *BEXW* TN39 .... 194 C8
Tilley La *HAIL* BN27 .... 164 A6
Tillingham Av *RYE* TN31 .... 113 H6
Tillingham La *RYE* TN31 .... 111 K5
Tillingham Vw *RYE* TN31 .... 109 J7
Tillingham Wy *PEV* BN24 .... 216 B6
Tilstone Cl *ROTT* BN2 .... 204 E1 ②
Tilstone St *ROTT* BN2 .... 7 D5
Tilsmore Cnr *HTHF* TN21 .... 99 K4
Tilsmore Rd *HTHF* TN21 .... 99 K3
Timberlaine Rd *PEV* BN24 .... 217 K7
Timberley Rd *LW/ROSE* BN22 ...... 229 J2
Timbers Ct *HAIL* BN27 .... 189 H4 ③
Timber Yard Cottages *LEW* BN7 .... 3 E4
Tindal Cl *BURH* RH15 .... 89 K8 ②
Tinker's La *UCK* TN22 .... 70 C7
 WADH TN5 .... 46 B8
Tintern Cl *BRI* BN1 .... 7 D1
 LW/ROSE BN22 .... 215 J8
Tisbury Rd *HOVE* BN3 .... 203 H5
Titchfield Cl *BURH* RH15 .... 119 K2
Tithe Barn Fld *WSEA* TN36 .... 141 K6 ②
Titian Rd *HOVE* BN3 .... 202 E4
Tiverton Dr *BEX* TN40 .... 195 K6
Tivoli Crs *BRI* BN1 .... 203 J2
Tivoli Crs North *BRI* BN1 .... 203 J1
Tivoli Pl *BRI* BN1 .... 203 J1
Tivoli Rd *BRI* BN1 .... 203 J1
Tolhurst La *WADH* TN5 .... 59 J3
Tolkien Rd *LGNY* BN23 .... 231 F1
Tollgate *PEAHV* BN10 .... 222 A2 ②
Tollgates *BAT* TN33 .... 136 B7
Toll La *UCK* TN22 .... 67 F2
Tollwood Pk *CROW* TN6 .... 53 K3
Tollwood Rd *CROW* TN6 .... 53 K3
Toll Wood Rd *HTHF* TN21 .... 129 K4
Tompset's Bank *FROW* RH18 ...... 35 K3
Tomtits La *FROW* RH18 .... 35 J2
Tonbridge Rd *RTWE/PEM* TN2 ...... 21 H4
Tonbridge Wy *RYE* TN31 .... 145 G1 ②
Tongdean Av *HOVE* BN3 .... 177 H8
Tongdean La *BRI* BN1 .... 177 J7
Tongdean Ri *BRI* BN1 .... 177 J7
Tongdean Rd *HOVE* BN3 .... 177 G8
Tongswood Dr *HAWK* TN18 ...... 63 J2
Top Cross Rd *BEX* TN40 .... 196 B4
Top Dr *UCK* TN22 .... 67 G5
Torcross Cl *ROTT* BN2 .... 205 F2
Torfield Rd *EAST* BN21 .... 10 A3 ②
Toronto Ter *LEW* BN7 .... 2 C4
 ROTT BN2 .... 7 D4
Torrance Cl *HOVE* BN3 .... 202 E2 ②
Tor Rd *PEAHV* BN10 .... 222 B1
Tor Rd West *PEAHV* BN10 .... 222 A1
Totland Rd *ROTT* BN2 .... 7 F3
Tottington Wy *SHOR* BN43 .... 200 E2 ②
Tott Yew Rd *EDN/EASTW* BN20 .... 215 F7
Tovey Cl *EAST* BN21 .... 229 J5
Tower Cl *EGRIN* RH19 .... 22 C1
 PEV BN24 .... 218 C5
Towergate *BRI* BN1 .... 203 K1
Tower Ride *UCK* TN22 .... 95 K2
Tower Rd *ROTT* BN2 .... 7 D4
 STLEO TN38 .... 4 A3
Tower Rd West *STLEO* TN38 ...... 197 J3
Towerscroft Av *SLVH* TN37 .... 169 J6
Tower St *HTHF* TN21 .... 100 B3
 RYE TN31 .... 113 J5 ③
Tower Vw *UCK* TN22 .... 95 K3 ③
Town Hi *RRTW* TN3 .... 33 J7
Trafalgar Cl *PEAHV* BN10 .... 222 B2 ①
 STLEO TN38 .... 169 G4

Trafalgar Ct *BRI* BN1 .... 6 C4 🔢
Trafalgar Ga *ROTT* BN2 .... 205 G8
Trafalgar La *BRI* BN1 .... 6 C4
Trafalgar Pl *BRI* BN1 .... 6 C4 🔢
Trafalgar St *BRI* BN1 .... 6 C4
Tram Rd *RYE* TN31 .... 144 C1
Transit Rd *NEWHV* BN9 .... 9 D3
Travellers La *RHAS* TN35 .... 171 F7
Trebilco Cl *RTWE/PEM* TN2 .... 20 D4 🔢
Treblers Rd *CROW* TN6 .... 54 B4
Tredcroft Rd *HOVE* BN3 .... 203 G1
Tree Tops Cl *ROTT* BN2 .... 206 B3
Tremola Av *ROTT* BN2 .... 220 E1
Trenches Rd *CROW* TN6 .... 53 H2
Treyford Cl *ROTT* BN2 .... 206 B2
The Triangle *EDN/EASTW* BN20 .... 215 F8 🔢
Trinity Cl *RTWE/PEM* TN2 .... 20 D7
Trinity Fld *RING/NEW* BN8 .... 155 K5
Trinity Pl *EAST* BN21 .... 10 C5
Trinity Rd *HPPT/KEY* BN6 .... 118 A3
Trinity St *ROTT* BN2 .... 7 D3
Trinity Trees *EAST* BN21 .... 10 C5
Tristan Gdns *SBGH/RUST* TN4 .... 19 H7 🔢
Troon Cl *SEAF* BN25 .... 224 B5 🔢
Trossachs Cl *LGNY* BN23 .... 216 E8
Troy Cl *CROW* TN6 .... 53 J2 🔢
Truleigh Cl *ROTT* BN2 .... 206 C4
Truleigh Dr *PTSD* BN41 .... 175 K7
Truleigh Wy *SHOR* BN43 .... 200 D2
Truman Dr *STLEO* TN38 .... 169 G5
Trumpet La *HAIL* BN27 .... 163 J1
Tubwell La *CROW* TN6 .... 54 B4
   HTHF TN21 .... 129 K1
Tudor Av *STLEO* TN38 .... 197 H4
Tudor Cl *EGRIN* RH19 .... 22 D4 🔢
   HOVE BN3 .... 202 E1
   SEAF BN25 .... 224 E7
Tudor Ct *RTWE/PEM* TN2 .... 29 J2 🔢
Tudor Gdns *BURH* RH15 .... 89 F7 🔢
Tudor Wk *UCK* TN22 .... 96 D6
Tugwell Rd *LW/ROSE* BN22 .... 230 A1
Tumulus Rd *ROTT* BN2 .... 221 F1
Tunbridge Wells Rd *CROW* TN6 .... 55 J5
   MAYF TN20 .... 55 K6
Tunnel Rd *RTW* TN1 .... 20 B6
Turkey La *BURH* RH15 .... 89 H8 🔢
Turkey Rd *BEXW* TN39 .... 194 C4
Turk's Br *HTHF* TN21 .... 74 A3
Turnberry Cl *STLEO* TN38 .... 197 H4
Turnberry Dr *HAIL* BN27 .... 189 F3
Turner Cl *BEX* TN40 .... 195 J6
   LGNY BN23 .... 230 E2 🔢
Turner Ct *EGRIN* RH19 .... 12 E8
Turners Green La *WADH* TN5 .... 44 B5
Turners Green Rd *WADH* TN5 .... 44 B4
Turners Wy *BURH* RH15 .... 89 F7 🔢
Turnpike Cl *PEAHV* BN10 .... 222 B3
   RING/NEW BN8 .... 156 B4
Turton Cl *ROTT* BN2 .... 7 F5
Tutts Barn La *LW/ROSE* BN22 .... 10 B2
Tuxford Rd *SBGH/RUST* TN4 .... 19 H8
Twineham Cl *ROTT* BN2 .... 205 G4
Twineham Rd *EAST* BN21 .... 229 J4
Twitten Cl *STHW* BN42 .... 201 H4 🔢
The Twitten *BURH* RH15 .... 89 H7 🔢
   CROW TN6 .... 53 G2
   STHW BN42 .... 201 H4
Twyford Crs *SLVH* TN37 .... 169 K7
Twyford Rd *BRI* BN1 .... 178 E5
Twyfords *CROW* TN6 .... 53 G2 🔢
Twyhurst Ct *EGRIN* RH19 .... 12 B8 🔢
Tye Cl *ROTT* BN2 .... 221 G3
Tyedean Rd *PEAHV* BN10 .... 221 J3
Tye Hill Rd *POLE* BN26 .... 187 J7
Tye Vw *PEAHV* BN10 .... 221 K2 🔢
Tylers La *UCK* TN22 .... 66 C2
Tyndale Av *BEXW* TN39 .... 194 B8

U

Uckfield Cl *ROTT* BN2 .... 205 G2
Uckfield Rd *CROW* TN6 .... 52 D5
   RING/NEW BN8 .... 155 G4
Uckham La *BAT* TN33 .... 136 E5
Udimore Rd *RYE* TN31 .... 109 K7
   RYE TN31 .... 112 K7
Undercliff *STLEO* TN38 .... 197 J5
Underdown Rd *STHW* BN42 .... 201 H3
Underhill *UCK* TN22 .... 67 H6
Underhill La *HPPT/KEY* BN6 .... 149 K3
Under Rd *HAIL* BN27 .... 162 C3
Union Cl *HAIL* BN27 .... 189 G1
Union Rd *ROTT* BN2 .... 7 D3
Union St *BRI* BN1 .... 6 C5 🔢
   STLEO TN38 .... 4 A5 🔢
Upland Rd *EDN/EASTW* BN20 .... 229 G8
Uplands Cl *BEXW* TN39 .... 194 E5
   UCK TN22 .... 95 J2
Uplands Pk *HTHF* TN21 .... 100 E2
Uplands Rd *BRI* BN1 .... 204 D1
Upper Abbey Rd *ROTT* BN2 .... 7 F6
Upper Av *EAST* BN21 .... 10 C3

Upper Bannings Rd *ROTT* BN2 .... 207 H8
Upper Bedford St *ROTT* BN2 .... 7 E6
Upper Belgrave Rd *SEAF* BN25 ...... 225 G6
Upper Bevendean Av *ROTT* BN2 .... 205 F2
Upper Broomgrove Rd *HAS* TN34 ..... 5 F1
Upper Carlisle Rd
   EDN/EASTW BN20 .... 236 C3
Upper Chalvington Pl *ROTT* BN2 ... 205 F6
Upper Church Rd *SLVH* TN37 .... 169 J7
Upper Chyngton Gdns
   SEAF BN25 .... 225 J6 🔢
Upper Clarence Rd *SLVH* TN37 .... 4 A2
Upper Cl *FROW* RH18 .... 35 K1
Upper Cumberland Wk *RTW* TN1..... 30 B2
The Upper Dr *HOVE* BN3 .... 203 H3
Upper Duke's Dr
   EDN/EASTW BN20 .... 236 D4
Upper Dunstan Rd
   SBGH/RUST TN4 .... 20 B5
Upper Gardner St *BRI* BN1 .... 6 C4 🔢
Upper Glen Rd *SLVH* TN37 .... 169 H6
Upper Gloucester Rd *BRI* BN1 ..... 6 B4 🔢
Upper Greenwoods La
   HTHF TN21 .... 101 H5
Upper Grosvenor Rd
   SBGH/RUST TN4 .... 20 B6
Upper Hamilton Rd *BRI* BN1 .... 6 A2
Upper Hollingdean Rd *BRI* BN1 .... 7 D1
Upper Horsebridge Rd *HAIL* BN27 .. 161 F8
Upper King's Dr
   EDN/EASTW BN20 .... 229 G2
Upper Kingston La *STHW* BN42 ...... 201 G2
Upper Lake *BAT* TN33 .... 136 D7
Upper Lewes Rd *ROTT* BN2 .... 7 D3
Upper Market St *HOVE* BN3 .... 203 J6 🔢
Upper Maze Hl *STLEO* TN38 .... 197 J3
Upper Nellington *RRTW* TN3 .... 19 F7
Upper North St *BRI* BN1 .... 6 B5 🔢
Upper Park Pl *ROTT* BN2 .... 7 D5 🔢
Upper Park Rd *SLVH* TN37 .... 4 A3
Upper Profit *RRTW* TN3 .... 18 E8
Upper Ratton Dr
   EDN/EASTW BN20 .... 229 G3
Upper Rock Gdns *ROTT* BN2 .... 7 D6
Upper St James's St *ROTT* BN2 .... 7 D6
Upper St Johns Rd *BURH* RH15 .... 89 G8
Upper Sea Rd *BEX* TN40 .... 195 J7
Upper Sherwood Rd *SEAF* BN25 .... 225 G7
Upper Shoreham Rd *SHOR* BN43 ... 200 B3
   STHW BN42 .... 201 G2
Upper South St *SLVH* TN37 .... 4 A3 🔢
Upper Station Rd *HTHF* TN21 .... 100 A4
Upper Stephens *RRTW* TN3............... 18 E8
Upper Stoneham *RING/NEW* BN8 ...... 3 F1
Upper St *EDN/EASTW* BN20 .... 235 F3
Upper Sudeley St *ROTT* BN2 .... 7 F6 🔢
Upperton Gdns *EAST* BN21 .... 10 B4
Upperton La *EAST* BN21 .... 10 B4
Upperton Rd *EAST* BN21 .... 10 A3
Upper Valley Rd *NEWHV* BN9 .... 8 B4
Upper Wellington Rd *ROTT* BN2 .... 7 E3
Upper Winfield Av *BRI* BN1 .... 178 A5
Upper Wish Hl *EDN/EASTW* BN20 ... 229 C3
Upton Av *STHW* BN42 .... 201 H2
Upton Quarry *RRTW* TN3 .... 18 D8 🔢
Upwick Rd *EDN/EASTW* BN20 .... 229 H8

V

Vale Av *BRI* BN1 .... 177 K4
   RTW TN1 .... 20 A8 🔢
   SBGH/RUST TN4 .... 19 K2
Valebridge Cl *BURH* RH15 .... 89 J5 🔢
Valebridge Dr *BURH* RH15 .... 89 J6 🔢
Valebridge Rd *BURH* RH15 .... 89 J6
Vale Cl *SEAF* BN25 .... 225 H1
Vale Gdns *PTSD* BN41 .... 202 A4
Valence Rd *LEW* BN7 .... 2 B4
Valentine Dr *BURH* RH15 .... 88 E7
Valerie Cl *PTSD* BN41 .... 202 A1
Vale Rd *BAT* TN33 .... 136 B6
   HWH RH16 .... 89 K1
   MAYF TN20 .... 72 B1
   PTSD BN41 .... 202 B4
   ROTT BN2 .... 207 G8
   RTW TN1 .... 20 A8
   SBGH/RUST TN4 .... 19 K2
   SEAF BN25 .... 225 G7
   SLVH TN37 .... 4 A2
The Vale *ROTT* BN2 .... 206 B6
Vale View Rd *HTHF* TN21 .... 100 B5 🔢
Vallance Cl *BURH* RH15 .... 88 E7
Vallance Gdns *HOVE* BN3 .... 203 F5
Vallance Rd *HOVE* BN3 .... 203 F5
Valley Cl *BRI* BN1 .... 177 H7
   NEWHV BN9 .... 8 B2
Valley Dene *NEWHV* BN9 .... 8 B3
Valley Dr *BRI* BN1 .... 177 H7
   SEAF BN25 .... 225 H6
Valley Ri *SEAF* BN25 .... 225 G7
Valley Rd *CROW* TN6 .... 53 H2
   LEW BN7 .... 2 A5

Valley Side Rd *HAS* TN34 .... 171 H8
Valley Vw *SBGH/RUST* TN4 .... 20 A1
Valley View Cl *CROW* TN6 .... 53 H2
Val Prinseps Rd *PEV* BN24 .... 217 K7
Vanguard Wy *CROW* TN6 .... 52 B4
   EGRIN RH19 .... 13 K6
   LING RH7 .... 14 A3
   POLE BN26 .... 212 C1
   RING/NEW BN8 .... 159 J1
   SEAF BN25 .... 226 D7
   SEAF BN25 .... 232 C2
   UCK TN22 .... 68 E3
   UCK TN22 .... 97 J8
Varndean Cl *BRI* BN1 .... 177 K8
Varndean Dr *BRI* BN1 .... 177 K8
Varndean Gdns *BRI* BN1 .... 177 K8
Varndean Holt *BRI* BN1 .... 178 A8
Varndean Rd *BRI* BN1 .... 177 K8
Vega Cl *HAIL* BN27 .... 189 J4
Ventnor Cl *LGNY* BN23 .... 216 C7
Ventnor Vis *HOVE* BN3 .... 203 G5
Venture Cl *BEX* TN40 .... 196 A7
Verbania Wy *EGRIN* RH19 .... 23 F2
Verdant Cl *SLVH* TN37 .... 4 B3
Vere Rd *BRI* BN1 .... 6 G2
Vermont Rd *SBGH/RUST* TN4 .... 19 G7 🔢
Vernon Av *PEAHV* BN10 .... 222 C5
   ROTT BN2 .... 205 K2
Vernon Cl *LGNY* BN23 .... 231 F4 🔢
Vernon Rd *RTW* TN1 .... 20 C5
   UCK TN22 .... 95 K5
Vernons Rd *RING/NEW* BN8 .... 93 G4
Vernon St *BRI* BN1 .... 6 A5
Veronica Wy *ROTT* BN2 .... 7 D6
Viaduct Rd *BRI* BN1 .... 6 C3
   ROTT BN2 .... 7 D3
Vian Av *LGNY* BN23 .... 231 G5
Vicarage Cl *NEWHV* BN9 .... 223 K1 🔢
   RING/NEW BN8 .... 155 H6
   SEAF BN25 .... 225 G8
Vicarage Dr *EDN/EASTW* BN20 ...... 229 J8
Vicarage La *BUR/ETCH* TN19 .... 74 C8
   EDN/EASTW BN20 .... 229 J8 🔢
   HAIL BN27 .... 161 F5
   HAIL BN27 .... 189 H3
   RHAS TN35 .... 139 F8
   ROTT BN2 .... 220 C2 🔢
Vicarage Ter *ROTT* BN2 .... 220 C2 🔢
Vicarage Wy *BUR/ETCH* TN19 .... 62 A8
   RING/NEW BN8 .... 155 J6
Victor Cl *SEAF* BN25 .... 224 E6
Victoria Av *BURH* RH15 .... 88 E8 🔢
   PEAHV BN10 .... 222 B5
   RHAS TN35 .... 171 F7
Victoria Cl *BURH* RH15 .... 88 E8 🔢
   BURH RH15 .... 119 F1
   POLE BN26 .... 214 E4
Victoria Dr *EAST* BN21 .... 229 H6
   EDN/EASTW BN20 .... 229 G5
Victoria Gdns *BURH* RH15 .... 118 E1
   EDN/EASTW BN20 .... 229 H7 🔢
Victoria Gv *HOVE* BN3 .... 203 H5 🔢
Victoria Pl *BRI* BN1 .... 6 A4 🔢
Victoria Rd *BEXW* TN39 .... 195 C7
   BRI BN1 .... 6 A4
   BURH RH15 .... 118 E1
   CROW TN6 .... 54 A3
   EDN/EASTW BN20 .... 229 G6 🔢
   HAIL BN27 .... 163 J6
   HAIL BN27 .... 189 H4
   MAYF TN20 .... 56 A8
   POLE BN26 .... 214 E4
   PTSD BN41 .... 202 A3
   RTW TN1 .... 20 B7 🔢
   SBGH/RUST TN4 .... 19 J2
   SHOR BN43 .... 200 B4
   SLVH TN37 .... 4 B5 🔢
   STHW BN42 .... 201 C4
Victoria St *BRI* BN1 .... 6 A4
Victoria Wy *BURH* RH15 .... 119 F1
   EGRIN RH19 .... 13 G6
   WSEA TN36 .... 143 G6
Victory Ms *ROTT* BN2 .... 205 H8
View Bank *RHAS* TN35 .... 199 C1
View Rd *PEAHV* BN10 .... 222 B3
View Ter *LING* RH7 .... 12 E3
Viking Cl *SEAF* BN25 .... 224 B5
The Village Barn *BRI* BN1 .... 177 K4
Village Ms *BEXW* TN39 .... 194 B7
The Village *EDN/EASTW* BN20 ..... 236 D3
Village Wy *BRI* BN1 .... 179 K5
Villa Rd *SLVH* TN37 .... 5 J4
Villiers Cl *ROTT* BN2 .... 206 B3
Vincent Cl *LGNY* BN23 .... 231 G4 🔢
Vinehall Cl *HAS* TN34 .... 170 D6

Vinehall Rd *RBTBR* TN32 .... 106 E5
The Vineries *BURH* RH15 .... 89 K8
  LGNY BN23 .... 230 E1 🔟
Vines Cross Rd *HTHF* TN21 .... 130 A3
  ROTT BN2 .... 205 G4
Vine Sq *LW/ROSE* BN22 .... 11 F1
Vine St *BRI* BN1 .... 6 C4 🔟
Vineyard La *WADH* TN5 .... 59 K1
Virgin's Cft *BAT* TN33 .... 136 D5
Virgin's La *BAT* TN33 .... 136 D5

W

Wade Cl *LGNY* BN23 .... 231 G4
Wadhurst Cl *LW/ROSE* BN22 .... 230 A1
  SLVH TN37 .... 169 J6
Wadhurst La *BAT* TN33 .... 135 J6
Wadhurst Ri *ROTT* BN2 .... 205 G6
Wadhurst Rd *CROW* TN6 .... 43 F8
  RRTW TN3 .... 42 C2
  WADH TN5 .... 43 F3
Wadlands Brook Rd *EGRIN* RH19 .... 12 B6
Wagg Cl *EGRIN* RH19 .... 22 F2
Waghorns La *UCK* TN22 .... 70 A6
Wainwright Cl *STLEO* TN38 .... 168 E8
Wainwright Rd *BEXW* TN39 .... 195 G7
Wainwright's La *WADH* TN5 .... 3 D3
Waites La *RHAS* TN35 .... 172 D6
Wakefield Rd *ROTT* BN2 .... 7 D2
Waldegrave Rd *BRI* BN1 .... 204 A1
Waldegrave St *HAS* TN34 .... 5 D4 🔟
Waldron Av *BRI* BN1 .... 178 E5
Waldron Cl *LW/ROSE* BN22 .... 229 J3
Waldron Rd *RING/NEW* BN8 .... 127 J6
Waldron Thorns *HTHF* TN21 .... 100 A5
Waldshut Rd *LEW* BN7 .... 2 A2
Walesbeech Rd *ROTT* BN2 .... 221 C3
Walker Cl *LGNY* BN23 .... 231 G4
Wallace Cl *RTWE/PEM* TN2 .... 30 A3
Wallands Crs *LEW* BN7 .... 2 C3
The Walled Gdn *UCK* TN22 .... 67 K7 🔟
Wallers *RRTW* TN3 .... 18 E4
Wall Hill Rd *FROW* RH18 .... 23 H6
Wallis Av *LGNY* BN23 .... 231 G4
Wallis Cl *CROW* TN6 .... 53 J2 🔟
Wallis Pl *LGNY* BN23 .... 231 F3
Wallis Wy *BURH* RH15 .... 88 E7 🔟
Wallsend Rd *PEV* BN24 .... 217 J5
Walmer Crs *ROTT* BN2 .... 205 H2
Walmer Rd *SEAF* BN25 .... 225 H7
Walnut Cl *BRI* BN1 .... 177 K8
  HTHF TN21 .... 100 B5
Walnut Tree Wk
  EDN/EASTW BN20 .... 229 G3
Walnut Wk *POLE* BN26 .... 215 F5
Walnut Wy *RTWE/PEM* TN2 .... 20 D3
Walpole Rd *ROTT* BN2 .... 7 E6
Walpole Ter *ROTT* BN2 .... 7 F5
Walshes Rd *CROW* TN6 .... 53 J4
Walsingham Cl *LW/ROSE* BN22 ... 215 J8 🔟
Walsingham Rd *HOVE* BN3 .... 202 E5
Walters Green Rd *RTON* TN11 ..... 17 G5
Walton Bank *BRI* BN1 .... 179 F6
Walton Cl *BEX* TN40 .... 196 B5
Walton Pk *BEXW* TN39 .... 194 E7
Wanderdown Cl *ROTT* BN2 .... 206 B7
Wanderdown Dr *ROTT* BN2 .... 206 B7
Wanderdown Rd *ROTT* BN2 .... 206 A7
Wanderdown Wy *ROTT* BN2 ..... 206 B7
Wannock Av *EDN/EASTW* BN20 . 214 E8
Wannock Cl *BEX* TN40 .... 196 B5
Wannock Gdns *EDN/EASTW* BN20 . 214 E8
  POLE BN26 .... 214 E8
Wannock La *EDN/EASTW* BN20 .. 214 E8
Wannock La *LW/ROSE* BN22 ...... 11 F2
  POLE BN26 .... 214 E6
Warbleton Cl *ROTT* BN2 .... 205 F6
Warburton Cl *EAST* BN21 .... 229 H3 🔟
  EGRIN RH19 .... 22 E2 🔟
  UCK TN22 .... 95 K3 🔟
Ward Cl *WADH* TN5 .... 44 A6
Wardsbrook Rd *WADH* TN5 ...... 60 B4
Ward's La *WADH* TN5 .... 45 G8
Ward Wy *BEXW* TN39 .... 195 F5
Warelands *BURH* RH15 .... 119 F2
Warenne Rd *HOVE* BN3 .... 176 B8
Wares Fld *UCK* TN22 .... 95 K7
Wares Rd *UCK* TN22 .... 95 K7
Warleigh Rd *BRI* BN1 .... 6 C2
Warmdene Av *BRI* BN1 .... 178 A5 🔟
Warmdene Cl *BRI* BN1 .... 178 A6 🔟
Warmdene Rd *BRI* BN1 .... 178 A5
Warmdene Wy *BRI* BN1 .... 178 A5
Warminster Rd *PEV* BN24 .... 218 A6
Warnham Ri *BRI* BN1 .... 178 B6
Warren Av *ROTT* BN2 .... 205 K2
Warren Cl *CROW* TN6 .... 53 F1
  EDN/EASTW BN20 .... 235 G2
  EDN/EASTW BN20 .... 236 C3
  HTHF TN21 .... 98 C5
  LEW BN7 .... 2 B5

Warrenwood *RING/NEW* BN8 ..... 92 E3
Warr Gn *LEW* BN7 .... 2 B2
Warrior Cl *PTSD* BN41 .... 202 A1
Warrior Gdns *SLVH* TN37 .... 4 A5
Warrior Sq *SLVH* TN37 .... 4 A5
Warrs Hill La *RING/NEW* BN8 .... 92 C2
Wartling Cl *STLEO* TN38 .... 169 G8
Wartling Dr *BEXW* TN39 .... 193 J6
Wartling Rd *HAIL* BN27 .... 192 A3
  LW/ROSE BN22 .... 11 E2
Warwick Cl *HAIL* BN27 .... 161 H8 🔟
Warwick Pk *RTWE/PEM* TN2 .... 30 D2
Warwick Rd *BEXW* TN39 .... 194 E6
  RTW TN1 .... 30 A1
  SEAF BN25 .... 225 F8 🔟
Washington Av *STLEO* TN38 .... 169 G5
Washington St *ROTT* BN2 .... 7 D4
Washwell La *WADH* TN5 .... 44 B8
Watchbell La *RYE* TN31 .... 113 J6 🔟
Watchbell St *RYE* TN31 .... 113 H6
Waterdown Rd *SBGH/RUST* TN4 .. 29 H2
Waterdyke Av *STHW* BN42 .... 201 H4 🔟
Waterfield *RTWE/PEM* TN2 ...... 30 A4
Waterford Cl *PEAHV* BN10 .... 222 B1
Watergate *BEXW* TN39 .... 195 G3
Watergate La *LEW* BN7 .... 3 D5 🔟
Waterhall Rd *BRI* BN1 .... 177 H5
Waterloo Cl *STLEO* TN38 .... 169 G4
Waterloo Pl *LEW* BN7 .... 3 D4 🔟
Waterloo Sq *POLE* BN26 .... 212 D8
Waterloo St *HOVE* BN3 .... 203 J6
Watermen's Cl *HAS* TN34 .... 4 C1
Watermill Cl *BEXW* TN39 .... 195 G3
  POLE BN26 .... 215 F6
Watermill Dr *STLEO* TN38 .... 168 E8
Watermill La *BEXW* TN39 .... 195 G3
  RHAS TN35 .... 172 B2
  RYE TN31 .... 88 B8
Waters Cottages *WADH* TN5 ..... 44 C7
Waterside *EGRIN* RH19 .... 23 F2
Waterside *HAS* TN34 .... 5 F1
Waterworks Rd *HAS* TN34 .... 5 D4
  LW/ROSE BN22 .... 10 C3
Watling Cl *STHW* BN42 .... 201 H4 🔟
Wattle's Wish *BAT* TN33 .... 136 C5
Watts Cl *WADH* TN5 .... 44 B7
Watts La *EAST* BN21 .... 10 A3
Watts' Palace La *RYE* TN31 .... 109 F3
Waverley Crs *BRI* BN1 .... 7 D1
Waverley Dr *RTWE/PEM* TN2 ... 21 F5
Waverley Rd *PEV* BN24 .... 218 A6
Wayfaring Down *POLE* BN26 .... 214 C8
Wayfield Av *HOVE* BN3 .... 202 D2
Wayfield Cl *HOVE* BN3 .... 202 E2 🔟
Wayford Cl *LGNY* BN23 .... 230 E1 🔟
Wayland Av *BRI* BN1 .... 177 H7
Wayland Hts *BRI* BN1 .... 177 H7
Wayside *BRI* BN1 .... 177 J5
  EDN/EASTW BN20 .... 235 F1
Wayside Wk *HTHF* TN21 .... 99 K5
Weald Cl *HOVE* BN3 .... 202 E3
Weald Cl *LEW* BN7 .... 2 C3 🔟
  RING/NEW BN8 .... 123 J7 🔟
Weald Dyke *SHOR* BN43 .... 200 C5
Wealden Cl *CROW* TN6 .... 39 H8
Wealden Cl *LW/ROSE* BN22 .... 229 H1
Wealden Pk *LW/ROSE* BN22 ... 229 H1
Wealden Wy *BEXW* TN39 .... 194 B5
Weald Ri *HWH* RH16 .... 90 A2
Weald Rd *BURH* RH15 .... 88 E3 🔟
The Weald *EGRIN* RH19 .... 12 D8
Weald Vw *RBTBR* TN32 .... 108 A2
  RING/NEW BN8 .... 123 H7
  WADH TN5 .... 44 B5
Wealdview Rd *HTHF* TN21 ...... 99 J4
Wealdway *CROW* TN6 .... 51 J1
  EDN/EASTW BN20 .... 228 D2
  HAIL BN27 .... 160 E4
  HRTF TN7 .... 38 C1
  HTHF TN21 .... 160 D3
  POLE BN26 .... 213 H7
  POLE BN26 .... 228 A1
  RING/NEW BN8 .... 127 H4

RRTW TN3 .... 18 B5
  UCK TN22 .... 67 J2
  UCK TN22 .... 97 G7
Weare Rd *SBGH/RUST* TN4 .... 20 C3
Weatherby Cl *EAST* BN21 .... 229 H3
Weavers Cl *BURH* RH15 .... 119 K2
Weavers La *POLE* BN26 .... 212 C5
Weavers Rock La *HTHF* TN21 ... 100 C6
Wedderburn Rd
  EDN/EASTW BN20 .... 229 G3
Week La *RING/NEW* BN8 .... 183 J1
Welbeck Av *HOVE* BN3 .... 202 D5
  SBGH/RUST TN4 .... 20 C3
  STLEO TN38 .... 197 H4 🔟
Welbeck Cl *BURH* RH15 .... 89 K7
  LW/ROSE BN22 .... 215 J8 🔟
Welbeck Dr *BURH* RH15 .... 89 J6
Welesmere Rd *ROTT* BN2 ..... 206 D8
Welland Cl *STHW* BN42 .... 53 J4
Wellcombe Crs *EDN/EASTW* BN20 .. 236 D4
Weller Rd *SBGH/RUST* TN4 .... 19 G7
Wellesley Cl *BEXW* TN39 ...... 194 C8
  CROW TN6 .... 53 F2
Wellesley Rd *EAST* BN21 ...... 10 C4 🔟
Wellfield *EGRIN* RH19 .... 23 G4
Wellgreen La *LEW* BN7 .... 181 J6
Wellhouse La *BURH* RH15 ..... 119 H4
Well House Pl *LEW* BN7 .... 2 C5 🔟
  LEW BN7 .... 2 C4 🔟
Wellingham La *RING/NEW* BN8 .. 155 F4
Wellington Ms *HAS* TN34 ..... 5 D4 🔟
Wellington Pk *SEAF* BN25 .... 225 H7
Wellington Pl *HAS* TN34 ...... 5 D5 🔟
Wellington Rd *HAS* TN34 ...... 5 E4
  NEWHV BN9 .... 223 K1
  PEAHV BN10 .... 222 D5 🔟
  PTSD BN41 .... 202 A5
  ROTT BN2 .... 7 D3
Wellington Sq *HAS* TN34 ..... 5 D4 🔟
Wellington St *LEW* BN7 .... 3 D4 🔟
  ROTT BN2 .... 7 E3
Wellington Town Rd *EGRIN* RH19 ... 12 B8
Wellis Gdns *STLEO* TN38 ...... 197 H3
Wellsbourne Rd *PEV* BN24 .... 216 B6
Wells Cl *EDN/EASTW* BN20 ... 236 C3 🔟
  LEW BN7 .... 121 C5
  RTW TN1 .... 20 A8 🔟
Wells Lea *EGRIN* RH19 .... 12 B8
Wells Meadow *EGRIN* RH19 ... 12 B8 🔟
Wendale Dr *PEAHV* BN10 ...... 222 C1
Wenthill Cl *EDN/EASTW* BN20 .. 235 F2
Went Hill Gdns *LW/ROSE* BN22 .. 215 G8
Went Hill Pk *SEAF* BN25 ...... 225 H8 🔟
Went La *EDN/EASTW* BN20 .... 235 G2 🔟
Went Wy *EDN/EASTW* BN20 .. 235 F2
Wentworth Cl *BEX* TN40 ...... 196 A6
  HAIL BN27 .... 188 E2
Wentworth St *ROTT* BN2 ..... 7 D6 🔟
Wentworth Wy *STLEO* TN38 .. 197 G3
Westaway Dr *BEXW* TN39 .... 195 F7
West Beeches Rd *CROW* TN6 .. 53 J1
Westbourne Gdns *HOVE* BN3 .. 203 F5
Westbourne Pl *HOVE* BN3 .... 203 F5
Westbourne St *HOVE* BN3 .... 203 F4
Westbourne Vls *HOVE* BN3 ... 202 E5
Westbrook La *RHAS* TN35 ..... 139 G6
Westbrook Wy *STHW* BN42 ... 201 J4
West Cl *POLE* BN26 .... 212 C6
  POLE BN26 .... 215 C4
Westcourt Dr *BEXW* TN39 .... 194 E8
Westdean Av *NEWHV* BN9 .... 8 A5
West Dean Ri *SEAF* BN25 ..... 225 H7
Westdene Cl *SLVH* TN37 ...... 169 K5 🔟
Westdene Dr *BRI* BN1 .... 177 H6
Westdown La *BUR/ETCH* TN19 .. 74 C4
West Down Rd *BEXW* TN39 ... 195 F6
Westdown Rd *SEAF* BN25 .... 224 E7
West Dr *ROTT* BN2 .... 7 D5
West End *HAIL* BN27 .... 163 F5
Westergate Rd *ROTT* BN2 .... 179 F7
Westerham Rd *LGNY* BN23 ... 230 E1
Westerleigh Cl *STLEO* TN38 .. 197 H3
Western Av *HAWK* TN18 ...... 63 F1
  POLE BN26 .... 215 C5
Western Gdns *CROW* TN6 .... 54 B4
Western Rd *BEX* TN40 .... 195 H8
  BRI BN1 .... 6 A5
  BURH RH15 .... 88 E8
  CROW TN6 .... 54 A4
  HAIL BN27 .... 189 F3
  HAWK TN18 .... 63 F1
  LEW BN7 .... 2 B4
  LW/ROSE BN22 .... 11 D3
  NEWHV BN9 .... 8 C4
  RING/NEW BN8 .... 93 G4
  RTW TN1 .... 20 C6
  SBGH/RUST TN4 .... 19 G2
  SHOR BN43 .... 200 B4
  SLVH TN37 .... 4 A5
  WADH TN5 .... 44 B5
Western St *BRI* BN1 .... 6 A5 🔟
Western Ter *BRI* BN1 .... 6 A5 🔟
Westfield Av *ROTT* BN2 ...... 207 G8
Westfield Av North *ROTT* BN2 .. 207 G8
Westfield Av South *ROTT* BN2 .. 207 G8

Westfield Cl *BRI* BN1 .... **178** B7
  MAYF TN20 .... **71** F5
  POLE BN26 .... **215** F4
Westfield Dr *POLE* BN26 .... **215** F4 ⑥
Westfield Crs *BRI* BN1 .... **178** B6
Westfield La *SLVH* TN37 .... **169** J4
Westfield Ri *ROTT* BN2 .... **207** G8
Westfield Rd *EAST* BN23 .... **229** J5
West Furlong La *HPPT/KEY* BN6 .... **118** A6
West Ga *LEW* BN7 .... **121** G5
Westgate St *LEW* BN7 .... **2** C5 ⑥
Westham Cl *BEXW* TN39 .... **194** D8 ⑥
Westham Dr *PEV* BN24 .... **218** C5
West Hl *EGRIN* RH19 .... **12** C5
  EGRIN RH19 .... **22** B3
Westhill Dr *BURH* RH15 .... **88** E8
West Hill Pl *BRI* BN1 .... **6** B4
West Hill Rd *BRI* BN1 .... **6** B4
  STLEO TN38 .... **197** H5
West Hill St *BRI* BN1 .... **6** B4
West Hoathly Rd *EGRIN* RH19 .... **22** A3
  EGRIN RH19 .... **22** B3
West Leigh *EGRIN* RH19 .... **22** D4
Westmeston Av *ROTT* BN2 .... **220** E1
Westminster Cl *LW/ROSE* BN22 .... **215** J8
Westminster Crs *HAS* TN34 .... **170** D7
Westmoreland Cl *STLEO* TN38 .... **169** G8
Westmount Cl *STHW* BN42 .... **201** G3 ⑥
West Park Av *SBGH/RUST* TN4 .... **20** A2
West Park Crs *BURH* RH15 .... **88** D7
Westpoint *RING/NEW* BN8 .... **93** G4
West Rd *POY/PYE* BN45 .... **148** C5
  PTSD BN41 .... **201** K4
West St *BRI* BN1 .... **6** B5
  BURH RH15 .... **88** E7
  EAST BN21 .... **10** B5
  EGRIN RH19 .... **22** C3
  HAS TN34 .... **5** E5
  HPPT/KEY BN6 .... **119** J8
  LING RH7 .... **12** E2
  MAYF TN20 .... **72** A2
  POLE BN26 .... **212** C7
  PTSD BN41 .... **202** A4
  ROTT BN2 .... **220** C2
  RYE TN31 .... **113** J6
  SEAF BN25 .... **232** A1 ⑥
  SHOR BN43 .... **200** B4
West Street La *HTHF* TN21 .... **129** K1
  HAIL BN27 .... **163** F5
West Undercliff *RYE* TN31 .... **113** G6
West Vw *HAS* TN34 .... **5** F7
  SEAF BN25 .... **232** A1
West View Gdns *EGRIN* RH19 .... **22** C3
Westville Rd *BEXW* TN39 .... **195** F7
West Wy *HOVE* BN3 .... **202** C1
Westway *RTWE/PEM* TN2 .... **20** A3
Westway Cl *PTSD* BN41 .... **175** H7 ⑥
Westway Gdns *PTSD* BN41 .... **175** H7
Westwood Rd *SBGH/RUST* TN4 .... **19** F6
Wharf Rd *EAST* BN21 .... **10** B4 ⑥
Whatlington Rd *BAT* TN33 .... **136** E5
Whatlington Wy *STLEO* TN38 .... **196** E1
Wheatfield Ct *SLVH* TN37 .... **169** K6 ⑥
Wheatfield Wy *ROTT* BN2 .... **179** G8
Wheatland Cl *PEAHV* BN10 .... **222** A1 ⑥
Wheatsheaf Cl *BURH* RH15 .... **88** E6
Wheatsheaf Gdns *LEW* BN7 .... **3** E3
Wheelers La *UCK* TN22 .... **70** B5
Wheel La *RHAS* TN35 .... **139** F8
Wheelwright Cl *LW/ROSE* BN22 .... **215** J7
Wheelwright La *BURH* RH15 .... **119** K2
Whichelo Pl *ROTT* BN2 .... **7** E4
Whin Croft Pk *CROW* TN6 .... **53** F3
Whippingham Rd *ROTT* BN2 .... **7** E2
Whippingham St *ROTT* BN2 .... **7** E2 ⑥
Whipping Post La *ROTT* BN2 .... **220** C2 ⑥
Whitbread Cl *HWY* BN23 .... **216** C7 ⑥
White Bear Pas
  SBGH/RUST TN4 .... **30** A1 ⑥
Whitebread La *RYE* TN31 .... **82** B3
Whitecross St *BRI* BN1 .... **6** C4 ⑥
Whitefield Rd *SBGH/RUST* TN4 .... **20** A5
Whitefriars Rd *HAS* TN34 .... **5** E3
Whitegate St *SBGH/RUST* TN4 .... **19** K3
Whitegates *RING/NEW* BN8 .... **122** B4 ⑥
Whitegates La *WADH* TN5 .... **43** J3
Whitehawk Cl *ROTT* BN2 .... **205** F5
Whitehawk Crs *ROTT* BN2 .... **205** F6
Whitehawk Hill Rd *ROTT* BN2 .... **7** F6
Whitehawk Rd *ROTT* BN2 .... **205** F5
Whitehawk Wy *ROTT* BN2 .... **205** G5
White Hill Av *BEXW* TN39 .... **194** D7
Whitehill Cl *CROW* TN6 .... **53** H2
White Hill Dr *BEXW* TN39 .... **194** D7
Whitehill Rd *CROW* TN6 .... **53** H3
Whitehouse Av *BEXW* TN39 .... **195** G4
Whitehouse La *HTHF* TN21 .... **88** E8
Whitelot Cl *STHW* BN42 .... **201** H2
Whitelot Wy *STHW* BN42 .... **201** H1
White Rock Gdns *HAS* TN34 .... **4** C5 ⑥
White Rock Rd *SLVH* TN37 .... **4** C5
White's Cl *HPPT/KEY* BN6 .... **118** C4
White's La *HAWK* TN18 .... **63** H1

White St *ROTT* BN2 .... **7** D5 ⑭
Whitethorn Dr *BRI* BN1 .... **177** G7
White Wy *LEW* BN7 .... **208** A2
  POLE BN26 .... **226** C2
Whiteway Cl *SEAF* BN25 .... **225** F5
Whiteway La *ROTT* BN2 .... **220** D1
Whitfeld La *RING/NEW* BN8 .... **154** B5
Whitley Rd *LW/ROSE* BN22 .... **11** D2
Whittingehame Gdns *BRI* BN1 .... **178** A3
Whittington's Wy *HAS* TN34 .... **170** E7
Whittlewood Cl *STLEO* TN38 .... **197** F1
Whybourne Crest *RTWE/PEM* TN2 .... **30** D2
Whydown Hl *BAT* TN33 .... **138** A5
Whydown Rd *BEXW* TN39 .... **194** A3
The Wickets *BURH* RH15 .... **89** F6
Wickham Av *BEXW* TN39 .... **195** G8
Wickham Dr *HPPT/KEY* BN6 .... **118** B6
Wickham Gdns *SBGH/RUST* TN4 .... **19** H6
Wickham Hl *HPPT/KEY* BN6 .... **118** C7
Wickham La *RING/NEW* BN8 .... **153** H1
Wickham Rock La *WSEA* TN36 .... **142** D6
Wickhurst Cl *PTSD* BN41 .... **201** J1
Wickhurst Ri *PTSD* BN41 .... **175** J8
Wickhurst Rd *PTSD* BN41 .... **201** J1
Wicklands Av *ROTT* BN2 .... **221** G2
Wick St *RING/NEW* BN8 .... **184** D6
Widbury Cl *RRTW* TN3 .... **18** D3 ⑥
Widdicombe Wy *ROTT* BN2 .... **205** F1
Wigmore Cl *BRI* BN1 .... **7** D1
Wilbury Av *HOVE* BN3 .... **203** H3
Wilbury Crs *HOVE* BN3 .... **203** H3
Wilbury Gdns *HOVE* BN3 .... **203** H3
Wilbury Gv *HOVE* BN3 .... **203** H5
Wilbury Rd *HOVE* BN3 .... **203** H4
Wilbury Vls *HOVE* BN3 .... **203** H4
Wilbury Av *STHW* BN42 .... **201** J3
Wilderness Gdns *RYE* TN31 .... **81** J4
Wilderness La *UCK* TN22 .... **70** A7
Wilderness Pk *CROW* TN6 .... **53** G1
Wilderness Ri *EGRIN* RH19 .... **12** E6
Wilderness Rd *HPPT/KEY* BN6 .... **118** A5
Wilderwick Rd *EGRIN* RH19 .... **12** E6
Wild Park Cl *ROTT* BN2 .... **179** F8
Wildwood *LGNY* BN23 .... **216** D7 ⑦
Wilfrid Rd *HOVE* BN3 .... **203** C3
Wilkinson Cl *ROTT* BN2 .... **206** C8
Wilkinson Wy *SEAF* BN25 .... **225** F7
Wilkins Wy *BEX* TN40 .... **196** A5
Willard Cl *LW/ROSE* BN22 .... **10** C1
Willetts Fld *RING/NEW* BN8 .... **159** H3
Willetts La *RRTW* TN3 .... **16** E7
William Rd *STLEO* TN38 .... **197** F4
Williams Rd *SHOR* BN43 .... **200** E3
William St *PTSD* BN41 .... **202** A4
  ROTT BN2 .... **6** C5 ⑭
  SBGH/RUST TN4 .... **20** A6
Willingdon Av *BEXW* TN39 .... **195** F7
  STLEO TN38 .... **169** H6
Willingdon Cl *EDN/EASTW* BN20 .... **229** G2 ⑥
  STLEO TN38 .... **169** H6
Willingdon Ct
  EDN/EASTW BN20 .... **215** F8 ⑥
Willingdon Dro *LGNY* BN23 .... **230** C2
  LW/ROSE BN22 .... **230** B2
Willingdon La *POLE* BN26 .... **228** B4
Willingdon Park Dr
  LW/ROSE BN22 .... **229** J1
Willingdon Rd *EAST* BN21 .... **229** H5 ⑥
  LW/ROSE BN22 .... **229** H2
  ROTT BN2 .... **205** F2
Willingdon Wy *LW/ROSE* BN22 .... **229** G3 ⑥
  STLEO TN38 .... **169** H6 ⑥
Willingford La *BUR/ETCH* TN19 .... **102** E1
Willoughby Crs *LW/ROSE* BN22 .... **11** E1
Willow Av *HAIL* BN27 .... **189** C2
Willow Bank *RBTBR* TN32 .... **78** B8
Willowbed Wk *HAS* TN34 .... **170** B6
Willowbrook Wy
  HPPT/KEY BN6 .... **119** G8 ⑥
Willow Cl *BUR/ETCH* TN19 .... **77** F3
  EGRIN RH19 .... **12** B8
  ROTT BN2 .... **100** B3
Willow Dr *BEXW* TN39 .... **194** B6
  POLE BN26 .... **215** F6
  SEAF BN25 .... **225** K8
Willow End *HAS* TN34 .... **170** C7
Willowfield Rd *LW/ROSE* BN22 .... **11** D3 ⑥
Willowfield Sq *LW/ROSE* BN22 .... **11** D4 ⑥
Willow La *WSEA* TN36 .... **143** H5
Willowmead *CROW* TN6 .... **53** G3
Willow Md *EGRIN* RH19 .... **22** D3
Willow Ms *RBTBR* TN32 .... **78** B8 ⑥
Willows Ri *UCK* TN22 .... **96** D6
The Willows *BURH* RH15 .... **89** H6
  RING/NEW BN8 .... **123** J6
Willow Stream Cl *RHAS* TN35 .... **140** C8
Willow Tree Rd *RTWE/PEM* TN2 .... **29** J2
Willow Wk *NEWHV* BN9 .... **8** C2
  RTWE/PEM TN2 .... **20** E3
Willow Wy *HPPT/KEY* BN6 .... **118** C4
Wilman Rd *SBGH/RUST* TN4 .... **20** A4
Wilmington Cl *BRI* BN1 .... **178** B6
  HPPT/KEY BN6 .... **118** B6
Wilmington Gdns *EAST* BN21 .... **10** C6 ⑥
Wilmington Pde *BRI* BN1 .... **178** A6 ⑥

Wilmington Rd *HAS* TN34 .... **5** E1
  NEWHV BN9 .... **8** B4
  SEAF BN25 .... **224** E7
Wilmington Sq *EAST* BN21 .... **10** C6 ⑥
Wilmington St *POLE* BN26 .... **213** J6
Wilmington Wy *BRI* BN1 .... **178** A6
Wilmot Rd *SHOR* BN43 .... **201** F3
Wilson Av *ROTT* BN2 .... **205** G7
  UCK TN22 .... **95** G4
Wilson Gv *UCK* TN22 .... **95** G4
Wilton Av *LW/ROSE* BN22 .... **216** A8
Wilton Rd *BEX* TN40 .... **195** H8
Wiltshire Wy *RTWE/PEM* TN2 .... **20** D4
Winchcombe Rd *LW/ROSE* BN22 .... **10** C3
Winchelsea Cl *SEAF* BN25 .... **225** K6 ⑥
Winchelsea La *RHAS* TN35 .... **171** H6
  RYE TN31 .... **141** K1
Winchelsea Rd *LW/ROSE* BN22 .... **11** F1
  RYE TN31 .... **113** H6
Winchester Rd *HAWK* TN18 .... **63** C1
Winchester St *BRI* BN1 .... **6** C2
Winchester Wy *LW/ROSE* BN22 .... **229** G1
Wincombe Rd *BRI* BN1 .... **203** J2 ⑥
Windermere Crs *LW/ROSE* BN22 .... **11** L2
Winding St *HAS* TN34 .... **5** F4 ⑦
Windlesham Av *HOVE* BN3 .... **6** A4
Windlesham Cl *PTSD* BN41 .... **201** K2
Windlesham Gdns *BRI* BN1 .... **6** A4
  SHOR BN43 .... **200** C3
Windlesham Rd *BRI* BN1 .... **6** A4
  SHOR BN43 .... **200** C3
Windmill Av *HPPT/KEY* BN6 .... **119** F8
Windmill Cl *EAST* BN21 .... **229** H5
  HOVE BN3 .... **202** E1
  HTHF TN21 .... **100** B3
Windmill Dr *BRI* BN1 .... **177** H5
  BURH RH15 .... **89** C7
Windmill Gn *PEV* BN24 .... **216** C6
Windmill La *EDN/EASTW* BN20 .... **234** E2
  EGRIN RH19 .... **12** B8
  EGRIN RH19 .... **23** C4
  WADH TN5 .... **43** K7
  WADH TN5 .... **44** E3
Windmill Pl *POLE* BN26 .... **215** F7
Windmill Rd *POLE* BN26 .... **215** F6
  STHW BN42 .... **201** H2
  STLEO TN38 .... **197** J1
Windmill St *ROTT* BN2 .... **7** D5
  RTWE/PEM TN2 .... **20** C8 ⑥
Windmill Ter *ROTT* BN2 .... **7** D4 ⑥
Windmill Vw *BRI* BN1 .... **178** B5
Windmill Wy *WSEA* TN36 .... **143** H4 ⑥
Windover Crs *LEW* BN7 .... **2** A3
Windover Wy *LW/ROSE* BN22 .... **215** G8 ⑥
Windsor Cl *HOVE* BN3 .... **177** F8
  HWH RH16 .... **90** A1
  SEAF BN25 .... **224** C5
Windsor Ct *CROW* TN6 .... **54** A5
Windsor Pl *CROW* TN6 .... **54** A3
  EGRIN RH19 .... **22** E5 ⑥
Windsor Rd *BEXW* TN39 .... **195** G7
  CROW TN6 .... **54** A3
  HAIL BN27 .... **189** C5
  SLVH TN37 .... **169** J8
Windsor St *BRI* BN1 .... **6** B5 ⑬
Windsor Wy *POLE* BN26 .... **215** F4
  WSEA TN36 .... **143** G7
Windward Quay *LGNY* BN23 .... **231** C3
Wineham Wy *BEX* TN40 .... **196** A7
Winfield Av *BRI* BN1 .... **178** A5
Winfield Cl *BRI* BN1 .... **178** A6 ⑥
  PTSD BN41 .... **175** K7
Wingate Cl *STLEO* TN38 .... **197** H2 ⑥
Wingle Tye Rd *BURH* RH15 .... **119** C3
Winkhurst Wy *BURH* RH15 .... **119** K2
Winkney Rd *LW/ROSE* BN22 .... **216** A8
Winscote Cl *CROW* TN6 .... **53** F2 ⑥
Winston Crs *LGNY* BN23 .... **230** E4 ⑥
Winston Dr *BEXW* TN39 .... **194** D7
Winstone Scott Av *RRTW* TN3 .... **18** C7 ⑥
Winterbourne Cl *HAS* TN34 .... **4** B4
  LEW BN7 .... **2** B5 ⑥
Winterbourne Hollow *LEW* BN7 .... **2** B5
Winterbourne La *LEW* BN7 .... **2** A5
Winterbourne Ms *LEW* BN7 .... **2** B5
Winterton Wy *SHOR* BN43 .... **200** E5
Winton Av *ROTT* BN2 .... **221** F1
Winton St *POLE* BN26 .... **212** C7
Wisden Av *BURH* RH15 .... **88** E6
Wiseacre *RRTW* TN3 .... **33** J8
Wish Hl *EDN/EASTW* BN20 .... **229** G2
Wishing Tree Cl *STLEO* TN38 .... **197** G1
Wishing Tree La *STLEO* TN38 .... **197** G1
Wishing Tree Rd *STLEO* TN38 .... **197** G1
Wishing Tree Rd North
  STLEO TN38 .... **169** H7
Wish Rd *EAST* BN21 .... **10** C5
  HOVE BN3 .... **202** D5
Wish Ward *RYE* TN31 .... **113** H6 ⑥
Wiston Rd *ROTT* BN2 .... **205** G4
Wiston Wy *ROTT* BN2 .... **205** G4
Withdean Av *BRI* BN1 .... **203** J1
Withdean Cl *BRI* BN1 .... **177** J8
Withdean Court Av *BRI* BN1 .... **177** J8
Withdean Crs *BRI* BN1 .... **177** K8
Withdean Ri *BRI* BN1 .... **177** J8

Withdean Rd *BRI* BN1 .... 203 J1
Witherenden Rd *MAYF* TN20............. 72 E2
Withy Bush *BURH* RH15 .... 88 E7 🖪
  BURH RH15 .... 88 E6 🖪
Withyham Av *ROTT* BN2 .... 221 F3
Withyham Cl *LW/ROSE* BN22 .... 230 A2
Withyham Rd *RRTW* TN3 .... 27 J5
Wittersham La *RYE* TN31................... 85 H6
Wittersham Rd *RYE* TN31 .... 85 J3
Wivelsfield Rd *HWH* RH16 .... 90 A1
  ROTT BN2 .... 207 F8
Woburn Cl *HAIL* BN27 .... 189 F2
Woburn Pl *BRI* BN1 .... 179 G6
Woburn Wy *LW/ROSE* BN22 .... 215 J8
Wode Rd *BAT* TN33 .... 165 K8
Wolfe Cl *CROW* TN6........................... 53 J5
Wolseley Rd *BRI* BN1 .... 178 E5
  PTSD BN41 .... 201 K3
  SBGH/RUST TN4 .... 20 C4
Wolstonbury Rd *HOVE* BN3 .... 6 A3 🖪
Wolstonbury Wy *BURH* RH15 .... 119 G1 🖪
Wolverstone Dr *BRI* BN1 .... 204 D1
Woodards Vw *SHOR* BN43.............. 200 A6
Woodbourne Av *BRI* BN1 .... 178 A7
Woodbrook Rd *HAS* TN34 .... 5 D1
Woodbury Av *EGRIN* RH19 .... 23 F3
Woodbury Cl *EGRIN* RH19 .... 23 F3
Woodbury Park Gdns
  SBGH/RUST TN4 .... 20 B6
Woodbury Park Rd
  SBGH/RUST TN4 .... 20 A6
Woodcombe *HAS* TN34 .... 170 C7
Woodcote Rd *FROW* RH18................. 35 J1
Woodcrest Rd *BURH* RH15 .... 119 F2
Woodcroft *BURH* RH15 .... 89 F6 🖪
Woodcroft Dr *EAST* BN21 .... 229 H4
Woodgate Meadow *LEW* BN7 .... 121 G4
Woodgate Rd *LW/ROSE* BN22 .... 11 D2
Woodhams Cl *BAT* TN33 .... 136 D7
Woodhill Pk *RTWE/PEM* TN2............ 21 J5
Woodhouse Rd *HOVE* BN3 .... 202 D4
Woodland Av *BURH* RH15 .... 89 J7
  HOVE BN5 .... 177 C7
  LW/ROSE BN22 .... 229 H3
Woodland Cl *BURH* RH15 .... 89 J7 🖪
  HOVE BN3 .... 203 G1 🖪
  SBGH/RUST TN4 .... 20 B4
Woodland Dr *HOVE* BN3 .... 177 C8
Woodland Ms *HTHF* TN21 .... 100 B5 🖪
Woodland Ri *BEX* TN40 .... 195 K7
Woodland Rd *SBGH/RUST* TN4 .... 20 C4
Woodlands *HOVE* BN3 .... 203 H1

Woodlands Cl *HAIL* BN27 .... 189 H1
  HPPT/KEY BN6 .... 119 F7 🖪
  HTHF TN21 .... 100 B6
  PEAHV BN10 .... 222 A2 🖪🖪
  UCK TN22... 95 K3
Woodlands Rd *EGRIN* RH19............... 12 E7
  HPPT/KEY BN6 .... 119 F7
The Woodlands *BRI* BN1 .... 177 K6
  HAS TN34.. 170 B6
Woodlands Wy *HAS* TN34 .... 170 B5 🖪
Woodland Vale Rd *STLEO* TN38 .... 4 A4
Woodland Wk *ROTT* BN2 .... 206 A7
Woodland Wy *BAT* TN33 .... 168 A7
  BRI BN1 .... 178 A7
  CROW TN6....................................... 53 H3
  HTHF TN21 .... 100 B5 🖪
  RHAS TN35 .... 172 D6
Wood La *HAIL* BN27 .... 164 B8
Woodleigh Rd *BURH* RH15 .... 89 J7
Woodpecker Crs *HPPT/KEY* BN6 ...... 88 D8
Woodpecker Dr *HAIL* BN27 .... 189 F3
Woodpecker Rd *LGNY* BN23 .... 230 C1
Woodruff Av *HOVE* BN3 .... 203 H1
Woodsgate Av *BEX* TN40 .... 195 H5
  BEXW TN39 .... 195 H5
Woodsgate Pk *BEXW* TN39 .... 195 F5
Woodsgate Wy *RTWE/PEM* TN2 ... 21 H5 🖪
Woods Hill Cl *EGRIN* RH19 .... 23 H5
Woods Hill La *EGRIN* RH19 .... 23 H5
Woodside *CROW* TN6......................... 53 G1
Woodside Av *BRI* BN1 .... 203 J1
Woodside Rd *SBGH/RUST* TN4 .... 19 H7
Woodside Wy *HAIL* BN27 .... 189 H1
Woodspring Cl *SLVH* TN37 .... 169 J6
Woodstock *EGRIN* RH19...................... 22 A1
Woodstock Rd *BEXW* TN39 .... 194 B5
Wood St *EGRIN* RH19 .... 22 B2
  RTW TN1 .... 20 B7
Woodview *SHOR* BN43..................... 200 C2
Woodview Cl *BRI* BN1 .... 178 E5
Woodville Rd *BEXW* TN39 .... 195 G8
Woodward Cl *LGNY* BN23 .... 231 F4 🖪
Woodwards Cl *BURH* RH15 .... 119 H2 🖪
Woolley Cl *SBGH/RUST* TN4 .... 19 K2
Woolley Rd *SBGH/RUST* TN4 .... 19 K2
Woolven Cl *BURH* RH15 .... 118 E2
Worcester Vls *HOVE* BN3 .... 202 B4
Wordsworth Dr *LGNY* BN23 .... 231 F1
Wordsworth Ri *EGRIN* RH19 .... 22 A2
Wordsworth St *HOVE* BN3 .... 203 F4
Workhouse La *WSEA* TN36 .... 141 K6

Worsham La *BEX* TN40...................... 196 A4
Worsted La *EGRIN* RH19................... 23 F4
Wray Cl *EGRIN* RH19 .... 23 H5
Wren Cl *HTHF* TN21.......................... 100 A4
Wren Ct *BAT* TN33 .... 137 F7 🖪
  STLEO TN38 .... 169 F8 🖪
Wrestwood Av *LW/ROSE* BN22....... 229 H2
Wrestwood Rd *BEX* TN40 .... 195 J5
Wrotham Cl *HAS* TN34 .... 170 B6
  LGNY BN23 .... 230 E2 🖪
Wroxham Rd *LGNY* BN23................. 216 C7
Wyatts La *RHWH* RH17...................... 48 B6
Wyberley Rd *BURH* RH15.................. 89 G7
Wybourne Ri *RTWE/PEM* TN2 .... 30 B2
Wychurst Gdns *BEX* TN40 .... 195 J5
Wykeham Rd *HAS* TN34 .... 4 C4
Wykeham Wy *BURH* RH15 .... 119 J1 🖪
Wyndham St *ROTT* BN2 .... 7 D6 🖪
Wynnes Ms *HOVE* BN3 .... 203 F4 🖪
The Wyshe *POY/PYE* BN45 .... 149 H5
Wythwood *HWH* RH16 .... 90 A2

Y

Yardley St *BRI* BN1 .... 6 C2
Yates Cl *RYE* TN31............................ 145 J1
Yeomans *RING/NEW* BN8 .... 156 B4
Yew Tree Cl *HAS* TN34 .... 170 B5
  HTHF TN21 .... 100 A5 🖪
  RING/NEW BN8................................ 156 A4
Yewtree La *CROW* TN6....................... 55 H3
Yew Tree Rd *SBGH/RUST* TN4 .... 20 A3
Yielding's Cl *EAST* BN21.................. 229 J6 🖪
York Av *EGRIN* RH19 .... 22 E3
  HOVE BN3 .... 6 A3
York Gdns *HAS* TN34 .... 5 D5 🖪
York Gv *BRI* BN1 .... 6 B3
York Hl *BRI* BN1.................................. 6 C3
York Pl *BRI* BN1 .... 6 C4
York Rd *BEX* TN40 .... 196 B6
  BRI BN1 .... 6 A4
  EAST BN21 .... 10 B5
  PEAHV BN10 .... 222 D5
  RTW TN1 .... 20 A7
  SLVH TN37 .... 4 A2
York Vls *BRI* BN1 .... 6 B3
Youngsmere Cl *BRI* BN1 .... 178 C5 🖪

Abbotsford School
  BURH RH15 .... 89 F5
A B C Cinema
  HAS TN34.. 5 D5
A B C Cinema
  RTW TN1 .... 20 A8
Adur District Council
  STHW BN42 .... 201 H4
Albion Doctors Surgery
  ROTT BN2 .... 7 D4
Aldrington House Hospital
  HOVE BN3 .... 202 E5
Alfriston County
Primary School
  POLE BN26 .... 212 C8
The Alfriston Gallery
  POLE BN26 .... 212 D8
All Saints Hospital
  EDN/EASTW BN20 .... 236 E4
All Saints Infant School
  BEXW TN39 .... 195 G4
All Saints Junior School
  RHAS TN35 .... 199 F1
Alwin Gallery
  SBGH/RUST TN4 .... 30 A1
Amberstone Hospital
  HAIL BN27 .... 161 J5
Ambulance Station
  LW/ROSE BN22 .... 10 C3
Arndale Shopping Centre
  EAST BN21 .... 10 C4
Arthur Blackman Clinic
  SLVH TN37 .... 169 J7
Ashdown Forest Health Centre
  FROW RH18..................................... 23 J8
Ashwyn Business Centre
  BURH RH15 .... 89 G6
Assembly Hall Theatre
  RTWE/PEM TN2 .... 20 B8
The Atman Clinic
  SBGH/RUST TN4 .... 20 A5

The Audrey Wickens
School of Music
  EAST BN21...................................... 10 A4
The Avenue Surgery
  BURH RH15 .... 119 F1
Bad Apple Theatre Co
  RTW TN1 .... 20 C7
Baldwins Hill CP School
  EGRIN RH19 .... 12 A8
Balfour Junior School
  BRI BN1 .... 178 B8
Bandstand
  EAST BN21 .... 11 D5
Barclays Business Centre
  HTHF TN21 .... 100 A3
Barcombe Primary School
  RING/NEW BN8.............................. 123 H6
The Barry Clinic
  SBGH/RUST TN4 .... 20 A5
Barton School
  STLEO TN38 .... 197 J2
Battle Abbey
Preparatory School
  BEX TN40.. 195 K6
Battle Abbey School
  BAT TN33 .... 136 D7
Battle Hospital
  BAT TN33 .... 136 A7
Battle & Langton School
  BAT TN33 .... 136 C7
Battle Museum
  BAT TN33 .... 136 D7
Beacon Community College
  CROW TN6....................................... 39 K8
Beacon Community College
  CROW TN6....................................... 53 J1
Beckley Gallery
  RYE TN31.. 83 G7
Beckley School
  RYE TN31.. 82 E7

Bedgebury Junior School
  CRBK TN17 .... 47 J2
Beeching Park
Industrial Estate
  BEXW TN39 .... 195 G7
Bellerbys College
  HOVE BN3 .... 203 H4
Bellerbys College Mayfield
  WADH TN5.. 43 J7
Bell Tower Industrial Estate
  ROTT BN2 .... 205 G7
Belmont Surgery
  WADH TN5.. 44 C7
Benfield County Junior School
  PTSD BN41 .... 202 B3
Benfield Valley Golf Course
  PTSD BN41 .... 176 B8
Bennett Memorial
Diocesan School
  SBGH/RUST TN4 .... 19 J5
Bentley Wildfowl
& Motor Museum
  RING/NEW BN8.............................. 126 B7
Bethany House Surgery
  HAIL BN27 .... 189 H2
Bevendean County Primary Sch
  ROTT BN2 .... 205 G2
Bexhill Amateur Athletic Club
  BEXW TN39 .... 195 G6
Bexhill C of E Primary
Junior School
  BEX TN40.. 195 H7
Bexhill College
  BEXW TN39 .... 195 F4
Bexhill Costume Museum
  BEX TN40.. 195 J7
Bexhill High School
  BEXW TN39 .... 195 G6
Bexhill Hospital
  BEX TN40.. 195 H5

Bexhill Leisure Centre
 BEXW TN39 .... **195** G6
Bexhill Sailing Club
 BEX TN40 .... **195** J8
Bexhill Squash Rackets Club
 BEX TN40 .... **195** K7
The Bishop Bell C of E School
 LGNY BN23 .... **231** F2
Bishops Down CP School
 SBGH/RUST TN4 .... **19** J6
Blackboys C of E School
 UCK TN22 .... **97** J5
Blackwell CP School
 EGRIN RH19 .... **12** C8
Blatchington Mill School
 HOVE BN3 .... **203** F2
Bodiam Castle (Nt)
 RBTBR TN32 .... **80** B3
Bodiam Manor School
 RBTBR TN32 .... **80** A3
Bodiam Primary School
 RBTBR TN32 .... **80** A3
Boltons Clinic
 MAYF TN20 .... **71** F5
Boltons Clinic
 STLEO TN38 .... **197** J2
**Booth Museum
 of Natural History**
 BRI BN1 .... **6** A2
Bourne County Primary School
 LW/ROSE BN22 .... **11** D4
Bowden House School
 SEAF BN25 .... **225** F7
Brambletye School
 EGRIN RH19 .... **23** G6
Braybon Business Park
 BURH RH15 .... **118** E1
Brede County Primary School
 RYE TN31 .... **109** K7
Brighton Business Centre
 BRI BN1 .... **6** C2
The Brighton Centre
 BRI BN1 .... **6** B5
Brighton College
 ROTT BN2 .... **7** E5
Brighton College of Technology
 BRI BN1 .... **6** C4
Brighton College of Technology
 HOVE BN3 .... **202** D3
Brighton College of Technology
 HOVE BN3 .... **203** G5
Brighton County Court
 ROTT BN2 .... **6** C5
Brighton Fishing Museum
 BRI BN1 .... **6** B6
Brighton General Hospital
 ROTT BN2 .... **7** F3
Brighton & Hove Council
 BRI BN1 .... **178** C5
Brighton & Hove Council
 HOVE BN3 .... **202** E2
Brighton & Hove Council
 HOVE BN3 .... **203** G4
Brighton & Hove Council
 HOVE BN3 .... **203** H5
Brighton & Hove Council
 PTSD BN41 .... **201** K2
Brighton & Hove Council
 PTSD BN41 .... **202** B3
Brighton & Hove Council
 ROTT BN2 .... **7** E3
Brighton & Hove Council
 ROTT BN2 .... **179** F8
Brighton & Hove Girls Day School
 BRI BN1 .... **6** A4
Brighton & Hove Golf Course
 HOVE BN3 .... **176** D5
**Brighton & Hove
 Progressive Synagogue**
 HOVE BN3 .... **203** J5
**Brighton Hove & Sussex
 6th Form College**
 HOVE BN3 .... **6** A2
**Brighton Islamic Centre
 & Mosque**
 HOVE BN3 .... **6** A3
Brighton Library & Museum
 BRI BN1 .... **6** C5
Brighton Municipal Market
 ROTT BN2 .... **7** D5
Brighton Racecourse
 ROTT BN2 .... **205** H3
Brighton Rugby Club
 BRI BN1 .... **177** G5

Brighton Technical College
 BRI BN1 .... **6** B2
Brighton Youth Centre
 ROTT BN2 .... **7** D5
Broad Oak Primary School
 HTHF TN21 .... **101** F1
Broadwater CP School
 RTWE/PEM TN2 .... **29** K3
Broadway Surgery
 ROTT BN2 .... **205** G7
The Brook Health Centre
 CROW TN6 .... **54** A2
Broomham School
 RHAS TN35 .... **140** E8
Broomhill Bank School
 RRTW TN3 .... **19** G5
Bross Estate
 NEWHV BN9 .... **9** E2
Buchanan Hospital
 STLEO TN38 .... **197** J2
Buckingham Middle School
 SHOR BN43 .... **200** D3
Burfield Park Industrial Estate
 HAIL BN27 .... **189** F4
Burgess Hill Clinic
 BURH RH15 .... **119** F1
Burgess Hill School
 BURH RH15 .... **119** H1
Burgess Hill Town Football Club
 BURH RH15 .... **89** H6
Burrswood Medical Centre
 RRTW TN3 .... **27** J3
Burwash School
 BUR/ETCH TN19 .... **75** K5
Buxted C of E Primary School
 UCK TN22 .... **68** B8
Camber Castle
 RYE TN31 .... **143** J1
Cambridge Gardens College
 HAS TN34 .... **4** C5
The Cameron Practice
 EAST BN21 .... **10** C5
Campion Gallery
 RYE TN31 .... **113** H6
Cardinal Newman School
 HOVE BN3 .... **203** J3
Carlton Hill CP School
 ROTT BN2 .... **7** D5
Castledean School
 BRI BN1 .... **204** C1
Catsfield C of E Primary School
 BAT TN33 .... **166** D3
Causeway Secondary School
 LW/ROSE BN22 .... **216** B8
The Cavendish School
 EAST BN21 .... **229** J6
Centenary Industrial Estate
 BRI BN1 .... **7** D1
The Central Hove Surgery
 HOVE BN3 .... **203** G5
Central Library
 EAST BN21 .... **10** B4
Chailey Comprehensive School
 RING/NEW BN8 .... **122** B4
**Chailey Heritage
 Clinical Services**
 RING/NEW BN8 .... **92** A4
Chailey Heritage School
 RING/NEW BN8 .... **92** A4
Chalklin Business Park
 RTWE/PEM TN2 .... **20** E3
Chantry CP School
 BEX TN40 .... **195** H6
Charlwoods Industrial Estate
 EGRIN RH19 .... **12** C8
Charter Medical Centre
 HOVE BN3 .... **203** J4
Charters Ancaster School
 BEX TN40 .... **195** K6
Chartham Park Golf Club
 EGRIN RH19 .... **12** A5
Chaucer Industrial Estate
 POLE BN26 .... **215** J5
Chelsea College
 SHOR BN43 .... **200** A4
Chiddingly CP School
 RING/NEW BN8 .... **159** H3
Chiddingly Cricket Club
 RING/NEW BN8 .... **159** H2
Child Clinic
 BRI BN1 .... **6** C5
Churchfields Industrial Estate
 STLEO TN38 .... **168** E7

Churchill Square Shopping Centre
 BRI BN1 .... **6** B5
Church of England School
 RHWH RH17 .... **49** F7
Church Surgery
 ROTT BN2 .... **7** E1
Churchwood Primary School
 STLEO TN38 .... **169** G8
Churchwood Surgery
 STLEO TN38 .... **169** G7
Cinema
 EAST BN21 .... **10** C4
Cinque Ports Surgery
 RYE TN31 .... **113** H5
Circe Health & Beauty Clinic
 UCK TN22 .... **95** J4
Civic Centre
 SHOR BN43 .... **200** D4
Clanricarde Medical Centre
 RTW TN1 .... **20** A8
Claremont CP School
 RTWE/PEM TN2 .... **30** B1
Claverham Community College
 BAT TN33 .... **136** A7
Clermont C P U School
 BRI BN1 .... **203** K1
Cliffe Business Centre
 LEW BN7 .... **3** E4
Cliffe Industrial Estate
 LEW BN7 .... **3** F5
Club House
 EDN/EASTW BN20 .... **236** A1
Cofe Primary School
 MAYF TN20 .... **56** B8
Coghurst Hall County Primary
 RHAS TN35 .... **171** F3
Coldean Junior & Infant School
 BRI BN1 .... **178** E5
Colebrook Industrial Estate
 RTWE/PEM TN2 .... **21** F2
The College of St Barnabas
 LING RH7 .... **12** D3
**Community Mental
 Health Centre**
 BURH RH15 .... **89** G7
The Congress Theatre
 EAST BN21 .... **10** C6
Conquest Hospital
 HAS TN34 .... **170** A5
Conway Court Clinic
 HOVE BN3 .... **203** G3
**Coombe Road County
 Primary Sch**
 ROTT BN2 .... **7** F1
**Cornerstones
 Independent School**
 HOVE BN3 .... **203** J5
Corn Exchange Theatre
 BRI BN1 .... **6** C5
The Cottage Clinic
 BEX TN40 .... **195** H8
Cottage Surgery
 PEAHV BN10 .... **222** B5
**Cottesmore St Marys
 RC Primary Schl**
 HOVE BN3 .... **203** J3
Count Primary School
 BURH RH15 .... **119** J2
County Hall
 LEW BN7 .... **3** D4
County Middle School
 STHW BN42 .... **201** J3
County Primary School
 BRI BN1 .... **204** C1
County Primary School
 RING/NEW BN8 .... **157** K5
Cradle Hill Cp School
 SEAF BN25 .... **225** H6
The Craftsman Gallery
 HPPT/KEY BN6 .... **119** K8
**Cross In Hand C of E
 Primary Sch**
 HTHF TN21 .... **99** K4
Crowborough Beacon Golf Club
 CROW TN6 .... **53** F3
**Crowborough War
 Memorial Hospital**
 CROW TN6 .... **53** G2
Crowhurst School
 BAT TN33 .... **168** A6
Crown Court
 HOVE BN3 .... **203** J5
Crown Prosecution Service
 EAST BN21 .... **10** B3

Cumnor House School
RHWH RH17 .... **49** F6

The Cyril Richings Business
Centre 202-210
SHOR BN43 .... **200** D4

Dale Hill Hotel & Golf Club
WADH TN5 .... **60** D2

Dallington School
HTHF TN21 .... **103** F8

Davigdor County Infants School
HOVE BN3 .... **203** J4

Denton County Primary School
NEWHV BN9 .... **9** E1

Devonshire Park Cricket Ground
EAST BN21 .... **10** B6

Devonshire Park Theatre
EAST BN21 .... **10** C6

Ditchling Gallery
HPPT/KEY BN6 .... **119** J8

Ditchling Health Centre
HPPT/KEY BN6 .... **119** K8

Ditchling Museum
HPPT/KEY BN6 .... **119** J8

Ditchling Primary School
HPPT/KEY BN6 .... **119** K8

Douglas Moat Practice
SBGH/RUST TN4 .... **30** A1

Downland Medical Centre
POLE BN26 .... **215** F5

Downlands School
HPPT/KEY BN6 .... **119** F8

Downs County First School
BRI BN1 .... **6** C2

Downs Junior School
BRI BN1 .... **6** C1

Downs Leisure Centre
SEAF BN25 .... **225** H7

Downs Park School
PTSD BN41 .... **202** A1

Downs Special School
EDN/EASTW BN20 .... **229** G7

Downs View School
ROTT BN2 .... **205** K3

Drusillas Zoo Park
POLE BN26 .... **212** E5

DSS
EAST BN21 .... **10** B4

DSS
ROTT BN2 .... **7** D5

Dudley Infants School
RHAS TN35 .... **5** F3

Dunnings Squash Club
EGRIN RH19 .... **22** C5

Durgates Industrial Estate
WADH TN5 .... **44** A6

The Eastbourne Clinic
EDN/EASTW BN20 .... **10** B5

Eastbourne College
EDN/EASTW BN20 .... **10** B6

Eastbourne College
EDN/EASTW BN20 .... **10** B5

Eastbourne College
EDN/EASTW BN20 .... **10** A6

Eastbourne College of Arts
& Tech
EAST BN21 .... **229** K4

Eastbourne County Court
EAST BN21 .... **10** B4

Eastbourne District
General Hospital
EAST BN21 .... **229** K4

Eastbourne Downs Golf Club
EDN/EASTW BN20 .... **236** A1

Eastbourne & Hailsham
Magistrates Court
EAST BN21 .... **10** A5

Eastbourne Health Authority
EAST BN21 .... **10** B3

Eastbourne Hospitals N H S Trust
EAST BN21 .... **10** C3

Eastbourne Pier
EAST BN21 .... **11** D5

Eastbourne Rugby
Football Club
LW/ROSE BN22 .... **229** J3

Eastbourne Saffrons
Sports Club
EAST BN21 .... **10** A5

Eastbourne Sovereign
Sailing Club Ltd
LW/ROSE BN22 .... **11** F3

Eastbourne United
Football Club
LW/ROSE BN22 .... **11** F2

East Court
EGRIN RH19 .... **22** D1

East Grinstead Health Clinic
EGRIN RH19 .... **22** C1

East Grinstead Sports Club
EGRIN RH19 .... **22** A6

East Hoathly C of E School
RING/NEW BN8 .... **127** H6

East Hoathly Surgery
RING/NEW BN8 .... **127** J6

East Sussex Brighton
& Hove Health Authority
LEW BN7 .... **3** D4

East Sussex County Council
HOVE BN3 .... **176** D8

East Sussex County Council
HTHF TN21 .... **100** C3

East Sussex County Council
LEW BN7 .... **2** B5

East Sussex County Council
LEW BN7 .... **3** E6

East Sussex County Council
LEW BN7 .... **3** D4

East Sussex County Council
NEWHV BN9 .... **8** C3

East Sussex County Council
NEWHV BN9 .... **9** E2

East Sussex County Council
PEAHV BN10 .... **222** B4

East Sussex County Council
PEAHV BN10 .... **222** D5

East Sussex County Council
POLE BN26 .... **215** F5

East Sussex County Council
ROTT BN2 .... **205** F5

East Sussex County Council
SEAF BN25 .... **225** F8

East Sussex County
Music School
LEW BN7 .... **2** C5

East Sussex Health Authority
NEWHV BN9 .... **9** D2

East Sussex National Golf Club
UCK TN22 .... **125** K3

E F International School
of English
SLVH TN37 .... **4** B5

Elm Grove CP School
ROTT BN2 .... **7** E3

Elphinstone Junior School
HAS TN34 .... **5** E2

Emerson College
FROW RH18 .... **24** B8

Enterprise Shopping Centre
EAST BN21 .... **10** B4

Escotts County Primary School
EGRIN RH19 .... **22** E2

Esperance Private Hospital
EAST BN21 .... **10** C5

Etchingham C of E
Primary School
BUR/ETCH TN19 .... **77** H1

Euro Business Park
NEWHV BN9 .... **9** D2

Eversfield Hospital
STLEO TN38 .... **197** H5

Evolution Health Centre
BRI BN1 .... **6** A4

Fairfax Gallery
RTW TN1 .... **30** A1

Fairfield Surgery
BUR/ETCH TN19 .... **75** J5

Fairlight County Primary School
ROTT BN2 .... **7** E2

Felix Gallery
LEW BN7 .... **3** D4

Fermor School
CROW TN6 .... **53** J1

Ferryfield Industrial Estate
NEWHV BN9 .... **9** E3

Filching Manor
POLE BN26 .... **228** C1

Filsham Valley
Secondary School
STLEO TN38 .... **197** G4

Firle C of E School
RING/NEW BN8 .... **184** B7

Firle Place
RING/NEW BN8 .... **184** D8

The Firs Surgery
HTHF TN21 .... **99** J3

The Fishermans Museum
HAS TN34 .... **5** F5

Fishersgate First School
PTSD BN41 .... **201** K4

Five Ashes Primary School
MAYF TN20 .... **71** F5

Fletching C of E School
UCK TN22 .... **65** K8

The Fold School
HOVE BN3 .... **202** C4

Fonthill Lodge School
EGRIN RH19 .... **22** A5

Fordcombe C of E
Primary School
RRTW TN3 .... **17** K6

Forest Row Business Park
FROW RH18 .... **23** K8

Forest Row C of E Infant School
FROW RH18 .... **35** K1

Fort
NEWHV BN9 .... **9** D5

Foxhill Surgery
PEAHV BN10 .... **222** A2

Framfield C of E School
UCK TN22 .... **96** D5

Frant C of E School
RRTW TN3 .... **30** B7

Freda Gardham Cp School
RYE TN31 .... **113** K5

Gallery
ROTT BN2 .... **7** E6

The Gallery
BEXW TN39 .... **195** G8

The Gallery
BRI BN1 .... **6** A5

The Gallery
HOVE BN3 .... **203** F4

The Gallery
SBGH/RUST TN4 .... **20** A1

Gattons CP School
BURH RH15 .... **88** E8

Gemini Business Centre
HOVE BN3 .... **203** F3

Gerald Dale Motor
Sports Centre
STLEO TN38 .... **169** G6

Glebe CP School
STHW BN42 .... **201** G4

Glennys Estate
LW/ROSE BN22 .... **11** E2

Glynde Palace
RING/NEW BN8 .... **184** A4

Goldsmith Leisure Centre
CROW TN6 .... **39** H7

Goldstone Junior School
HOVE BN3 .... **202** D2

The Good Start School
POY/PYE BN45 .... **148** B6

Graham Gallery
SBGH/RUST TN4 .... **20** A8

Graham Whitehouse Practice
BURH RH15 .... **88** E7

Granary Business Centre
HAIL BN27 .... **160** E5

Grays County Infants School
NEWHV BN9 .... **9** D4

Greenfield School
FROW RH18 .... **35** G2

Green Street Clinic
EAST BN21 .... **229** H7

Grosvenor Medical Centre
RTW TN1 .... **20** A7

Grovelands County
Primary School
HAIL BN27 .... **189** F2

Grove Park School
CROW TN6 .... **53** C2

The Grove School
STLEO TN38 .... **197** C2

Guestling School
RHAS TN35 .... **171** K3

Guestling Surgery
RHAS TN35 .... **171** K3

Hailsham School
HAIL BN27 .... **189** G3

Hailsham Town Council
HAIL BN27 .... **189** H4

Hailsham Whitehouse
CP School
HAIL BN27 .... **189** G3

Ham Business Centre
SHOR BN43 .... **200** D4

Hamilton Lodge School
ROTT BN2 .... **7** F5

Hammerwood Park
EGRIN RH19 .... **24** C1

Hampden Park Infants School
LW/ROSE BN22 .... **229** K1
Hampden Park
Secondary School
LW/ROSE BN22 .... **229** K1
Hampden Park Sports Centre
LW/ROSE BN22 .... **229** J1
Hamsey CP School
RING/NEW BN8 .... **153** K3
Hangleton County Junior
& Infant School
HOVE BN3 .... **202** D1
Hankham CP School
PEV BN24 .... **216** C3
Harlands Farm County
Primary School
UCK TN22 .... **95** K6
Harvington Business Park
LW/ROSE BN22 .... **230** A3
Hassocks County Infant School
HPPT/KEY BN6 .... **119** F7
Hassocks Golf Club
HPPT/KEY BN6 .... **118** E6
Hasting Medical Centre
HAS TN34 .... **5** D4
Hastings Castle
HAS TN34 .... **5** E4
Hastings College of Arts
& Technology
HAS TN34 .... **5** F3
Hastings College of Arts
& Technology
STLEO TN38 .... **197** J5
Hastings Education College
STLEO TN38 .... **197** G4
Hastings Golf Club
BAT TN33 .... **169** G3
Hastings Indoor Market
HAS TN34 .... **5** D5
Hastings Museum & Art Gallery
HAS TN34 .... **4** C5
Hastings & St Leonards
Sailing Club
STLEO TN38 .... **197** J5
Hastings Town Football Club
HAS TN34 .... **170** D7
Hawkes Farm Cp School
HAIL BN27 .... **189** G1
Hawkhurst C of E
Primary School
HAWK TN18 .... **63** F3
Hawkhurst Squash Club
HAWK TN18 .... **62** E1
Hazel Cottage Clinic
ROTT BN2 .... **205** K3
Hazel Court School
LGNY BN23 .... **216** C8
Heathfield C of E
Primary School
HTHF TN21 .... **100** D5
Heathfield School
HTHF TN21 .... **100** E4
Helenswood Lower School
SLVH TN37 .... **170** A4
Helenswood Upper School
HAS TN34 .... **170** D7
Hellingly CP School
HAIL BN27 .... **160** E6
Hellingly Hospital
HAIL BN27 .... **161** J6
Herbert Hone Clinic
ROTT BN2 .... **7** D3
Herne School
CROW TN6 .... **53** H3
Herons Dale School
SHOR BN43 .... **201** F2
Herstmonceux Castle
HAIL BN27 .... **191** J2
Herstmonceux C of E School
HAIL BN27 .... **163** F6
High Beech Hotel
& Country Club
STLEO TN38 .... **169** G5
Highfield Business Park
STLEO TN38 .... **168** E7
Highfield County Junior School
LW/ROSE BN22 .... **230** A2
High Hurstwood C of E School
UCK TN22 .... **68** C2
High Schools
BRI BN1 .... **6** A4
Highwoods Golf Club Ltd
BEXW TN39 .... **194** E4

Hillcrest School
RHAS TN35 .... **171** H6
Hillside School
PTSD BN41 .... **202** A1
Hippodrome Bingo
BRI BN1 .... **6** B5
Hoddern County Junior School
PEAHV BN10 .... **222** A3
Hollington Junior School
STLEO TN38 .... **169** H7
Hollington Lodge Country Club
SLVH TN37 .... **169** H4
Holmbush County Infants School
SHOR BN43 .... **201** F2
Holmewood House School
RRTW TN3 .... **28** E1
Homecare Business Centre
LEW BN7 .... **3** E4
Home Farm Business Centre
BRI BN1 .... **178** E8
Homeopathic Hospital
RTW TN1 .... **20** A8
Horsted Keynes C of E School
RHWH RH17 .... **48** A5
Hospital
HAWK TN18 .... **62** D1
Hove Business Centre
HOVE BN3 .... **203** G3
Hove General Hospital
HOVE BN3 .... **203** F4
Hove Medical Centre
HOVE BN3 .... **202** C1
Hove Metal Galleries
HOVE BN3 .... **6** A3
Hove Park Upper School
HOVE BN3 .... **203** F2
Hove Polyclinic
HOVE BN3 .... **202** E2
Hove Rugby Football Club
HOVE BN3 .... **203** G2
How We Lived Then
Museum of Shops
EAST BN21 .... **10** C5
Hubbard School
EGRIN RH19 .... **22** C2
Hurstpierpoint College
HPPT/KEY BN6 .... **118** B3
Hurstwood Park Hospital
HWH RH16 .... **90** C1
Icklesham Primary School
WSEA TN36 .... **141** J5
Iford & Kingston C of E School
LEW BN7 .... **181** J6
The Imber Sports Centre
EGRIN RH19 .... **12** B8
The Indooer Market
HAS TN34 .... **5** D5
Indoor Market
SLVH TN37 .... **4** A5
Inglesea School
STLEO TN38 .... **169** G7
Inside Out Theatre Co Ltd
STLEO TN38 .... **4** A4
International Lawn Tennis Centre
EAST BN21 .... **10** C5
Jarvis Brook Cp School
CROW TN6 .... **54** A4
Jempsons Trading Estate
RYE TN31 .... **113** H6
Kent & Sussex Hospital
SBGH/RUST TN4 .... **20** A7
King Offa CP School
BEXW TN39 .... **195** G6
Kings Manor School
SHOR BN43 .... **201** G3
Kingstanding Business Park
RTON TN11 .... **21** F1
Kingston Buci School
SHOR BN43 .... **200** D3
Kingswood Surgery
RTWE/PEM TN2 .... **20** C8
Knoll Business Centre
HOVE BN3 .... **202** C3
Lamberhurst C of E School
RRTW TN3 .... **33** K5
Lamberhurst Golf Club
RRTW TN3 .... **33** K5
Lamberhurst Surgery
RRTW TN3 .... **33** J6
Langney CP School
LGNY BN23 .... **231** F2
Langney Shopping Centre
LGNY BN23 .... **216** D8

Langney Sports Club
LGNY BN23 .... **217** G8
Langton Green Cp School
RRTW TN3 .... **18** C7
Lansdowne Road Clinic
RTW TN1 .... **20** B7
Law Courts
ROTT BN2 .... **7** D5
Lawn Tennis Club
EAST BN21 .... **10** C5
Leap Cross Small
Business Centre
HAIL BN27 .... **189** F1
Lewes Business Centre
LEW BN7 .... **3** D3
Lewes Castle & Museums
LEW BN7 .... **2** C4
Lewes District Council
NEWHV BN9 .... **8** C2
Lewes District Council
SEAF BN25 .... **225** F8
Lewes Gallery
LEW BN7 .... **2** C5
Lewes Grammar School
LEW BN7 .... **2** C5
Lewes Leisure Centre
LEW BN7 .... **3** E5
Lewes Little Theatre
LEW BN7 .... **2** C4
Lewes Magistrates Court
LEW BN7 .... **3** D4
Lewes Sports Club
LEW BN7 .... **2** B6
Lewes Tertiary College
LEW BN7 .... **3** D5
Lewes Victoria Hospital
LEW BN7 .... **2** A4
Lewes Wallands Cp School
LEW BN7 .... **2** A3
Lexden Lodge Industrial Estate
CROW TN6 .... **54** B3
Life Boat Museum
EAST BN21 .... **10** C6
Lindfield School
LW/ROSE BN22 .... **229** J1
Liongate Clinic
SBGH/RUST TN4 .... **20** A6
Little Common Primary School
BEXW TN39 .... **194** C7
Little Horsted School
UCK TN22 .... **125** J2
Little Ridge School
SLVH TN37 .... **169** K6
Little Ridge Surgery
SLVH TN37 .... **169** K6
Little Theatre
SEAF BN25 .... **232** A1
London Meed CP School
BURH RH15 .... **119** G2
Longhill School
ROTT BN2 .... **206** B7
Longley Industrial Estate
BRI BN1 .... **6** B3
Lower Glen Surgery
SLVH TN37 .... **169** J7
L T C International College
EAST BN21 .... **10** A5
Malthouse Business Park
RYE TN31 .... **112** C1
Manor Cp School
UCK TN22 .... **95** K3
Manor Farm Business Centre
POY/PYE BN45 .... **148** C6
Manor Field CP School
BURH RH15 .... **89** J7
Manor House Hospital
HOVE BN3 .... **203** F4
Manor Oak Surgery
HTHF TN21 .... **129** K4
Manor Park Medical Centre
POLE BN26 .... **214** E5
Marefield Leisure Centre
UCK TN22 .... **67** G7
Maresfield Bonners School
UCK TN22 .... **67** H7
Marine Clinic
ROTT BN2 .... **220** D2
Mark Cross C of E School
CROW TN6 .... **42** A8
Market Place
BURH RH15 .... **119** G1
Marlborough House School
HAWK TN18 .... **62** E1

Marlipins Museum
  SHOR BN43 .... **200** B5
Marshlands CP School
  HAIL BN27 .... **189** J3
Martins Oak Surgery
  BAT TN33 .... **136** D7
Mayfield Gallery
  MAYF TN20 .... **56** B8
Maynards Green Cp School
  HTHF TN21 .... **130** A1
Meadows Memorial School
  SBGH/RUST TN4 .... **19** K1
The Meadows Surgery
  BURH RH15 .... **88** D7
The Mead School
  RTWE/PEM TN2 .... **30** A2
Meads School
  EGRIN RH19 .... **22** C4
The Meads Surgery
  UCK TN22 .... **95** J4
The Medical Centre
  PEV BN24 .... **218** A6
Meeching Valley Cp School
  NEWHV BN9 .... **8** B3
Megabowl
  BEX TN40 .... **196** B7
Memorial Art Gallery
  HAS TN34 .... **5** D5
Mercateria Business Centre
  STLEO TN38 .... **4** A6
Meridian CP School
  PEAHV BN10 .... **222** B2
Meridian Leisure Centre
  PEAHV BN10 .... **222** B4
Meridian Surgery
  PEAHV BN10 .... **222** A3
The Mews Clinic
  EAST BN21 .... **10** A3
Michael Hall School
  FROW RH18 .... **35** H2
Michelham Priory
  HAIL BN27 .... **188** A4
Middle Street Primary School
  BRI BN1 .... **6** B5
Mid Sussex Golf Club
  HPPT/KEY BN6 .... **120** C6
Mile Oak Clinic
  PTSD BN41 .... **175** J8
Mile Oak Junior School
  PTSD BN41 .... **175** J8
Millbrook Business Park
  CROW TN6 .... **54** B3
Mill View Hospital
  HOVE BN3 .... **202** D2
Moatfield Surgery
  EGRIN RH19 .... **22** C1
Moira House School
  EDN/EASTW BN20 .... **236** D2
Morley Street Health Centre
  ROTT BN2 .... **7** D4
The Mosque
  STLEO TN38 .... **4** A5
Motcombe County
  Infant School
  EAST BN21 .... **229** H6
Moulscoomb Clinic
  ROTT BN2 .... **179** F8
Moulsecoomb County
  Junior Sch
  ROTT BN2 .... **179** F8
Mountfield & Whatlington C of E
  Primary School
  RBTBR TN32 .... **106** D4
Mount Pleasant Hospital
  SLVH TN37 .... **169** H7
Mount School
  WADH TN5 .... **43** H5
Mowden School
  HOVE BN3 .... **203** J2
Museum
  SHOR BN43 .... **200** A4
Museum of Local History
  HAS TN34 .... **5** E4
Netherfield C of E
  Primary School
  BAT TN33 .... **135** G1
Nevill Golf Club
  RTWE/PEM TN2 .... **30** D4
Newhaven Flea Market
  NEWHV BN9 .... **8** C4
Newhaven Health Centre
  NEWHV BN9 .... **9** D3
Newhaven Town Council
  NEWHV BN9 .... **8** C3

Newick Health Centre
  RING/NEW BN8 .... **93** H4
Newick House Special School
  BURH RH15 .... **119** J2
Newick School
  RING/NEW BN8 .... **93** G5
Newlands Preparatory School
  SEAF BN25 .... **225** J7
Newlands Senior School
  SEAF BN25 .... **225** H7
New Life School
  EGRIN RH19 .... **22** B1
Newmans Loner School
  HOVE BN3 .... **203** J3
New Venture Theatre
  BRI BN1 .... **6** A5
Ninfield C of E School
  BAT TN33 .... **166** A6
Northbourne Medical Centre
  SHOR BN43 .... **200** D3
Northease Manor School
  LEW BN7 .... **208** B2
North Farm Industrial Estate
  RTWE/PEM TN2 .... **20** E2
Northfield Business Park
  HAIL BN27 .... **159** K7
Northiam Primary School
  RYE TN31 .... **81** K6
Nutley Primary School
  UCK TN22 .... **50** C7
Oakmeads Community School
  BURH RH15 .... **119** G1
Ocklynge County Junior School
  EAST BN21 .... **229** H5
Odeon Cinema
  BRI BN1 .... **6** B5
Old Grammar School
  LEW BN7 .... **2** C4
The Old Museum
  RYE TN31 .... **110** D1
Old Salehurst School
  RBTBR TN32 .... **78** B6
Old School Surgery
  SEAF BN25 .... **232** A1
Old Town Art Gallery
  HAS TN34 .... **5** E4
The Open University
  EGRIN RH19 .... **22** C2
Orchard Business Centre
  RTWE/PEM TN2 .... **20** D3
Ore Business Park
  HAS TN34 .... **5** F2
Our Lady of Lourdes School
  ROTT BN2 .... **220** C1
Ovingdean Hall School
  ROTT BN2 .... **206** A7
Park College Eastbourne
  EAST BN21 .... **229** J4
Parklands Junior
  & Infant School
  LW/ROSE BN22 .... **229** J2
Park Mead School
  HAIL BN27 .... **187** K3
Parkside County
  Primary School
  HTHF TN21 .... **100** C6
Park View Leisure Centre
  HOVE BN3 .... **202** D4
Pashley Down County
  Infant Sch
  EDN/EASTW BN20 .... **229** G7
Patcham CP School
  BRI BN1 .... **178** A5
Patcham First School
  BRI BN1 .... **177** K5
Patcham High School
  BRI BN1 .... **178** A5
Patcham House School
  BRI BN1 .... **177** K5
The Pavilion Clinic
  BRI BN1 .... **6** A5
Paxton Business Centre
  HOVE BN3 .... **202** C3
Peacehaven Infant School
  PEAHV BN10 .... **222** A4
Peacehaven Sports Centre
  PEAHV BN10 .... **222** C4
Peacehaven Town Council
  PEAHV BN10 .... **222** B3
Peacock Industrial Estate
  HOVE BN3 .... **203** J4
Peasmarsh C of E
  Primary School
  RYE TN31 .... **112** B2

Pebsham Primary School
  BEX TN40 .... **196** B6
Pells C of E Infant School
  LEW BN7 .... **2** B3
Pells Primary School
  LEW BN7 .... **2** C3
Pembury Hospital
  RTWE/PEM TN2 .... **21** G4
Pembury Primary School
  RTWE/PEM TN2 .... **21** K3
Penns Gallery
  EAST BN21 .... **10** B5
Peter Gladwin School
  PTSD BN41 .... **201** K1
Pevensey Bay Sailing Club
  PEV BN24 .... **231** K1
Pevensey Castle
  PEV BN24 .... **217** J5
Pevensey & Westham
  C of E Primary School
  PEV BN24 .... **217** H5
Phoenix Industrial Estate
  LEW BN7 .... **3** D3
The Picture House
  UCK TN22 .... **95** J4
The Piltdown Golf Club
  UCK TN22 .... **94** E1
Playden School
  RYE TN31 .... **113** J1
Plumpton New Primary School
  LEW BN7 .... **121** H6
Polegate CP School
  POLE BN26 .... **215** F4
Polegate Town Council Office
  POLE BN26 .... **214** E6
Portland Business Park
  HOVE BN3 .... **202** C4
Portland Industrial Estate
  HOVE BN3 .... **202** D3
Portland Road Industrial Estate
  HOVE BN3 .... **202** C3
Portland Surgery
  HOVE BN3 .... **202** E4
Portslade Community College
  PTSD BN41 .... **175** K8
Portslade Community College
  PTSD BN41 .... **201** K2
Portslade Community College
  STHW BN42 .... **201** J1
Portslade Health Centre
  PTSD BN41 .... **202** A4
Practice
  SBGH/RUST TN4 .... **30** A1
Premier Gallery
  EAST BN21 .... **10** B5
Preston Furniture Gallery
  BRI BN1 .... **204** A1
Preston Park Clinic
  BRI BN1 .... **6** C1
Preston Park Surgery
  BRI BN1 .... **6** C2
Prince Regent
  Swimming Complex
  BRI BN1 .... **6** C5
The Princes Royal Hospital
  HWH RH16 .... **90** B1
Priory Hill Shopping Centre
  HAS TN34 .... **5** D4
Priory School
  LEW BN7 .... **3** D5
Punnetts Town School
  HTHF TN21 .... **101** H5
Queensdown School
  BRI BN1 .... **178** D8
Queens Park County
  Primary School
  ROTT BN2 .... **7** E5
Queen Victoria Hospital
  N H S Trust
  EGRIN RH19 .... **12** D8
Quintin Medical Centre
  HAIL BN27 .... **161** H8
Ranalah Estate
  NEWHV BN9 .... **9** E2
Ratton County
  Secondary School
  EAST BN21 .... **229** H4
Red Lake CP School
  RHAS TN35 .... **171** G7
Regent Business Centre
  BURH RH15 .... **118** E1
Rich Industrial Estate
  NEWHV BN9 .... **9** E1

Ringmer Business Centre
RING/NEW BN8 .... **156** A5
Ringmer CP School
RING/NEW BN8 .... **155** K6
Ringmer Football Club
RING/NEW BN8 .... **155** J6
Ringmer Parish Council
RING/NEW BN8 .... **155** J6
Riverbank Business Centre
SHOR BN43 .... **200** A4
River Lodge Surgery
LEW BN7 .... **3** D4
Riverside Business Centre
SHOR BN43 .... **200** C5
Riverside Industrial Estate
LEW BN7 .... **3** D3
Robertsbridge Community College
RBTBR TN32 .... **77** K7
Roborough Day Hospital
EAST BN21 .... **10** C3
Robsack Infant School
STLEO TN38 .... **197** F1
Rock & Bowl Bowling Alley
EGRIN RH19 .... **22** C2
Rocks Park CP School
UCK TN22 .... **95** H3
Rockys Leisure Centre
HAS TN34 .... **4** C5
Rodmell Primary School
LEW BN7 .... **208** D2
Roebuck House Surgery
HAS TN34 .... **5** F4
Roedean School
ROTT BN2 .... **205** K8
Rose Hill School
SBGH/RUST TN4 .... **19** J6
Roselands County Infants School
LW/ROSE BN22 .... **11** D2
Rother District Council
BAT TN33 .... **136** C6
Rotherfield CP School
CROW TN6 .... **55** F3
Rotherfield Surgery
CROW TN6 .... **55** F3
Rottingdean Football Club
ROTT BN2 .... **206** C8
Rottingdean Primary School
ROTT BN2 .... **220** D1
Rottingdean Surgery
ROTT BN2 .... **206** B8
Royal Alexandra Hospital
BRI BN1 .... **6** B4
Royal Ashdown Forest Golf Club
FROW RH18 .... **36** A2
Royal Eastbourne Golf Club
EDN/EASTW BN20 .... **236** D1
Royal George Clinic
BURH RH15 .... **88** E8
Royal Hippodrome Theatre
LW/ROSE BN22 .... **11** D4
Royal Sussex County Hospital Nhs Trust
ROTT BN2 .... **7** F6
Royal Victoria Place Shopping Centre
RTW TN1 .... **20** B7
Rudyard Kipling Primary School
ROTT BN2 .... **206** B4
Rugby Club
EGRIN RH19 .... **22** A6
Rusthall Medical Centre
SBGH/RUST TN4 .... **19** F7
Rutherfords Business Park
BAT TN33 .... **137** H4
Rye Art Gallery
RYE TN31 .... **113** J6
Rye Bay Club House
WSEA TN36 .... **143** G6
Rye Castle Museum
RYE TN31 .... **113** J6
Rye Community Clinic
RYE TN31 .... **113** H6
Rye Football & Cricket Club
RYE TN31 .... **113** J5
Rye Golf Club
RYE TN31 .... **114** D8
Rye Harbour Sailing Club
RYE TN31 .... **114** C8
Rye Industrial Estate
RYE TN31 .... **113** K7
Sackville School
EGRIN RH19 .... **22** E2

Sacred Heart School
RTWE/PEM TN2 .... **20** E7
Sacred Heart School
WADH TN5 .... **43** K6
St Andrews C of E Infant School
LW/ROSE BN22 .... **11** E1
St Andrews C of E School
HOVE BN3 .... **203** G5
St Andrews Medical Centre
SBGH/RUST TN4 .... **20** A2
St Andrews School
EDN/EASTW BN20 .... **236** D4
St Andrews Surgery
LEW BN7 .... **3** D5
St Annes Special School
LEW BN7 .... **2** B5
St Aubyns School
ROTT BN2 .... **220** D2
St Augustine School
SBGH/RUST TN4 .... **20** A4
St Barnabas C of E Primary School
RTW TN1 .... **20** B6
St Bartholomews C of E Primary School
BRI BN1 .... **6** C3
St Bedes School
EDN/EASTW BN20 .... **236** E4
St Bedes School
HAIL BN27 .... **187** J3
St Bernadettes First Middle Va School
BRI BN1 .... **203** K1
St Christophers School
HOVE BN3 .... **203** F4
St Dominics Gallery
HPPT/KEY BN6 .... **119** J8
St Faith Clinic
ROTT BN2 .... **205** F7
St Georges School
RTWE/PEM TN2 .... **21** G6
St Giles College
EDN/EASTW BN20 .... **10** B6
St Gregorys RC School
SBGH/RUST TN4 .... **20** A4
St James's Junior & Infant School
RTWE/PEM TN2 .... **20** C7
St Johns Church School
CROW TN6 .... **38** E7
St Johns Infant School
SBGH/RUST TN4 .... **20** A6
St Johns Primary School
SBGH/RUST TN4 .... **20** B4
St Johns Residential School
ROTT BN2 .... **7** F5
St John the Baptist RC Primary School
ROTT BN2 .... **7** F5
St Josephs RC School
LW/ROSE BN22 .... **11** E2
St Leonards C of E Primary School
STLEO TN38 .... **197** H4
St Leonards Football Club
HAS TN34 .... **5** E1
St Lukes Junior & Infant School
ROTT BN2 .... **7** E4
St Lukes School
SBGH/RUST TN4 .... **20** C4
St Lukes Swimming Pool
ROTT BN2 .... **7** E4
St Marks C of E Primary School
ROTT BN2 .... **205** F6
St Marks C of E Primary School
SBGH/RUST TN4 .... **29** H2
St Marks C of E Primary School
UCK TN22 .... **70** A6
St Martins C of E Primary School
ROTT BN2 .... **7** E2
St Mary Magdalene School
BEX TN40 .... **195** K5
St Mary Magdalene School
BRI BN1 .... **6** A5
St Marys C of E School
EGRIN RH19 .... **22** B1
St Marys Hall School for Girls
ROTT BN2 .... **7** F6
St Marys Primary Catholic School
CROW TN6 .... **53** H1
St Marys RC School
PTSD BN41 .... **202** A4
St Marys School
BEX TN40 .... **195** K5

St Marys School
HTHF TN21 .... **130** A2
St Mary the Virgin School
HRTF TN7 .... **25** K7
St Michaels Cp School
HRTF TN7 .... **26** D6
St Nicholas & St. Mary School
SHOR BN43 .... **200** D3
St Pancras RC Primary School
LEW BN7 .... **2** B4
St Pauls C of E Infant School
RRTW TN3 .... **19** F7
St Pauls C of E Junior School
SBGH/RUST TN4 .... **19** F7
St Pauls C of E School
BRI BN1 .... **6** B4
St Pauls School
SLVH TN37 .... **4** B3
St Peters County Infant School
PTSD BN41 .... **202** A5
St Peters Primary School
RING/NEW BN8 .... **92** C7
St Peters Primary School
RTWE/PEM TN2 .... **20** C8
St Peters RC School
EGRIN RH19 .... **22** A2
St Peters R C School
SHOR BN43 .... **200** D3
St Phillips R C Primary School
UCK TN22 .... **95** J6
St Richards School
BEX TN40 .... **195** K7
St Thomas A Becket RC Infants School
EAST BN21 .... **10** B2
St Thomas A Becket RC Junior School
EAST BN21 .... **10** B2
St Thomas C of E Primary School
RRTW TN3 .... **28** A5
St Thomas C of E Primary School
WSEA TN36 .... **143** F4
St Vincent School
STLEO TN38 .... **197** G5
St Wilfrids RC School
BURH RH15 .... **119** G1
Salehurst C of E Primary School
RBTBR TN32 .... **78** B7
Saltdean County Primary School
ROTT BN2 .... **221** F1
Salvation Army
LW/ROSE BN22 .... **11** D4
Sandown Court School
RTWE/PEM TN2 .... **20** E5
Sandown School
RHAS TN35 .... **171** F7
Saxonborough Surgery
CROW TN6 .... **53** H1
Saxon Mount School
STLEO TN38 .... **197** G4
The Seaford Business Centre
SEAF BN25 .... **225** F8
Seaford CP School
SEAF BN25 .... **225** F7
Seaford Day Hospital
SEAF BN25 .... **225** G8
Seaford Golf Club
SEAF BN25 .... **225** G5
Seaford Head Community College
SEAF BN25 .... **232** C1
Seaford Head Community College
SEAF BN25 .... **232** B1
Seaford Head Lower School
SEAF BN25 .... **232** B1
Seaford Health Centre
SEAF BN25 .... **225** F8
Seaford Sports & Leisure Centre
SEAF BN25 .... **225** F8
Sea Life Centre
ROTT BN2 .... **7** D6
Sea Road Surgery
BEX TN40 .... **195** J8
Seaside Medical Centre
LW/ROSE BN22 .... **11** D3
Secondary School
ROTT BN2 .... **205** F5
Sedlescombe C of E School
BAT TN33 .... **138** A2

Sedlescombe Golf Club
BAT TN33 .... **138** A6
The Seven Dials Medical Centre
BRI BN1 .... **6** A4
Shankill Surgery
RHAS TN35 .... **171** G7
Sheddindean Business Centre
BURH RH15 .... **89** F6
Sheddingdean First School
BURH RH15 .... **89** G6
Sheila Cashin Gallery
BRI BN1 .... **6** B4
Sheriffs Gallery
HAIL BN27 .... **189** H4
Sherwood Park Infant School
RTWE/PEM TN2 .... **20** D5
Sherwood Park Primary School
RTWE/PEM TN2 .... **20** D5
The Ship Street Surgery
EGRIN RH19 .... **22** C3
Shoreham Beach County
First School
SHOR BN43 .... **200** D5
Shoreham College
SHOR BN43 .... **201** G4
Shoreham County First School
SHOR BN43 .... **200** B3
Shoreham Football Club
PTSD BN41 .... **202** A4
Shoreham Health Centre
SHOR BN43 .... **200** B4
Sidley Primary School
BEXW TN39 .... **195** H5
Sidley Sports Club
BEXW TN39 .... **195** H4
Sidley Surgery
BEXW TN39 .... **195** G4
Silverhill Natural Health Centre
STLEO TN38 .... **197** J1
Silver Springs Medical Practice
SLVH TN37 .... **4** A4
Simpsons Industrial Estate
RYE TN31 .... **114** A8
The Skinners School
SBGH/RUST TN4 .... **20** A5
Skippers Hill Manor
Preparatory School
MAYF TN20 .... **71** F3
Somerhill County Junior School
HOVE BN3 .... **203** J5
Southdown Business Park
LEW BN7 .... **3** D3
Southdown CP School
NEWHV BN9 .... **8** C3
South Downs Health Clinic
BRI BN1 .... **6** B4
South Malling Primary School
LEW BN7 .... **3** D2
Southover C of E Primary School
LEW BN7 .... **2** C5
South Saxon Howe Surgery
STLEO TN38 .... **197** F4
Southway County Junior School
HPPT/KEY BN6 .... **88** D8
Southwick Business Centre
PTSD BN41 .... **201** H5
Southwick Manor Hall
County First School
STHW BN42 .... **201** J4
Spa Industrial Park
RTWE/PEM TN2 .... **20** E3
Speldhurst Primary School
RRTW TN3 .... **18** E4
Spinney School
HTHF TN21 .... **99** H8
Springfield Industrial Estate
RHWH RH17 .... **90** B6
Squash Club
EAST BN21 .... **10** A5
Squires Farm Industrial Estate
UCK TN22 .... **127** G2
Stafford County Junior School
LW/ROSE BN22 .... **10** C1
Stanford Junior School
BRI BN1 .... **6** B2
Stanley Deason Leisure Centre
ROTT BN2 .... **205** G6
Staplecross School
RBTBR TN32 .... **108** A1
Stevenson Gallery
RYE TN31 .... **113** H6
Stewart Gallery
BEX TN40 .... **195** H8

Stone Cross CP School
PEV BN24 .... **216** B6
Stonegate C of E Primary School
WADH TN5 .... **59** H6
Stonelands School of Ballet
& Theatre
HOVE BN3 .... **203** G5
Summerfields Business Centre
SLVH TN37 .... **4** B4
Summerfield Sports Centre
HAS TN34 .... **4** B4
Sussex County Cricket Club
HOVE BN3 .... **203** H4
Sussex Eye Hospital
ROTT BN2 .... **7** F6
Sussex House Industrial Estate
HOVE BN3 .... **202** E3
Sussex Nuffield Hospital
HOVE BN3 .... **202** E5
Sussex Nuffield Hospital
ROTT BN2 .... **205** K3
Sussex Private Clinic
STLEO TN38 .... **197** J3
The Sussex Toy
& Model Museum
BRI BN1 .... **6** C4
Sussex University
LEW BN7 .... **3** E3
Sutton Industrial Park
WSEA TN36 .... **143** G4
Swan Barn Business Centre
HAIL BN27 .... **189** J5
Sydney West Sports Centre
BURH RH15 .... **89** G7
Synagogue
EAST BN21 .... **10** C4
Synogogue
BRI BN1 .... **6** B6
TA Centre
LW/ROSE BN22 .... **11** D3
Teacher Training Sch
HAS TN34 .... **5** E3
Telscombe Cliffs Primary School
PEAHV BN10 .... **221** K3
Temple Grove with
St Nicholas School
UCK TN22 .... **52** A8
Tennis Club
CROW TN6 .... **53** G1
Thomas Peacocke
Community College
RYE TN31 .... **113** H5
Ticehurst Clinic
HOVE BN3 .... **203** F5
Ticehurst C of E Primary School
WADH TN5 .... **60** B3
Tideway School
NEWHV BN9 .... **8** B4
Tilling Green School
RYE TN31 .... **113** G6
Tobias School of Art
EGRIN RH19 .... **22** C5
Tollgate Junior School
LGNY BN23 .... **230** E4
Torfield School
HAS TN34 .... **5** F3
Towner Art Gallery & Local History
Museum
EDN/EASTW BN20 .... **229** J8
Tree Tops Tree Surgery
STLEO TN38 .... **169** G8
Trinity Theatre
& Arts Association
RTW TN1 .... **20** A8
Tunbridge Wells Borderers
Sports Club
RTWE/PEM TN2 .... **30** A3
Tunbridge Wells Centre
RTW TN1 .... **20** A7
Tunbridge Wells Golf Club
SBGH/RUST TN4 .... **19** J8
Tunbridge Wells Grammar
School for Boys
SBGH/RUST TN4 .... **20** A3
Tunbridge Wells Grammar
School for Girls
SBGH/RUST TN4 .... **19** K5
Tunbridge Wells Hockey Club
RTW TN1 .... **30** B2
Tunbridge Wells
Independent Hospital
RRTW TN3 .... **17** K8

Tunbridge Wells Museum
& Art Gallery
SBGH/RUST TN4 .... **20** A7
Tunbridge Wells Nuffield Hospital
RTWE/PEM TN2 .... **20** D8
Tunbridge Wells Sports Centre
SBGH/RUST TN4 .... **20** A4
Uckfield Civic Centre
UCK TN22 .... **95** J4
Uckfield Community Hospital
UCK TN22 .... **95** K5
Uckfield Community School
UCK TN22 .... **95** K3
Uckfield Holy Cross School
UCK TN22 .... **95** J4
Uckfield Rugby Football Club
UCK TN22 .... **96** A3
Uckfield Sports Centre
UCK TN22 .... **95** J4
University
EDN/EASTW BN20 .... **10** A6
University of Brighton
BRI BN1 .... **179** H6
University of Brighton
EAST BN21 .... **10** B3
University of Brighton
EDN/EASTW BN20 .... **236** D4
University of Brighton
EDN/EASTW BN20 .... **236** D2
University of Brighton
ROTT BN2 .... **204** D1
University of Sussex
BRI BN1 .... **179** J4
Uplands Community College
WADH TN5 .... **44** B7
Uplands School
BRI BN1 .... **204** D1
Utopia Leisure Centre
UCK TN22 .... **95** K3
Vals Swim School
BEXW TN39 .... **195** G3
Varndean College
BRI BN1 .... **178** A8
Varndean High School
BRI BN1 .... **178** B8
Venture Industrial Park
STLEO TN38 .... **197** H1
Vicarage Field Surgery
HAIL BN27 .... **189** H3
Virgin Cinemas
BRI BN21 .... **205** F8
Virgin Cinemas
LGNY BN23 .... **231** G2
Wadhurst Business Park
WADH TN5 .... **43** H4
Wadhurst C of E Primary School
WADH TN5 .... **44** B6
Warrior Square Surgery
SLVH TN37 .... **4** A5
Waterhall Golf Course
BRI BN1 .... **177** G4
Waytefield Clinic
BRI BN1 .... **203** K1
Wealden College
CROW TN6 .... **53** H3
Wealden District Council
HAIL BN27 .... **189** H3
Wealden Industrial Estate
CROW TN6 .... **54** A3
Websters Gallery
EAST BN21 .... **11** D4
Welfare Clinic
HOVE BN3 .... **202** D1
Wellington Square
Medical Centre
HAS TN34 .... **5** D5
Wellhurst Golf & Country Club
HAIL BN27 .... **161** F1
Westdene Primary School
BRI BN1 .... **177** H6
Westerleigh School
STLEO TN38 .... **197** H3
Westham Medical Centre
PEV BN24 .... **217** H6
West Hove Middle School
HOVE BN3 .... **202** D4
West Kent College
of Further Edu
SBGH/RUST TN4 .... **20** A4
West Pier (Under Repair)
BRI BN1 .... **6** A6
West Rise Junior & Infant School
LGNY BN23 .... **230** D1

West St Leonards County
  Primary School
    STLEO TN38 .... 197 G3
West Sussex County Council
    SHOR BN43 .... 200 E4
West Terrace Clinic
    EAST BN21 .... 10 B5
Wheel Park Farm
  Industrial Estate
    RHAS TN35 .... 139 F7
The White Gallery
    HOVE BN3 .... 203 H5
Whitehawk Clinic
    ROTT BN2 .... 205 G6
The Whitehawk College
    EAST BN21 .... 10 C4
Whitehawk Infant School
    ROTT BN2 .... 205 F5
Whitehawk Junior School
    ROTT BN2 .... 205 F5
Whitehill County Infant School
    CROW TN6 .... 53 J2
White Rock Theatre
    HAS TN34 .... 4 C5

William Parker Lower School
    HAS TN34 .... 170 A7
William Parker Upper School
    HAS TN34 .... 170 A7
Willingdon CP School
    EDN/EASTW BN20 .... 215 F8
Willingdon Golf Club
    EDN/EASTW BN20 .... 229 G4
Willingdon School
    POLE BN26 .... 214 E7
Willingdon Trees Primary School
    LW/ROSE BN22 .... 215 J8
The Willow Surgery
    ROTT BN2 .... 205 G2
Windlesham School
    HOVE BN3 .... 6 A2
Windmills County Junior School
    HPPT/KEY BN6 .... 119 F8
Window Gallery
    BRI BN1 .... 6 B3
Winifred Lee Health Centre
    LW/ROSE BN22 .... 11 E2
Winter Gardens
    EAST BN21 .... 10 C5

Wish Tower Puppet Museum
    EAST BN21 .... 10 C6
Wish Valley Surgery
    HAWK TN18 .... 63 F3
Wittersham Primary School
    TENT TN30 .... 84 D1
Woodingdean Primary School
    ROTT BN2 .... 205 K3
Workshop Gallery
    EAST BN21 .... 10 C4
Worthing District
  Health Authority
    SHOR BN43 .... 200 C4
Worthing & Southlands
  Hospitals N H S Trust
    SHOR BN43 .... 200 E3
Wych Cross Place
    FROW RH18 .... 35 G7
Yeowart Business Centre
    UCK TN22 .... 95 H5
YMCA
    BRI BN1 .... 6 B4

Notes